RADIANT

TONY VALENTE

CONTENTS

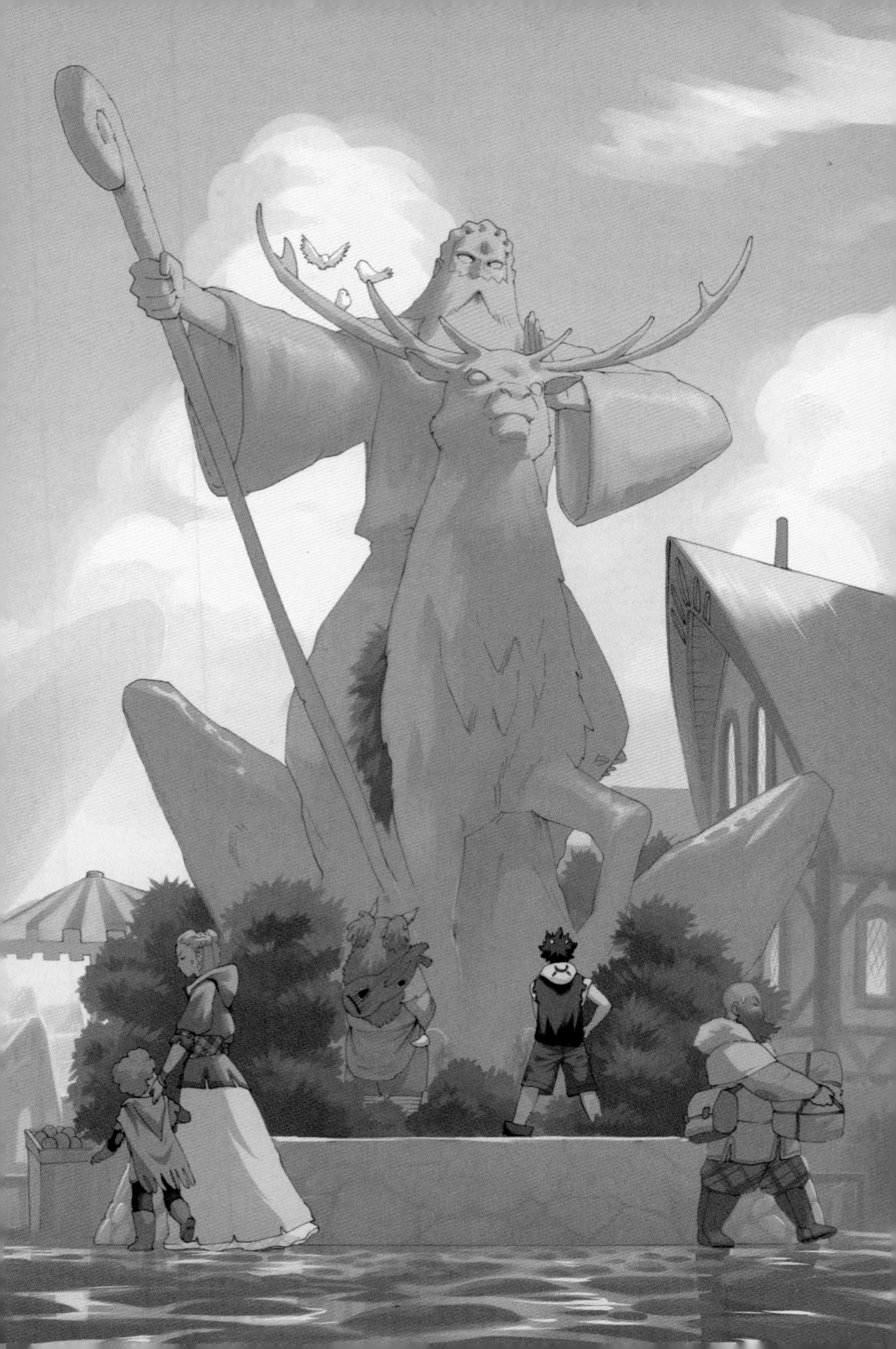

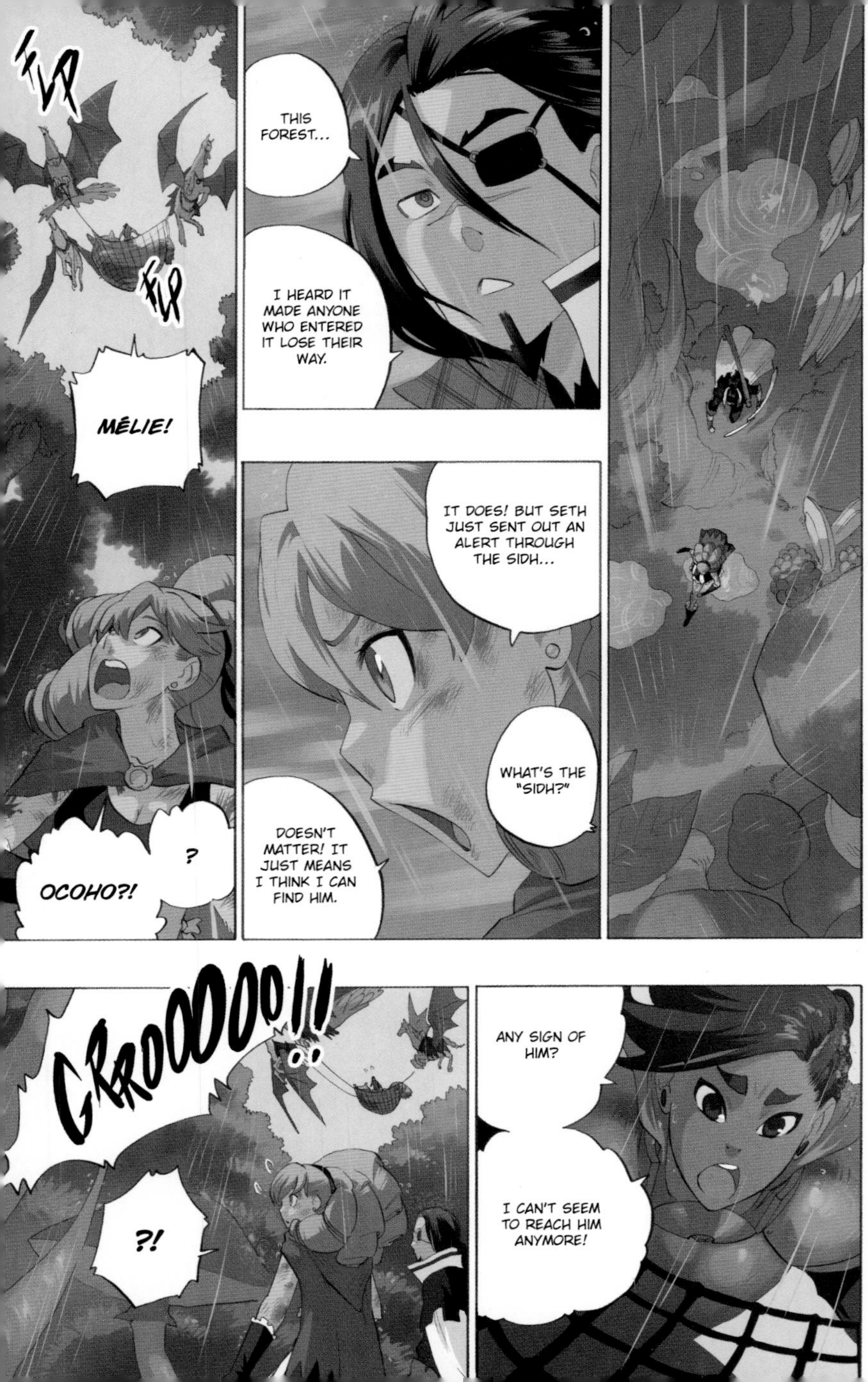
THIS FOREST...
I HEARD IT MADE ANYONE WHO ENTERED IT LOSE THEIR WAY.
IT DOES! BUT SETH JUST SENT OUT AN ALERT THROUGH THE SIDH...
WHAT'S THE "SIDH?"
DOESN'T MATTER! IT JUST MEANS I THINK I CAN FIND HIM.
FLP
FLP
MÊLIE!
?
OCOHO?!
ANY SIGN OF HIM?
I CAN'T SEEM TO REACH HIM ANYMORE!
GRROOOOO!!!
?!

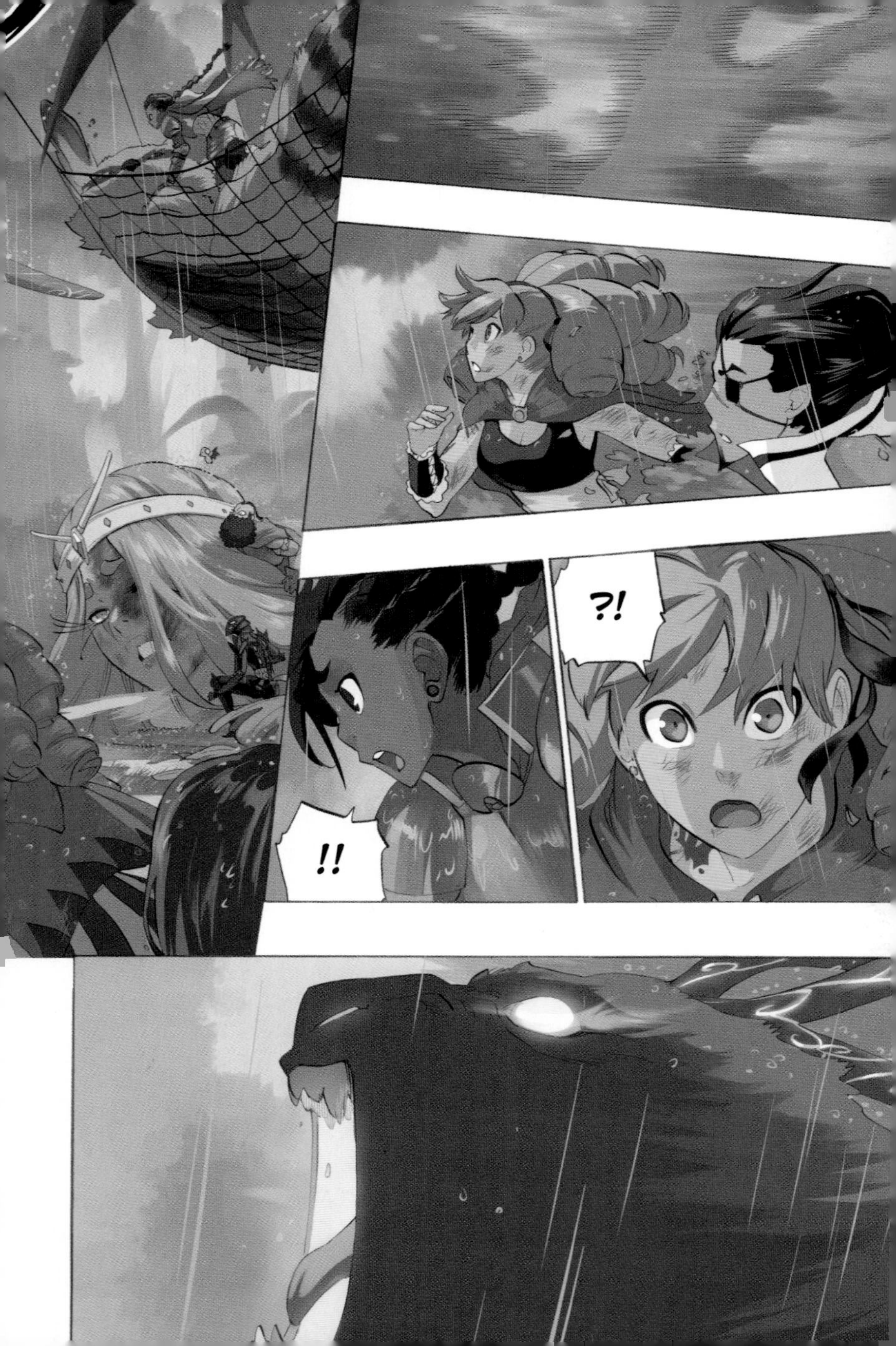
?!
!!

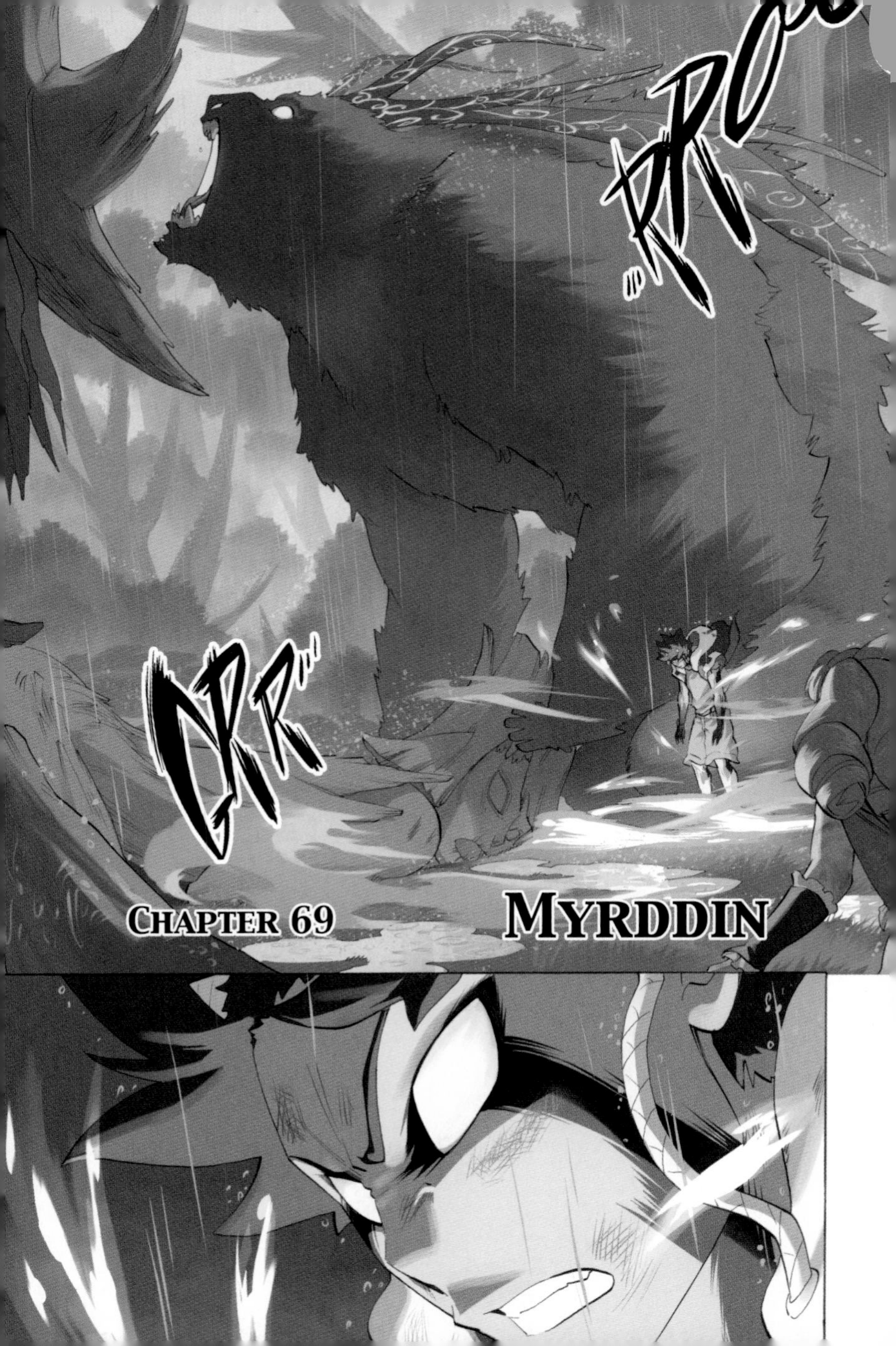
Chapter 69
Myrddin

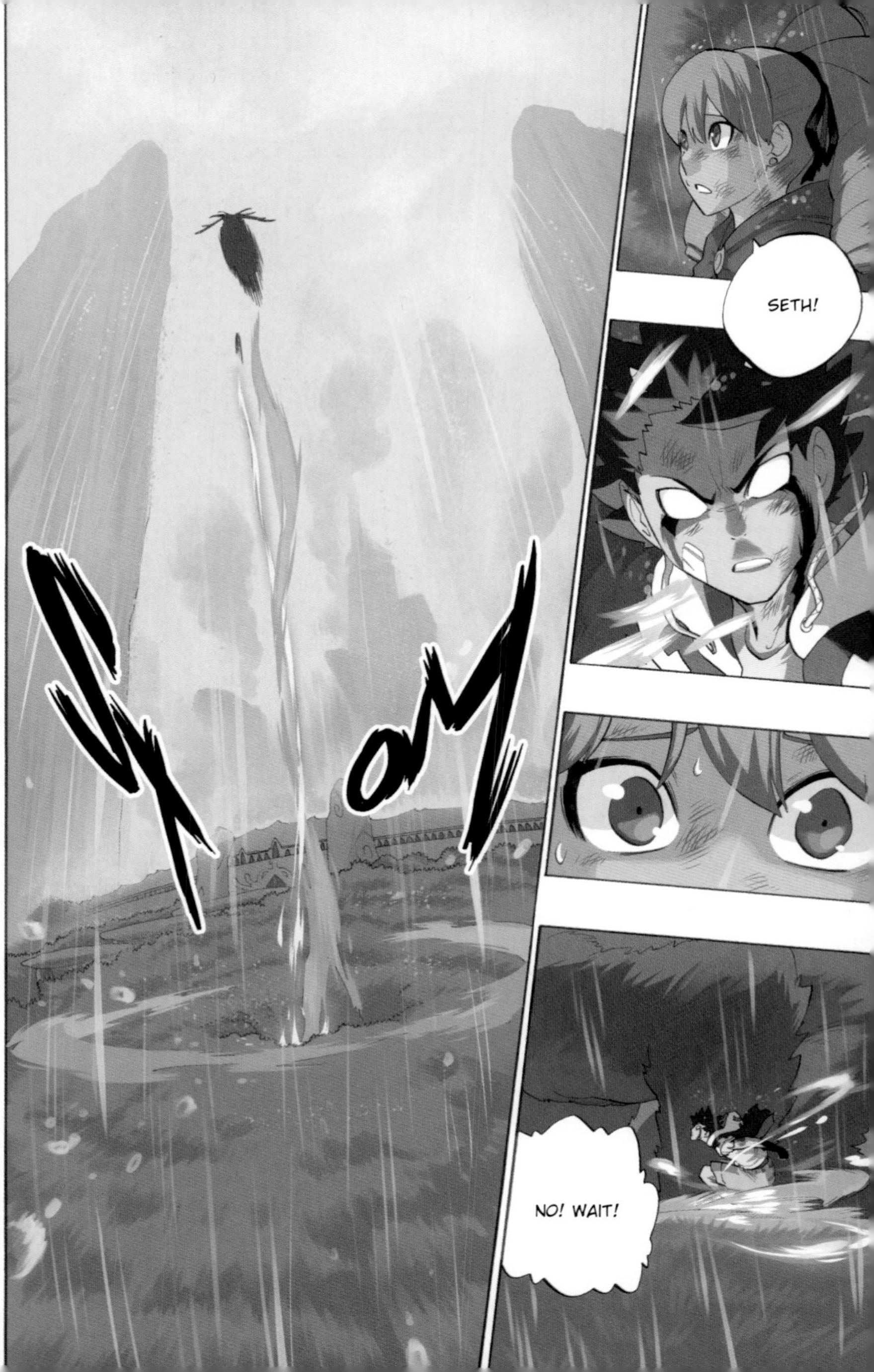
SETH!
NO! WAIT!

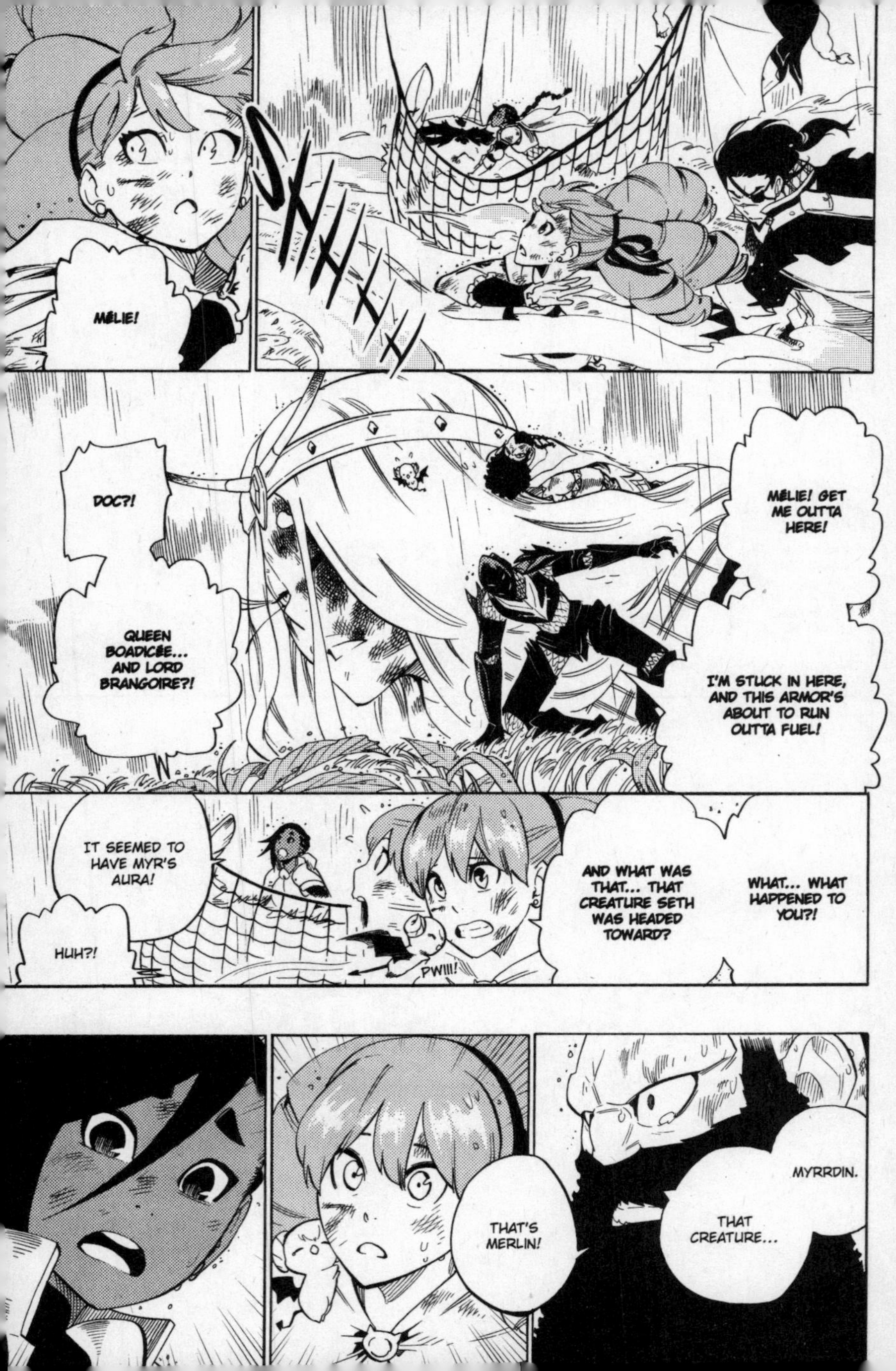
SHHHHH
MÉLIE!
MÉLIE! GET ME OUTTA HERE!
I'M STUCK IN HERE, AND THIS ARMOR'S ABOUT TO RUN OUTTA FUEL!
DOC?!
QUEEN BOADICÉE... AND LORD BRANGOIRE?!
WHAT... WHAT HAPPENED TO YOU?!
AND WHAT WAS THAT... THAT CREATURE SETH WAS HEADED TOWARD?
PWIII!
IT SEEMED TO HAVE MYR'S AURA!
HUH?!
MYRRDIN.
THAT CREATURE...
THAT'S MERLIN!

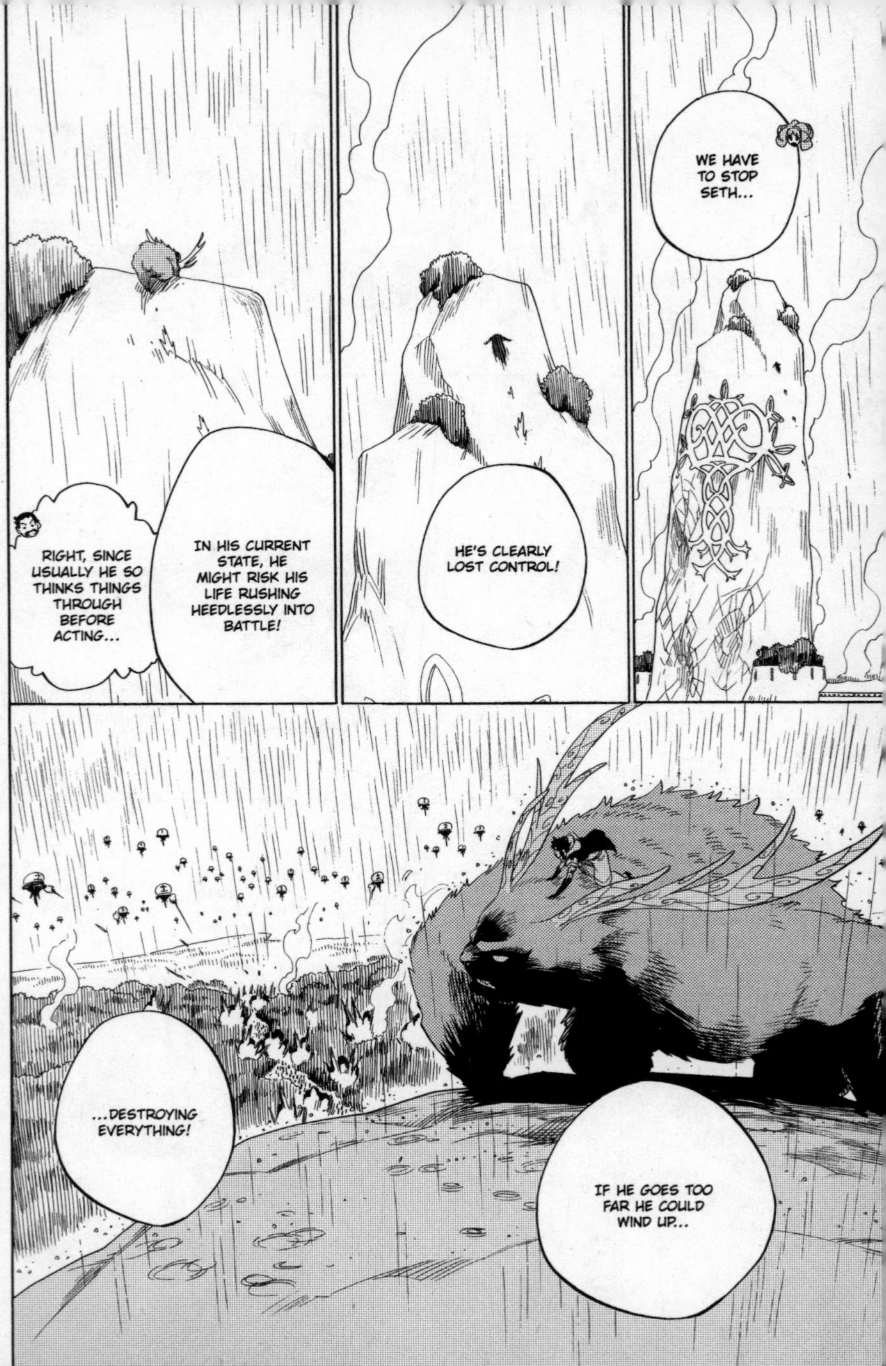
WE HAVE TO STOP SETH...
HE'S CLEARLY LOST CONTROL!
IN HIS CURRENT STATE, HE MIGHT RISK HIS LIFE RUSHING HEEDLESSLY INTO BATTLE!
RIGHT, SINCE USUALLY HE SO THINKS THINGS THROUGH BEFORE ACTING...
IF HE GOES TOO FAR HE COULD WIND UP...
...DESTROYING EVERYTHING!

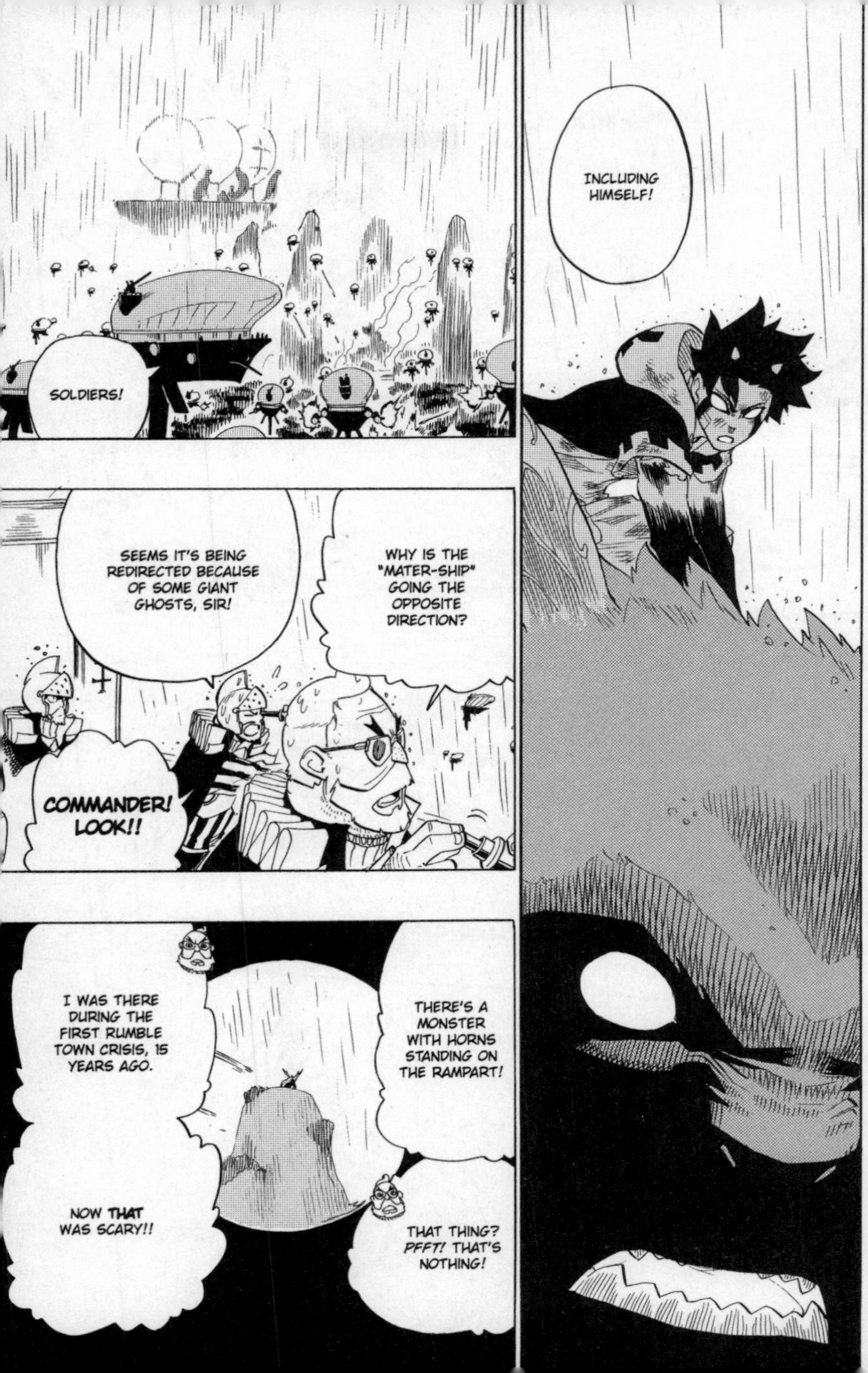
INCLUDING HIMSELF!
SOLDIERS!
WHY IS THE "MATER-SHIP" GOING THE OPPOSITE DIRECTION?
SEEMS IT'S BEING REDIRECTED BECAUSE OF SOME GIANT GHOSTS, SIR!
COMMANDER! LOOK!!
THERE'S A MONSTER WITH HORNS STANDING ON THE RAMPART!
THAT THING? *PFFT!* THAT'S NOTHING!
I WAS THERE DURING THE FIRST RUMBLE TOWN CRISIS, 15 YEARS AGO.
NOW THAT WAS SCARY!!

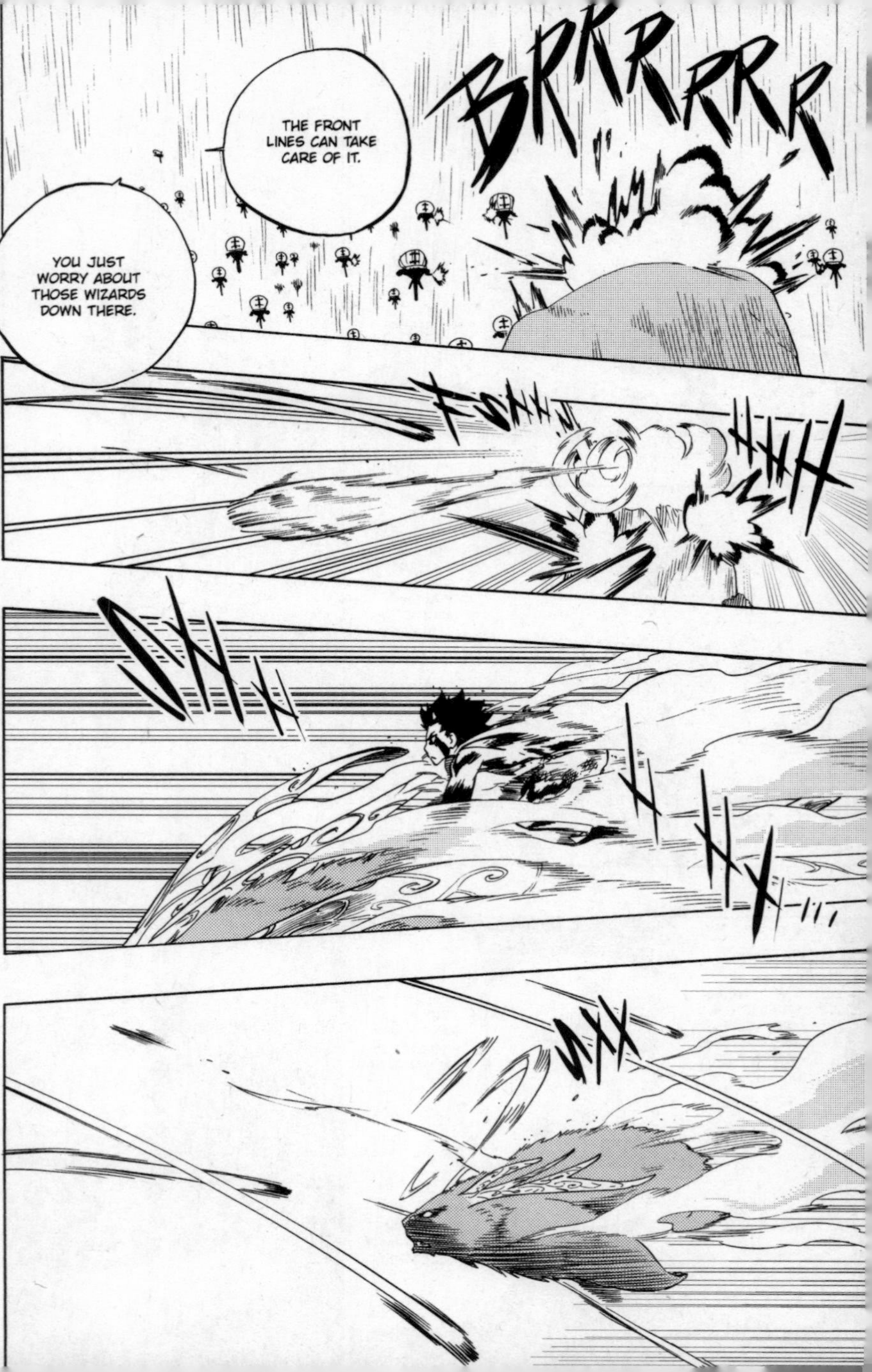
BRKRRRR
THE FRONT LINES CAN TAKE CARE OF IT.
YOU JUST WORRY ABOUT THOSE WIZARDS DOWN THERE.
FSHH
HHH
SHHH
SHH

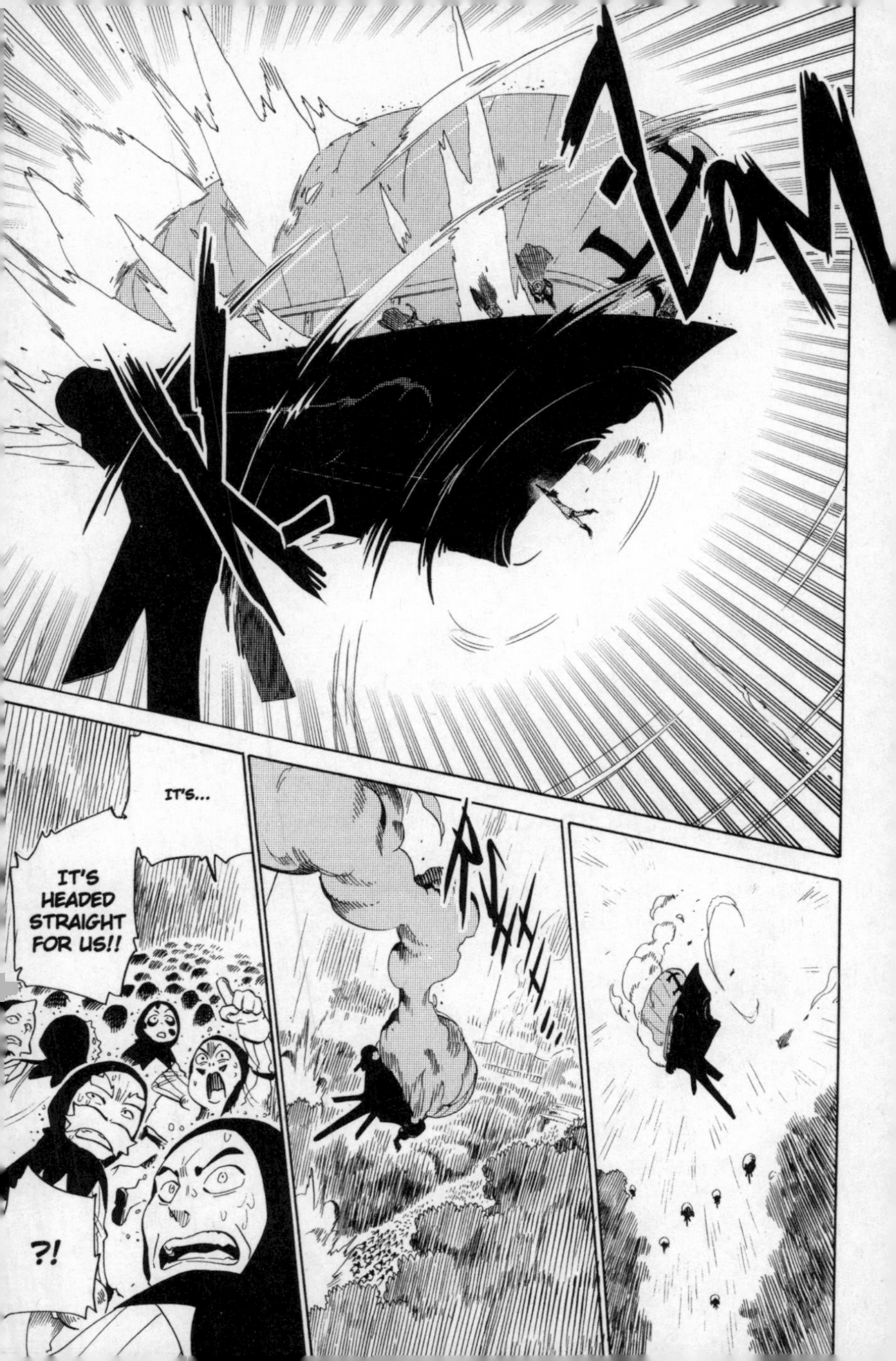
IT'S...
IT'S HEADED STRAIGHT FOR US!!
?!

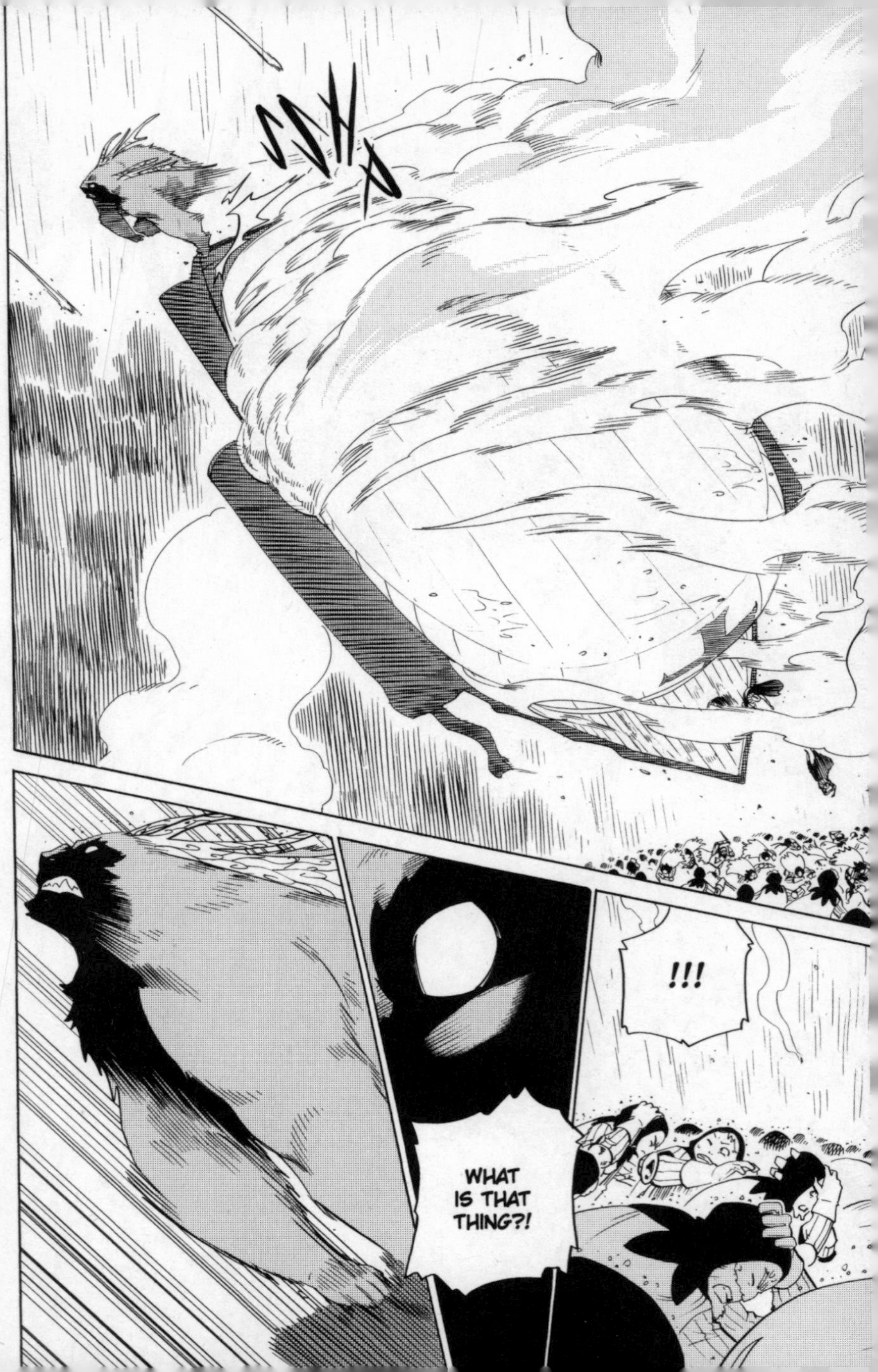
!!!
WHAT IS THAT THING?!

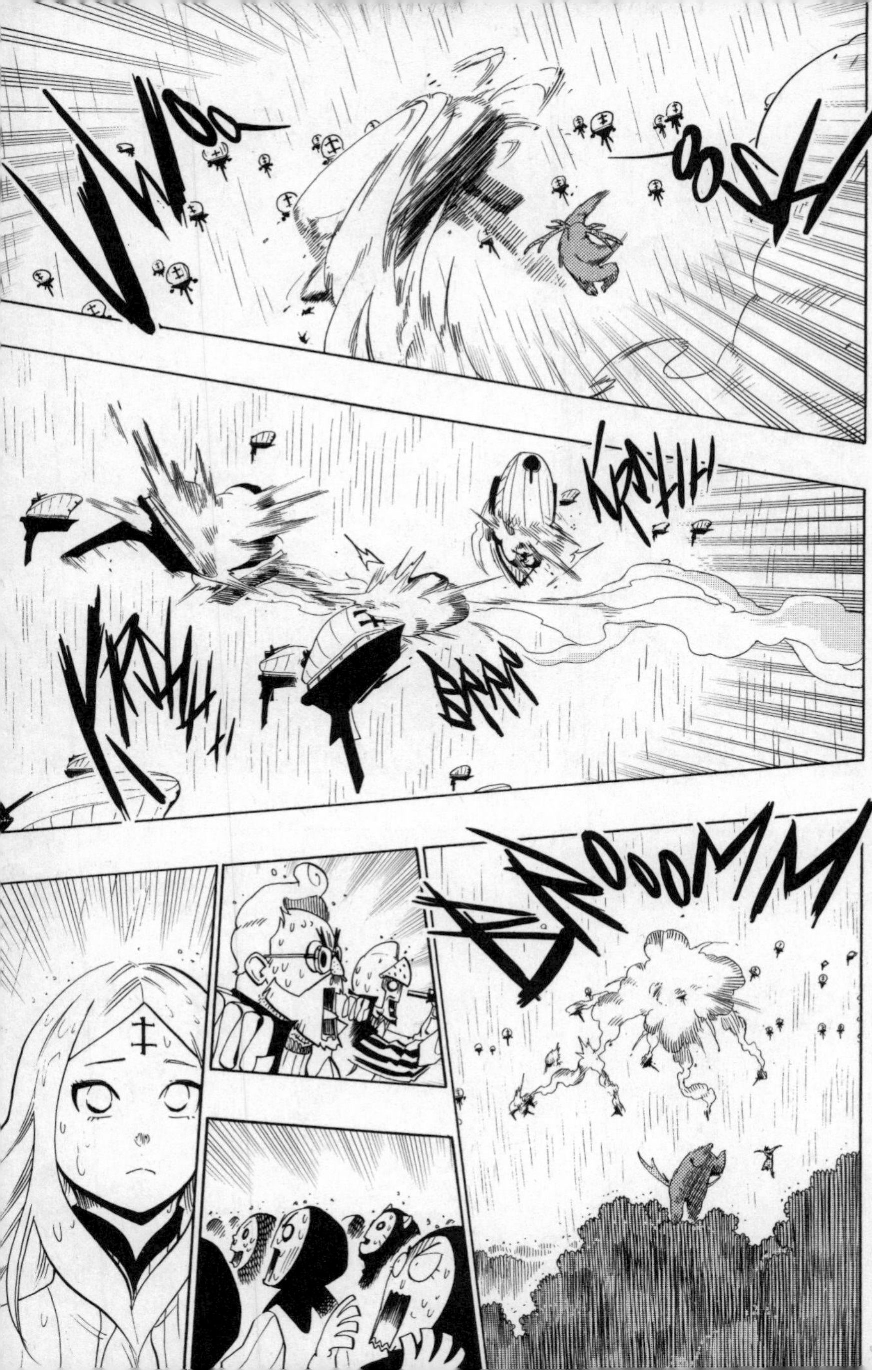
VWOO
OOSH
KRSHH
BRRR
KRSHH
BROOOMM

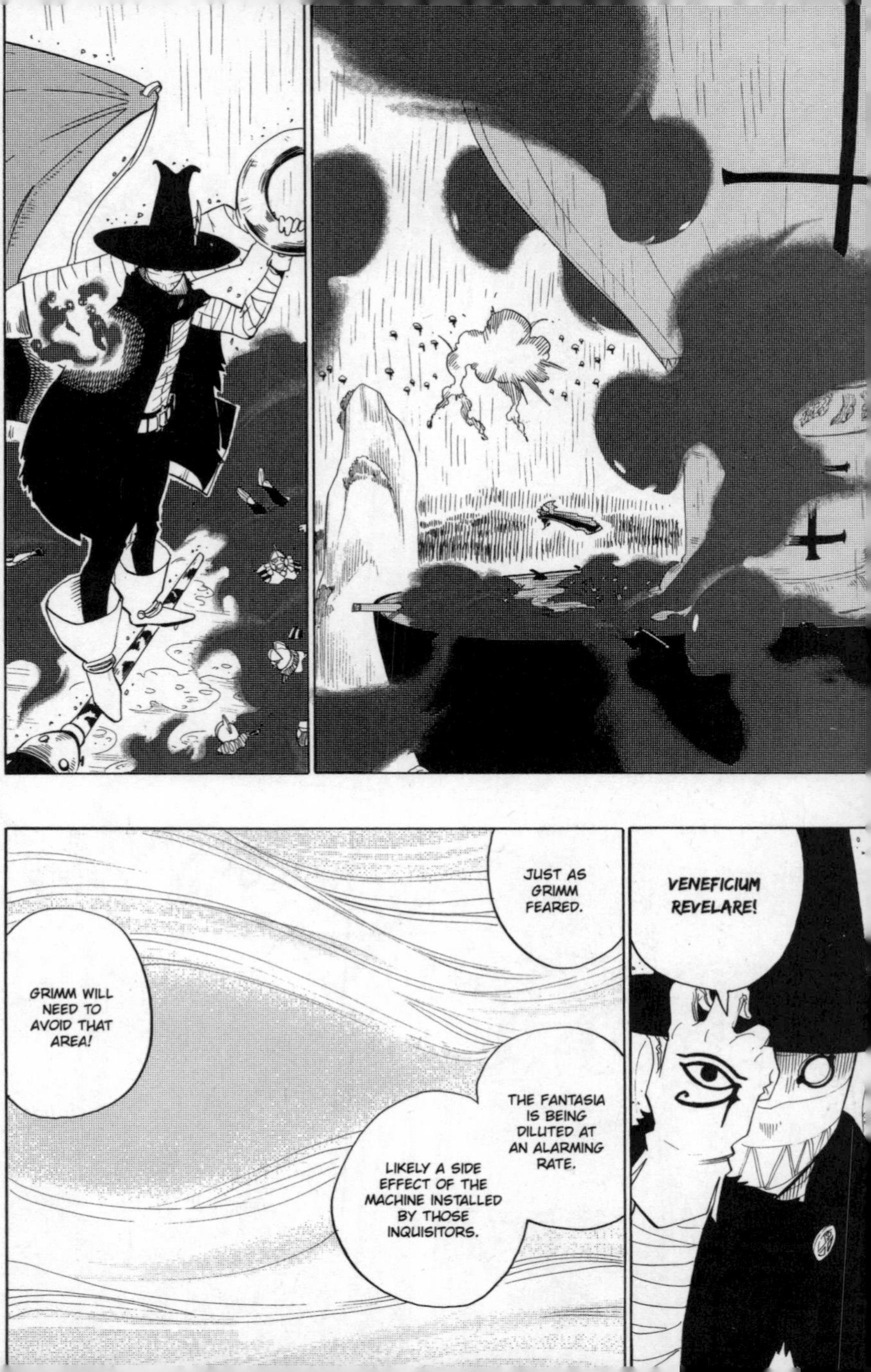
VENEFICIUM REVELARE!
JUST AS GRIMM FEARED.
THE FANTASIA IS BEING DILUTED AT AN ALARMING RATE.
LIKELY A SIDE EFFECT OF THE MACHINE INSTALLED BY THOSE INQUISITORS.
GRIMM WILL NEED TO AVOID THAT AREA!

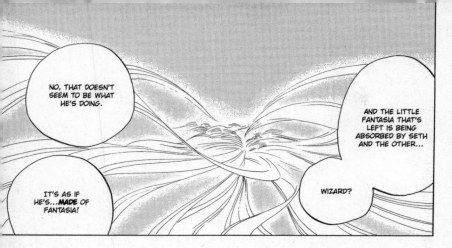

AND THE LITTLE FANTASIA THAT'S LEFT IS BEING ABSORBED BY SETH AND THE OTHER...
WIZARD?
NO, THAT DOESN'T SEEM TO BE WHAT HE'S DOING.
IT'S AS IF HE'S...**MADE** OF FANTASIA!
GOOD THING THAT SHIP IS OUT OF THEIR REACH.
A SHIP THAT SIZE CRASHING HERE WOULD BE A DISASTER ON BOTH SIDES.
OH, HORNED WIZARD, SEE THE POSITION YOU'VE PUT GRIMM IN?
RENDERED POWERLESS DUE TO THE LACK OF FANTASIA...
SO HE CAN ONLY SIT HERE AND WATCH AS EVERYTHING UNFOLDS...

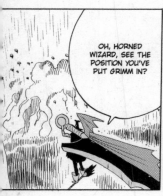

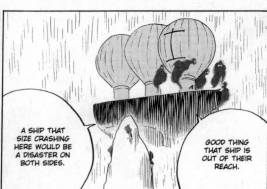

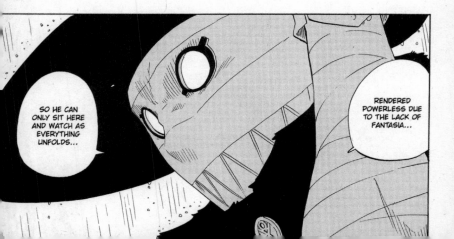

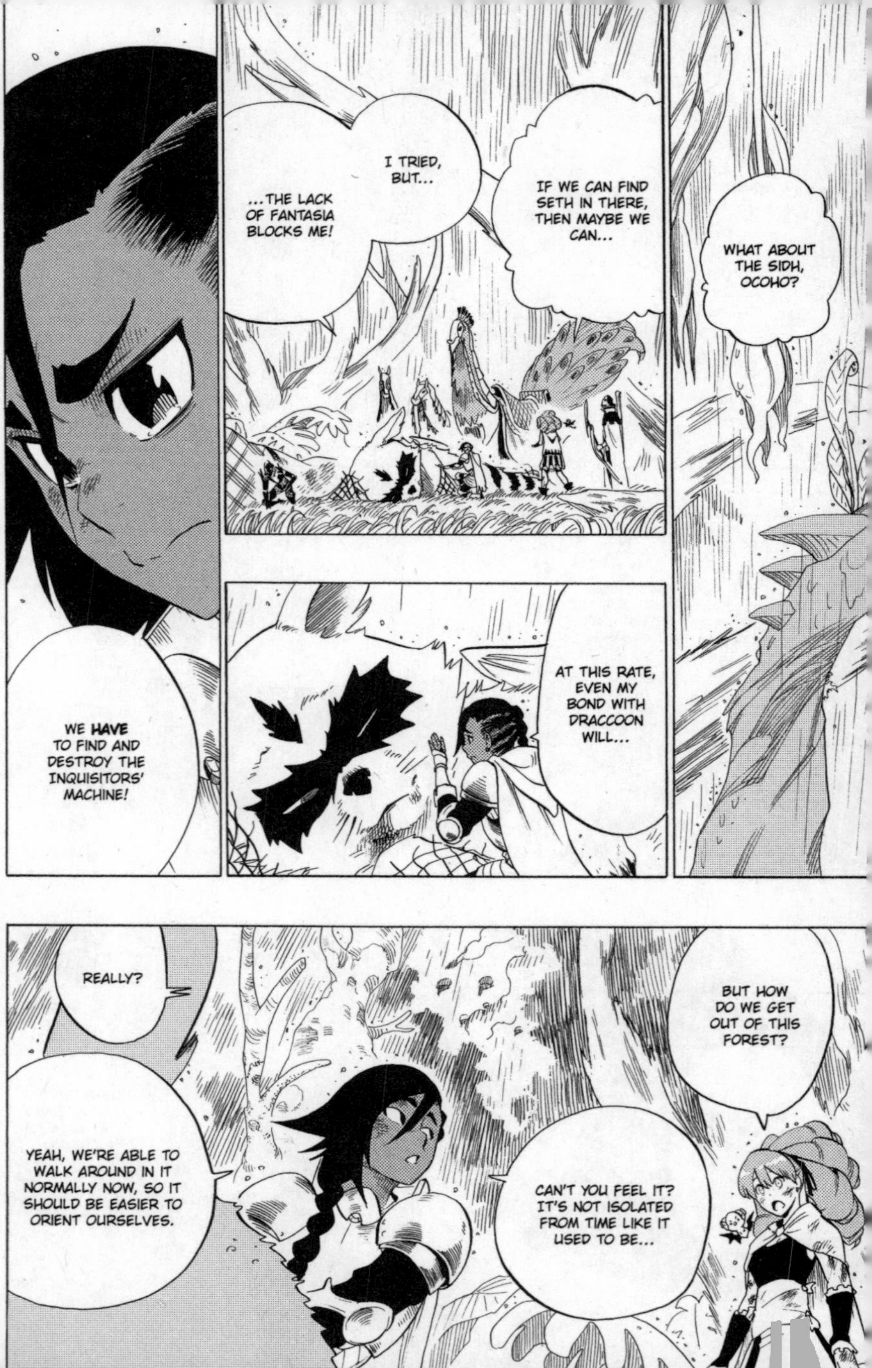
WHAT ABOUT THE SIDH, OCOHO?
I TRIED, BUT...
...THE LACK OF FANTASIA BLOCKS ME!
IF WE CAN FIND SETH IN THERE, THEN MAYBE WE CAN...
AT THIS RATE, EVEN MY BOND WITH DRACCOON WILL...
WE **HAVE** TO FIND AND DESTROY THE INQUISITORS' MACHINE!
BUT HOW DO WE GET OUT OF THIS FOREST?
CAN'T YOU FEEL IT? IT'S NOT ISOLATED FROM TIME LIKE IT USED TO BE...
REALLY?
YEAH, WE'RE ABLE TO WALK AROUND IN IT NORMALLY NOW, SO IT SHOULD BE EASIER TO ORIENT OURSELVES.

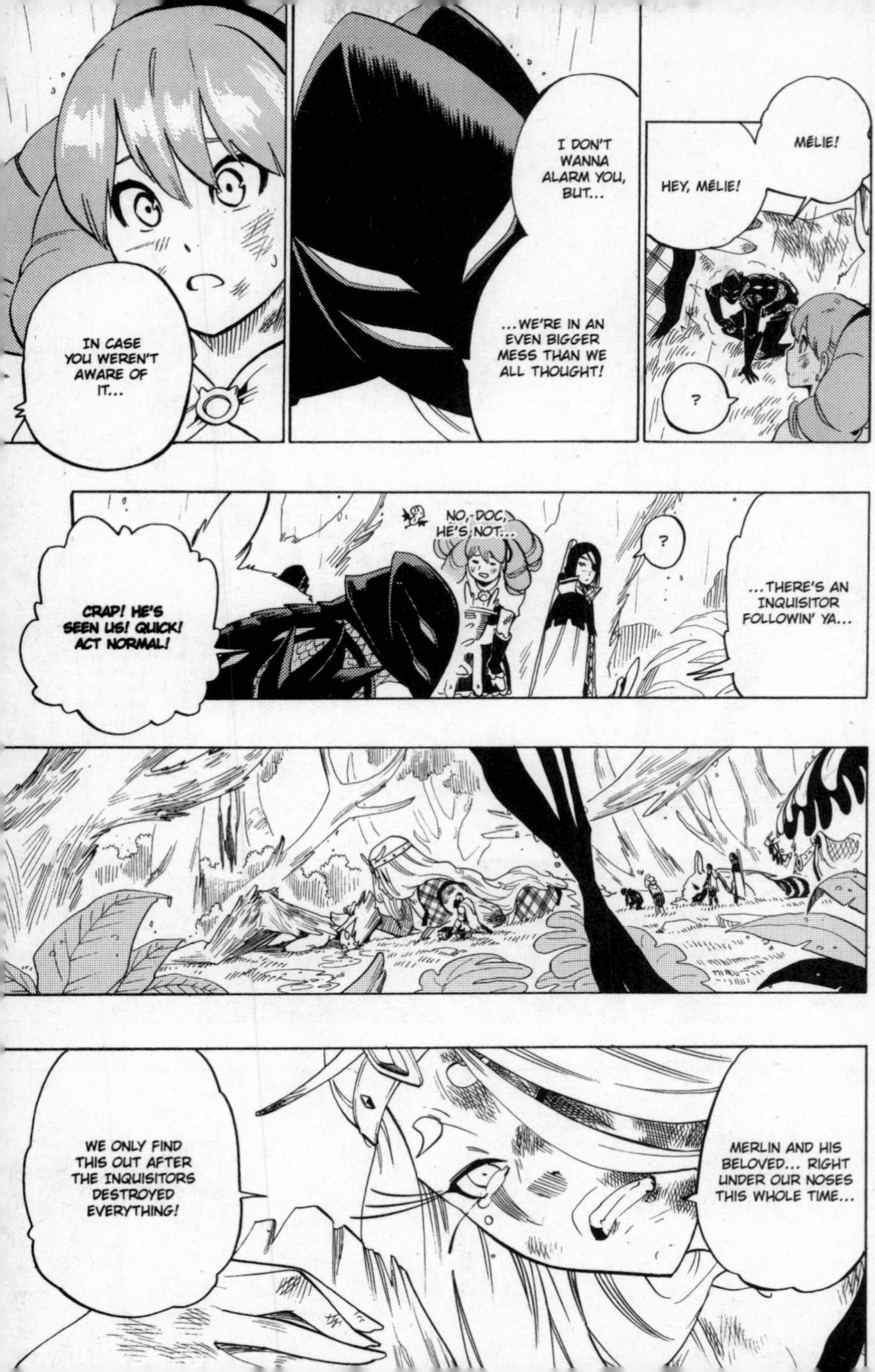
MÉLIE!
HEY, MÉLIE!
?
I DON'T WANNA ALARM YOU, BUT...
...WE'RE IN AN EVEN BIGGER MESS THAN WE ALL THOUGHT!
IN CASE YOU WEREN'T AWARE OF IT...
...THERE'S AN INQUISITOR FOLLOWIN' YA...
?
NO, DOC, HE'S NOT...
CRAP! HE'S SEEN US! QUICK! ACT NORMAL!
MERLIN AND HIS BELOVED... RIGHT UNDER OUR NOSES THIS WHOLE TIME...
WE ONLY FIND THIS OUT AFTER THE INQUISITORS DESTROYED EVERYTHING!

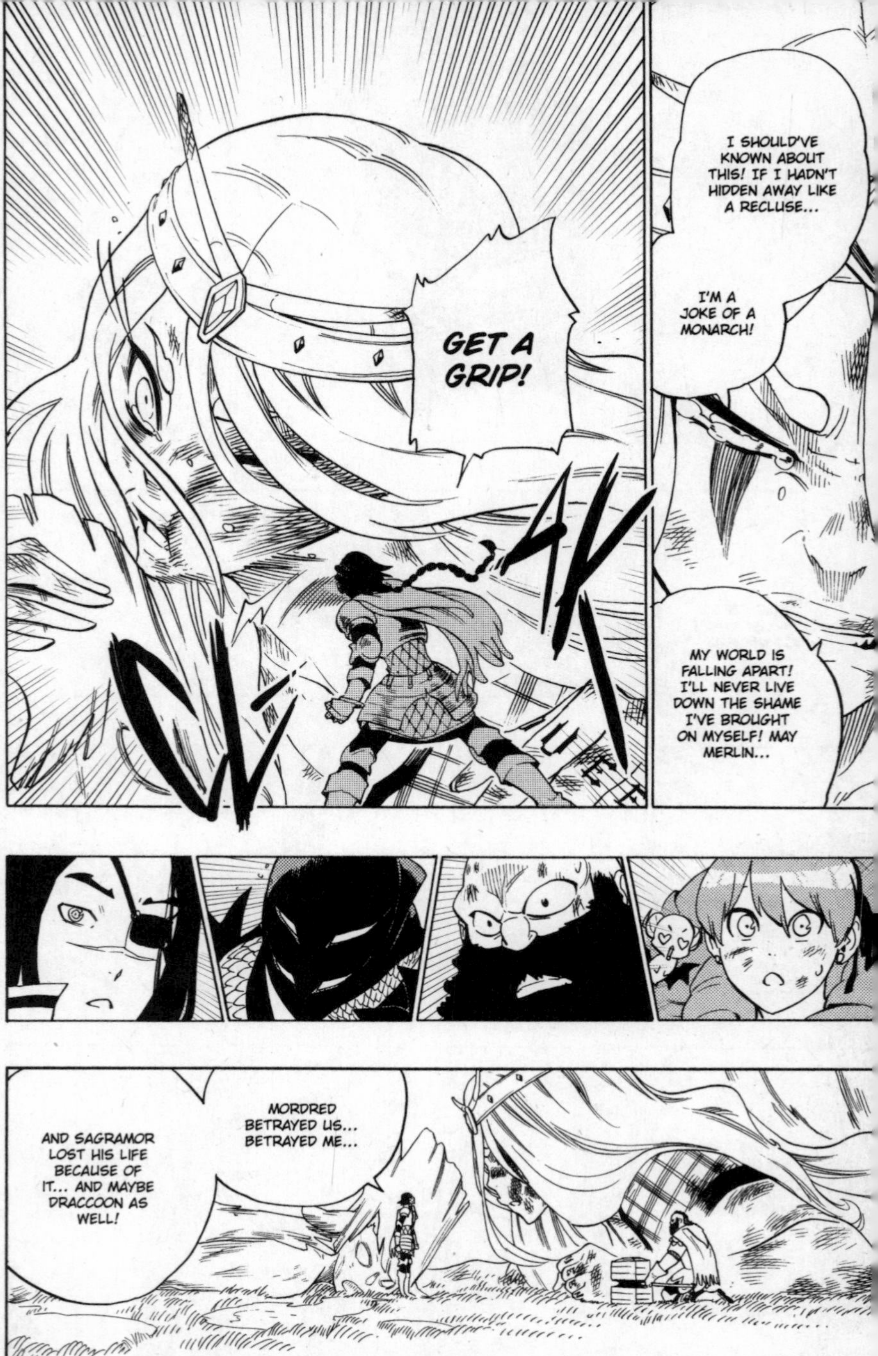
I SHOULD'VE KNOWN ABOUT THIS! IF I HADN'T HIDDEN AWAY LIKE A RECLUSE...
I'M A JOKE OF A MONARCH!
MY WORLD IS FALLING APART! I'LL NEVER LIVE DOWN THE SHAME I'VE BROUGHT ON MYSELF! MAY MERLIN...
GET A GRIP!
MORDRED BETRAYED US... BETRAYED ME...
AND SAGRAMOR LOST HIS LIFE BECAUSE OF IT... AND MAYBE DRACCOON AS WELL!

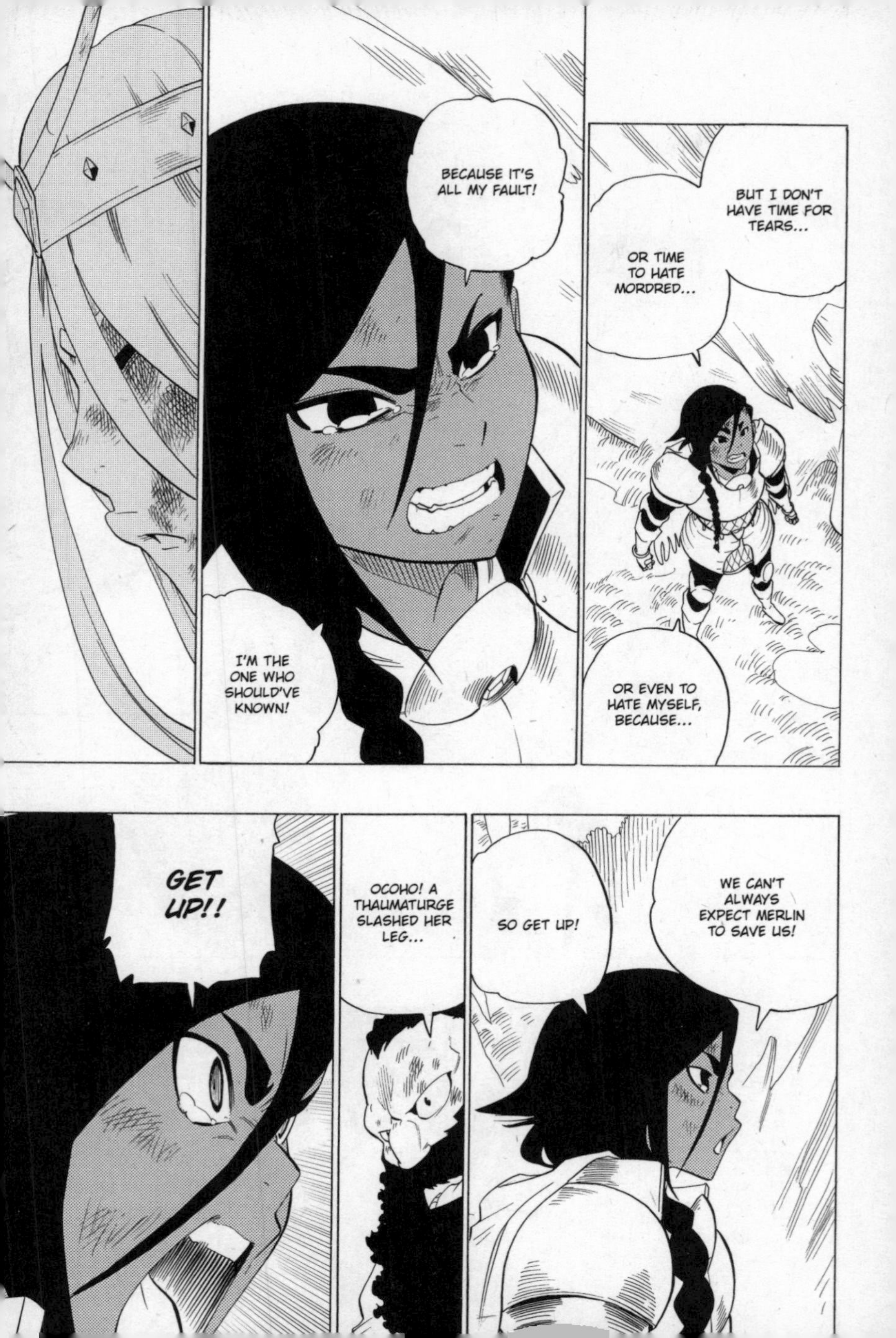
BUT I DON'T HAVE TIME FOR TEARS...
OR TIME TO HATE MORDRED...
OR EVEN TO HATE MYSELF, BECAUSE...
BECAUSE IT'S ALL MY FAULT!
I'M THE ONE WHO SHOULD'VE KNOWN!
WE CAN'T ALWAYS EXPECT MERLIN TO SAVE US!
SO GET UP!
OCOHO! A THAUMATURGE SLASHED HER LEG...
GET UP!!

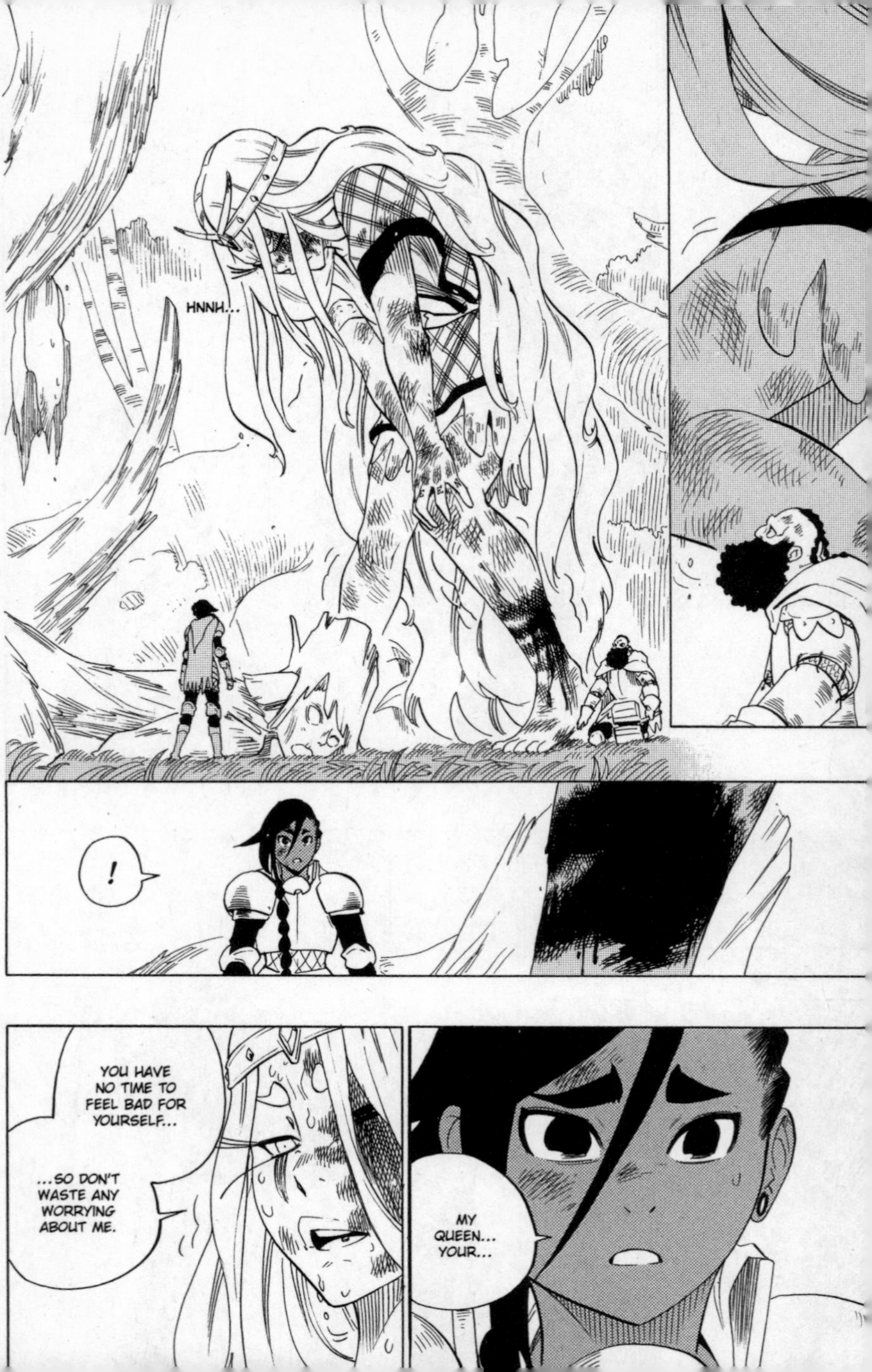
HNNH...
!
MY QUEEN... YOUR...
YOU HAVE NO TIME TO FEEL BAD FOR YOURSELF...
...SO DON'T WASTE ANY WORRYING ABOUT ME.

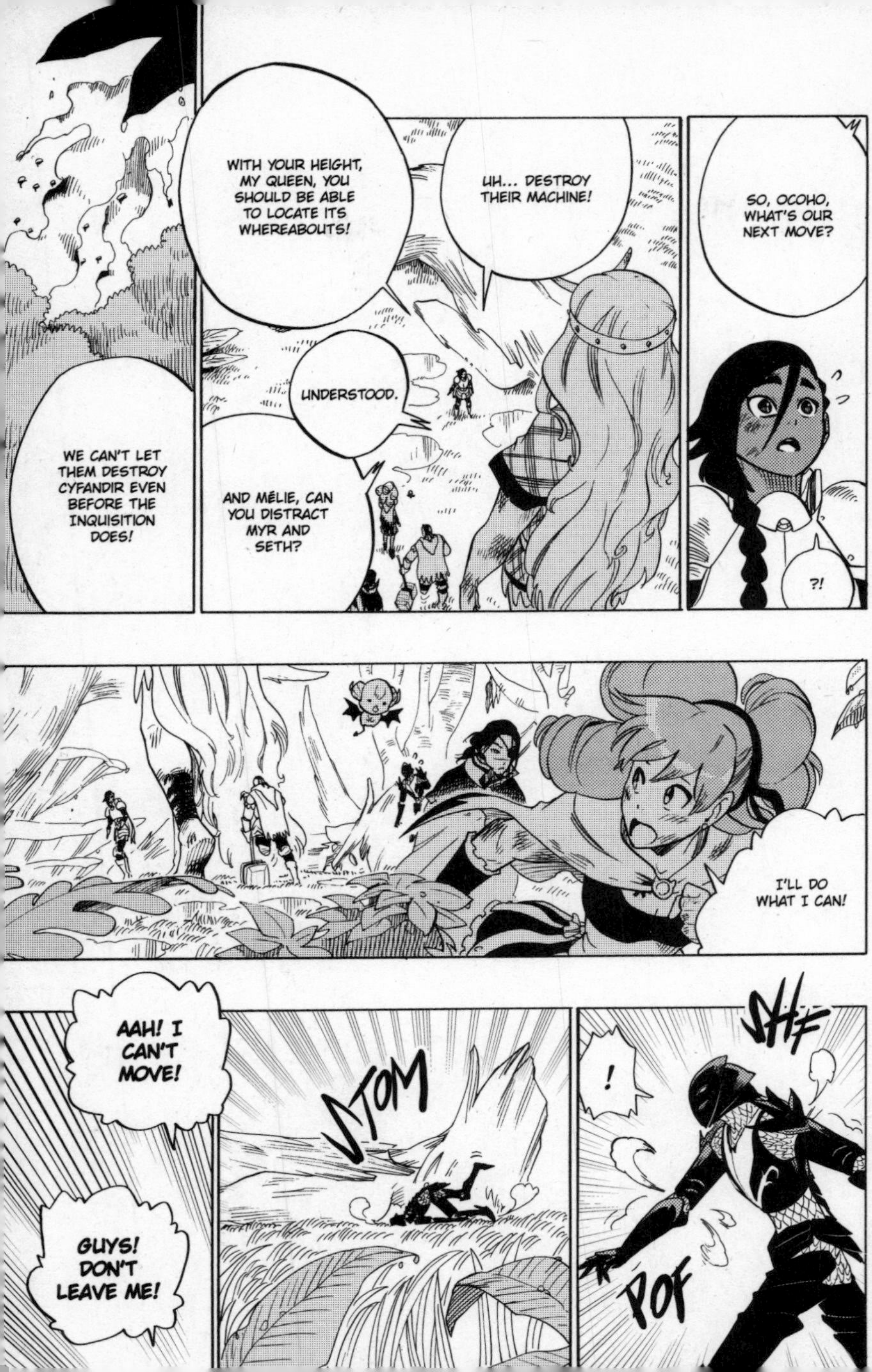
SO, OCOHO, WHAT'S OUR NEXT MOVE?
?!
UH... DESTROY THEIR MACHINE!
WITH YOUR HEIGHT, MY QUEEN, YOU SHOULD BE ABLE TO LOCATE ITS WHEREABOUTS!
UNDERSTOOD.
AND MÉLIE, CAN YOU DISTRACT MYR AND SETH?
WE CAN'T LET THEM DESTROY CYFANDIR EVEN BEFORE THE INQUISITION DOES!
I'LL DO WHAT I CAN!
SHF
!
POF
STOM
AAH! I CAN'T MOVE!
GUYS! DON'T LEAVE ME!

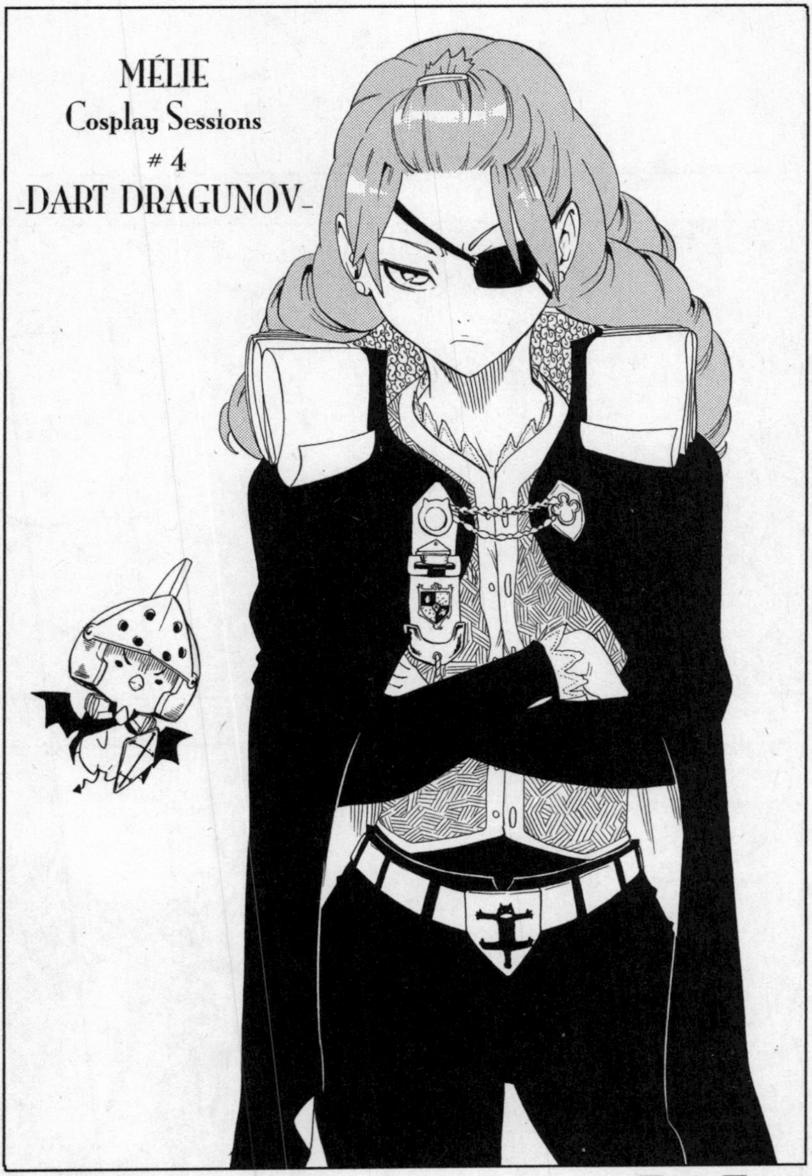
MÉLIE
Cosplay Sessions
4
-DART DRAGUNOV-

Chapter 70

Tin Toy

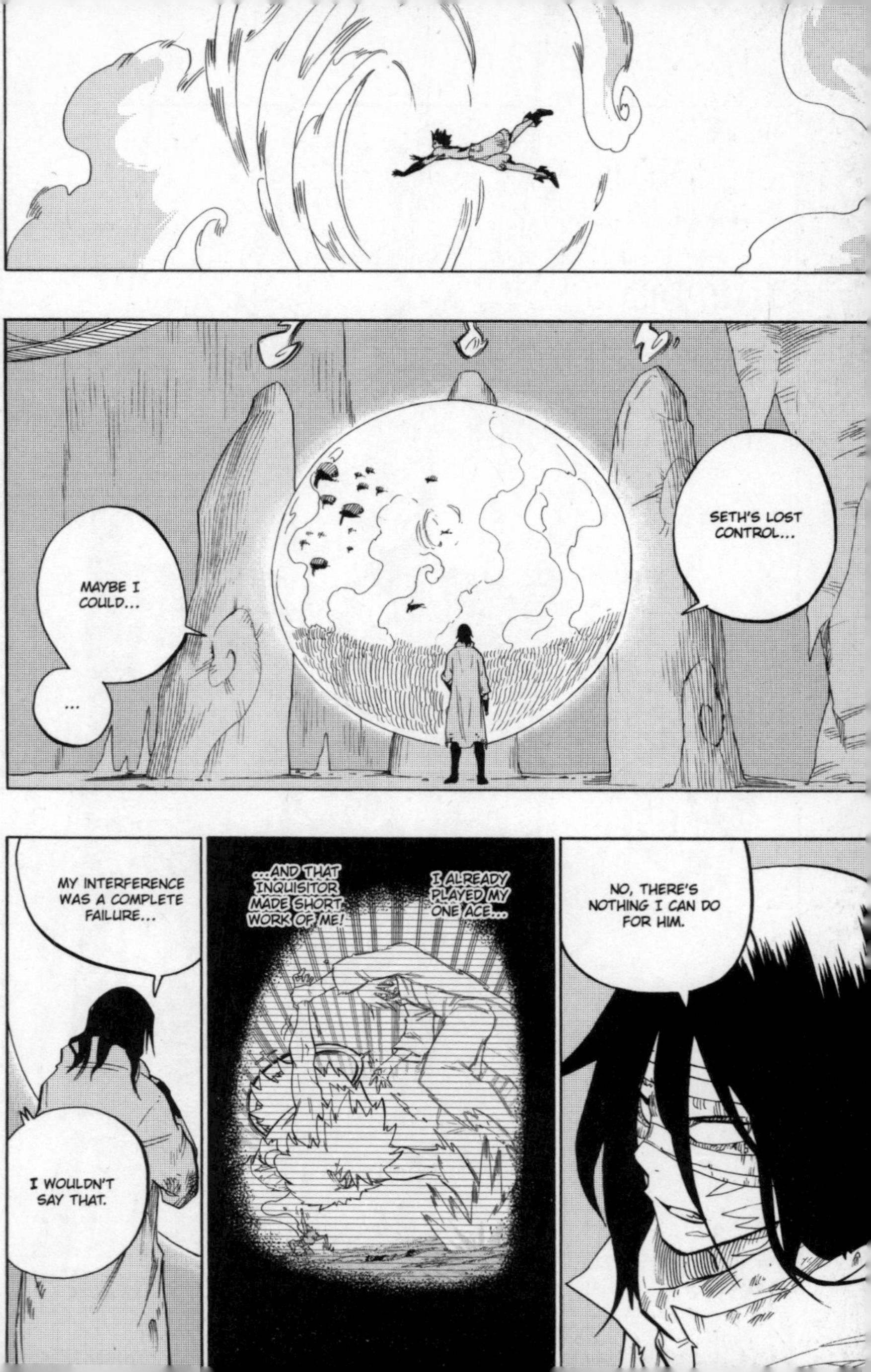
SETH'S LOST CONTROL...
MAYBE I COULD...
...
NO, THERE'S NOTHING I CAN DO FOR HIM.
I ALREADY PLAYED MY ONE ACE...
...AND THAT INQUISITOR MADE SHORT WORK OF ME!
MY INTERFERENCE WAS A COMPLETE FAILURE...
I WOULDN'T SAY THAT.

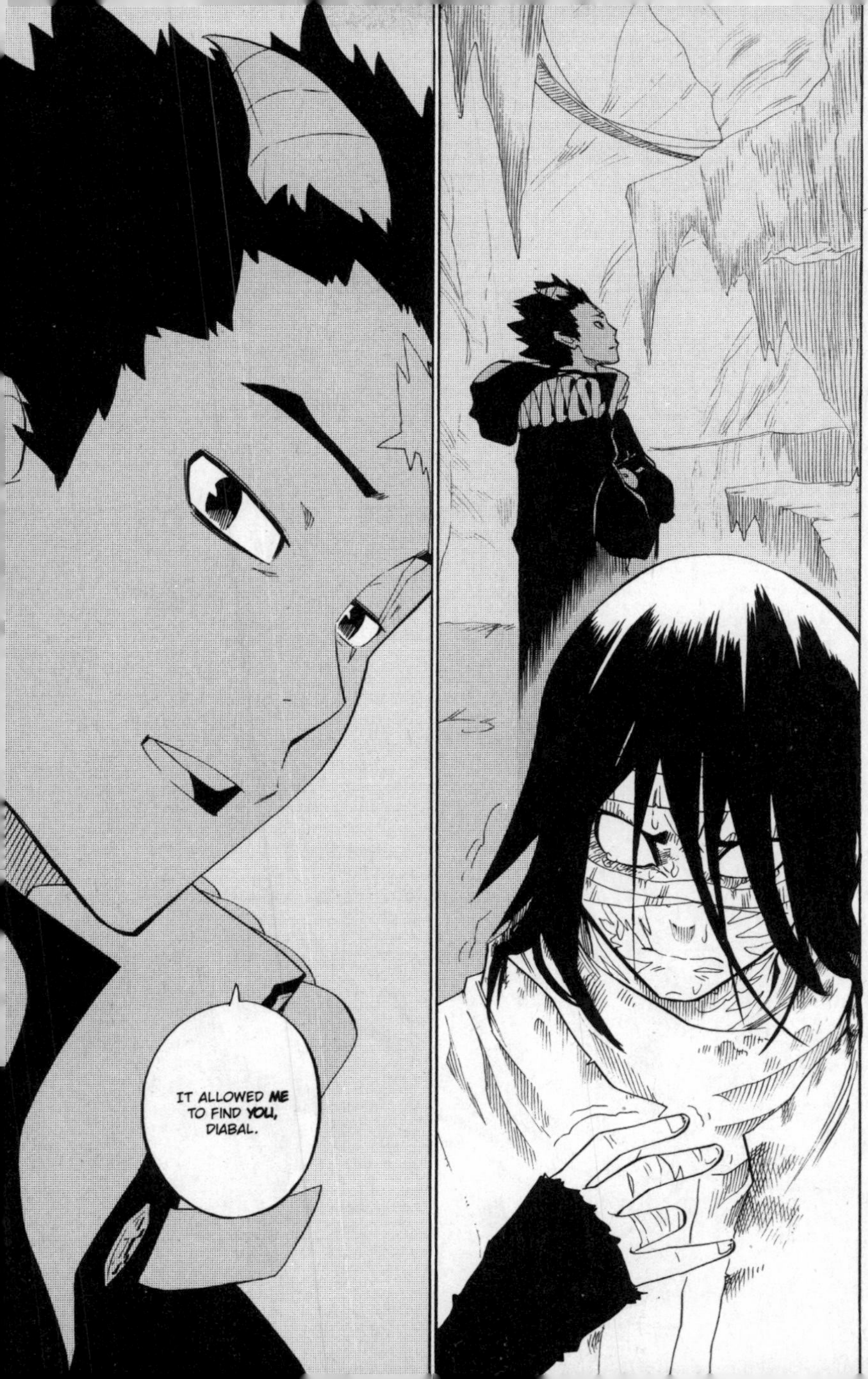
IT ALLOWED ME TO FIND YOU, DIABAL.

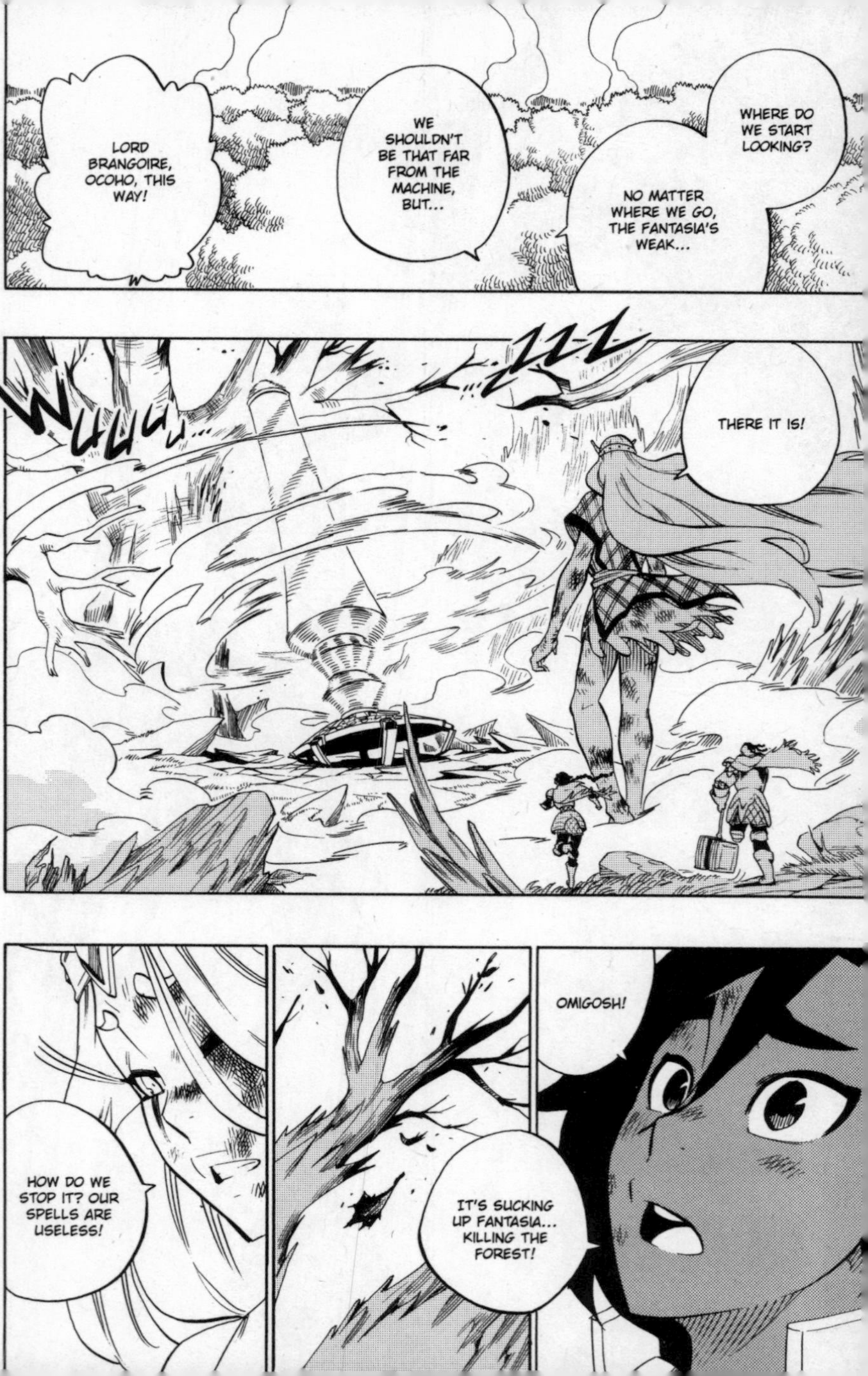
WHERE DO WE START LOOKING?
NO MATTER WHERE WE GO, THE FANTASIA'S WEAK...
WE SHOULDN'T BE THAT FAR FROM THE MACHINE, BUT...
LORD BRANGOIRE, OCOHO, THIS WAY!
THERE IT IS!
ZZZ
WUUUU...
OMIGOSH!
IT'S SUCKING UP FANTASIA... KILLING THE FOREST!
HOW DO WE STOP IT? OUR SPELLS ARE USELESS!

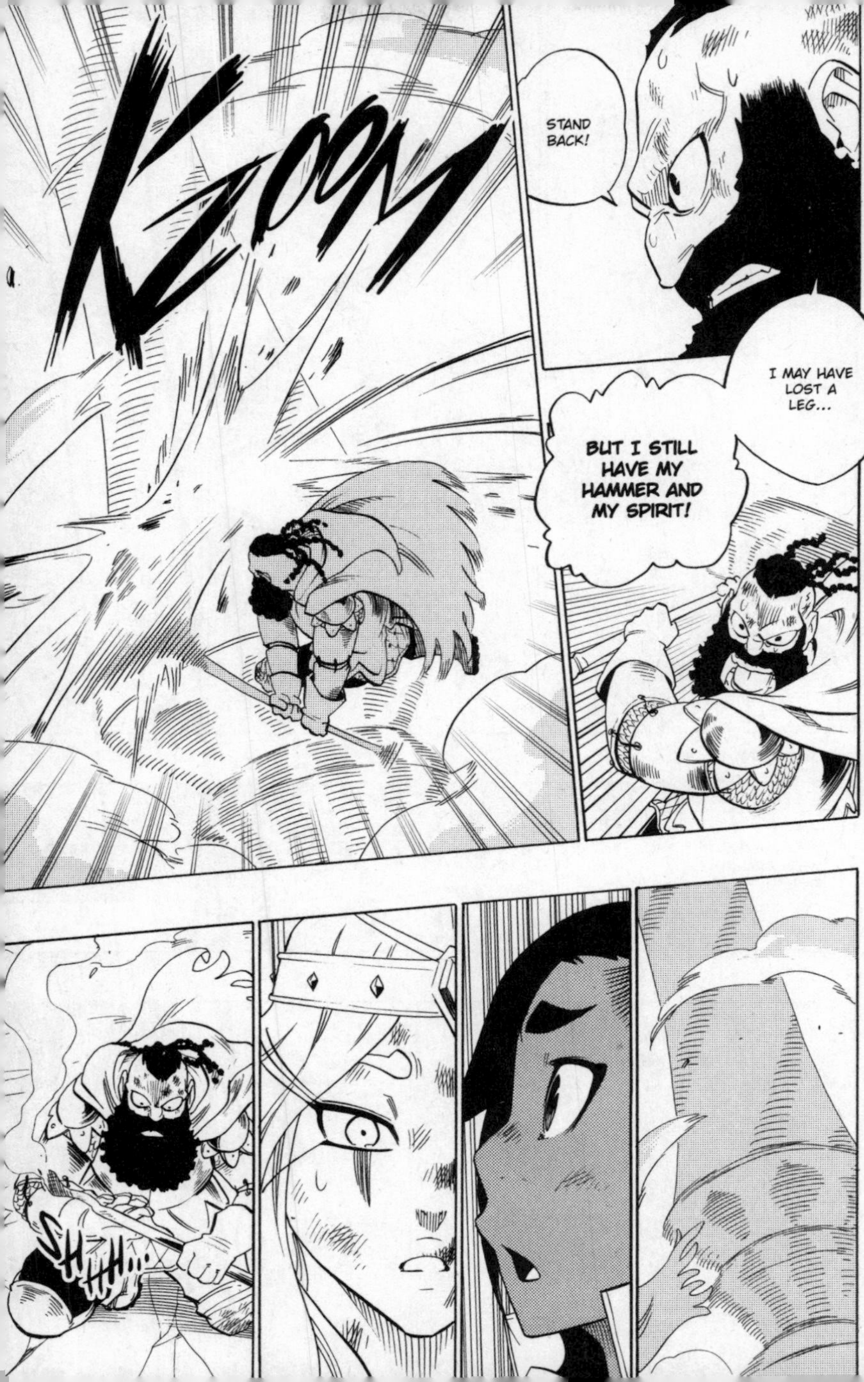
STAND BACK!
KZOOM
I MAY HAVE LOST A LEG...
BUT I STILL HAVE MY HAMMER AND MY SPIRIT!
SHHH...

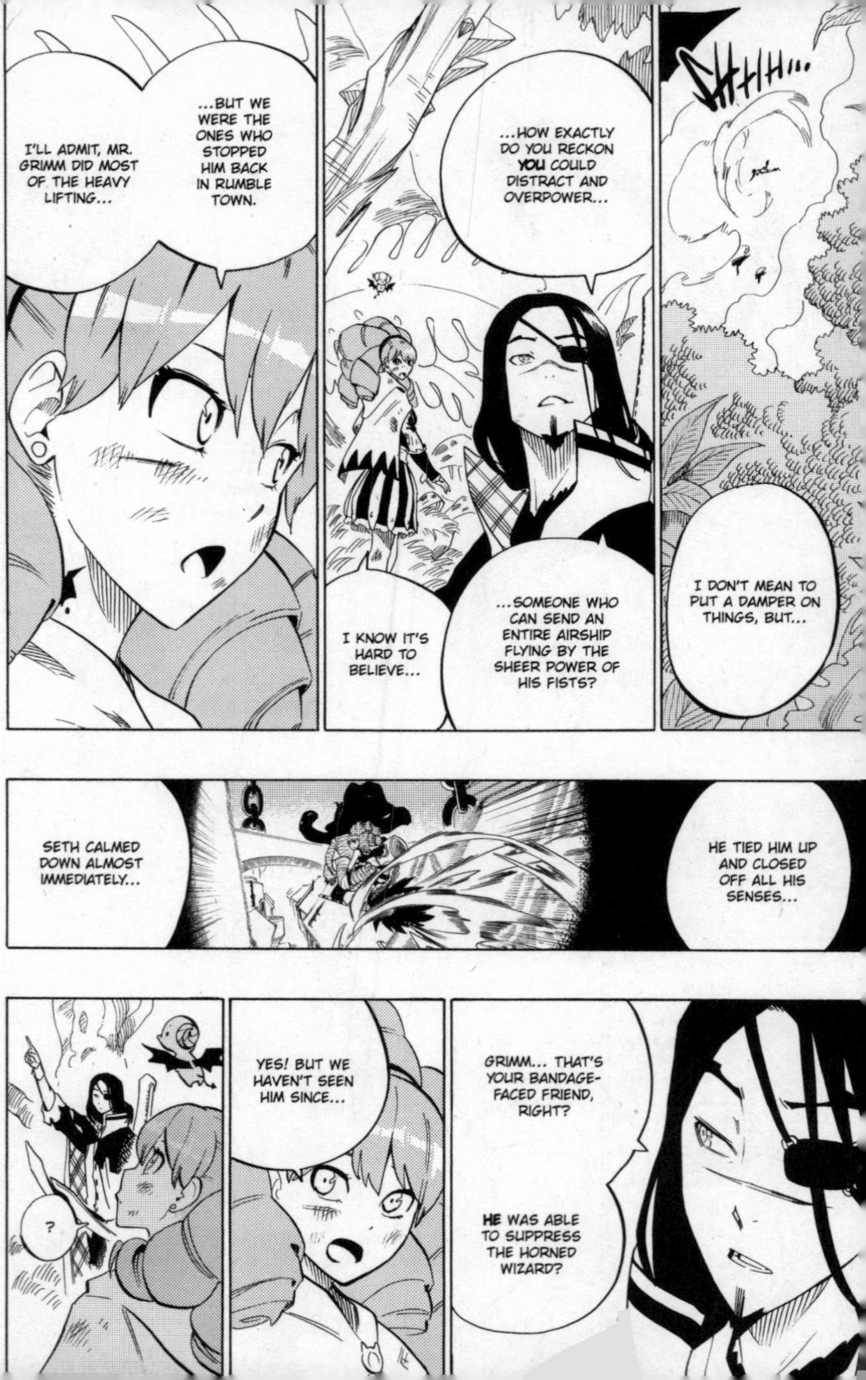
SHHH...
I DON'T MEAN TO PUT A DAMPER ON THINGS, BUT...
...HOW EXACTLY DO YOU RECKON **YOU** COULD DISTRACT AND OVERPOWER...
...SOMEONE WHO CAN SEND AN ENTIRE AIRSHIP FLYING BY THE SHEER POWER OF HIS FISTS?
I KNOW IT'S HARD TO BELIEVE...
I'LL ADMIT, MR. GRIMM DID MOST OF THE HEAVY LIFTING...
...BUT WE WERE THE ONES WHO STOPPED HIM BACK IN RUMBLE TOWN.
HE TIED HIM UP AND CLOSED OFF ALL HIS SENSES...
SETH CALMED DOWN ALMOST IMMEDIATELY...
GRIMM... THAT'S YOUR BANDAGE-FACED FRIEND, RIGHT?
HE WAS ABLE TO SUPPRESS THE HORNED WIZARD?
YES! BUT WE HAVEN'T SEEN HIM SINCE...
?

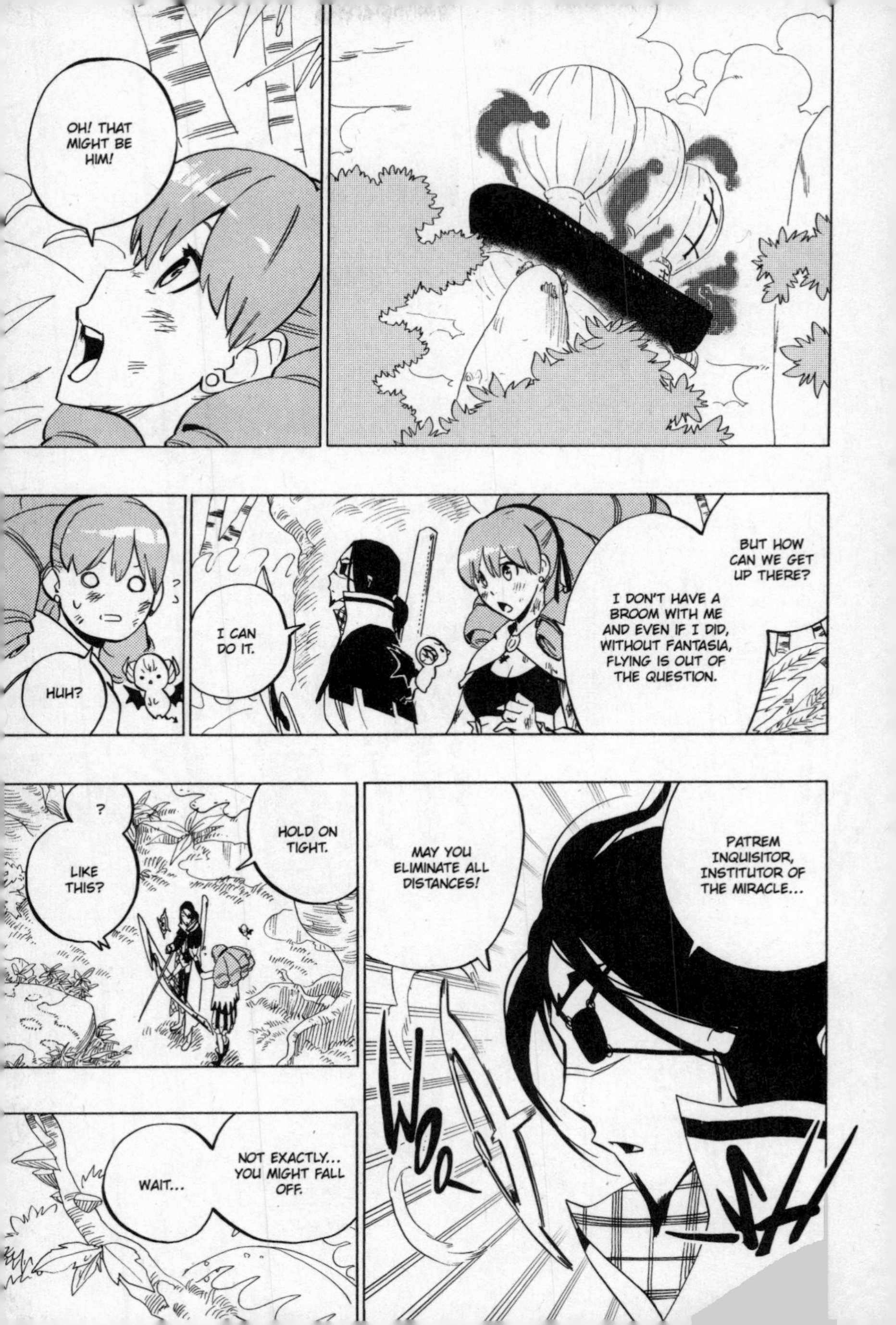
OH! THAT MIGHT BE HIM!
BUT HOW CAN WE GET UP THERE?
I DON'T HAVE A BROOM WITH ME AND EVEN IF I DID, WITHOUT FANTASIA, FLYING IS OUT OF THE QUESTION.
I CAN DO IT.
HUH?
PATREM INQUISITOR, INSTITUTOR OF THE MIRACLE...
MAY YOU ELIMINATE ALL DISTANCES!
HOLD ON TIGHT.
?
LIKE THIS?
NOT EXACTLY... YOU MIGHT FALL OFF.
WAIT...

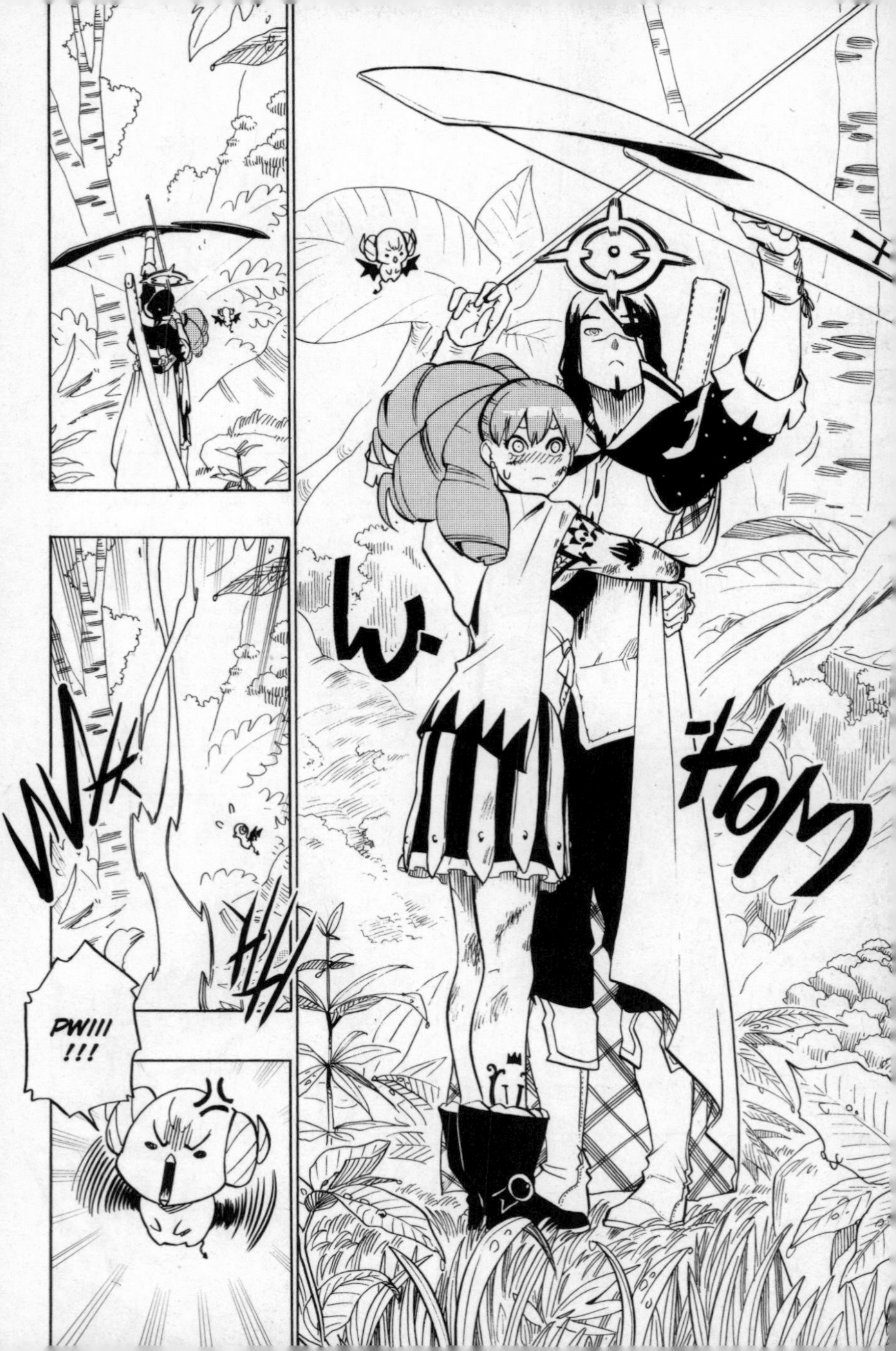
PWIII
!!!

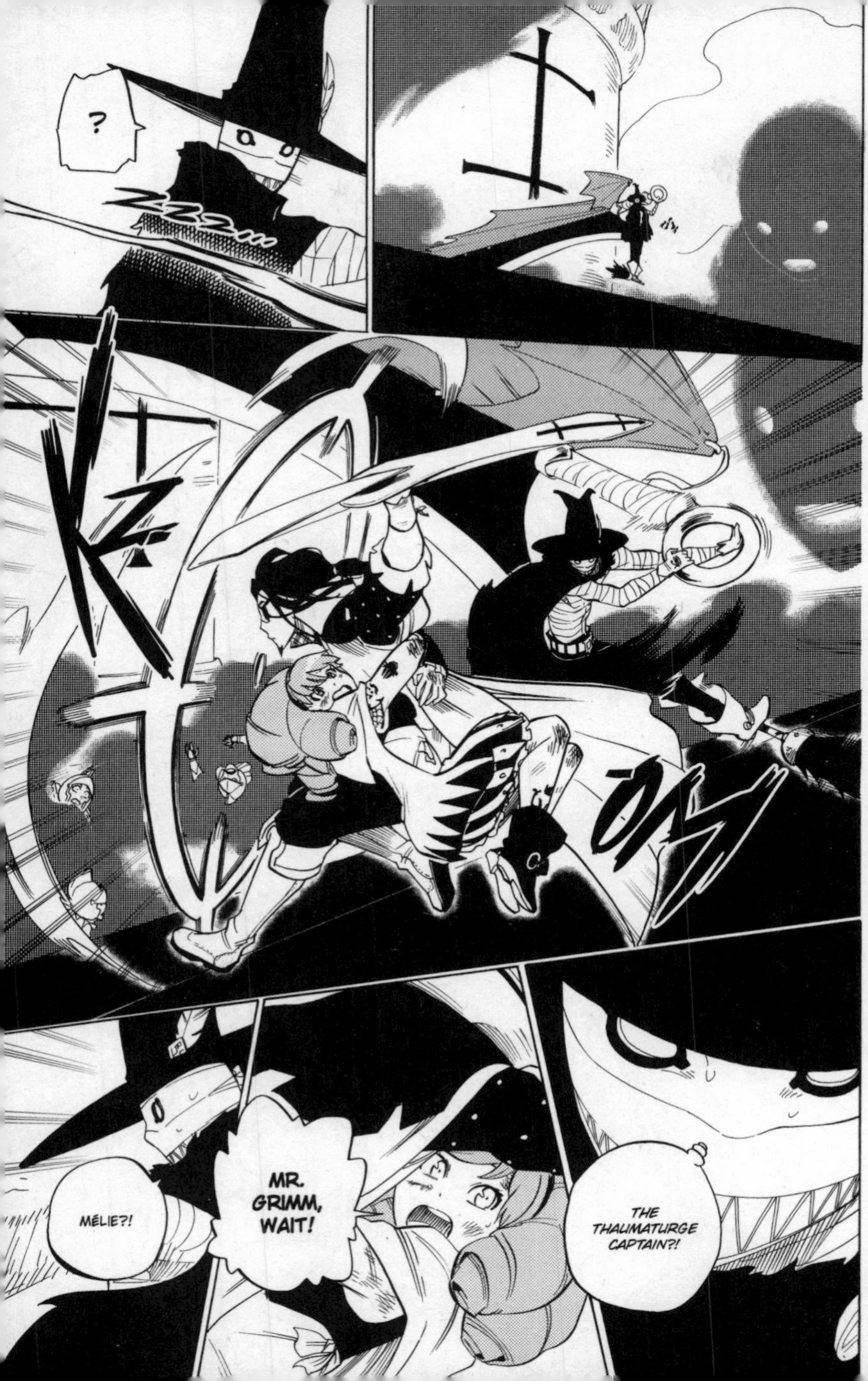
?
THE THAUMATURGE CAPTAIN?!
MR. GRIMM, WAIT!
MÉLIE?!

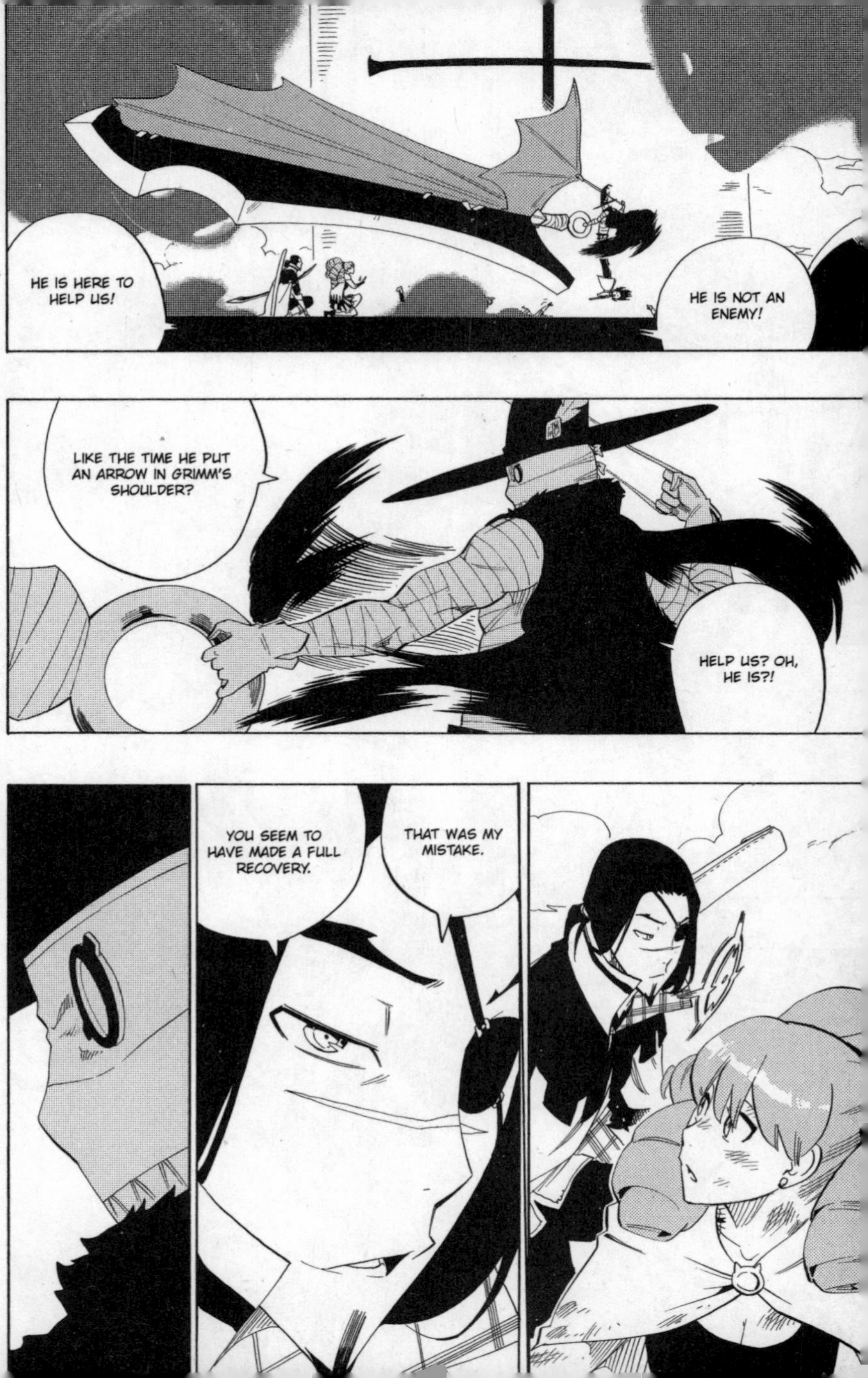
HE IS NOT AN ENEMY!
HE IS HERE TO HELP US!
HELP US? OH, HE IS?!
LIKE THE TIME HE PUT AN ARROW IN GRIMM'S SHOULDER?
THAT WAS MY MISTAKE.
YOU SEEM TO HAVE MADE A FULL RECOVERY.

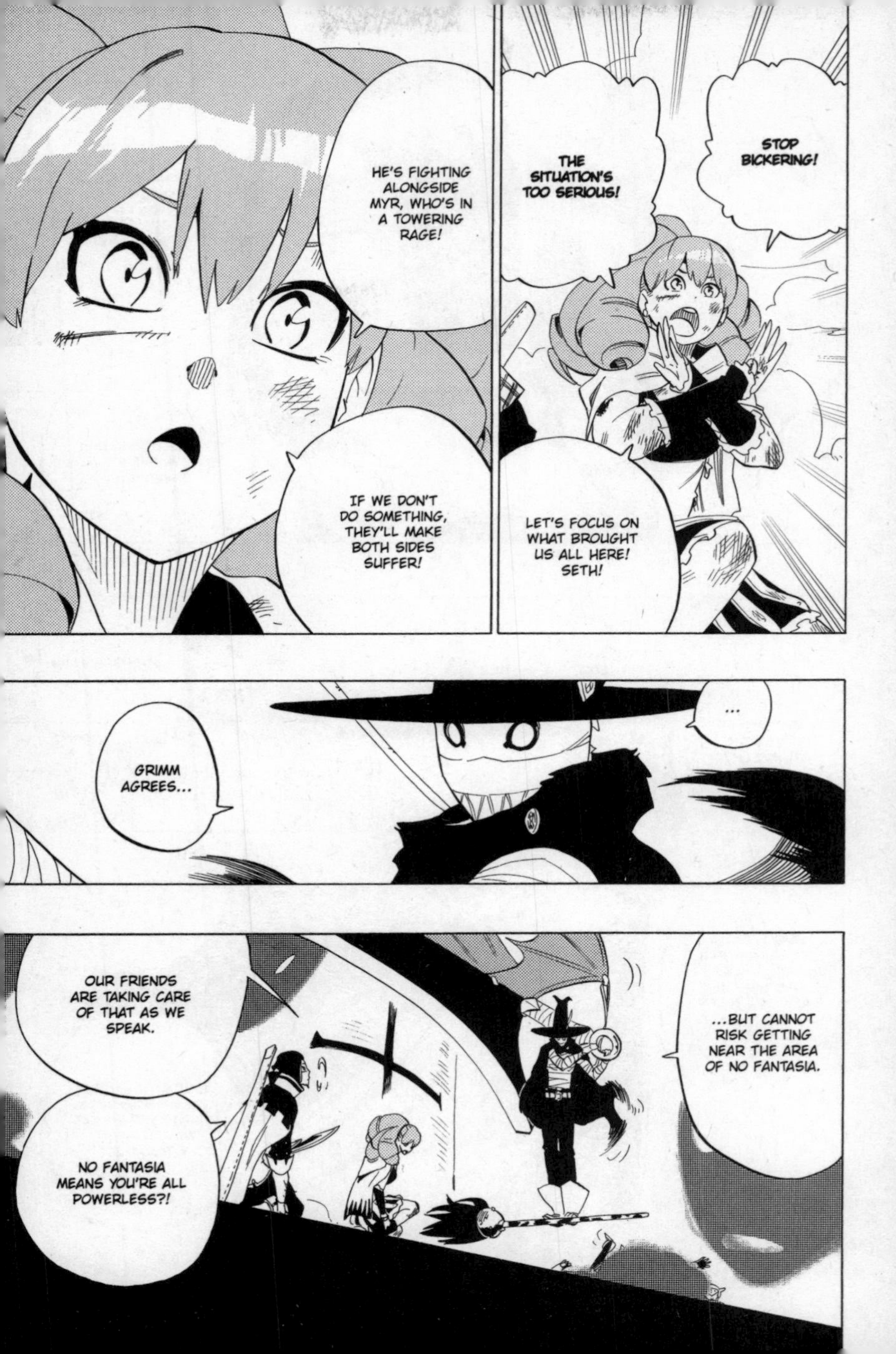
STOP BICKERING!
THE SITUATION'S TOO SERIOUS!
LET'S FOCUS ON WHAT BROUGHT US ALL HERE! SETH!
HE'S FIGHTING ALONGSIDE MYR, WHO'S IN A TOWERING RAGE!
IF WE DON'T DO SOMETHING, THEY'LL MAKE BOTH SIDES SUFFER!
...
GRIMM AGREES...
...BUT CANNOT RISK GETTING NEAR THE AREA OF NO FANTASIA.
OUR FRIENDS ARE TAKING CARE OF THAT AS WE SPEAK.
NO FANTASIA MEANS YOU'RE ALL POWERLESS?!

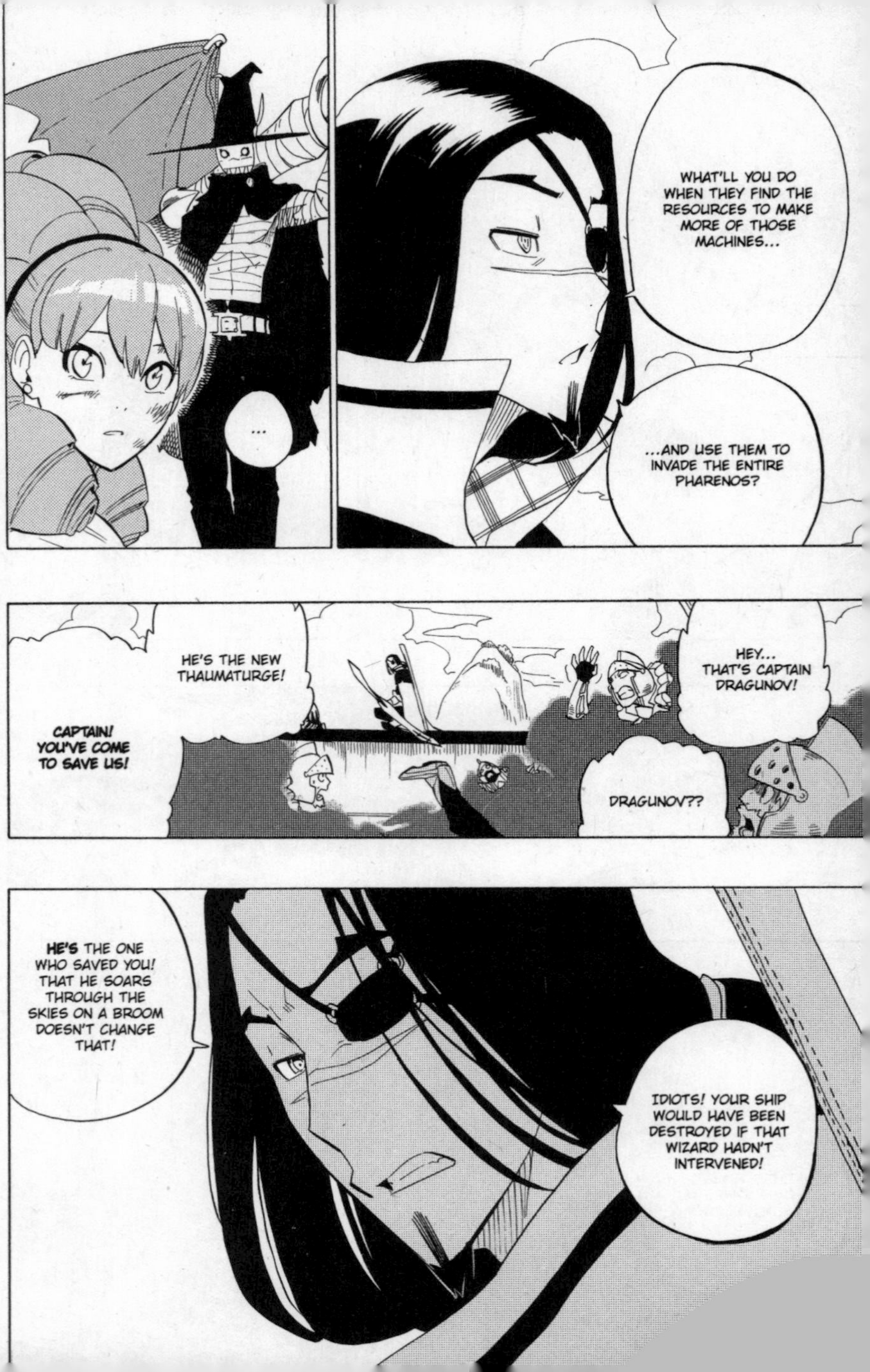
WHAT'LL YOU DO WHEN THEY FIND THE RESOURCES TO MAKE MORE OF THOSE MACHINES...
...AND USE THEM TO INVADE THE ENTIRE PHARENOS?
...
HEY... THAT'S CAPTAIN DRAGUNOV!
DRAGUNOV??
HE'S THE NEW THAUMATURGE!
CAPTAIN! YOU'VE COME TO SAVE US!
IDIOTS! YOUR SHIP WOULD HAVE BEEN DESTROYED IF THAT WIZARD HADN'T INTERVENED!
HE'S THE ONE WHO SAVED YOU! THAT HE SOARS THROUGH THE SKIES ON A BROOM DOESN'T CHANGE THAT!

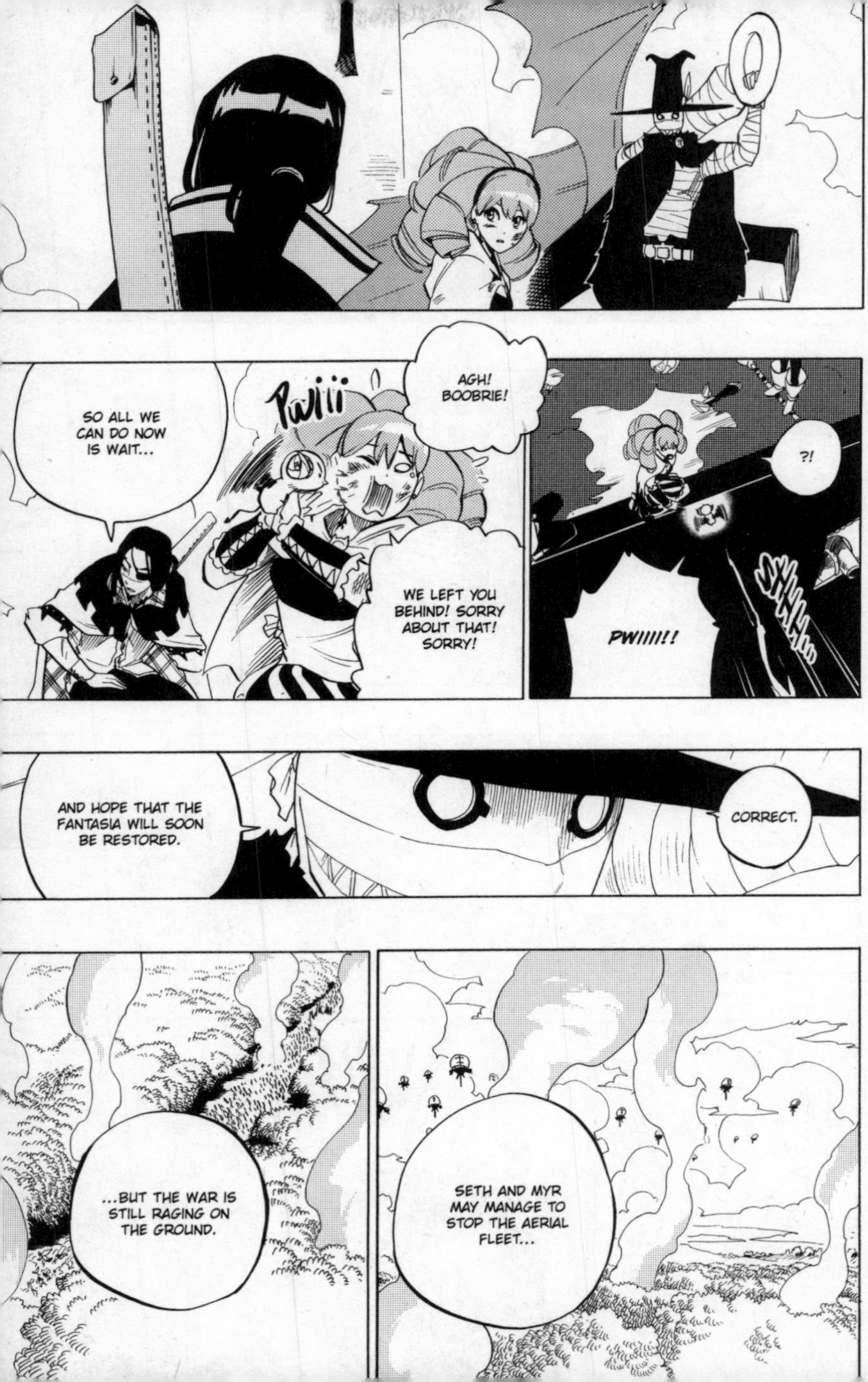
?!
PWIIII!!
AGH! BOOBRIE!
PWiii
SO ALL WE CAN DO NOW IS WAIT...
WE LEFT YOU BEHIND! SORRY ABOUT THAT! SORRY!
CORRECT.
AND HOPE THAT THE FANTASIA WILL SOON BE RESTORED.
SETH AND MYR MAY MANAGE TO STOP THE AERIAL FLEET...
...BUT THE WAR IS STILL RAGING ON THE GROUND.

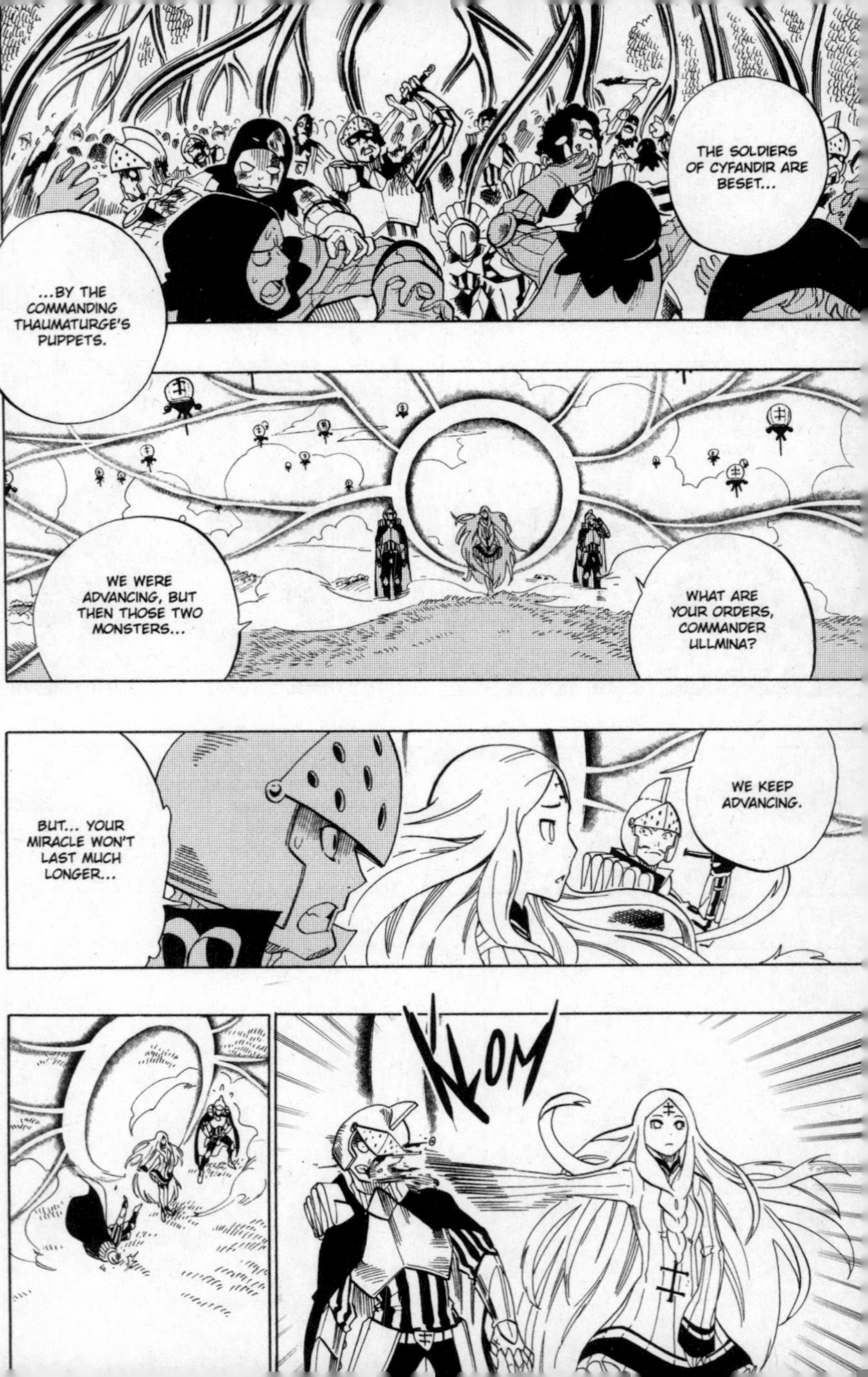
THE SOLDIERS OF CYFANDIR ARE BESET...
...BY THE COMMANDING THAUMATURGE'S PUPPETS.
WHAT ARE YOUR ORDERS, COMMANDER ULLMINA?
WE WERE ADVANCING, BUT THEN THOSE TWO MONSTERS...
WE KEEP ADVANCING.
BUT... YOUR MIRACLE WON'T LAST MUCH LONGER...
KLOM

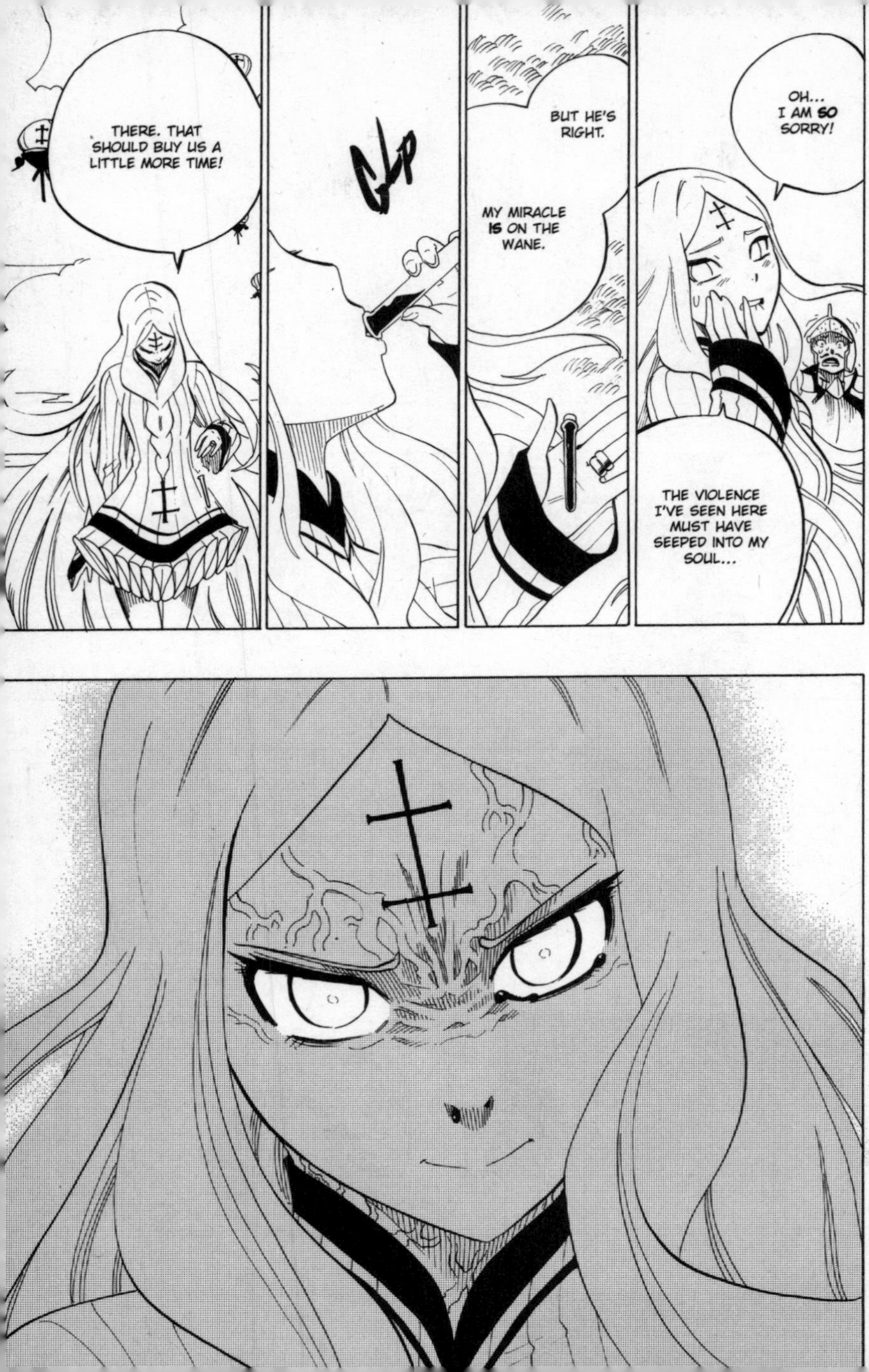
OH... I AM SO SORRY!
THE VIOLENCE I'VE SEEN HERE MUST HAVE SEEPED INTO MY SOUL...
BUT HE'S RIGHT.
MY MIRACLE IS ON THE WANE.
THERE. THAT SHOULD BUY US A LITTLE MORE TIME!

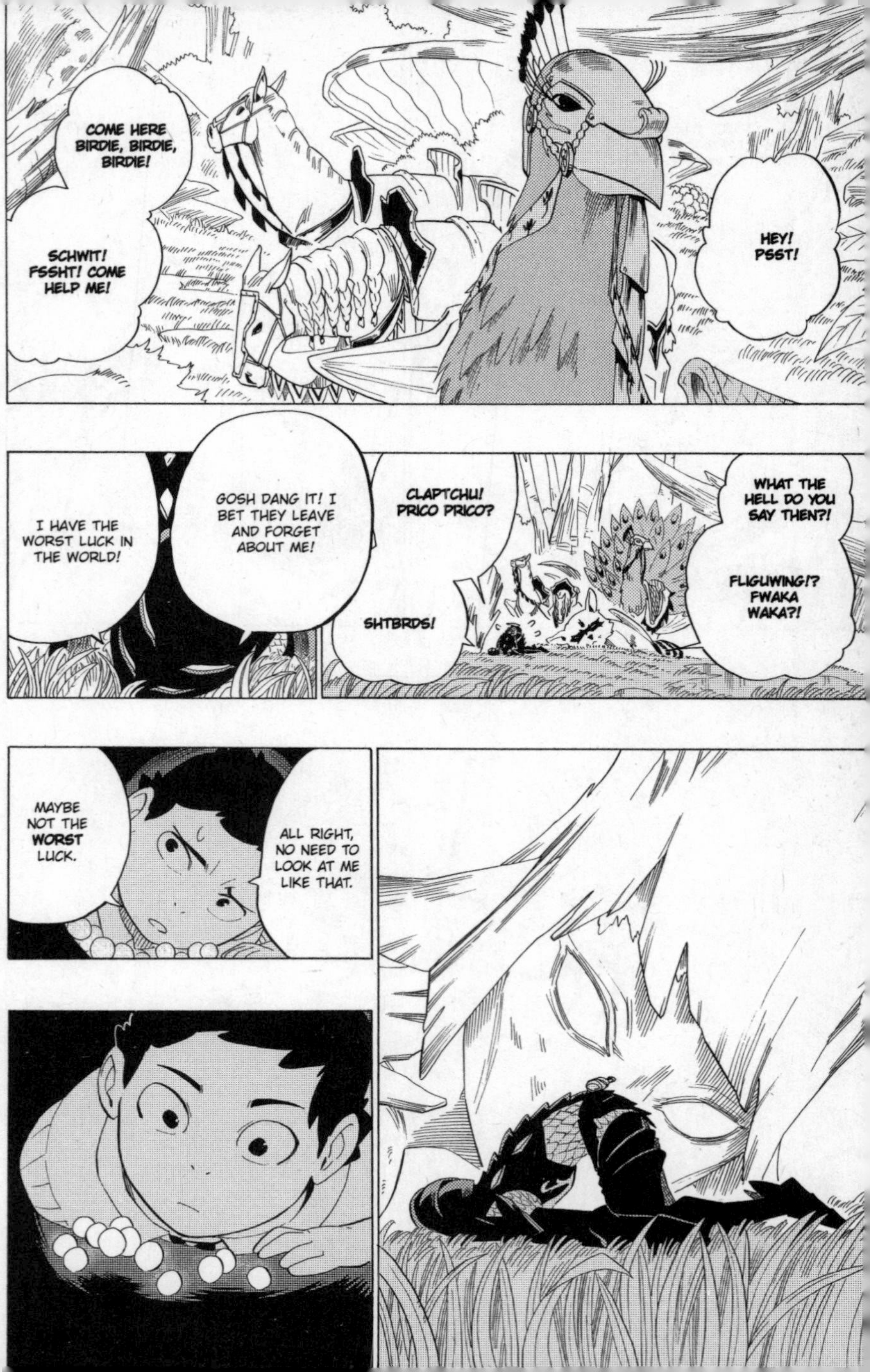
HEY! PSST!
COME HERE BIRDIE, BIRDIE, BIRDIE!
SCHWIT! FSSHT! COME HELP ME!
WHAT THE HELL DO YOU SAY THEN?!
FLIGUWING!? FWAKA WAKA?!
CLAPTCHU! PRICO PRICO?
SHTBRDS!
GOSH DANG IT! I BET THEY LEAVE AND FORGET ABOUT ME!
I HAVE THE WORST LUCK IN THE WORLD!
ALL RIGHT, NO NEED TO LOOK AT ME LIKE THAT.
MAYBE NOT THE **WORST** LUCK.

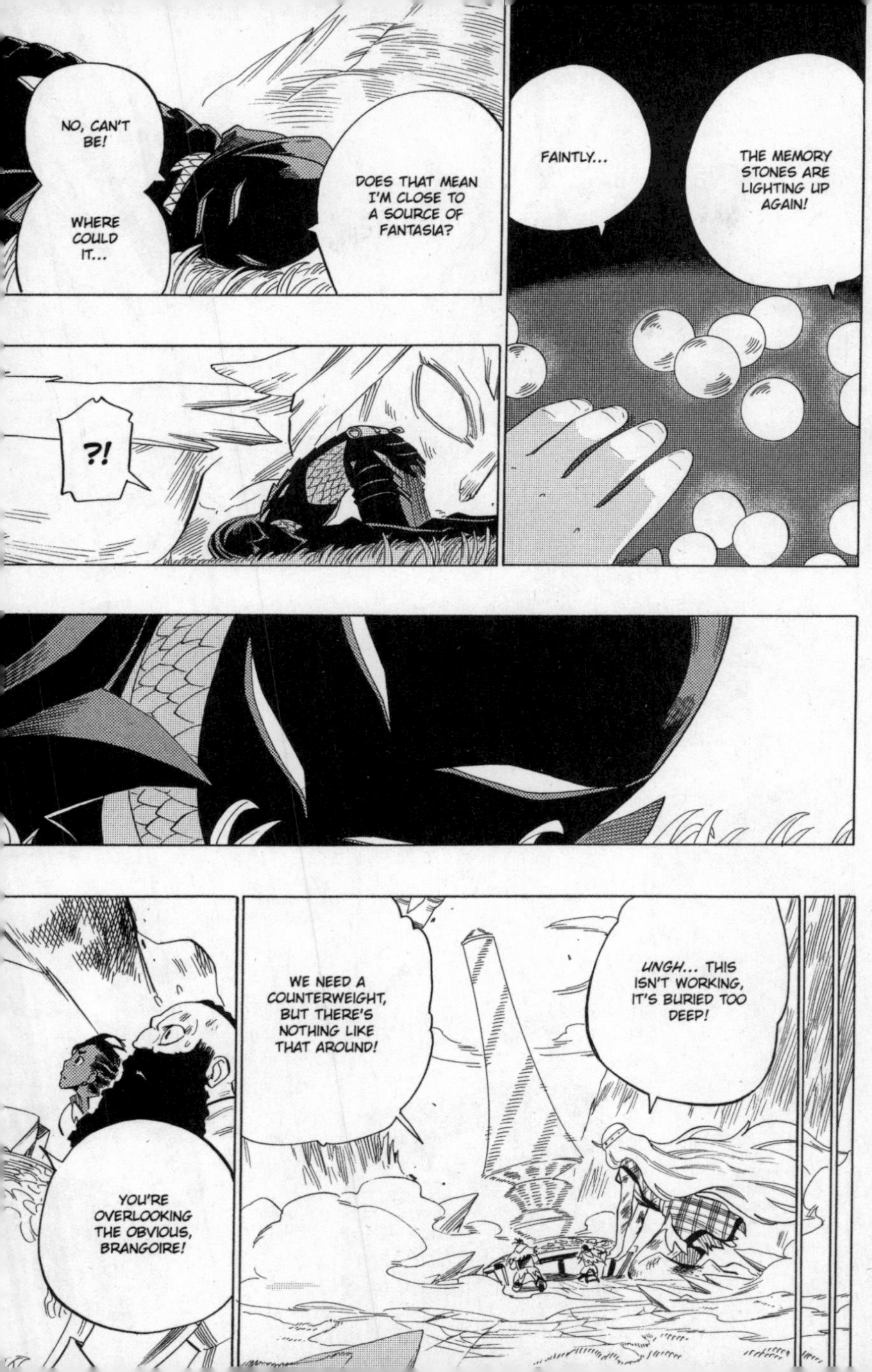
THE MEMORY STONES ARE LIGHTING UP AGAIN!
FAINTLY...
DOES THAT MEAN I'M CLOSE TO A SOURCE OF FANTASIA?
NO, CAN'T BE!
WHERE COULD IT...
?!
UNGH... THIS ISN'T WORKING, IT'S BURIED TOO DEEP!
WE NEED A COUNTERWEIGHT, BUT THERE'S NOTHING LIKE THAT AROUND!
YOU'RE OVERLOOKING THE OBVIOUS, BRANGOIRE!

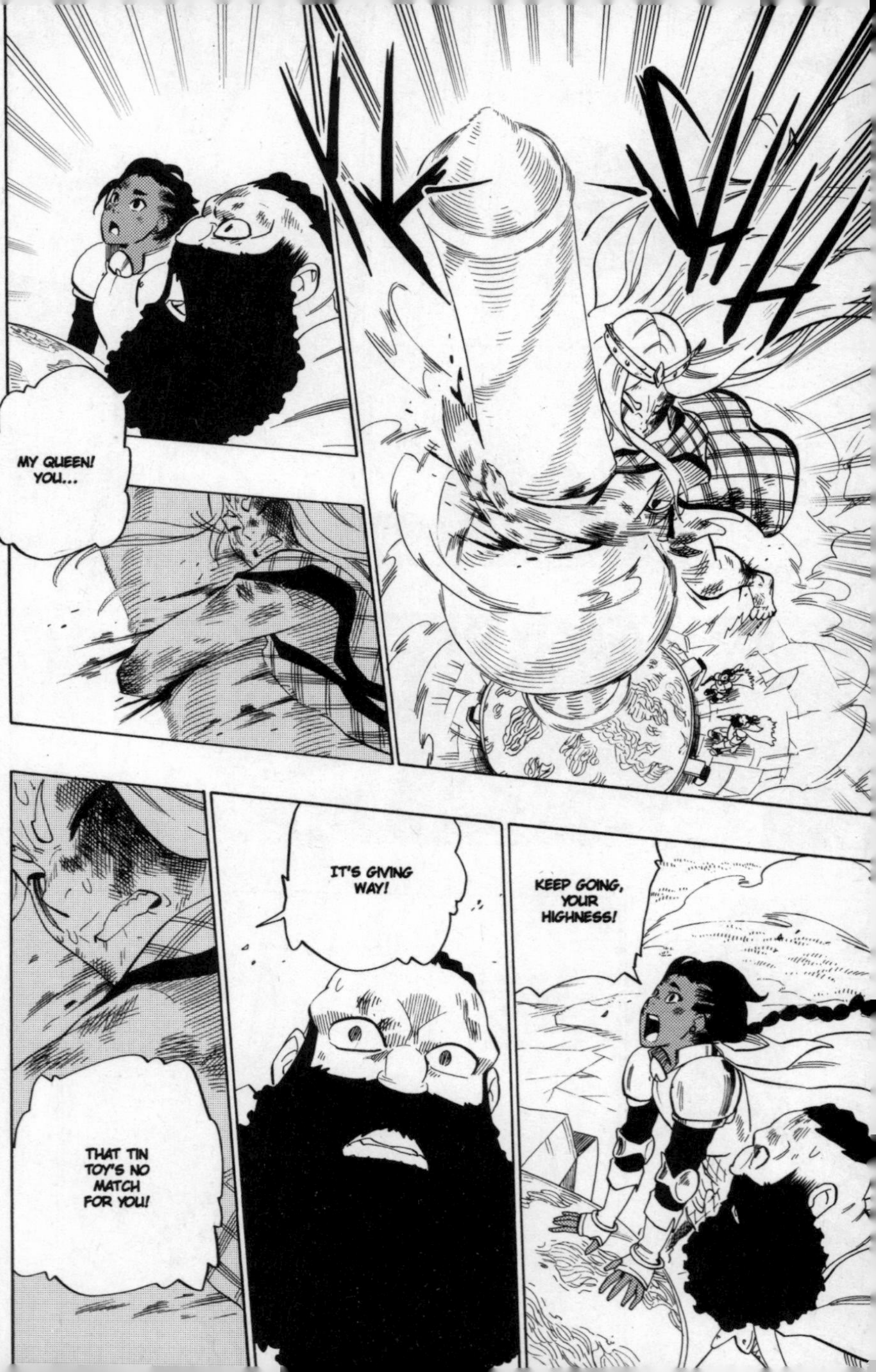
MY QUEEN! YOU...
KEEP GOING, YOUR HIGHNESS!
IT'S GIVING WAY!
THAT TIN TOY'S NO MATCH FOR YOU!

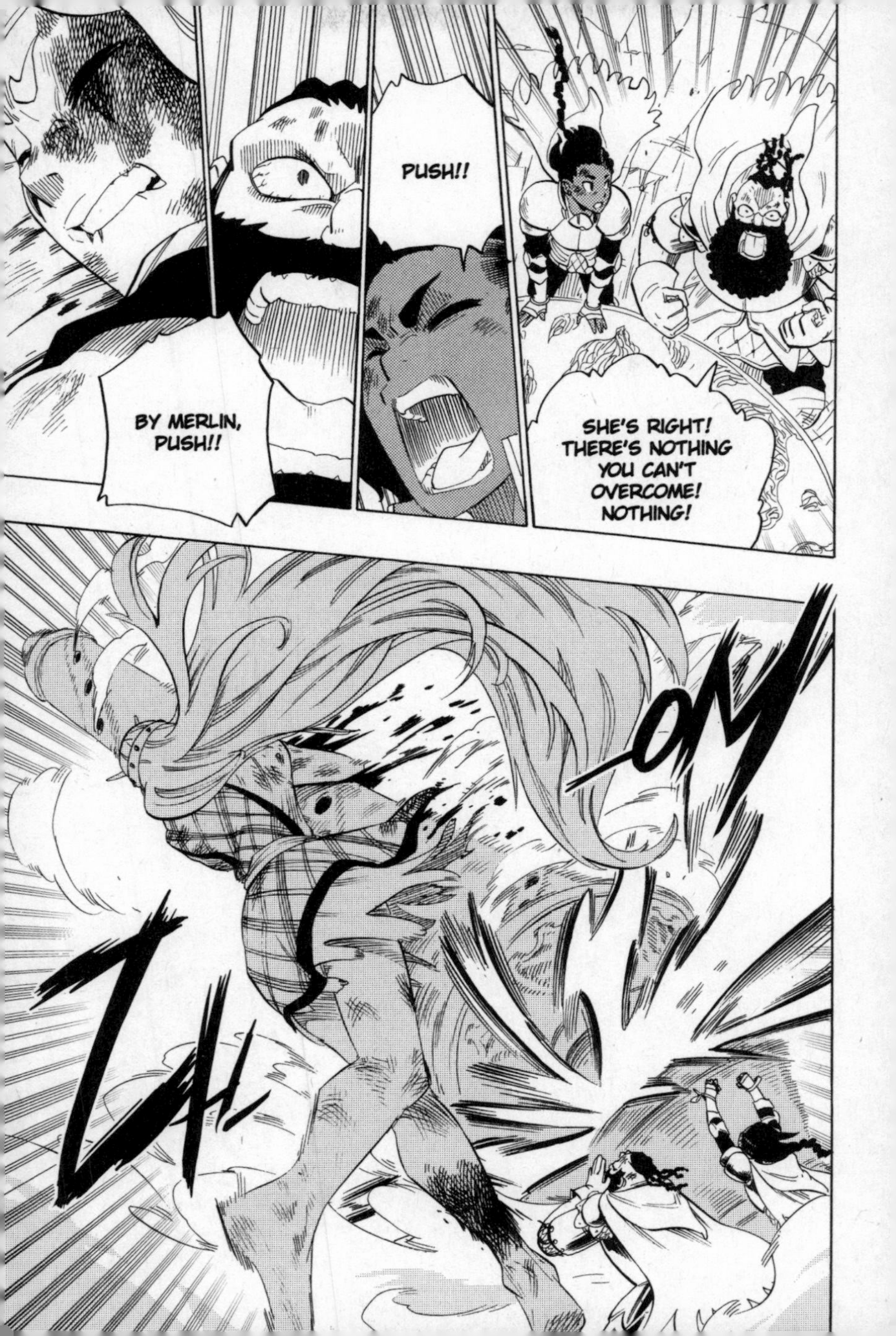
SHE'S RIGHT! THERE'S NOTHING YOU CAN'T OVERCOME! NOTHING!
PUSH!!
BY MERLIN, PUSH!!

PEACOCK-DRAGONS,
ALWAYS READY FOR A
BUTT-OFF.

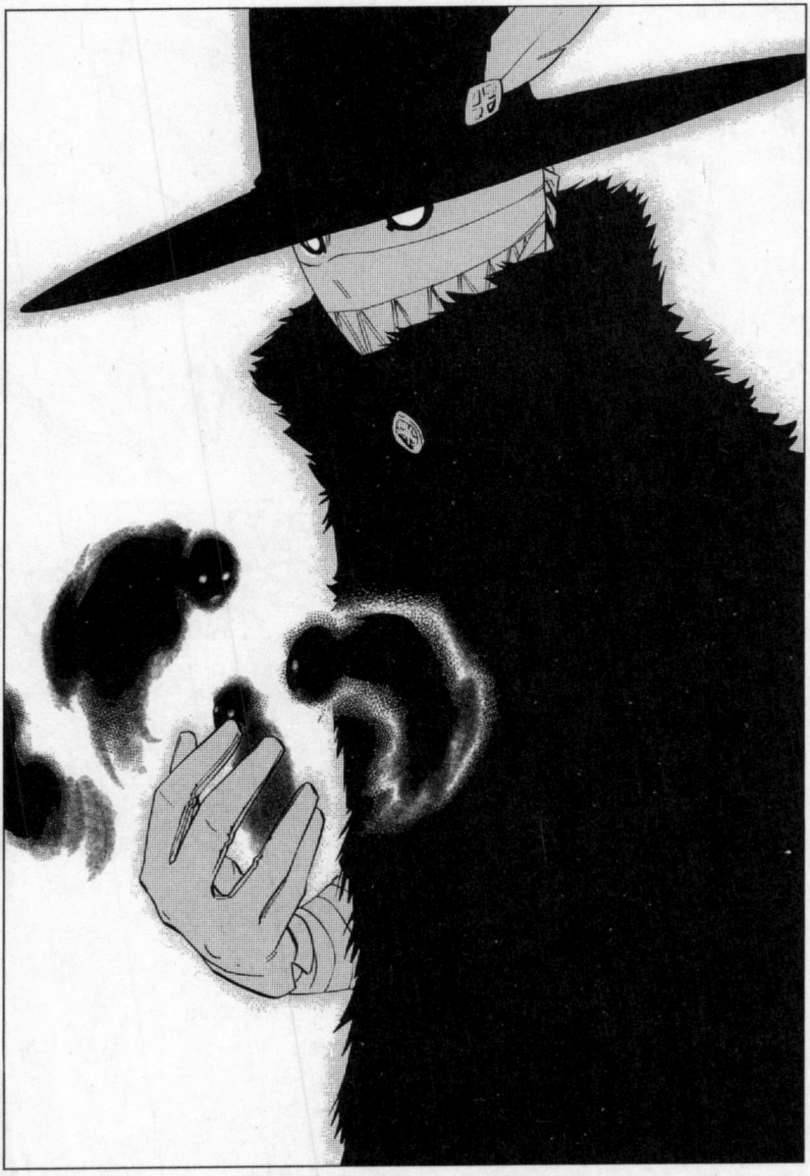

Chapter 71 **A Soul Black to the Core**

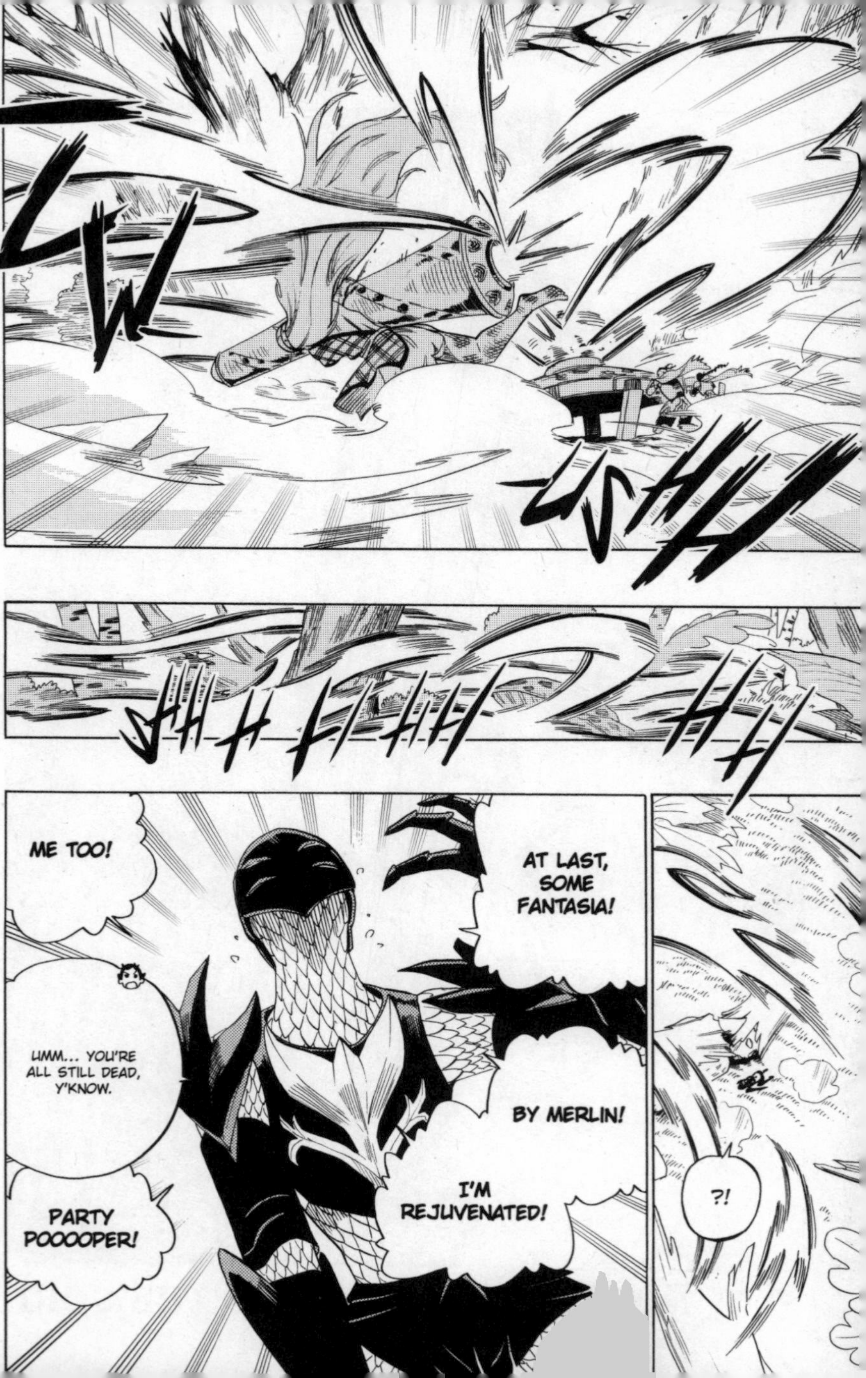
?!
AT LAST, SOME FANTASIA!
ME TOO!
BY MERLIN!
UMM... YOU'RE ALL STILL DEAD, Y'KNOW.
I'M REJUVENATED!
PARTY POOOOPER!

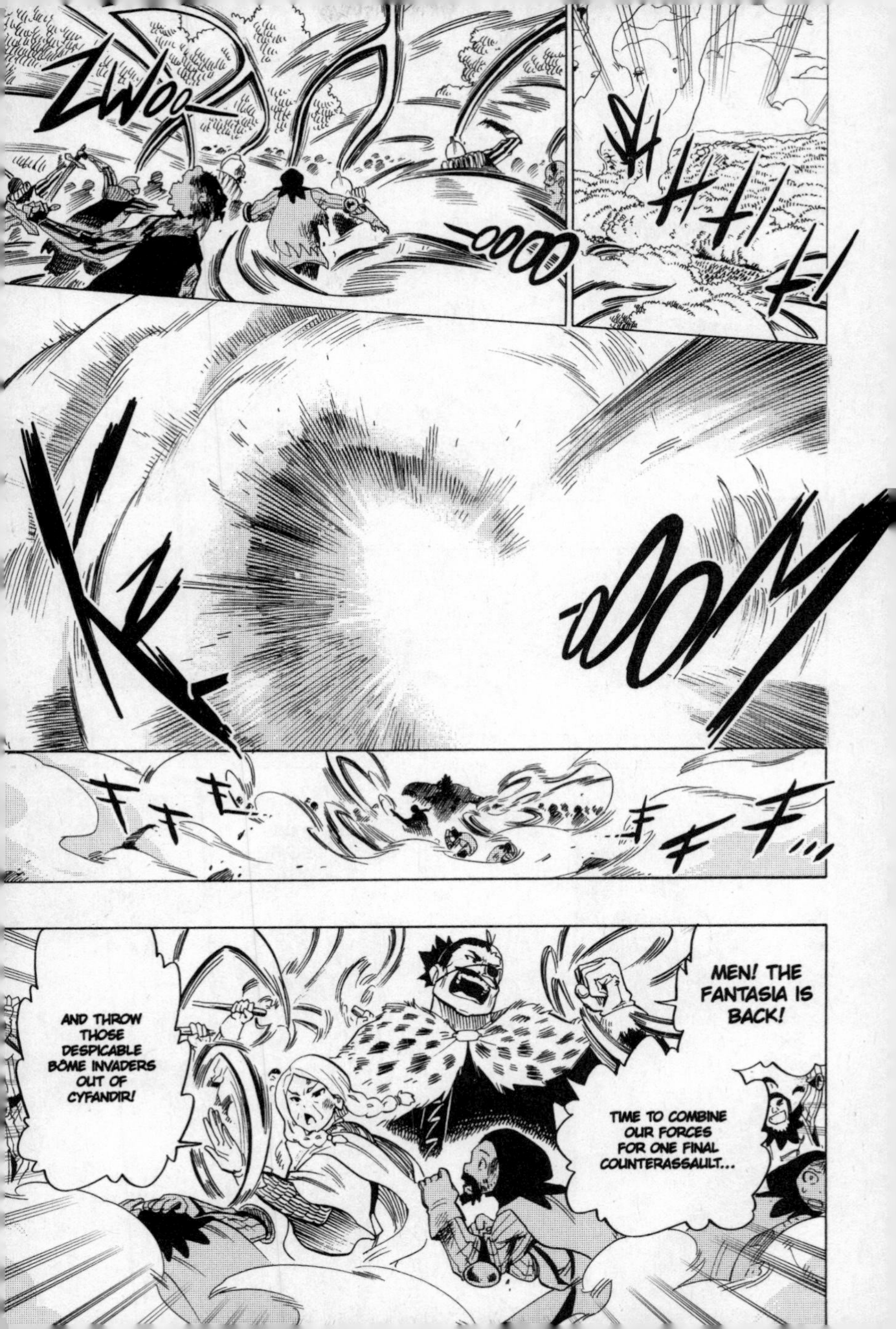

MEN! THE FANTASIA IS BACK!
TIME TO COMBINE OUR FORCES FOR ONE FINAL COUNTERASSAULT...
AND THROW THOSE DESPICABLE BÔME INVADERS OUT OF CYFANDIR!

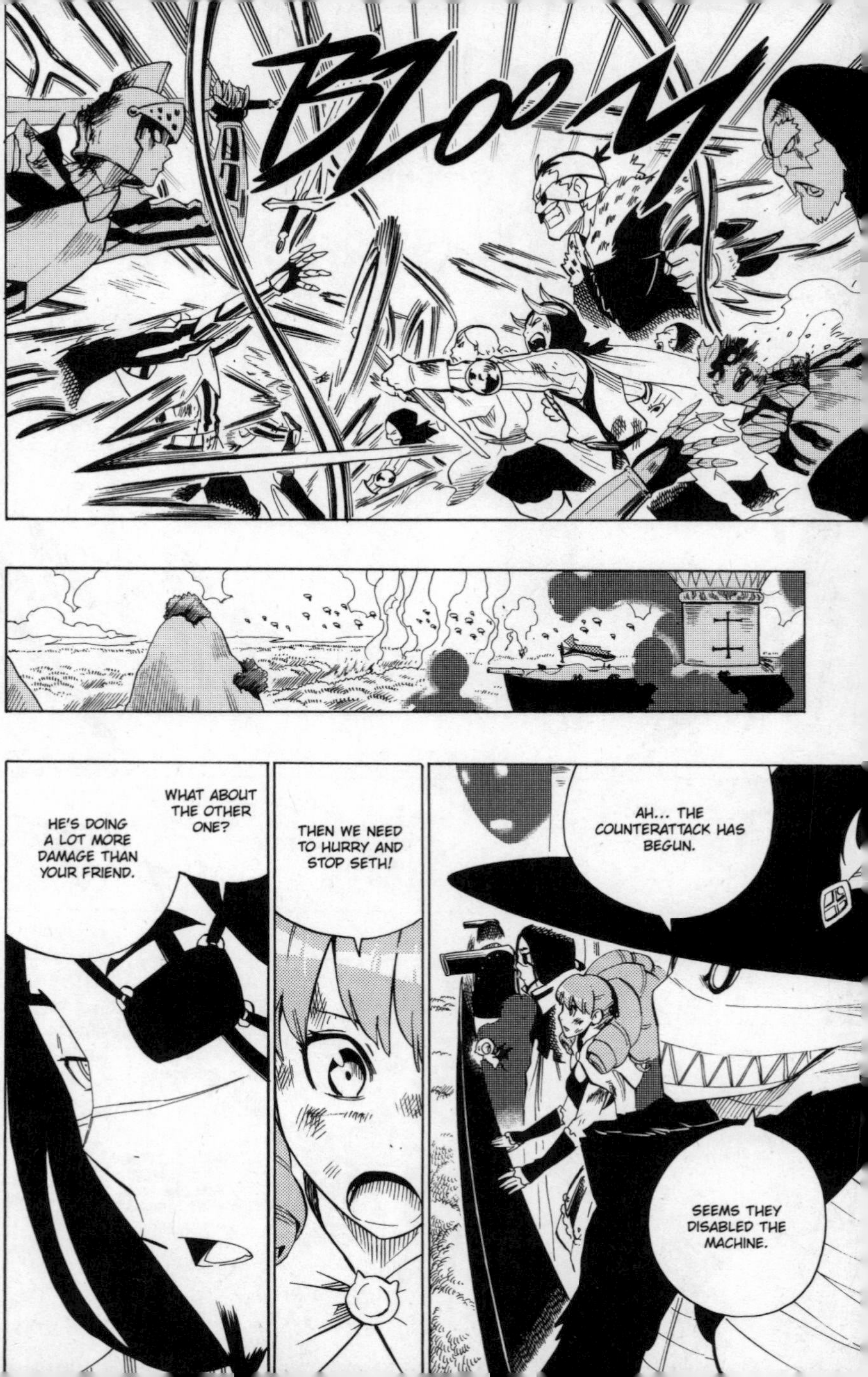
BZOOM
AH... THE COUNTERATTACK HAS BEGUN.
SEEMS THEY DISABLED THE MACHINE.
THEN WE NEED TO HURRY AND STOP SETH!
WHAT ABOUT THE OTHER ONE?
HE'S DOING A LOT MORE DAMAGE THAN YOUR FRIEND.

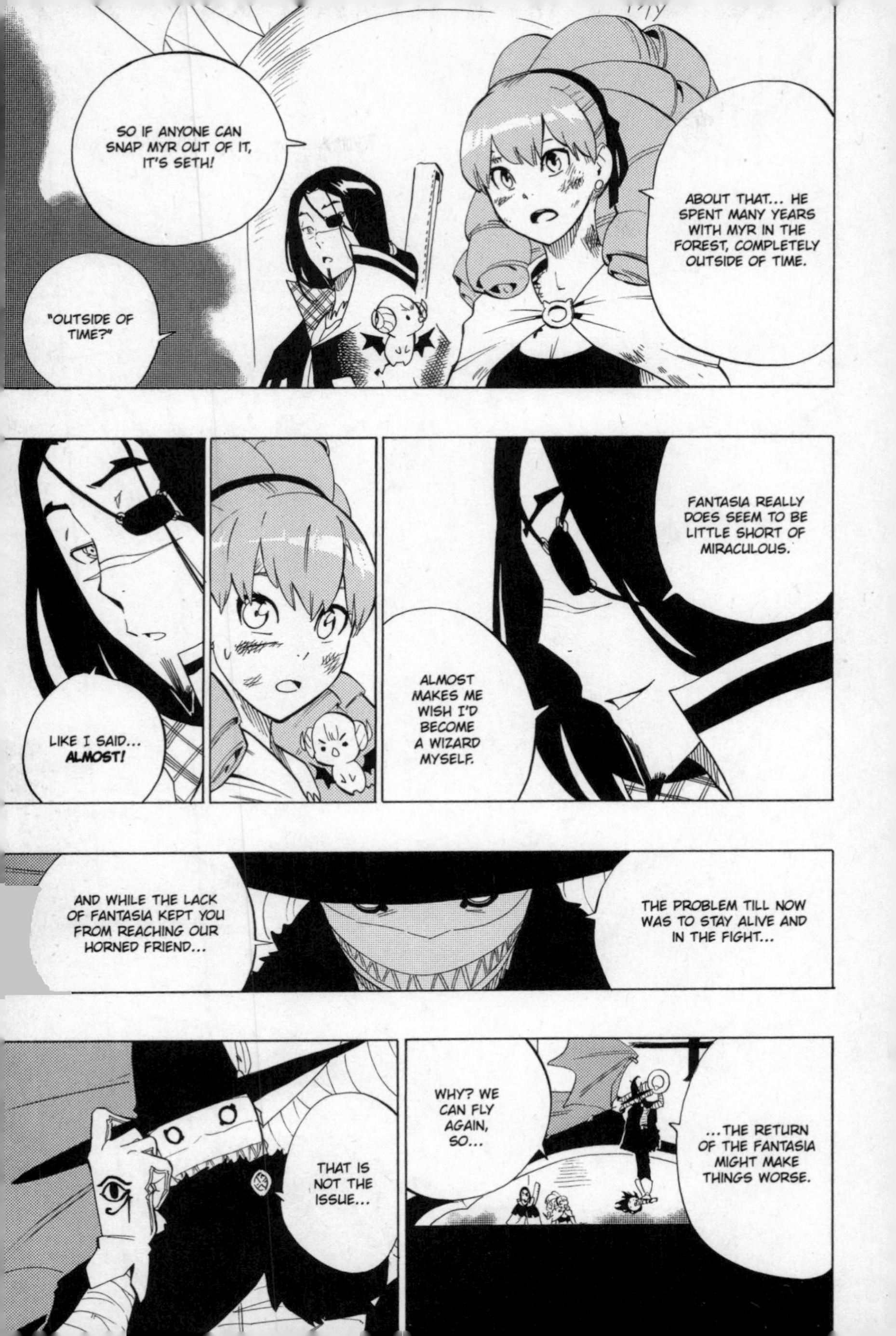
SO IF ANYONE CAN SNAP MYR OUT OF IT, IT'S SETH!
ABOUT THAT... HE SPENT MANY YEARS WITH MYR IN THE FOREST, COMPLETELY OUTSIDE OF TIME.
"OUTSIDE OF TIME?"
FANTASIA REALLY DOES SEEM TO BE LITTLE SHORT OF MIRACULOUS.
ALMOST MAKES ME WISH I'D BECOME A WIZARD MYSELF.
LIKE I SAID... **ALMOST!**
THE PROBLEM TILL NOW WAS TO STAY ALIVE AND IN THE FIGHT...
AND WHILE THE LACK OF FANTASIA KEPT YOU FROM REACHING OUR HORNED FRIEND...
WHY? WE CAN FLY AGAIN, SO...
...THE RETURN OF THE FANTASIA MIGHT MAKE THINGS WORSE.
THAT IS NOT THE ISSUE...

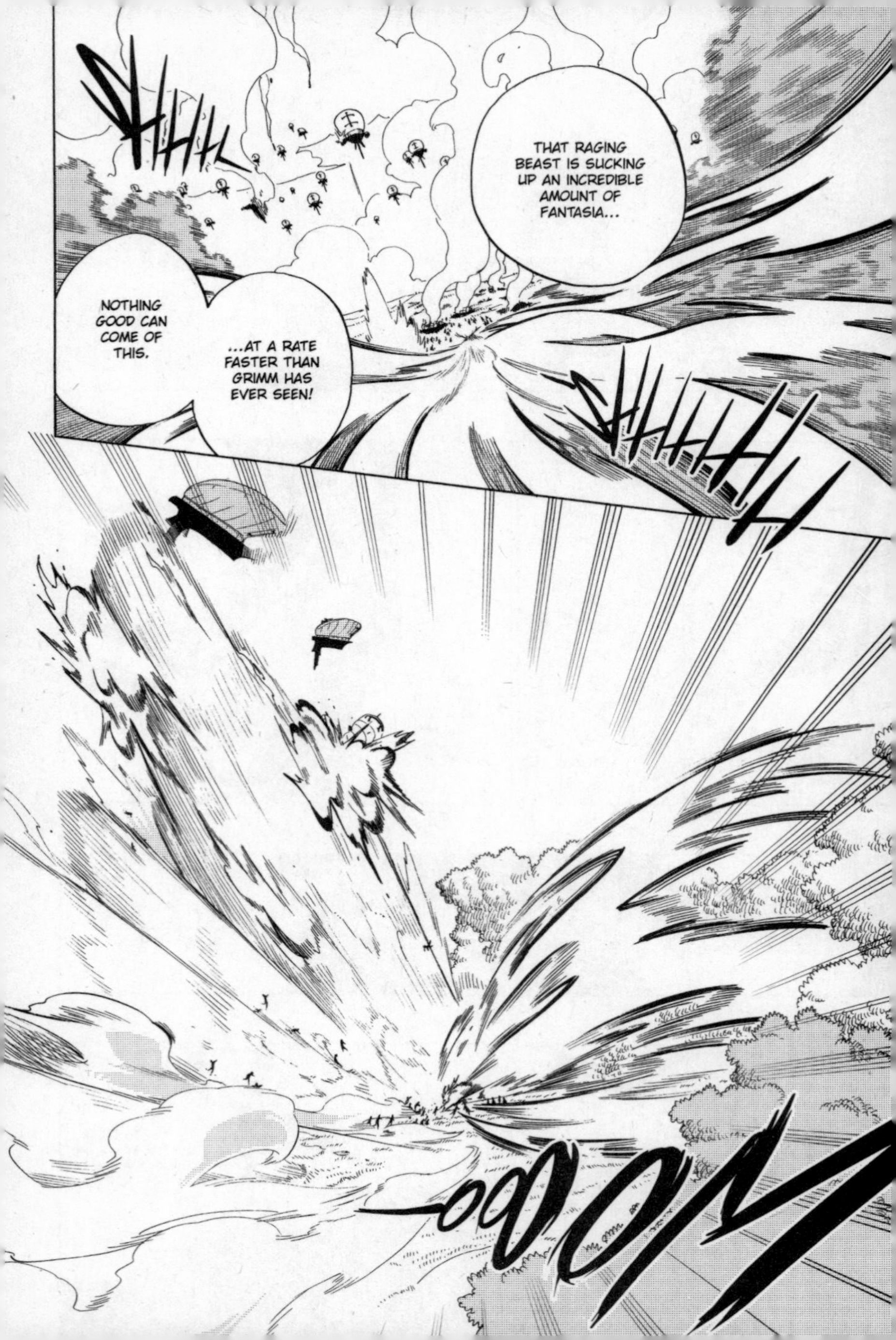
THAT RAGING BEAST IS SUCKING UP AN INCREDIBLE AMOUNT OF FANTASIA...
...AT A RATE FASTER THAN GRIMM HAS EVER SEEN!
NOTHING GOOD CAN COME OF THIS.

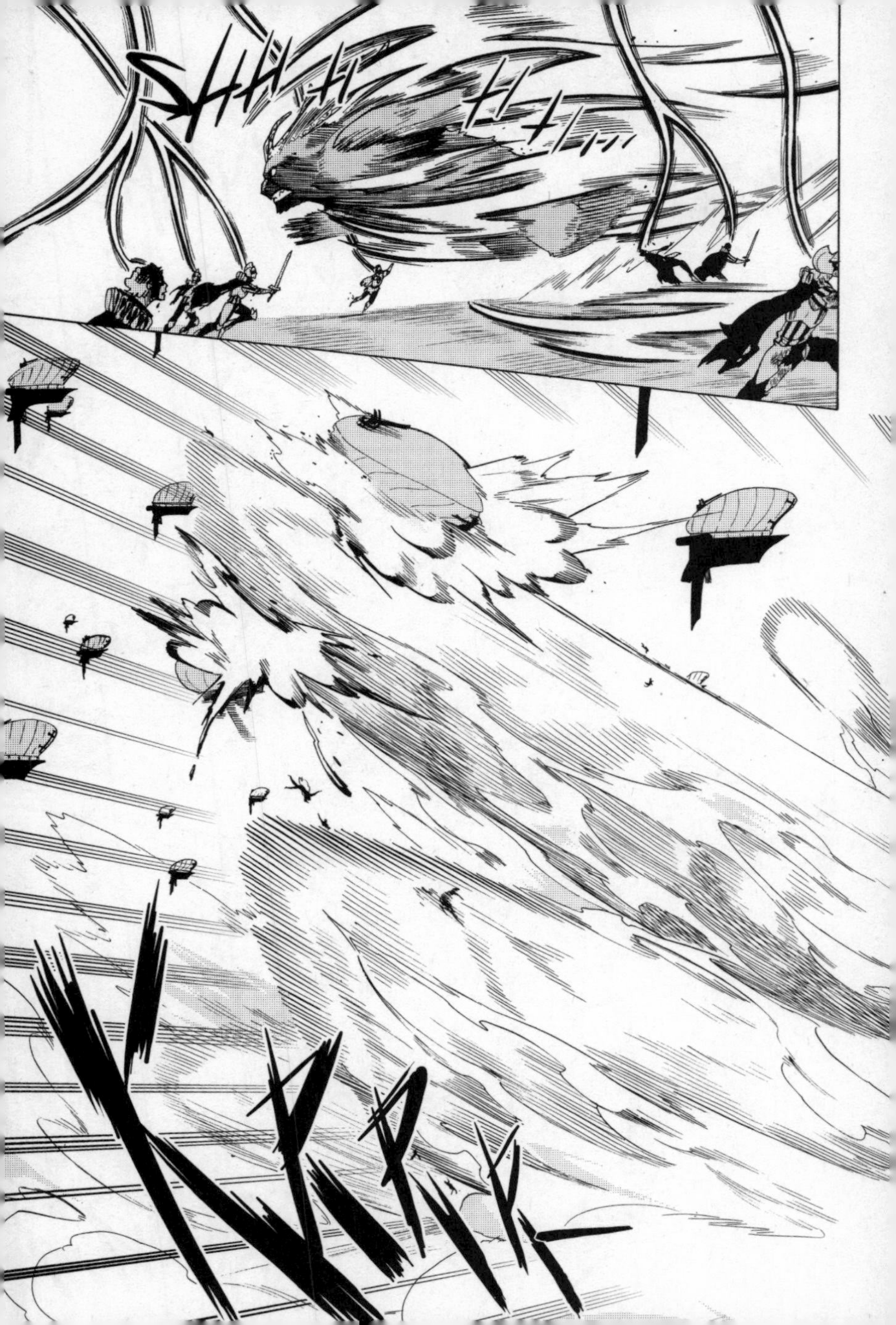

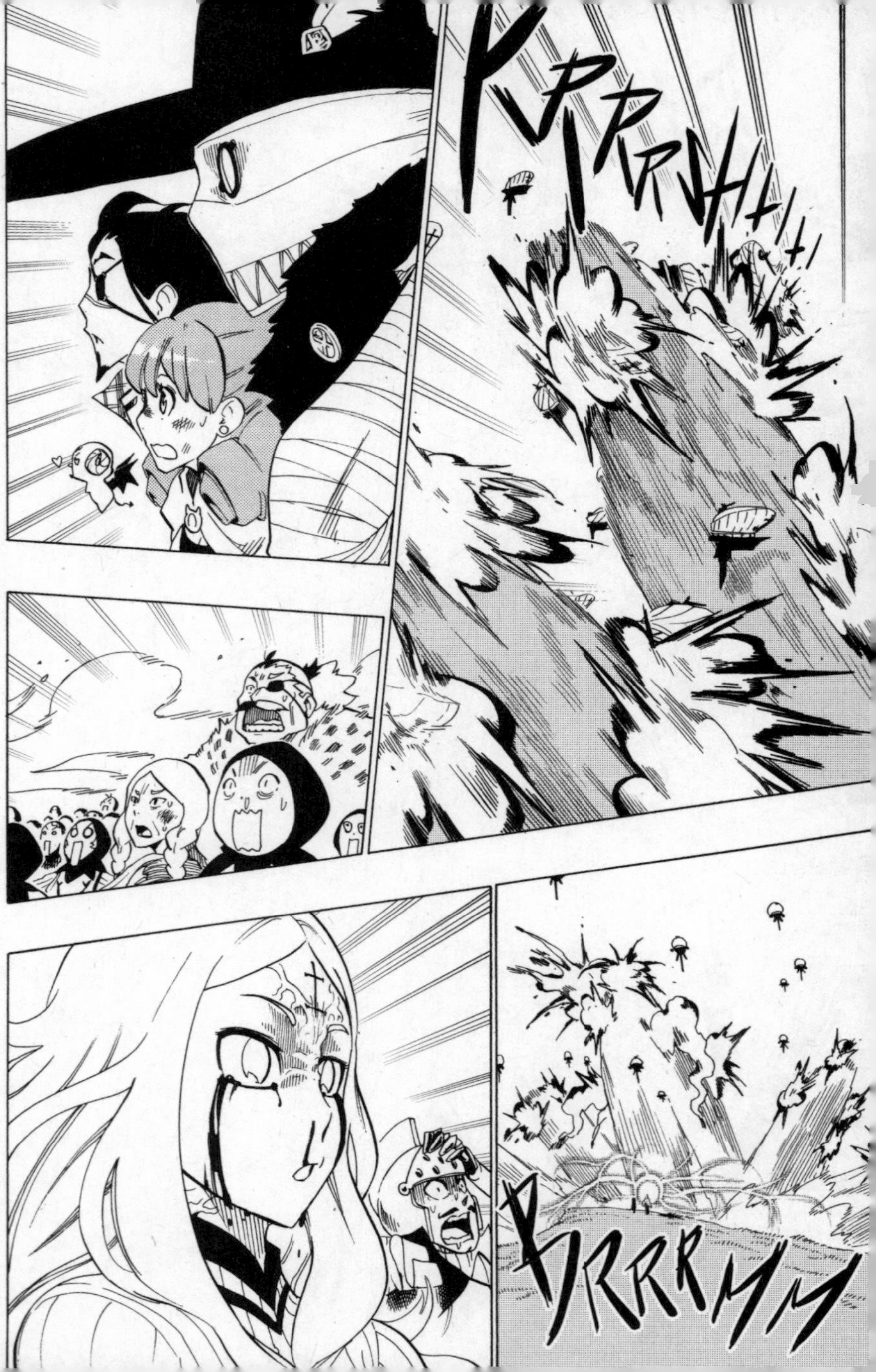
KRRRSHHH
BRRRMM

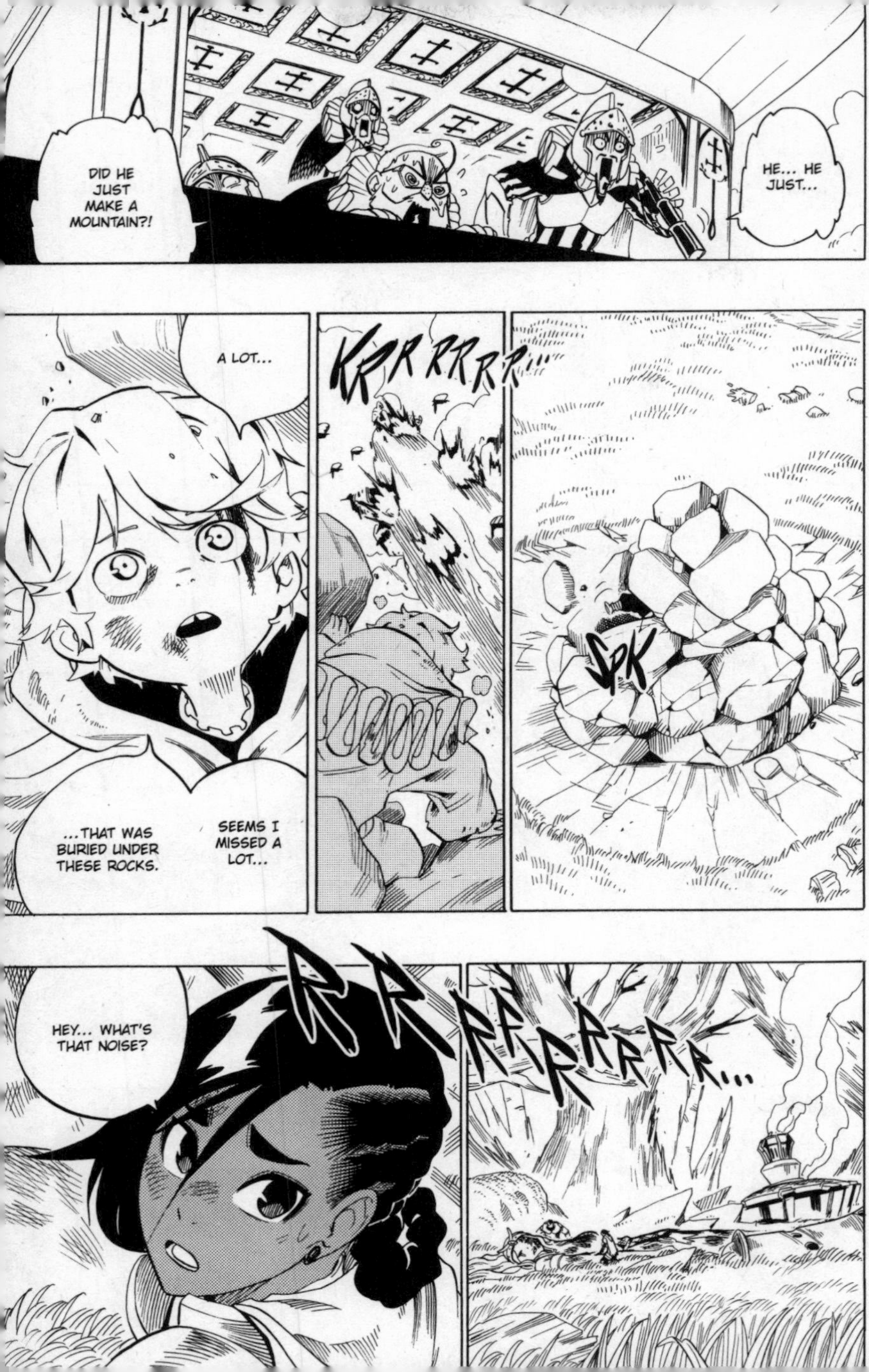

HE... HE JUST...
DID HE JUST MAKE A MOUNTAIN?!
SPK
KRRRRRRR...
A LOT...
SEEMS I MISSED A LOT...
...THAT WAS BURIED UNDER THESE ROCKS.
RRRRRRRRRR...
HEY... WHAT'S THAT NOISE?

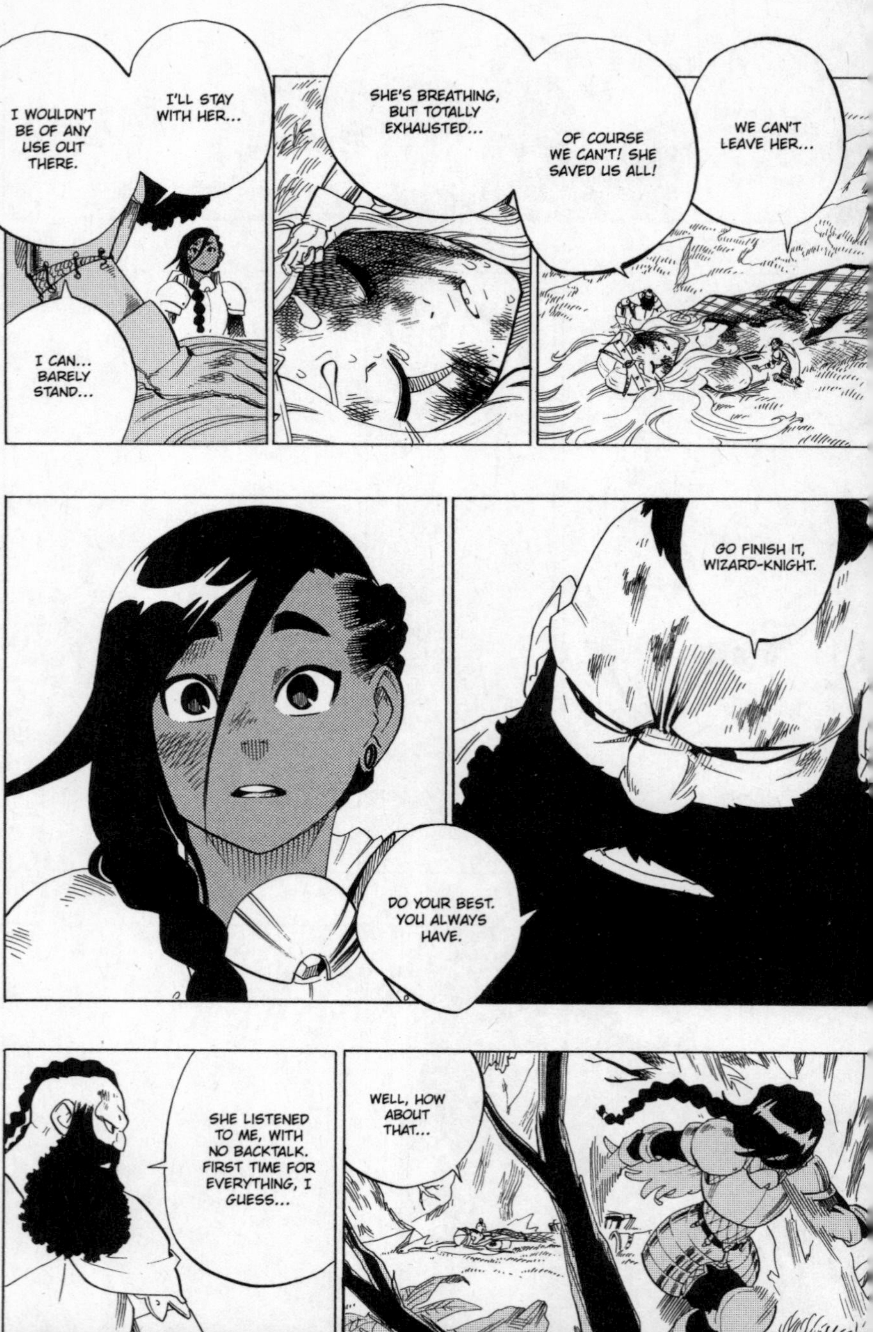
WE CAN'T LEAVE HER...
OF COURSE WE CAN'T! SHE SAVED US ALL!
SHE'S BREATHING, BUT TOTALLY EXHAUSTED...
I'LL STAY WITH HER...
I WOULDN'T BE OF ANY USE OUT THERE.
I CAN... BARELY STAND...
GO FINISH IT, WIZARD-KNIGHT.
DO YOUR BEST. YOU ALWAYS HAVE.
WELL, HOW ABOUT THAT...
SHE LISTENED TO ME, WITH NO BACKTALK. FIRST TIME FOR EVERYTHING, I GUESS...

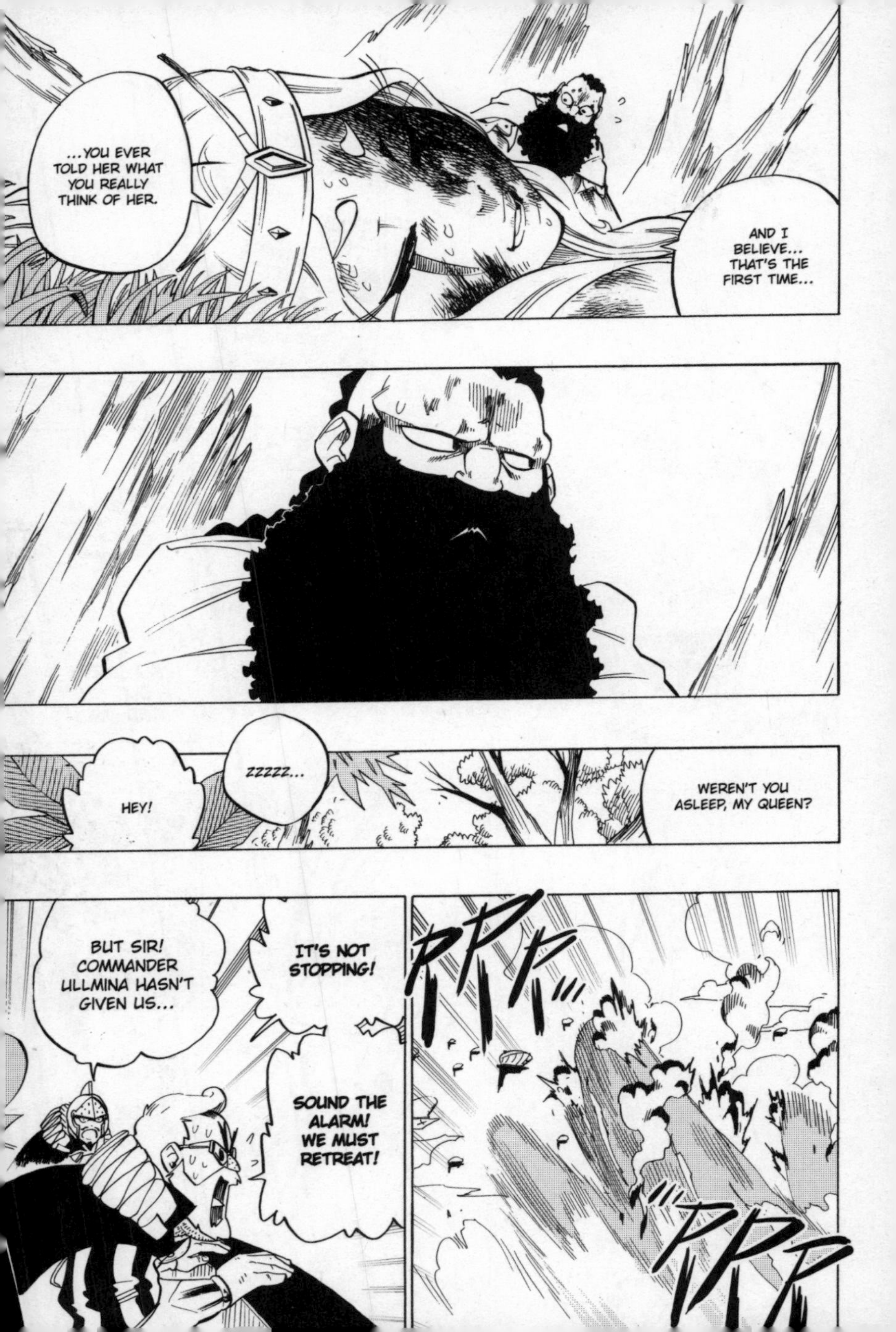
AND I BELIEVE... THAT'S THE FIRST TIME...
...YOU EVER TOLD HER WHAT YOU REALLY THINK OF HER.
WEREN'T YOU ASLEEP, MY QUEEN?
ZZZZZ...
HEY!
IT'S NOT STOPPING!
BUT SIR! COMMANDER ULLMINA HASN'T GIVEN US...
SOUND THE ALARM! WE MUST RETREAT!

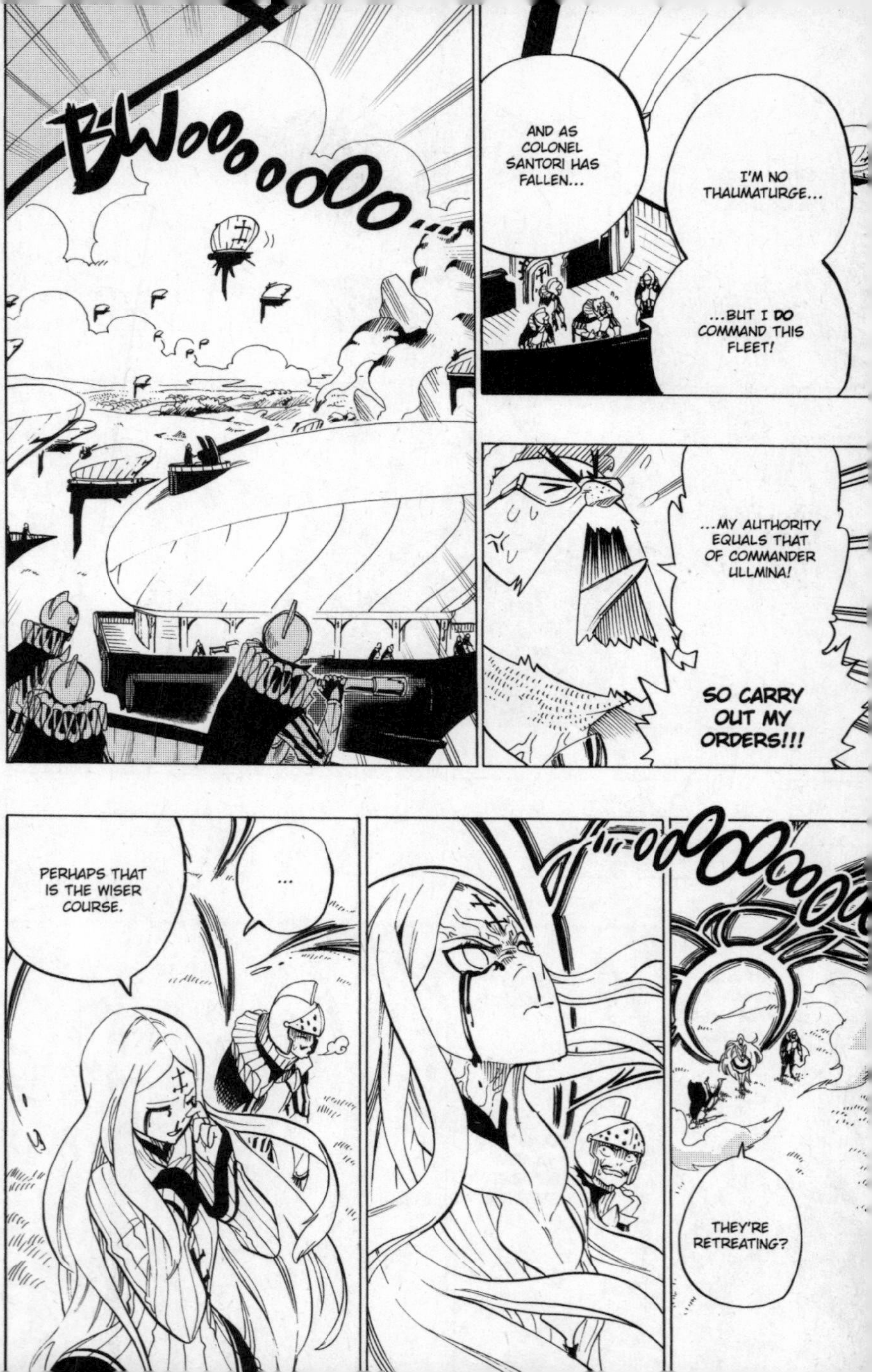
I'M NO THAUMATURGE...
...BUT I DO COMMAND THIS FLEET!
AND AS COLONEL SANTORI HAS FALLEN...
...MY AUTHORITY EQUALS THAT OF COMMANDER ULLMINA!
SO CARRY OUT MY ORDERS!!!
BWOOOOOOOO...
...OOOOOOOOOO
THEY'RE RETREATING?
...
PERHAPS THAT IS THE WISER COURSE.

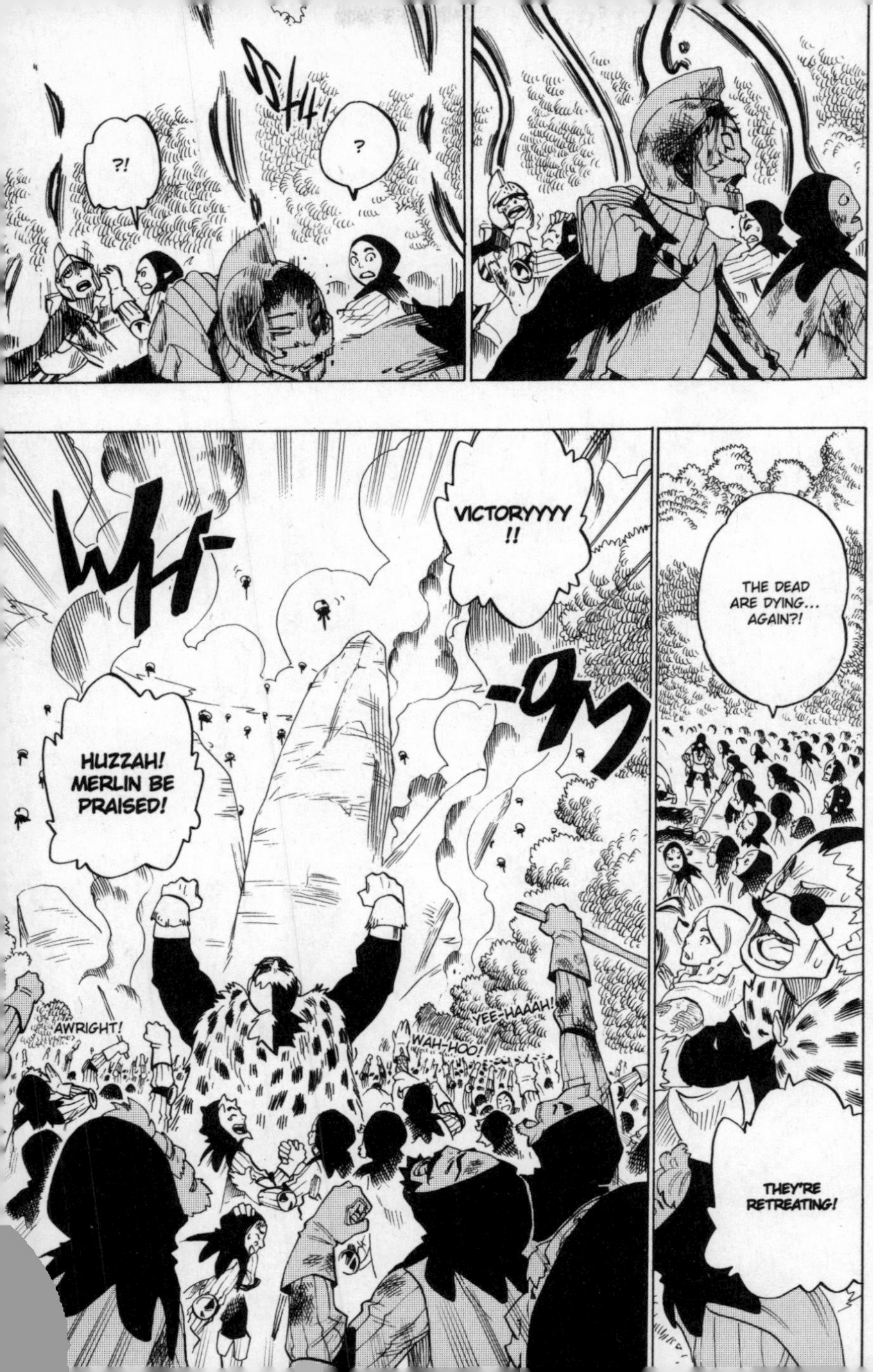
?
?!
THE DEAD ARE DYING... AGAIN?!
THEY'RE RETREATING!
VICTORYYYY !!
HUZZAH! MERLIN BE PRAISED!
YEE-HAAAH!
WAH-HOO!
AWRIGHT!

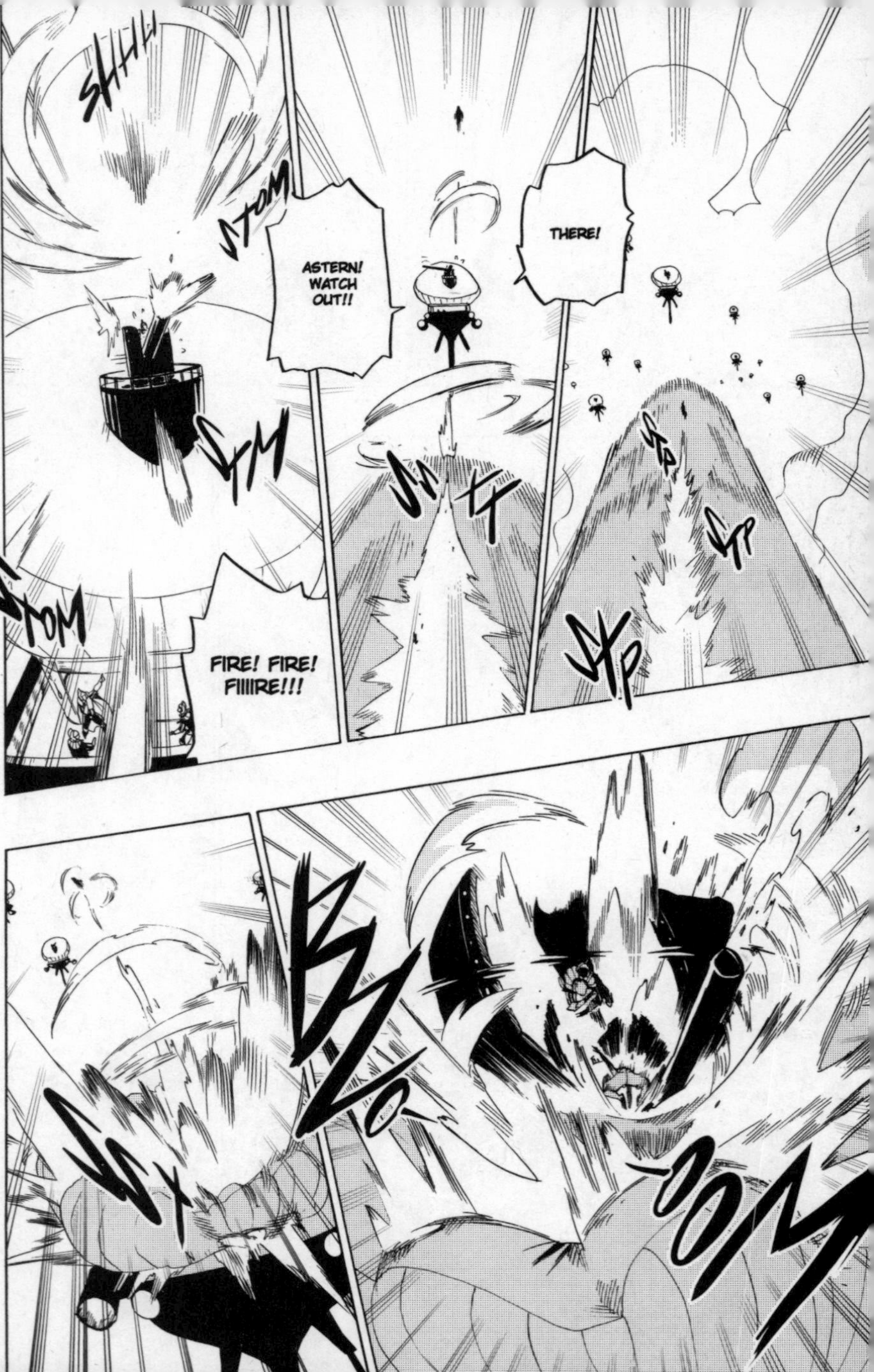

THERE!
ASTERN! WATCH OUT!!
STOM
STOM
FIRE! FIRE! FIIIRE!!!

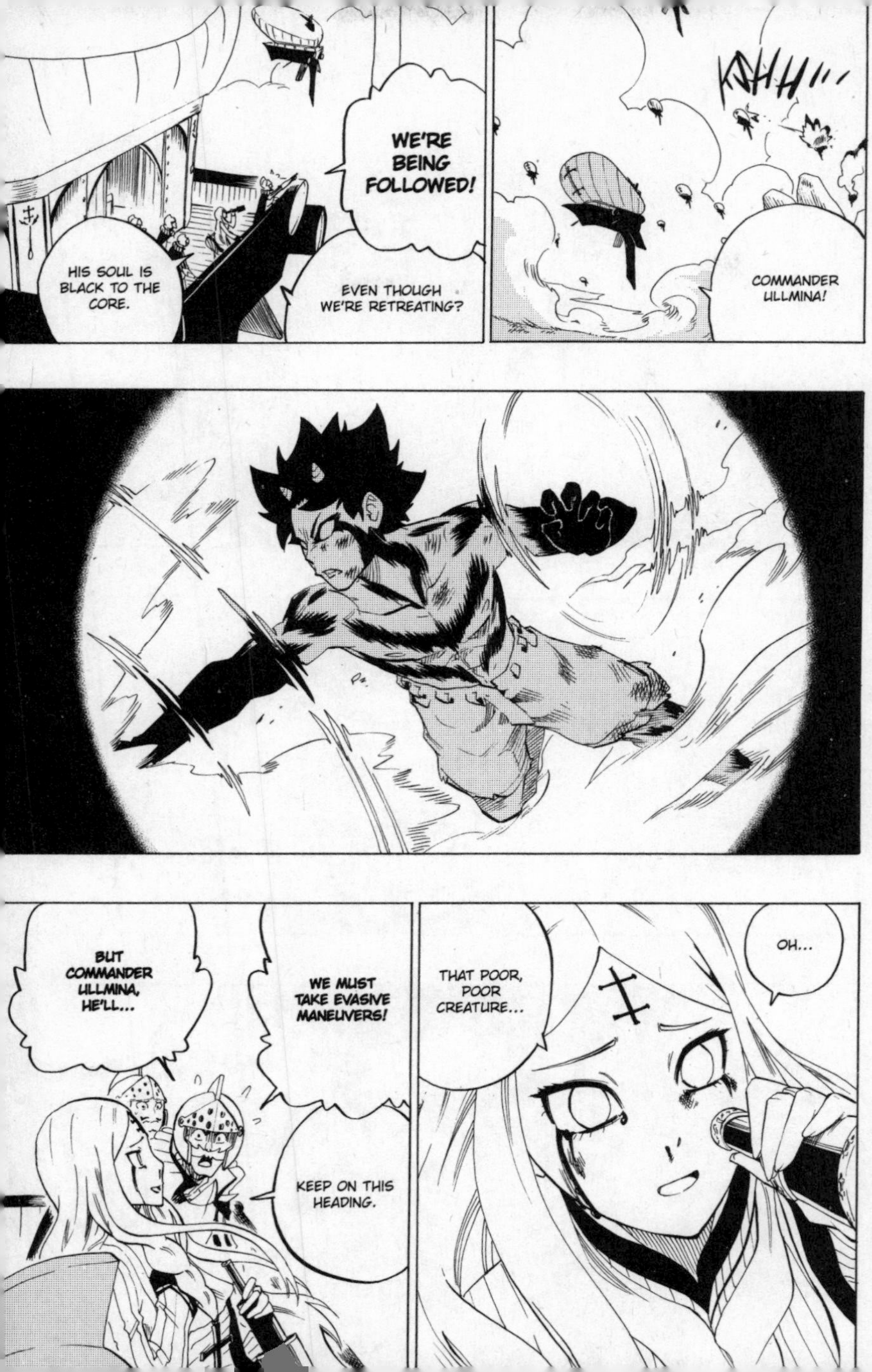
KSHH
COMMANDER ULLMINA!
WE'RE BEING FOLLOWED!
EVEN THOUGH WE'RE RETREATING?
HIS SOUL IS BLACK TO THE CORE.
OH...
THAT POOR, POOR CREATURE...
WE MUST TAKE EVASIVE MANEUVERS!
BUT COMMANDER ULLMINA, HE'LL...
KEEP ON THIS HEADING.

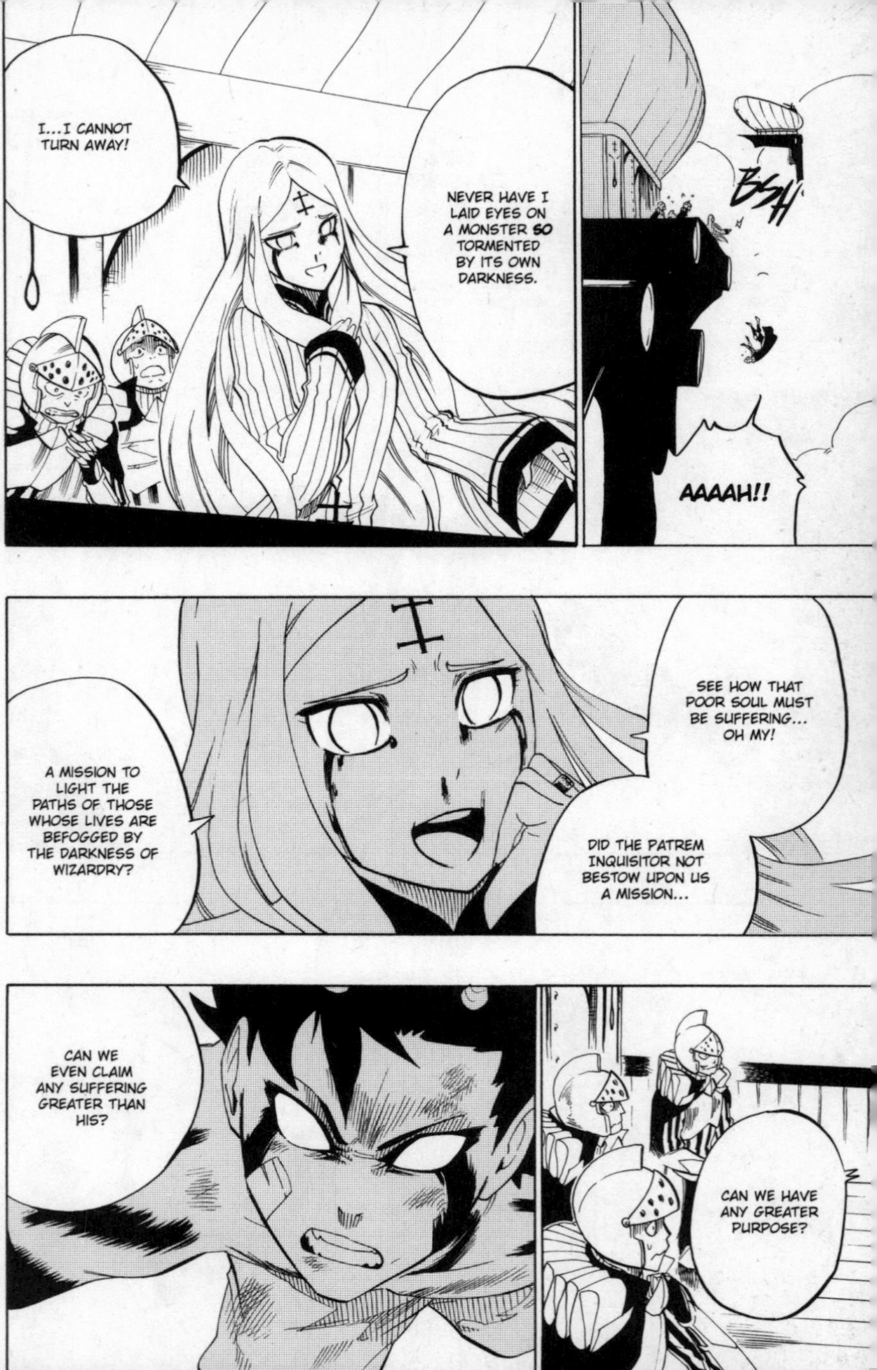
BSH
AAAAH!!
NEVER HAVE I LAID EYES ON A MONSTER SO TORMENTED BY ITS OWN DARKNESS.
I...I CANNOT TURN AWAY!
SEE HOW THAT POOR SOUL MUST BE SUFFERING... OH MY!
DID THE PATREM INQUISITOR NOT BESTOW UPON US A MISSION...
A MISSION TO LIGHT THE PATHS OF THOSE WHOSE LIVES ARE BEFOGGED BY THE DARKNESS OF WIZARDRY?
CAN WE HAVE ANY GREATER PURPOSE?
CAN WE EVEN CLAIM ANY SUFFERING GREATER THAN HIS?

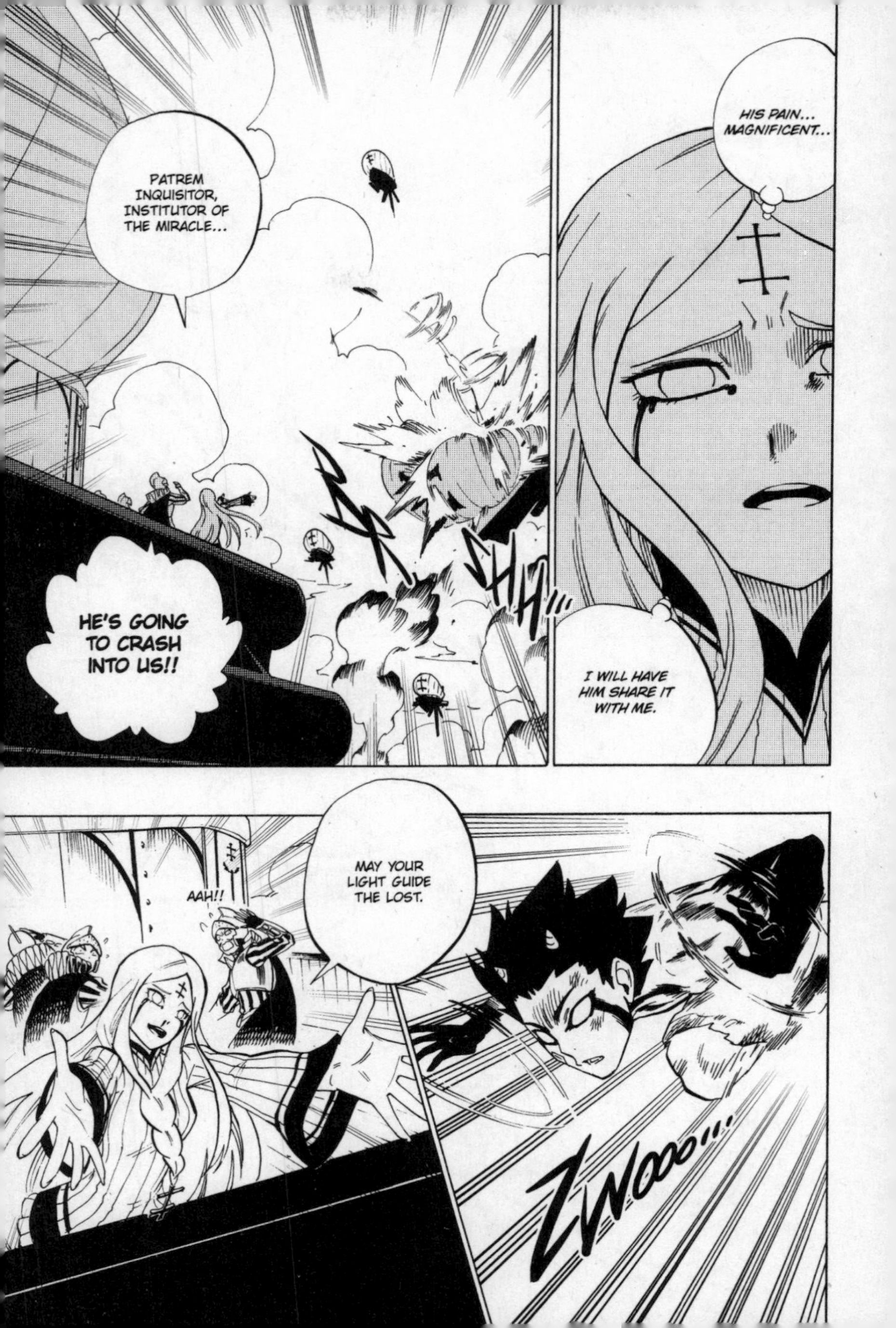
HIS PAIN... MAGNIFICENT...
I WILL HAVE HIM SHARE IT WITH ME.
PATREM INQUISITOR, INSTITUTOR OF THE MIRACLE...
HE'S GOING TO CRASH INTO US!!
MAY YOUR LIGHT GUIDE THE LOST.
AAH!!
ZWOOO...

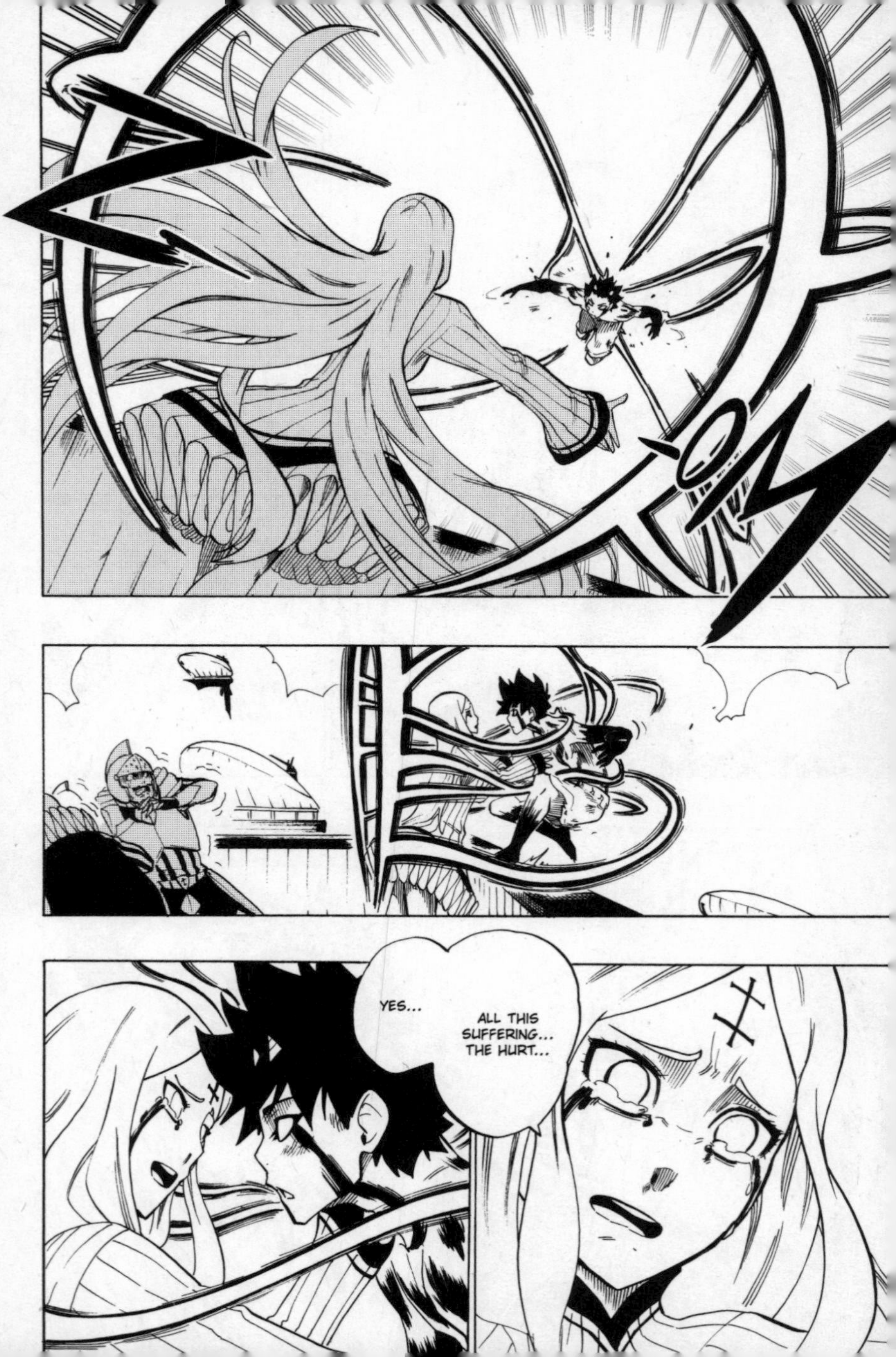
YES...
ALL THIS SUFFERING... THE HURT...

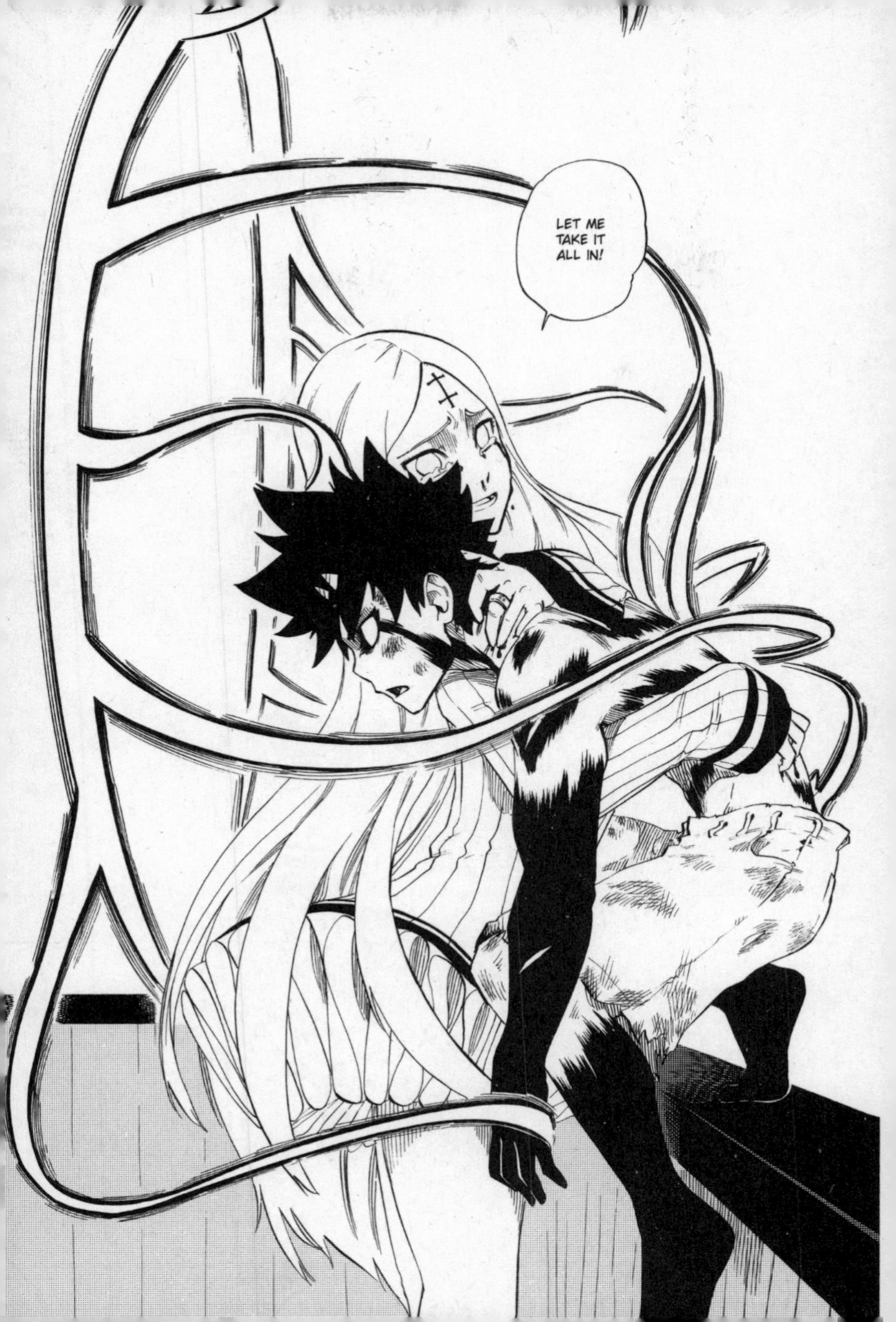
LET ME TAKE IT ALL IN!

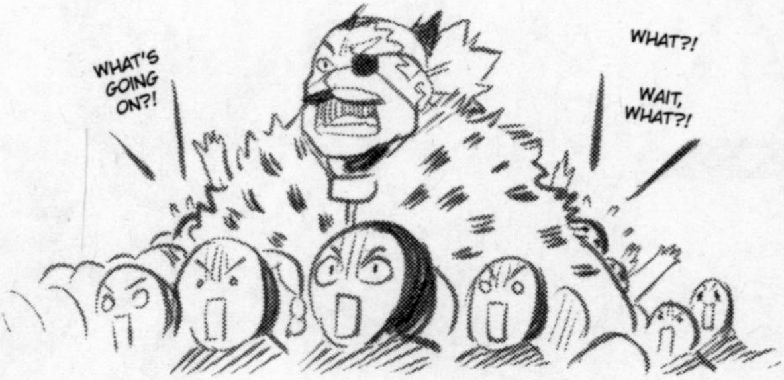
WHAT?!
WAIT, WHAT?!
WHAT'S GOING ON?!

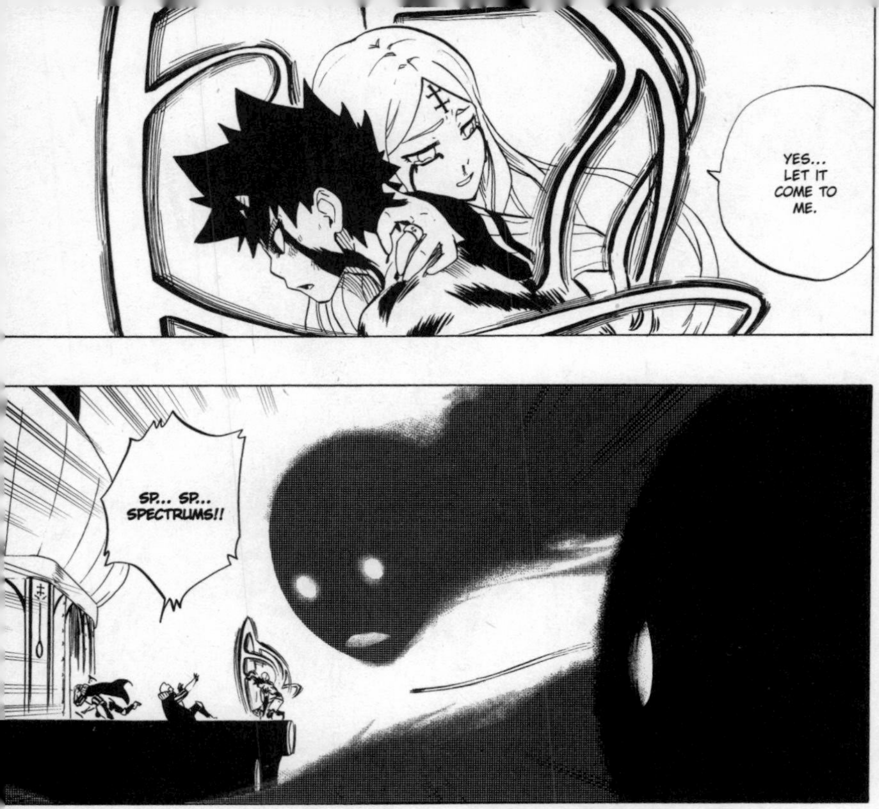
YES... LET IT COME TO ME.
SP... SP... SPECTRUMS!!

Chapter 72 All Must Die

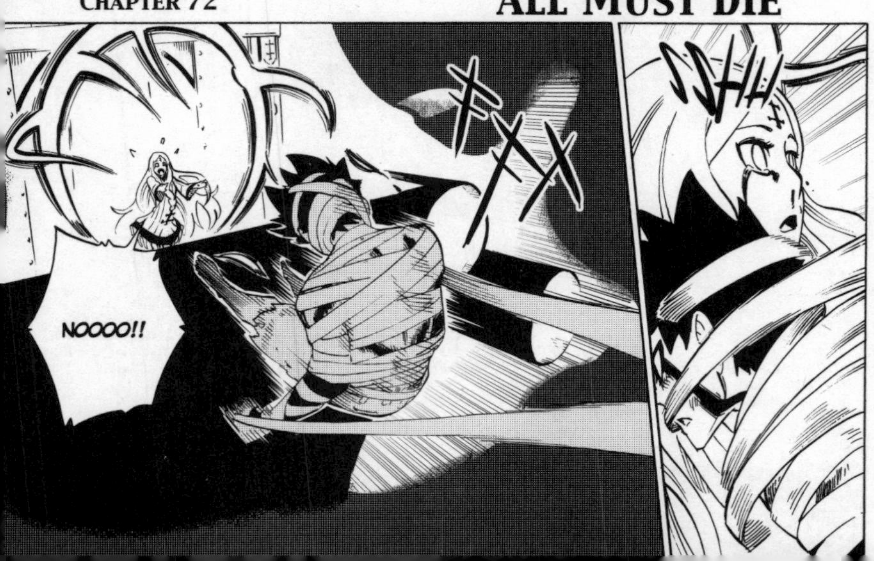
NOOOO!!

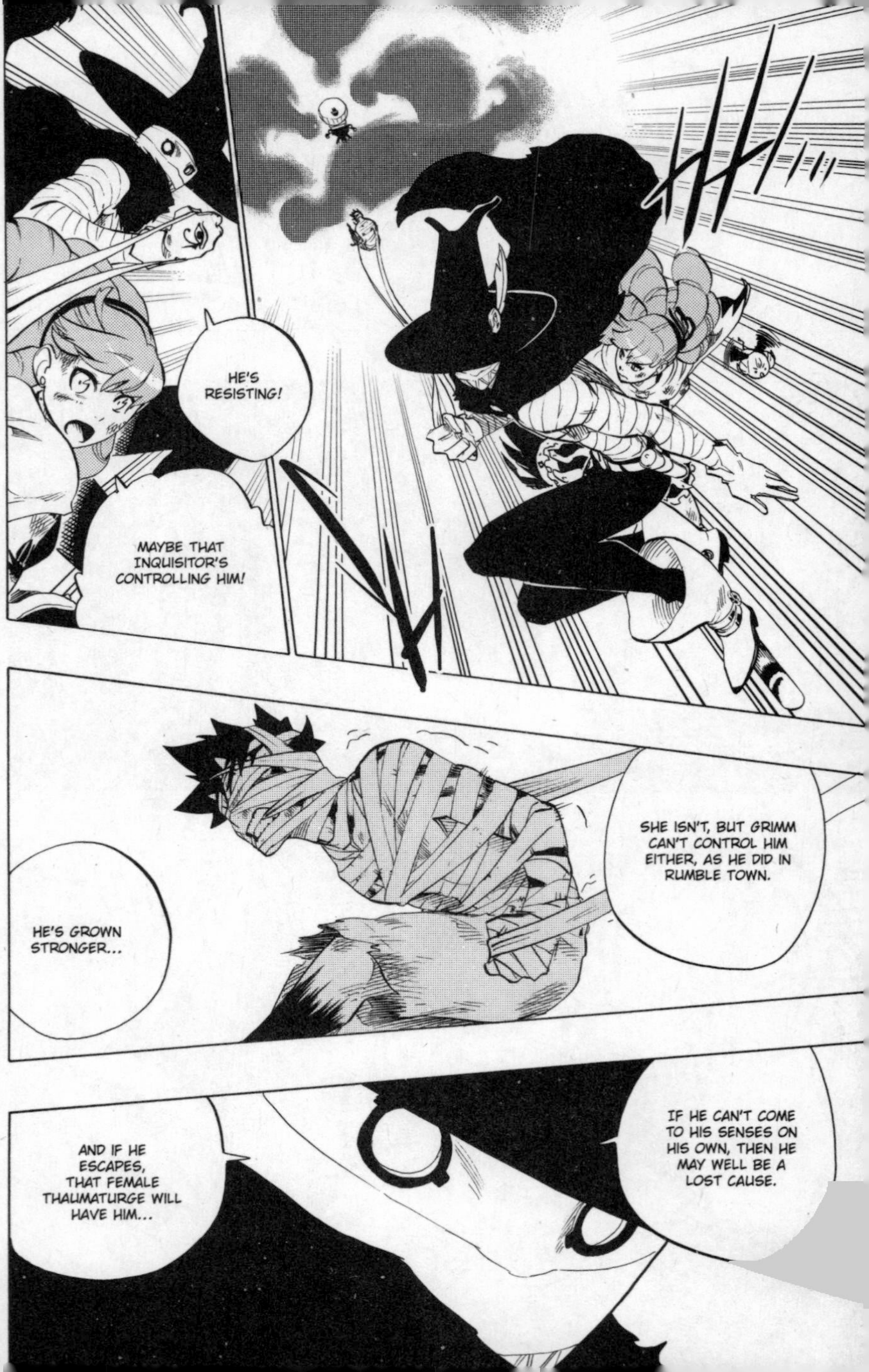
HE'S RESISTING!
MAYBE THAT INQUISITOR'S CONTROLLING HIM!
SHE ISN'T, BUT GRIMM CAN'T CONTROL HIM EITHER, AS HE DID IN RUMBLE TOWN.
HE'S GROWN STRONGER...
IF HE CAN'T COME TO HIS SENSES ON HIS OWN, THEN HE MAY WELL BE A LOST CAUSE.
AND IF HE ESCAPES, THAT FEMALE THAUMATURGE WILL HAVE HIM...

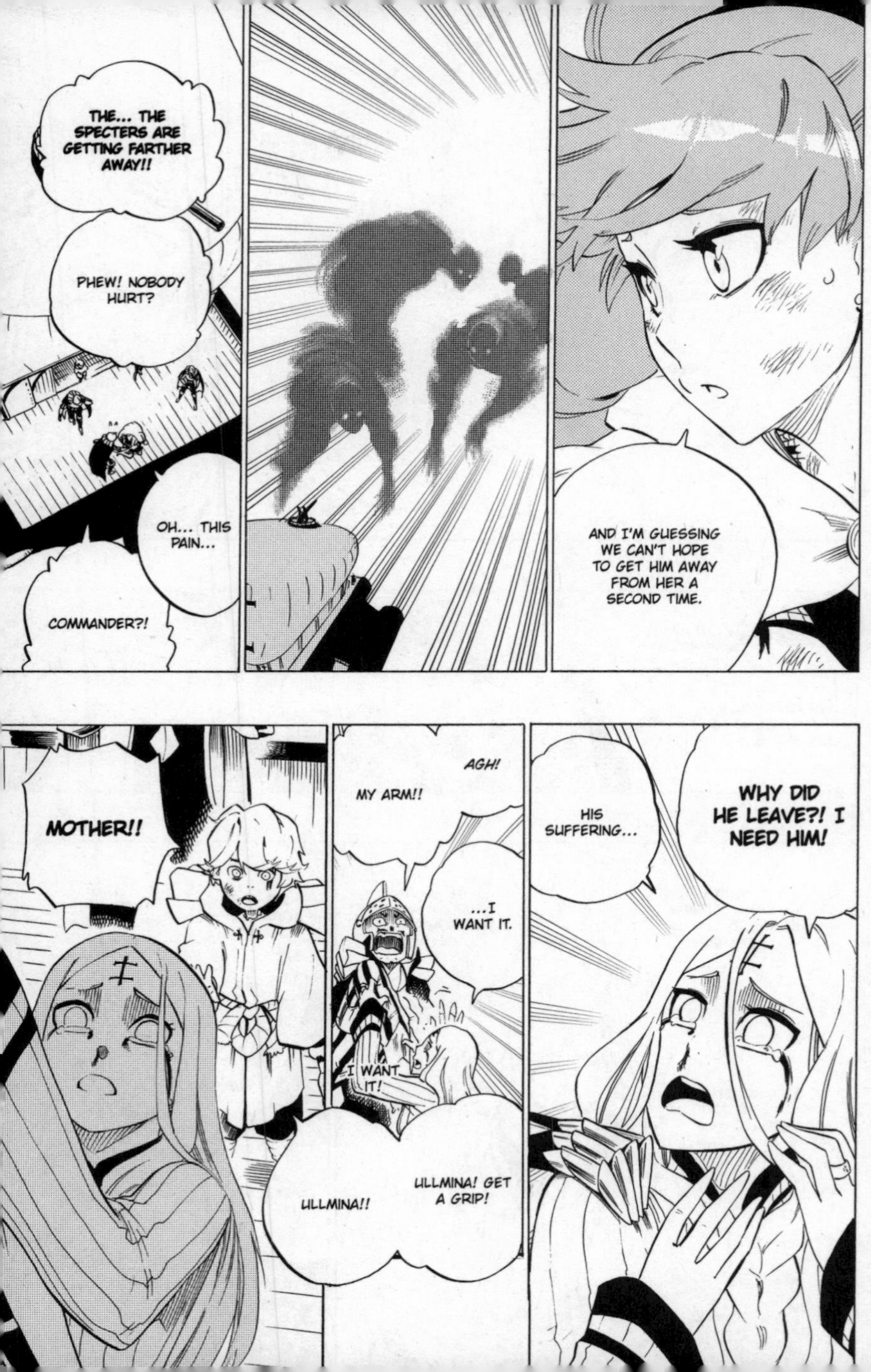
AND I'M GUESSING WE CAN'T HOPE TO GET HIM AWAY FROM HER A SECOND TIME.
THE... THE SPECTERS ARE GETTING FARTHER AWAY!!
PHEW! NOBODY HURT?
OH... THIS PAIN...
COMMANDER?!
WHY DID HE LEAVE?! I NEED HIM!
HIS SUFFERING...
AGH!
MY ARM!!
...I WANT IT.
I WANT IT!
ULLMINA! GET A GRIP!
ULLMINA!!
MOTHER!!

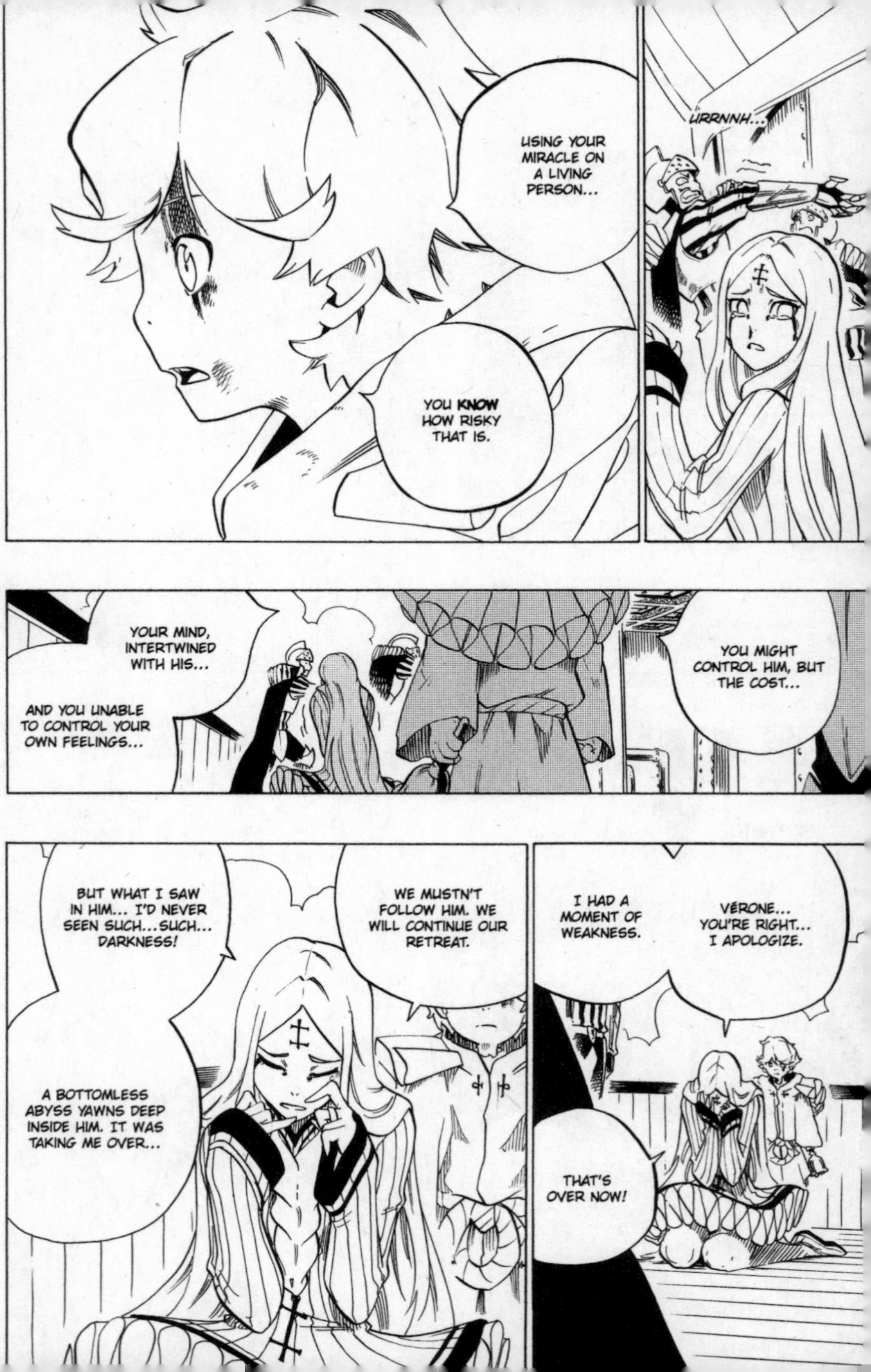
URRNNH...
USING YOUR MIRACLE ON A LIVING PERSON...
YOU **KNOW** HOW RISKY THAT IS.
YOU MIGHT CONTROL HIM, BUT THE COST...
YOUR MIND, INTERTWINED WITH HIS...
AND YOU UNABLE TO CONTROL YOUR OWN FEELINGS...
VÉRONE... YOU'RE RIGHT... I APOLOGIZE.
I HAD A MOMENT OF WEAKNESS.
THAT'S OVER NOW!
WE MUSTN'T FOLLOW HIM. WE WILL CONTINUE OUR RETREAT.
BUT WHAT I SAW IN HIM... I'D NEVER SEEN SUCH...SUCH... DARKNESS!
A BOTTOMLESS ABYSS YAWNS DEEP INSIDE HIM. IT WAS TAKING ME OVER...

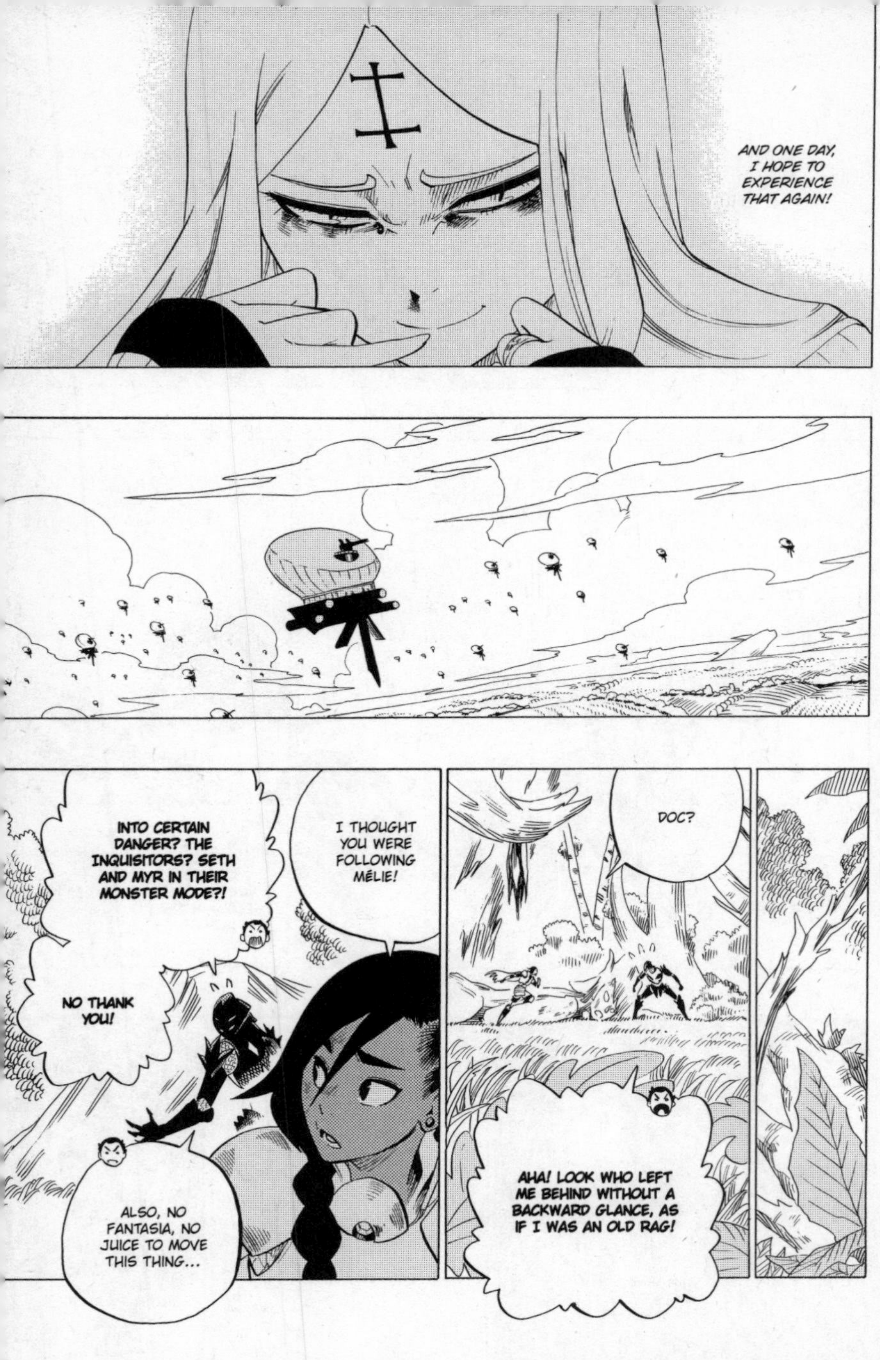
AND ONE DAY, I HOPE TO EXPERIENCE THAT AGAIN!
DOC?
AHA! LOOK WHO LEFT ME BEHIND WITHOUT A BACKWARD GLANCE, AS IF I WAS AN OLD RAG!
I THOUGHT YOU WERE FOLLOWING MÉLIE!
INTO CERTAIN DANGER? THE INQUISITORS? SETH AND MYR IN THEIR MONSTER MODE?!
NO THANK YOU!
ALSO, NO FANTASIA, NO JUICE TO MOVE THIS THING...

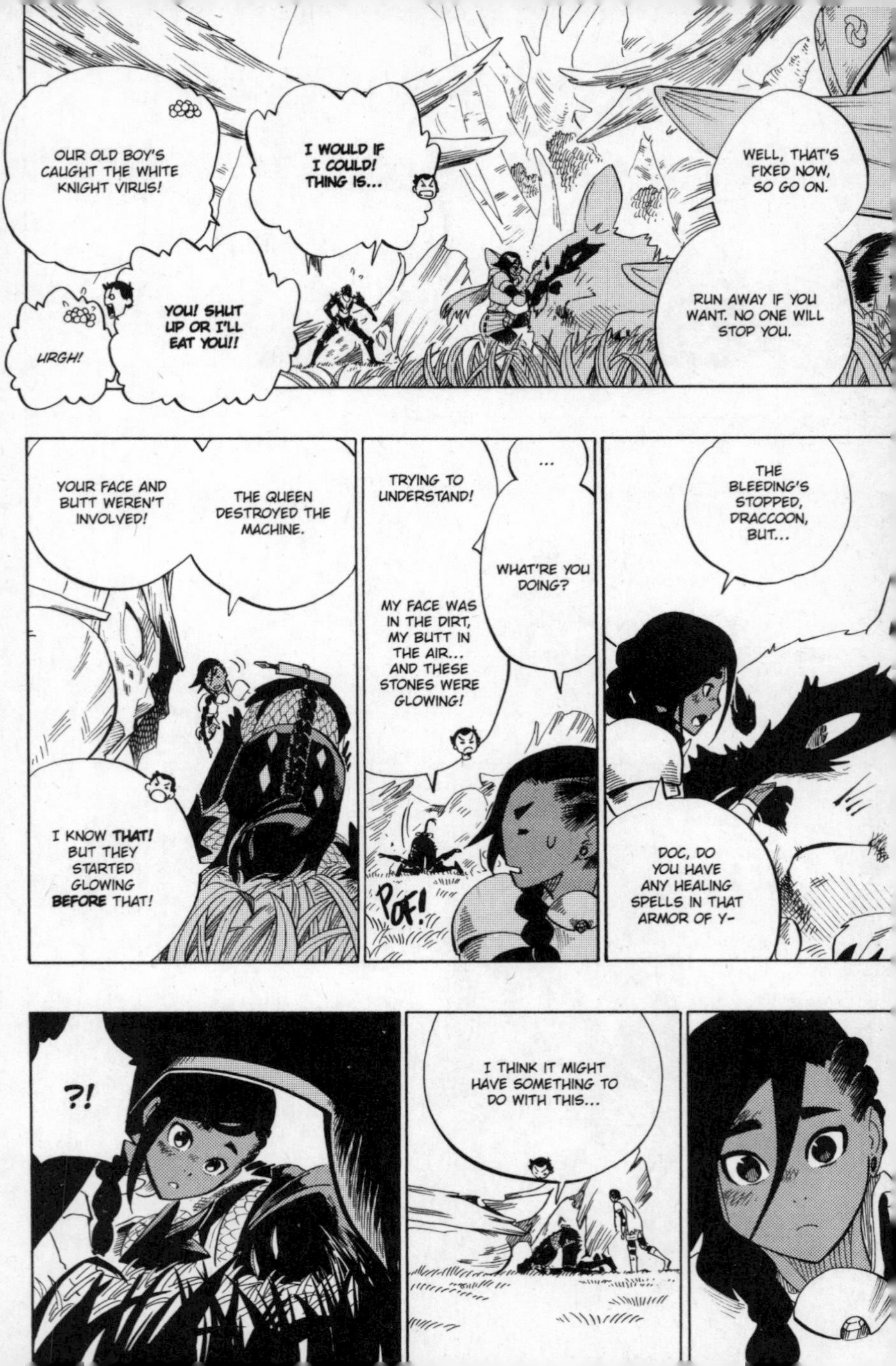
WELL, THAT'S FIXED NOW, SO GO ON.
RUN AWAY IF YOU WANT. NO ONE WILL STOP YOU.
I WOULD IF I COULD! THING IS...
OUR OLD BOY'S CAUGHT THE WHITE KNIGHT VIRUS!
YOU! SHUT UP OR I'LL EAT YOU!!
URGH!
THE BLEEDING'S STOPPED, DRACCOON, BUT...
DOC, DO YOU HAVE ANY HEALING SPELLS IN THAT ARMOR OF Y-
...
WHAT'RE YOU DOING?
TRYING TO UNDERSTAND!
MY FACE WAS IN THE DIRT, MY BUTT IN THE AIR... AND THESE STONES WERE GLOWING!
POF!
THE QUEEN DESTROYED THE MACHINE.
YOUR FACE AND BUTT WEREN'T INVOLVED!
I KNOW **THAT**! BUT THEY STARTED GLOWING **BEFORE** THAT!
I THINK IT MIGHT HAVE SOMETHING TO DO WITH THIS...
?!

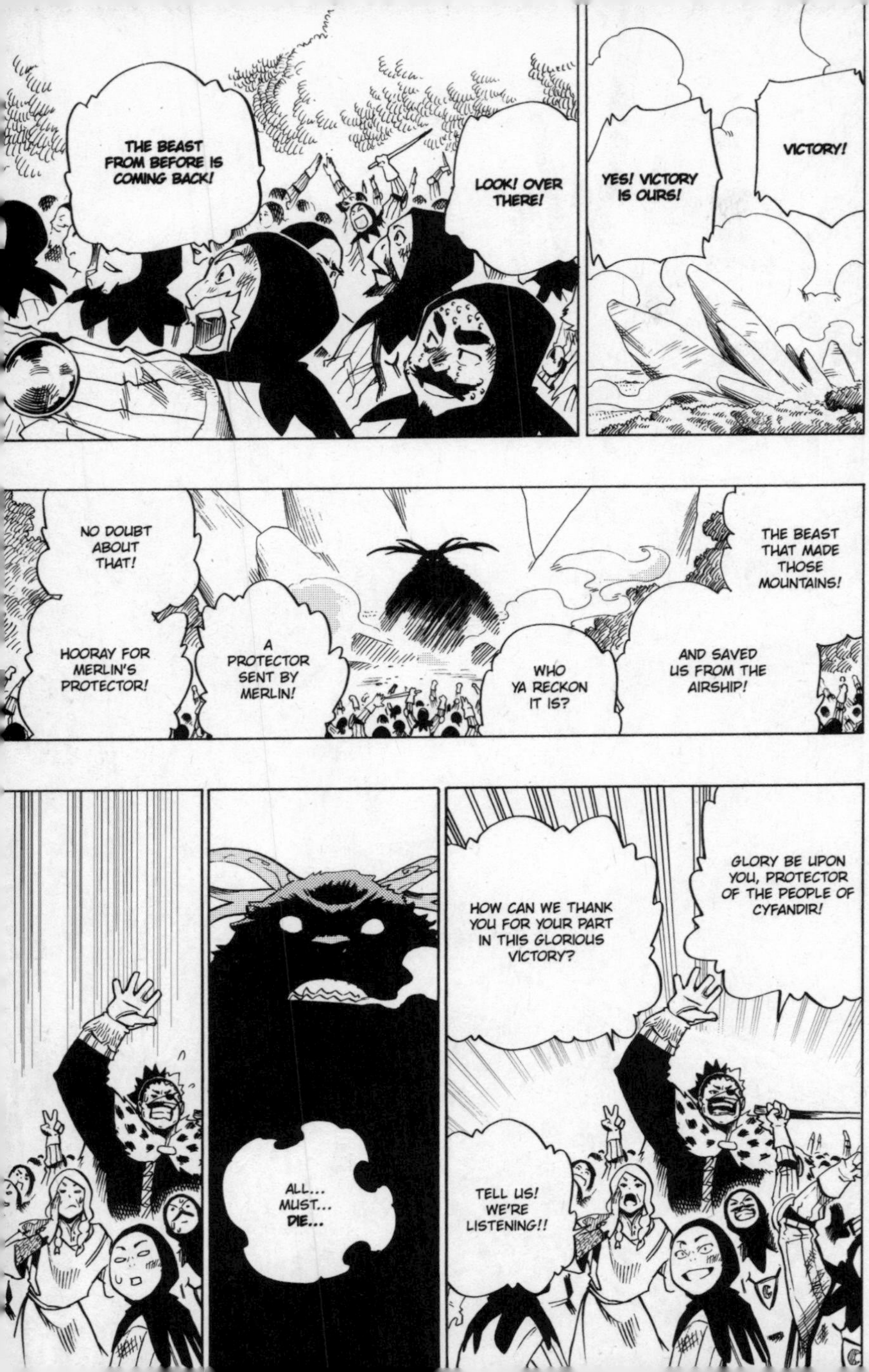
VICTORY!
YES! VICTORY IS OURS!
LOOK! OVER THERE!
THE BEAST FROM BEFORE IS COMING BACK!
THE BEAST THAT MADE THOSE MOUNTAINS!
AND SAVED US FROM THE AIRSHIP!
WHO YA RECKON IT IS?
A PROTECTOR SENT BY MERLIN!
NO DOUBT ABOUT THAT!
HOORAY FOR MERLIN'S PROTECTOR!
GLORY BE UPON YOU, PROTECTOR OF THE PEOPLE OF CYFANDIR!
HOW CAN WE THANK YOU FOR YOUR PART IN THIS GLORIOUS VICTORY?
TELL US! WE'RE LISTENING!!
ALL... MUST... DIE...

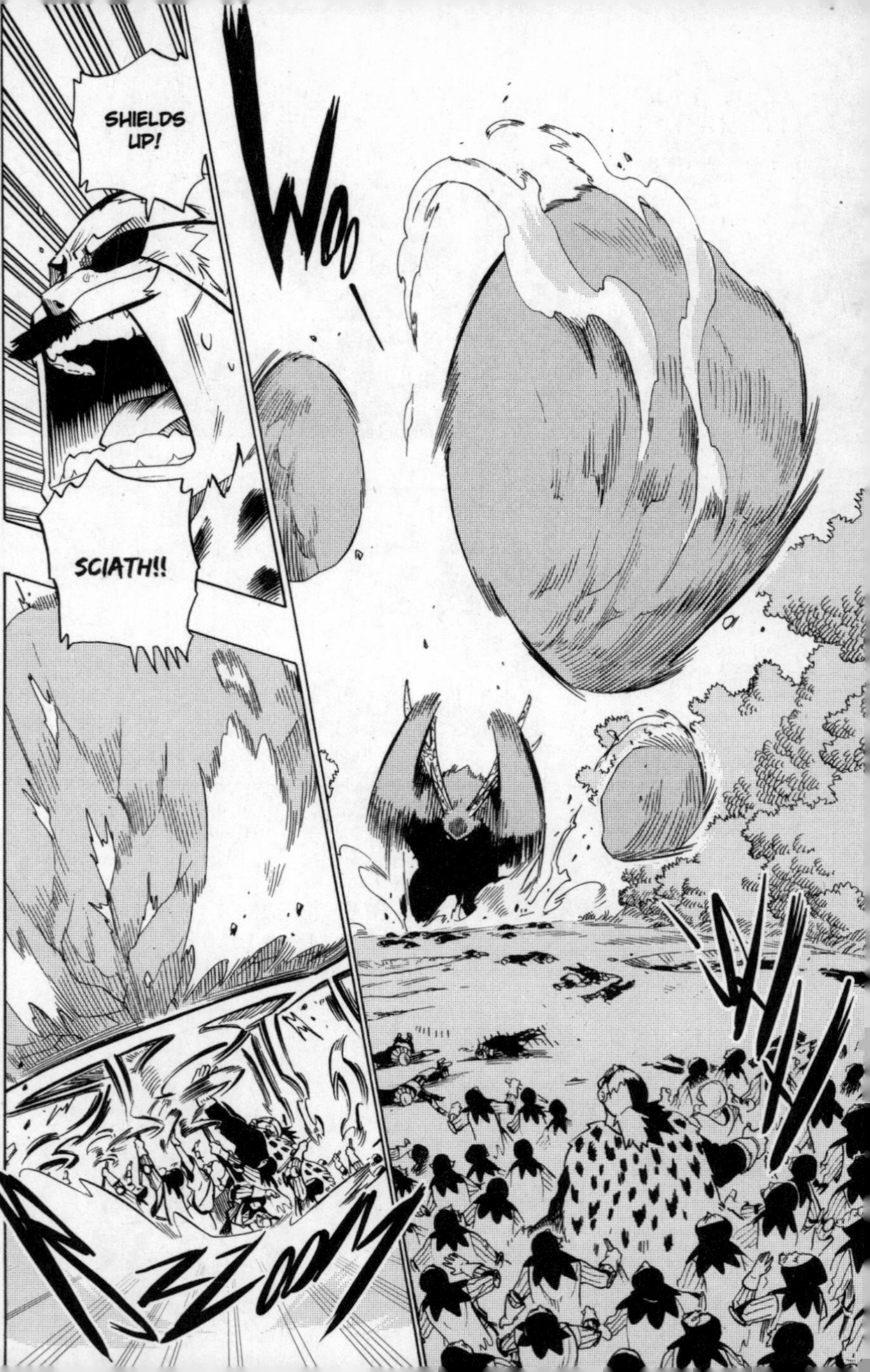
SHIELDS UP!
SCIATH!!
WOOO
ZZZOOM

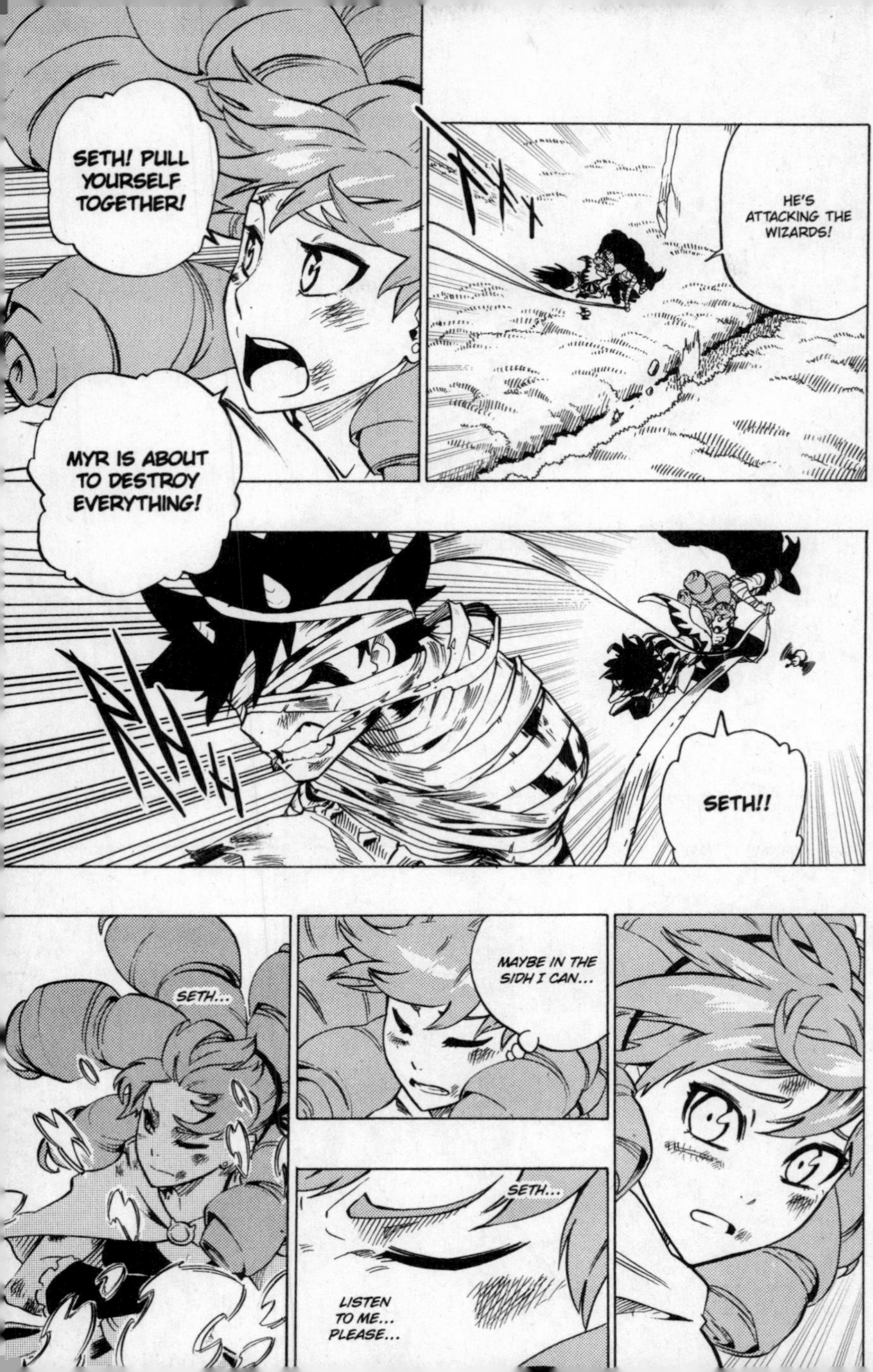
HE'S ATTACKING THE WIZARDS!
SETH! PULL YOURSELF TOGETHER!
MYR IS ABOUT TO DESTROY EVERYTHING!
SETH!!
MAYBE IN THE SIDH I CAN...
SETH...
LISTEN TO ME... PLEASE...
SETH...

WOOo...   ...OOOW

WHAT IS...

SETH?!

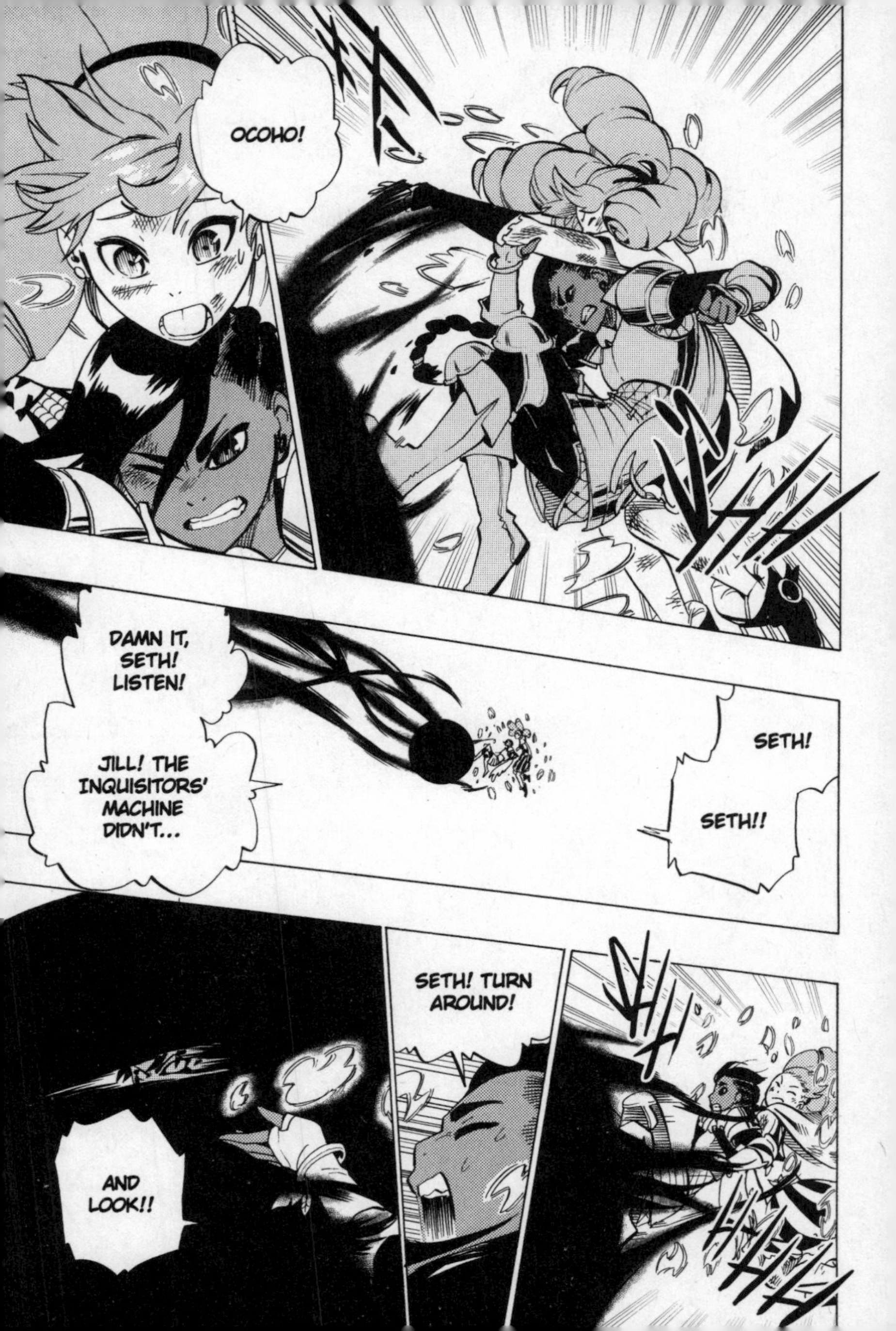
OCOHO!
SETH!
SETH!!
DAMN IT, SETH! LISTEN!
JILL! THE INQUISITORS' MACHINE DIDN'T...
SETH! TURN AROUND!
AND LOOK!!

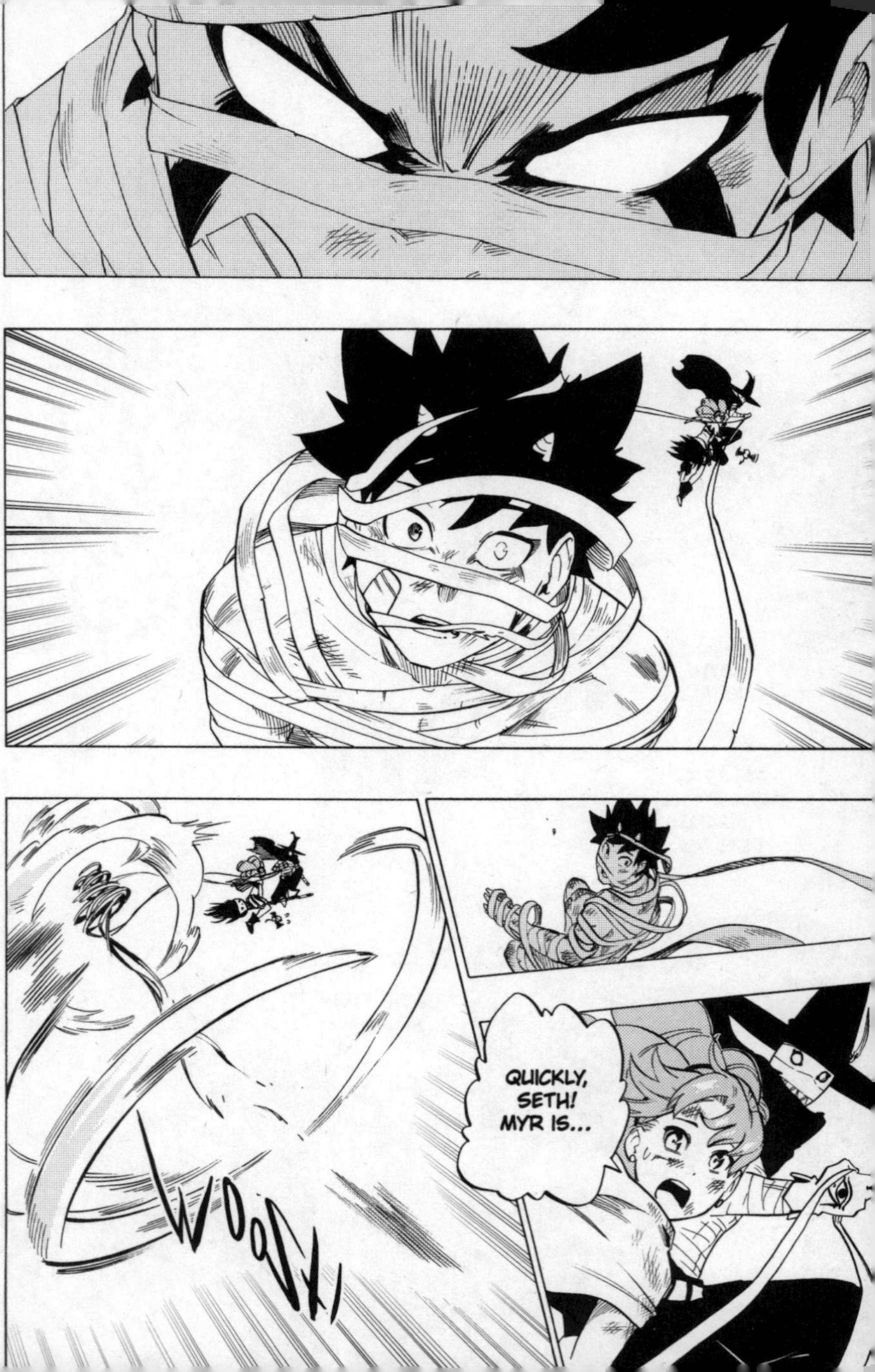
QUICKLY, SETH! MYR IS...

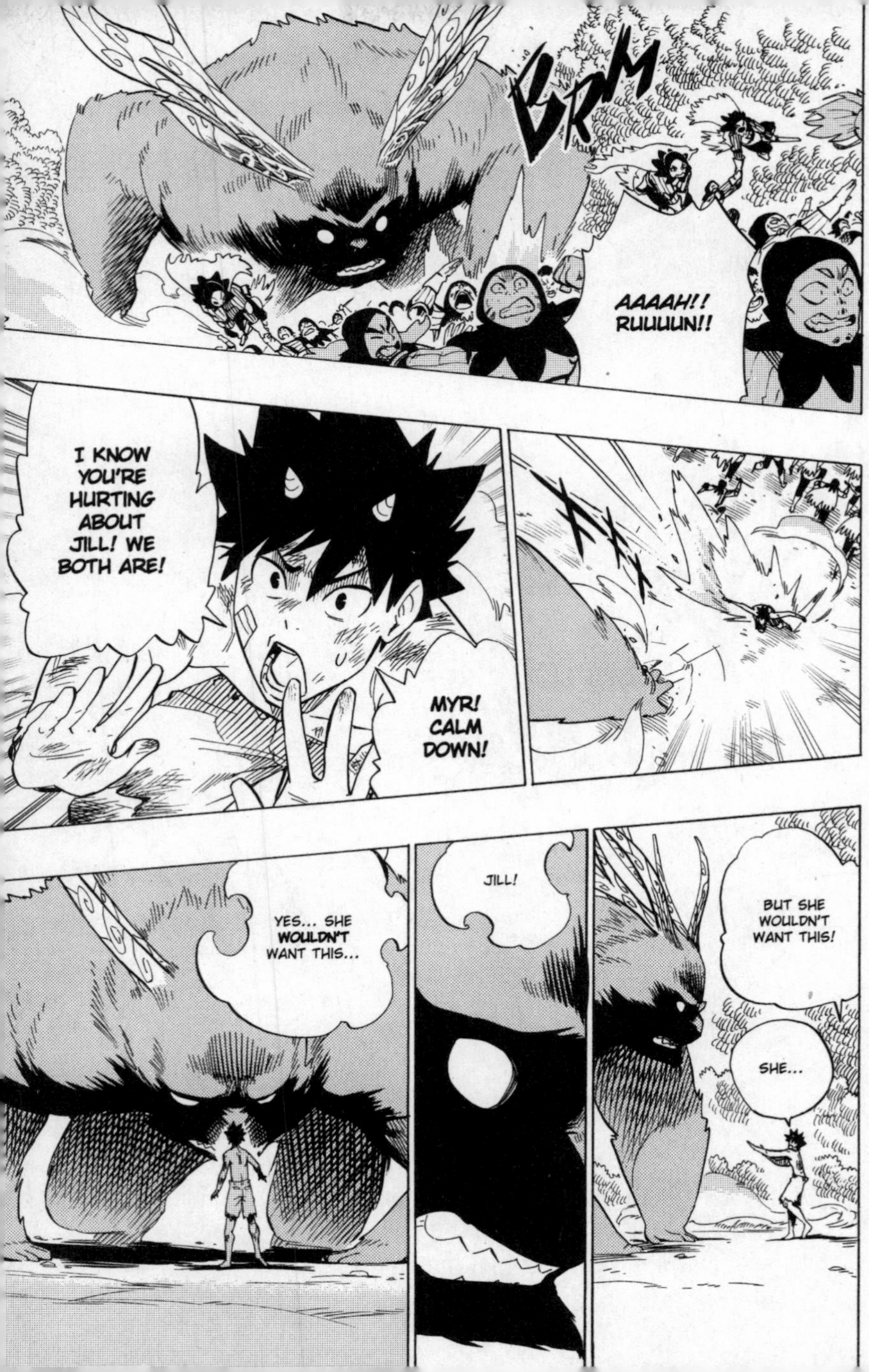
BRM
AAAAH!! RUUUUN!!
MYR! CALM DOWN!
I KNOW YOU'RE HURTING ABOUT JILL! WE BOTH ARE!
BUT SHE WOULDN'T WANT THIS!
SHE...
JILL!
YES... SHE WOULDN'T WANT THIS...

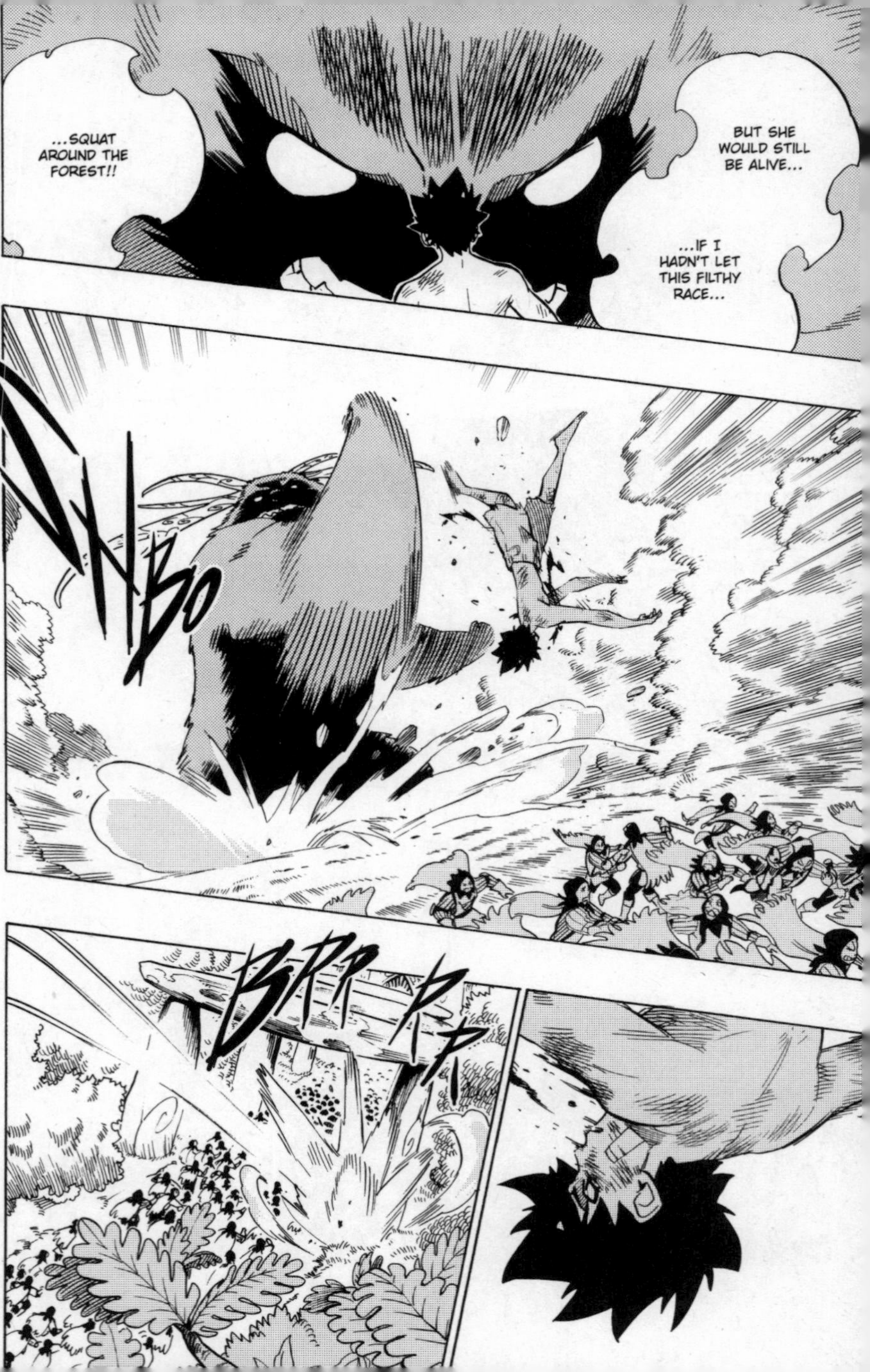
BUT SHE WOULD STILL BE ALIVE...
...IF I HADN'T LET THIS FILTHY RACE...
...SQUAT AROUND THE FOREST!!

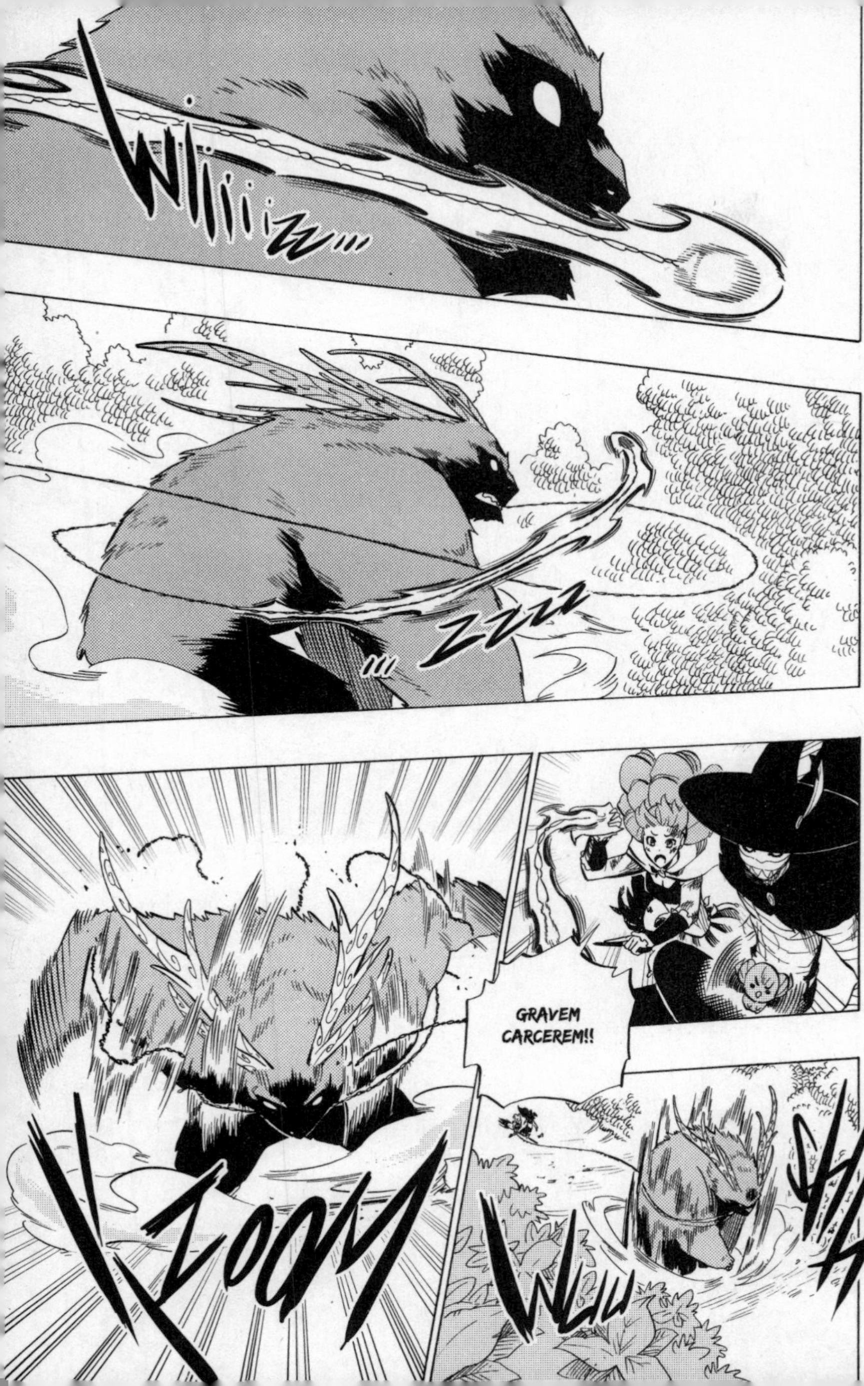
WHiiiizzz...
...ZZZZ
GRAVEM CARCEREM!!
KZOOOM
SHHH
WUUU

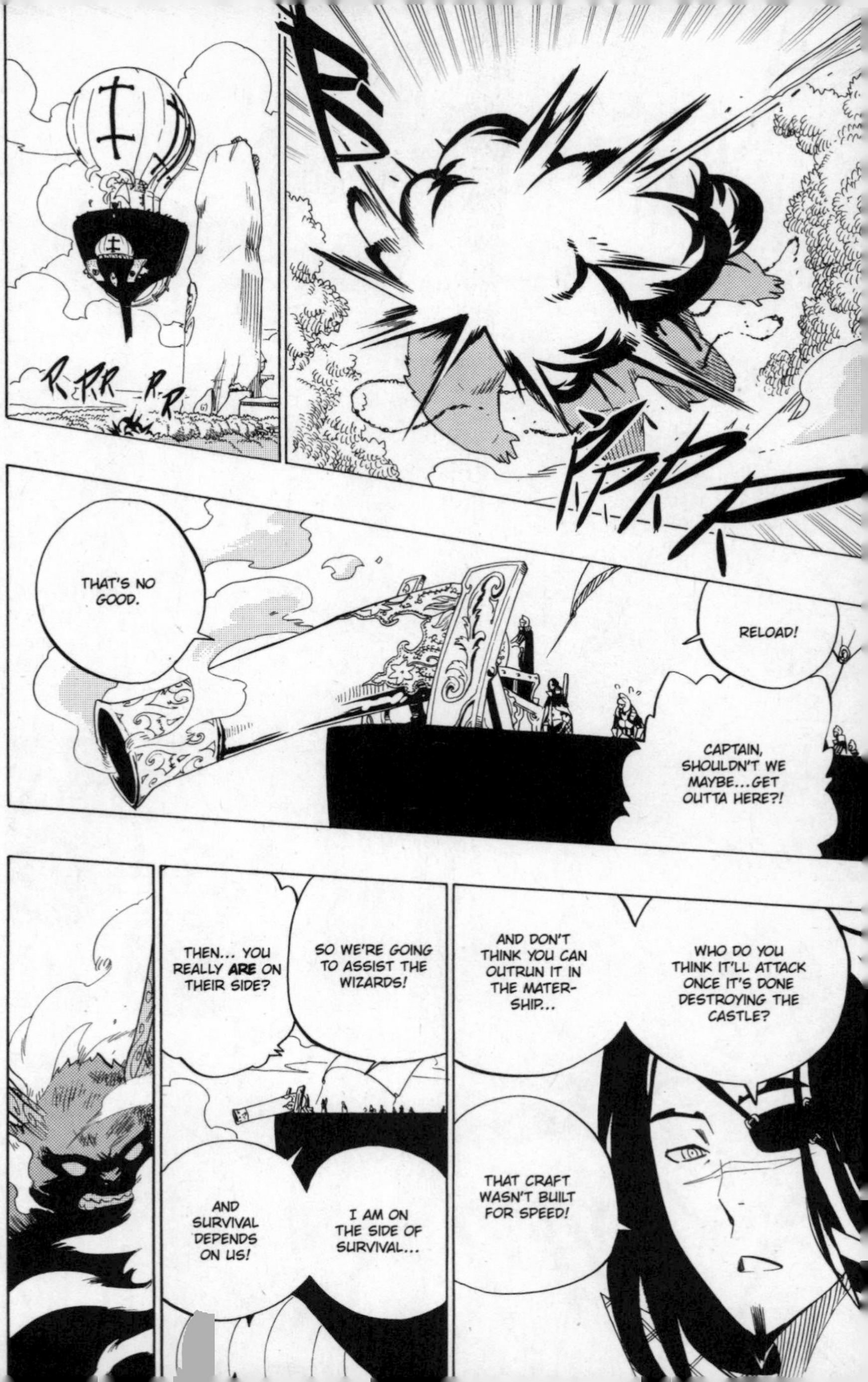
RELOAD!
CAPTAIN, SHOULDN'T WE MAYBE...GET OUTTA HERE?!
THAT'S NO GOOD.
WHO DO YOU THINK IT'LL ATTACK ONCE IT'S DONE DESTROYING THE CASTLE?
AND DON'T THINK YOU CAN OUTRUN IT IN THE MATER-SHIP...
THAT CRAFT WASN'T BUILT FOR SPEED!
SO WE'RE GOING TO ASSIST THE WIZARDS!
THEN... YOU REALLY **ARE** ON THEIR SIDE?
I AM ON THE SIDE OF SURVIVAL...
AND SURVIVAL DEPENDS ON US!

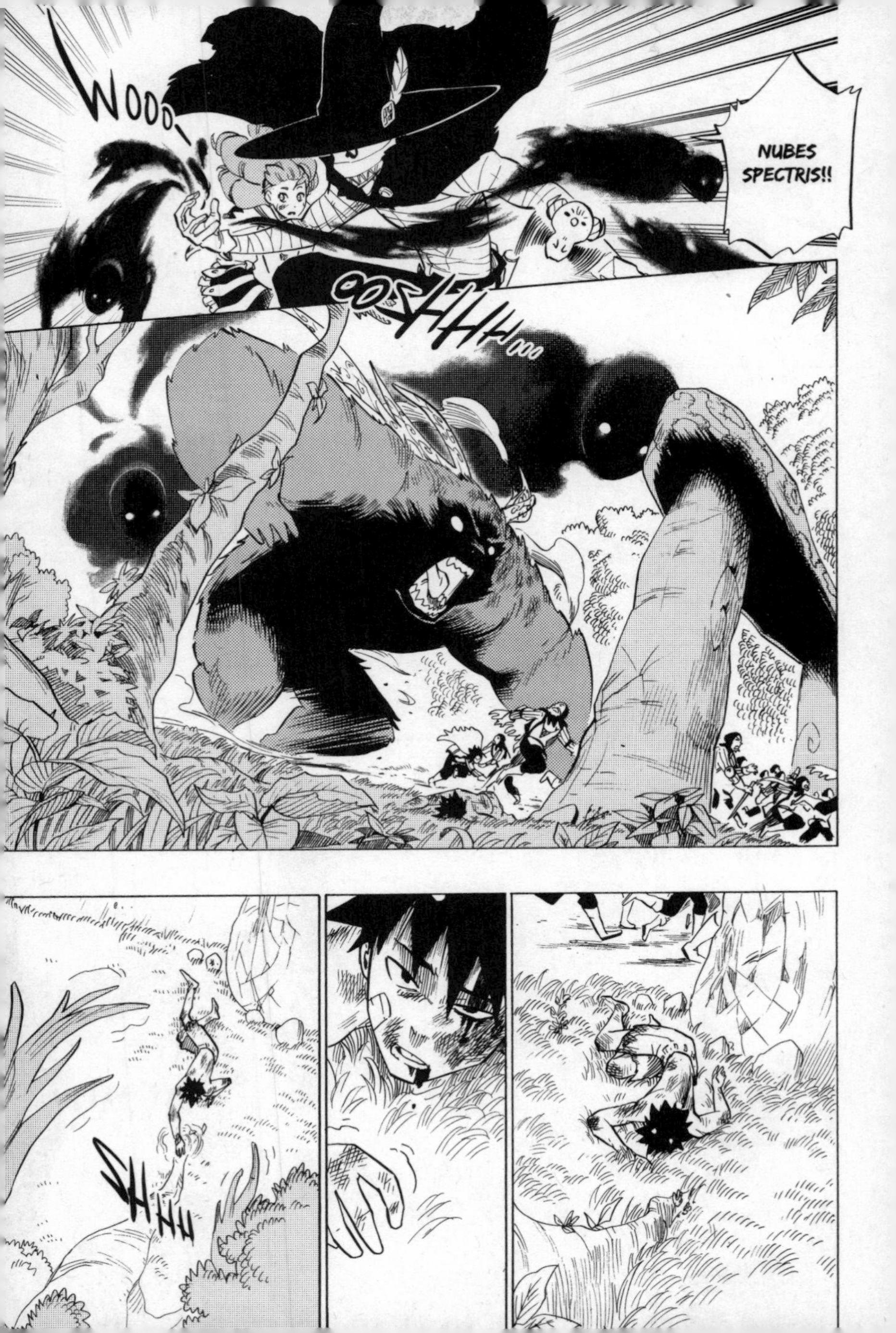
NUBES SPECTRIS!!
WOOO
SHHH

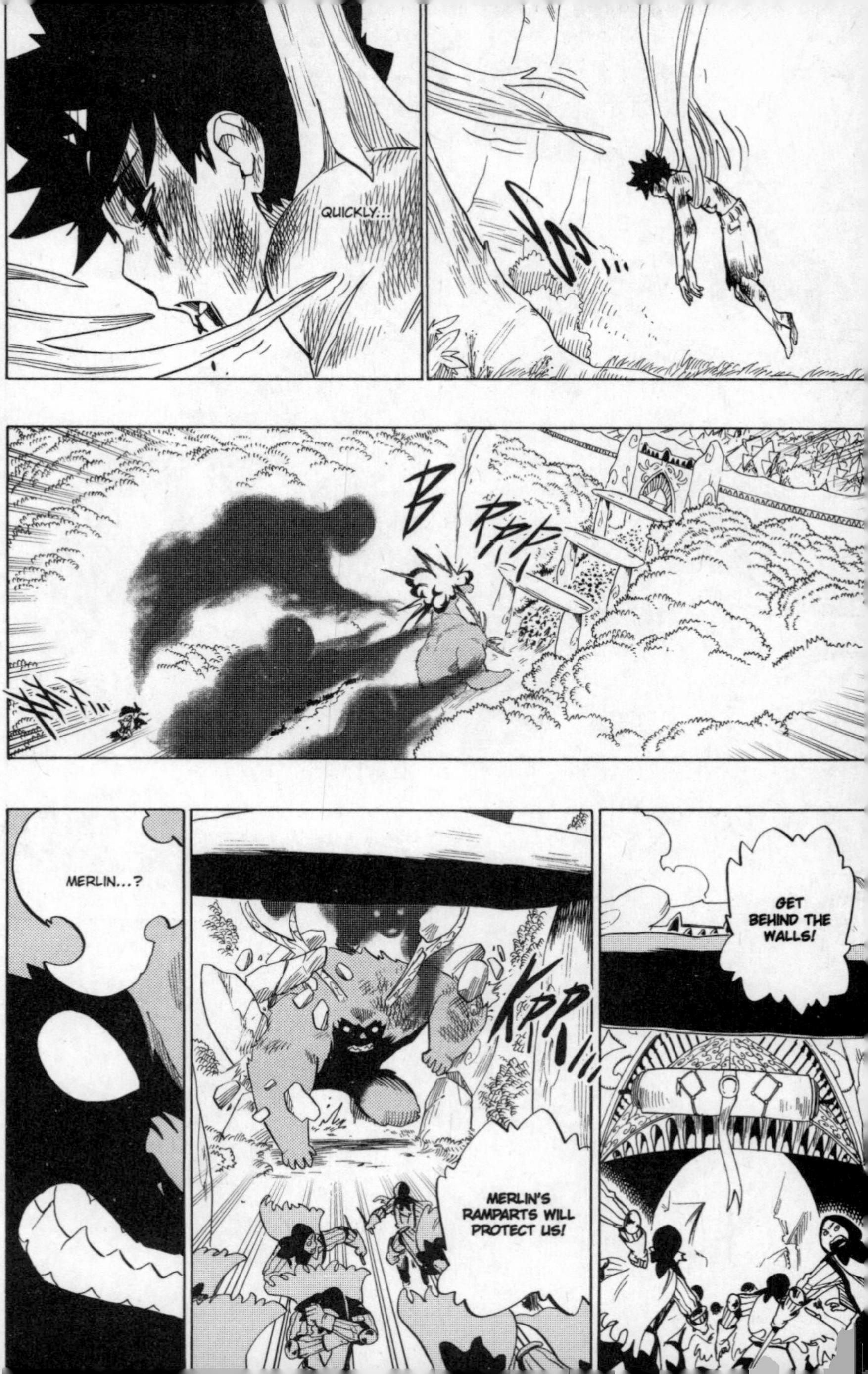
QUICKLY...
GET BEHIND THE WALLS!
KPP!!
MERLIN'S RAMPARTS WILL PROTECT US!
MERLIN...?

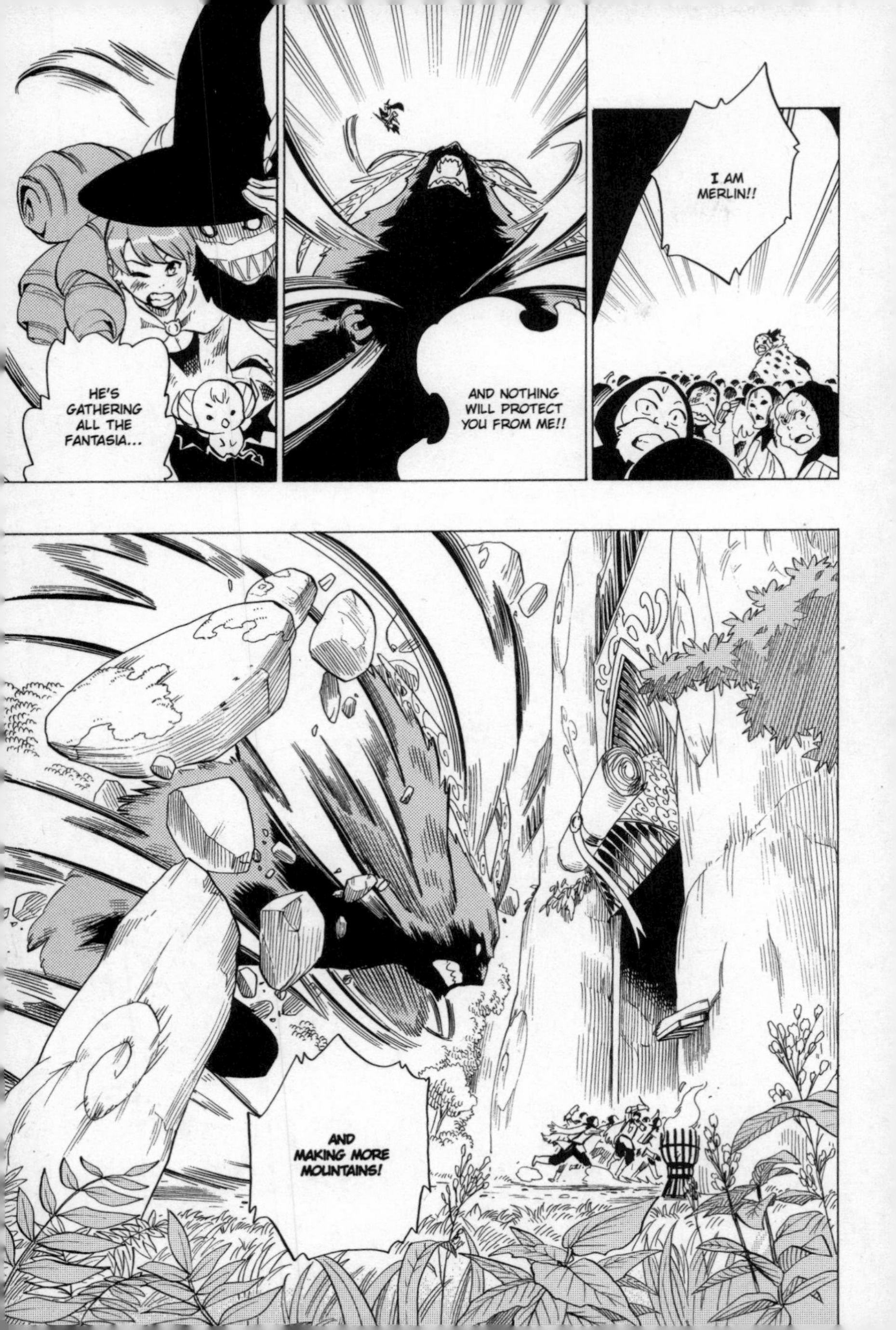
I AM MERLIN!!
AND NOTHING WILL PROTECT YOU FROM ME!!
HE'S GATHERING ALL THE FANTASIA...
AND MAKING MORE MOUNTAINS!

EVEN AGAINST TWO ENEMIES, A
PEACOCK-DRAGON NEVER ADMITS
DEFEAT!

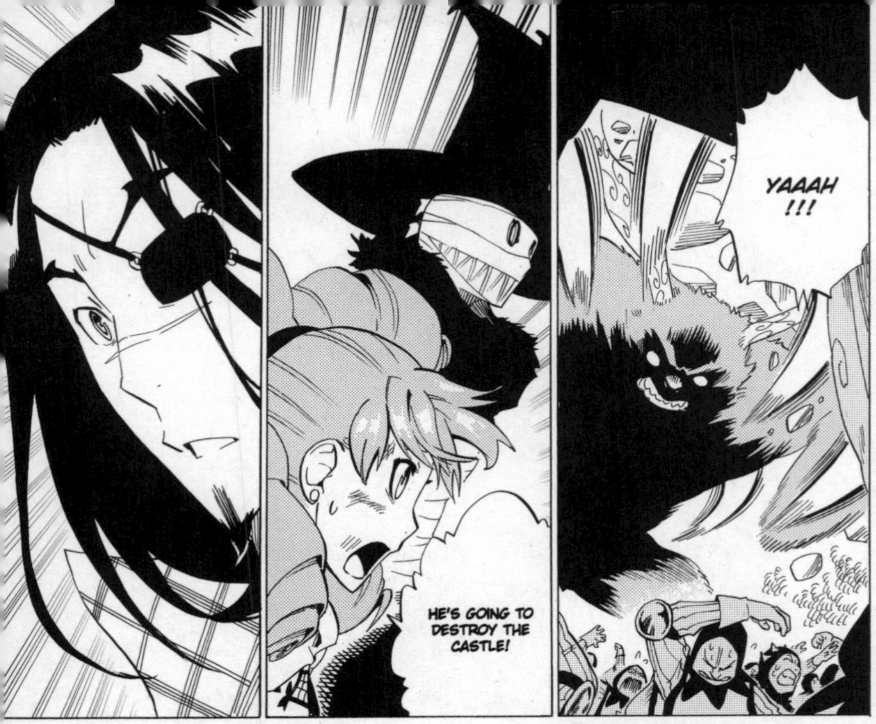
YAAAH !!!
HE'S GOING TO DESTROY THE CASTLE!

Chapter 73 Sacrificed

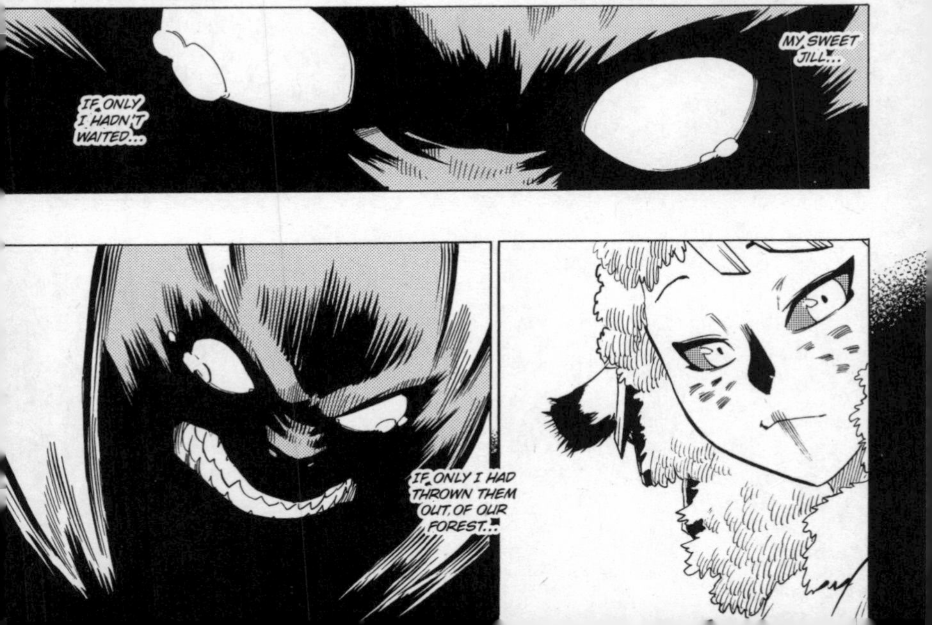
MY SWEET JILL...
IF ONLY I HADN'T WAITED...
IF ONLY I HAD THROWN THEM OUT OF OUR FOREST...

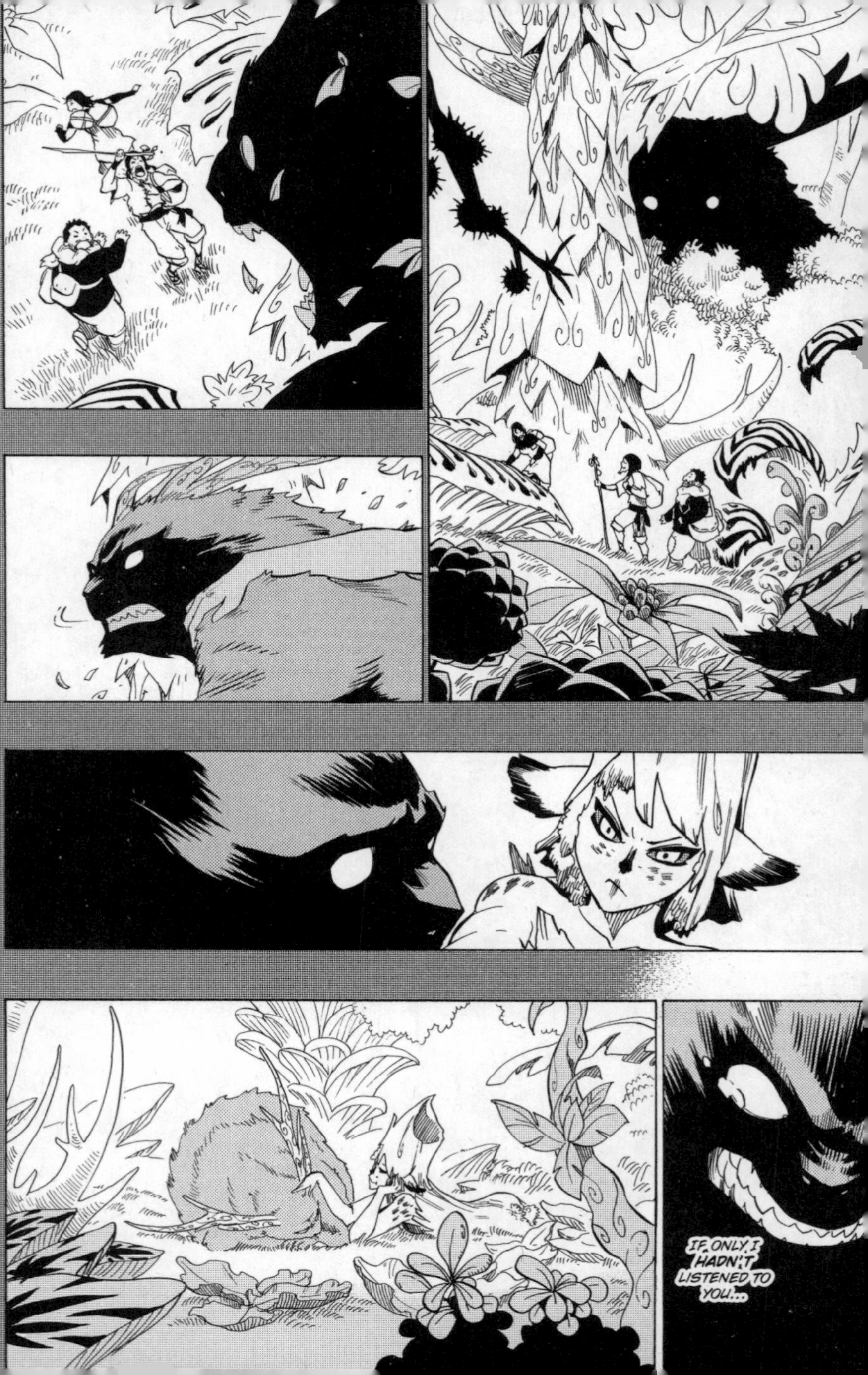
IF ONLY I HADN'T LISTENED TO YOU...

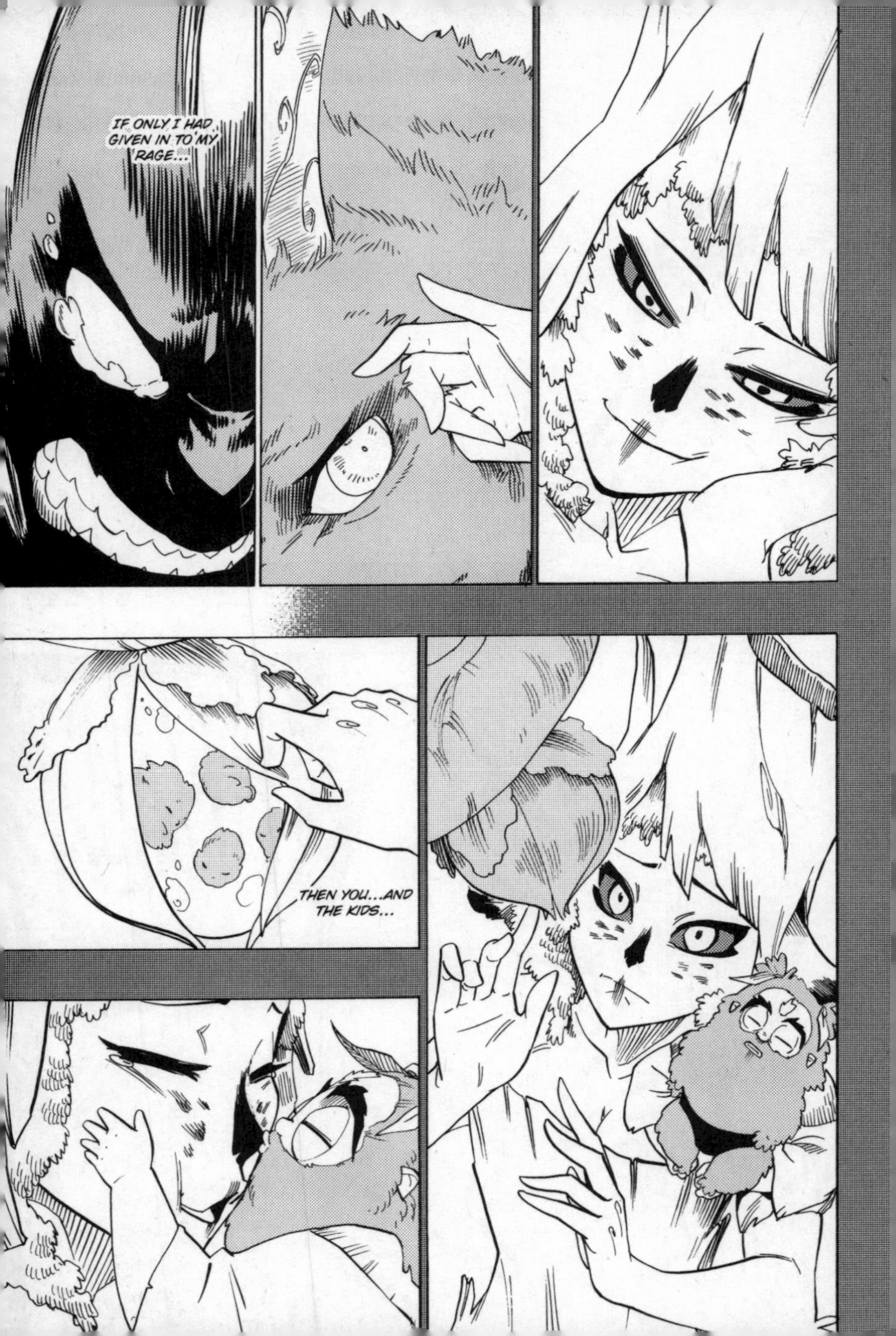
IF ONLY I HAD GIVEN IN TO MY RAGE...
THEN YOU...AND THE KIDS...

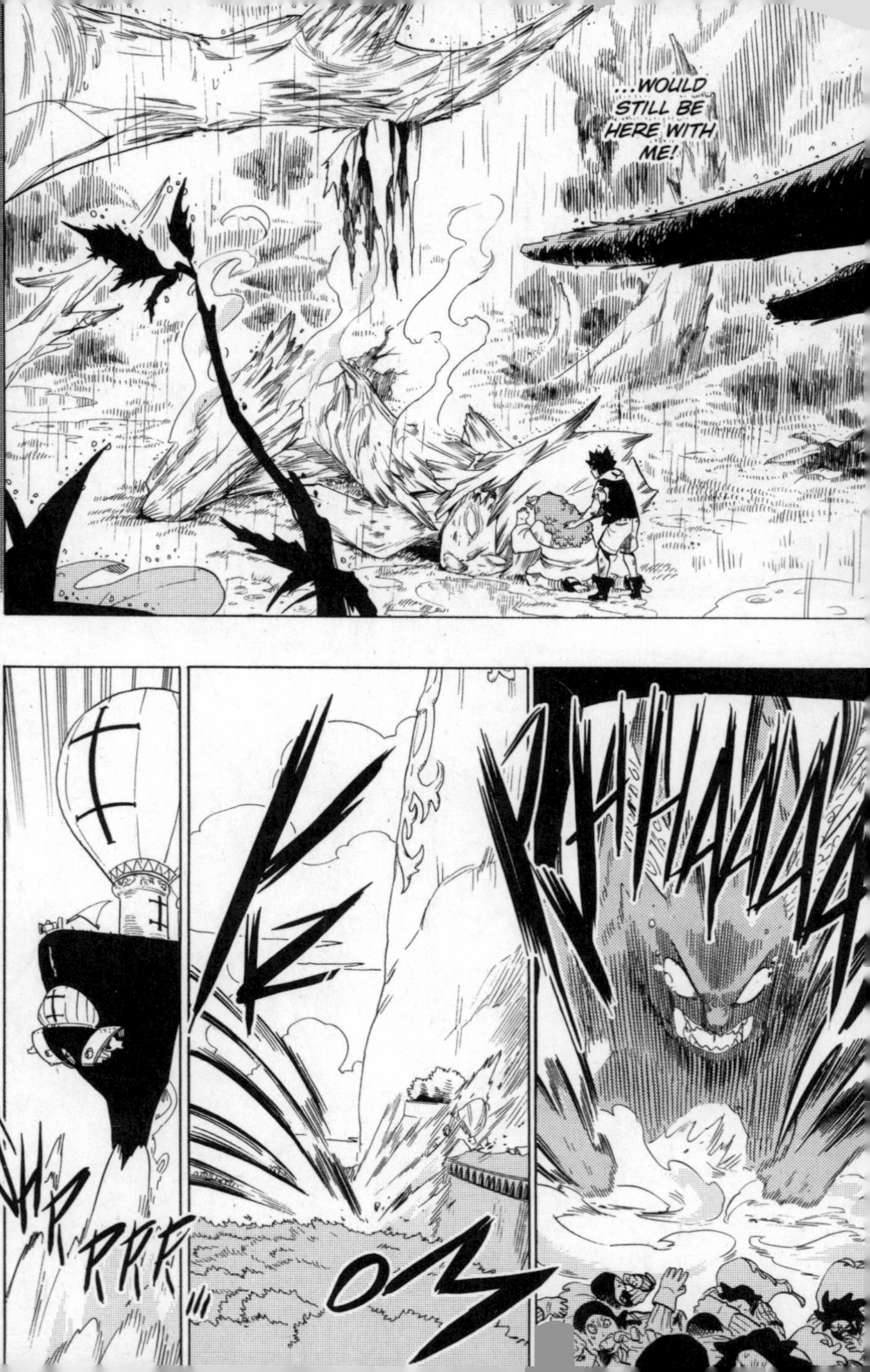
...WOULD STILL BE HERE WITH ME!
WHAAAAA
VRRRRRMMM
ZZZ
SHPRRF...

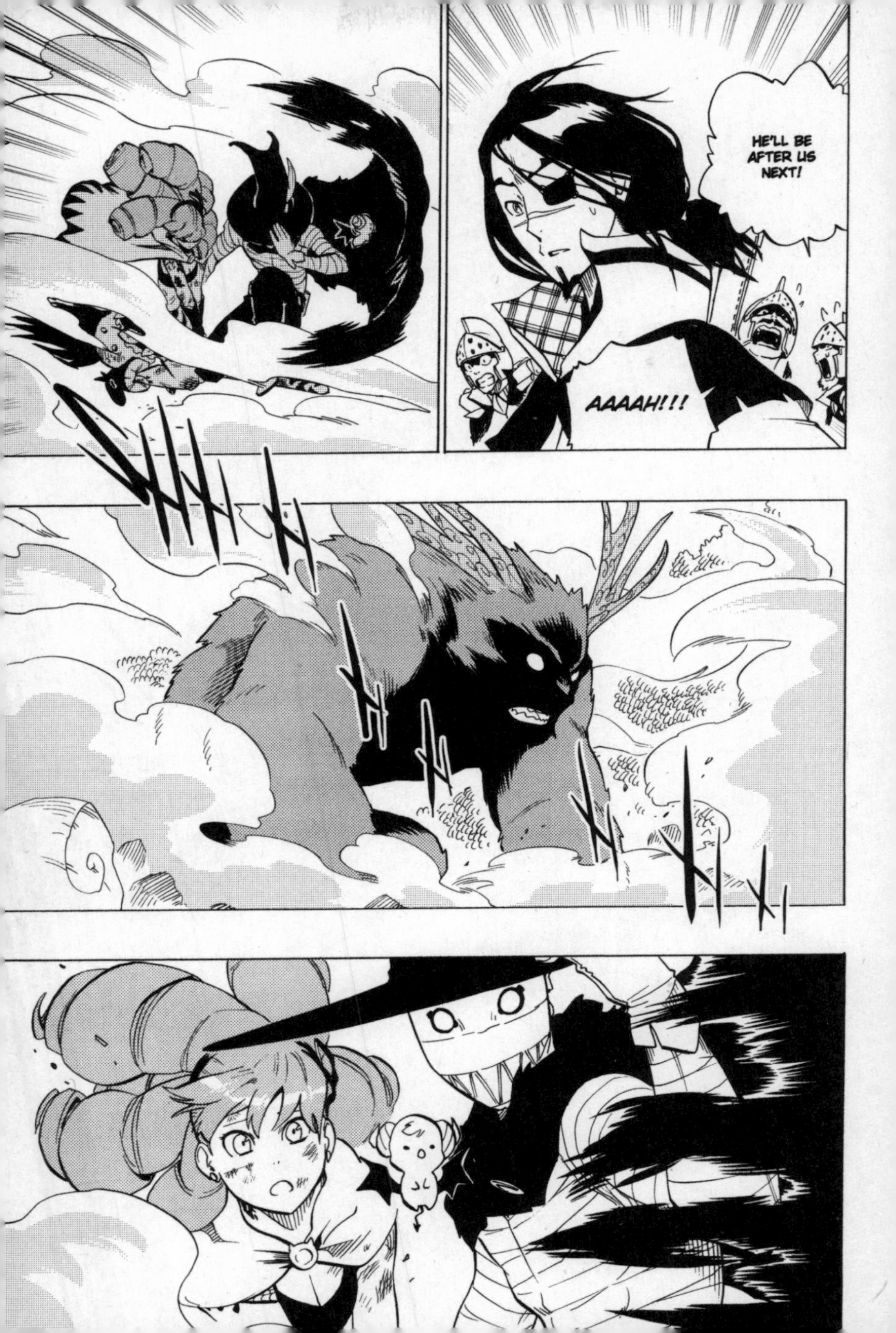
HE'LL BE AFTER US NEXT!
AAAAH!!!

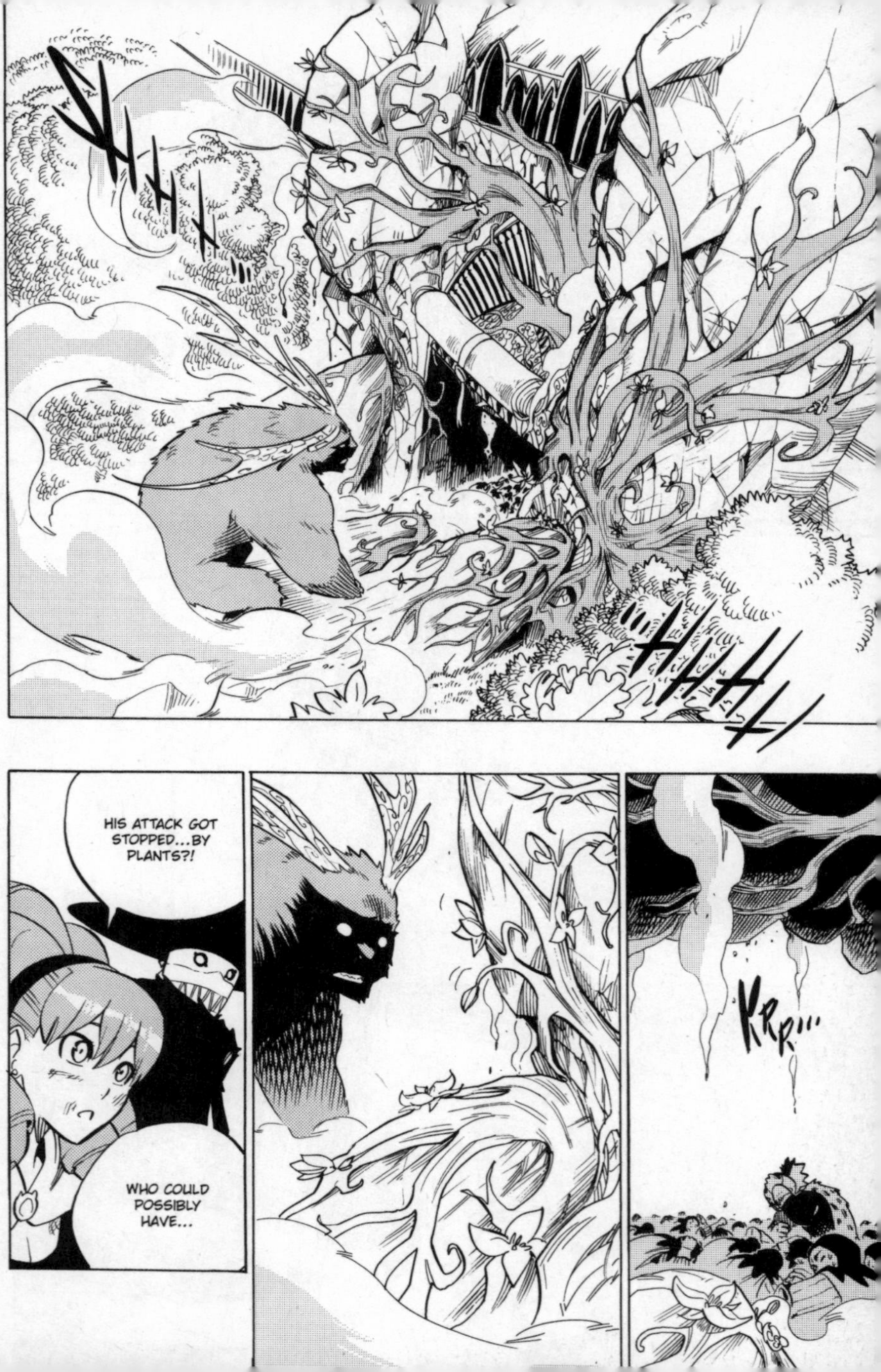
KRR...
HIS ATTACK GOT STOPPED...BY PLANTS?!
WHO COULD POSSIBLY HAVE...

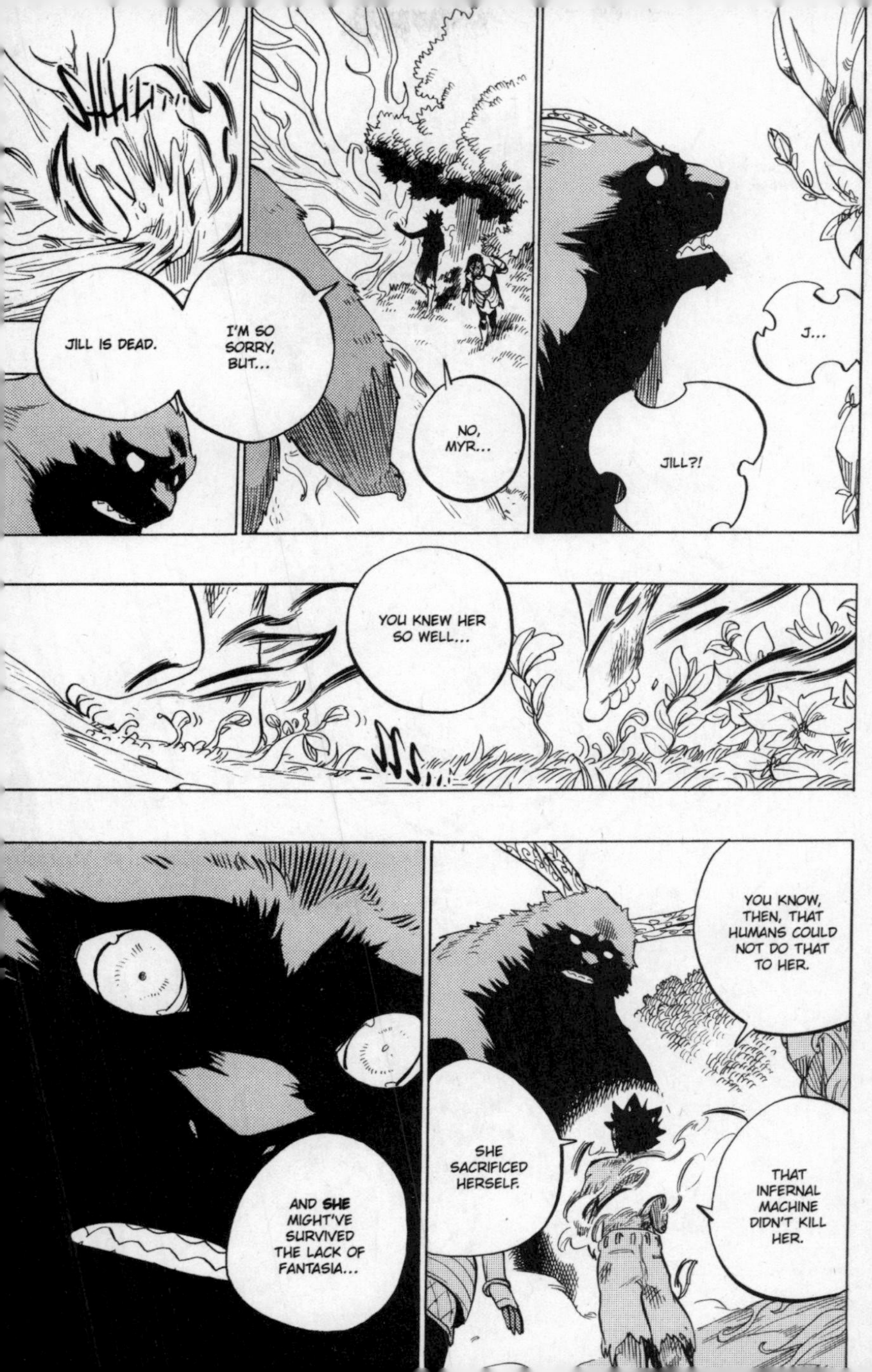
J...
JILL?!
NO, MYR...
I'M SO SORRY, BUT...
JILL IS DEAD.
YOU KNEW HER SO WELL...
YOU KNOW, THEN, THAT HUMANS COULD NOT DO THAT TO HER.
THAT INFERNAL MACHINE DIDN'T KILL HER.
SHE SACRIFICED HERSELF.
AND **SHE** MIGHT'VE SURVIVED THE LACK OF FANTASIA...

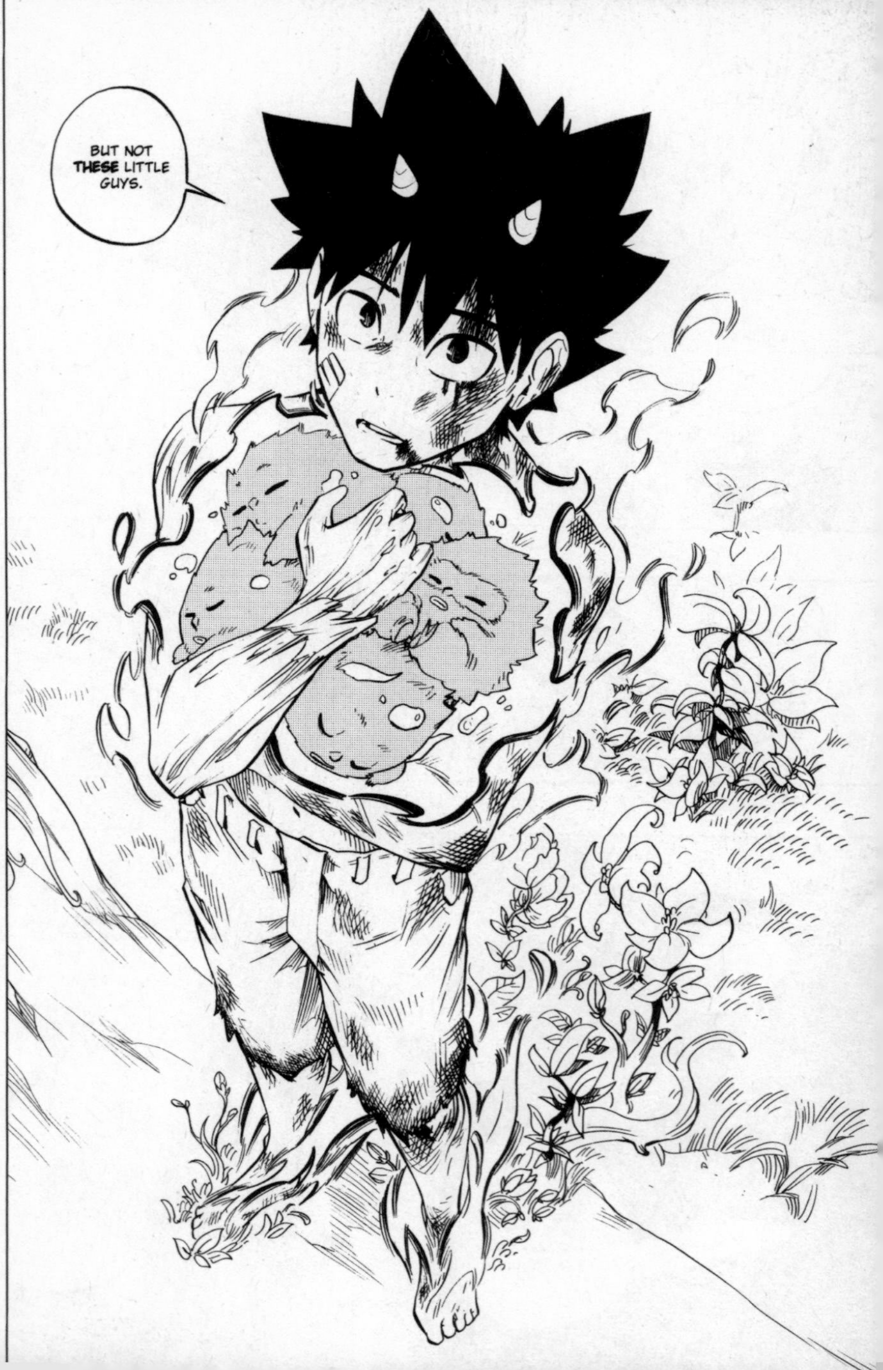
BUT NOT **THESE** LITTLE GUYS.

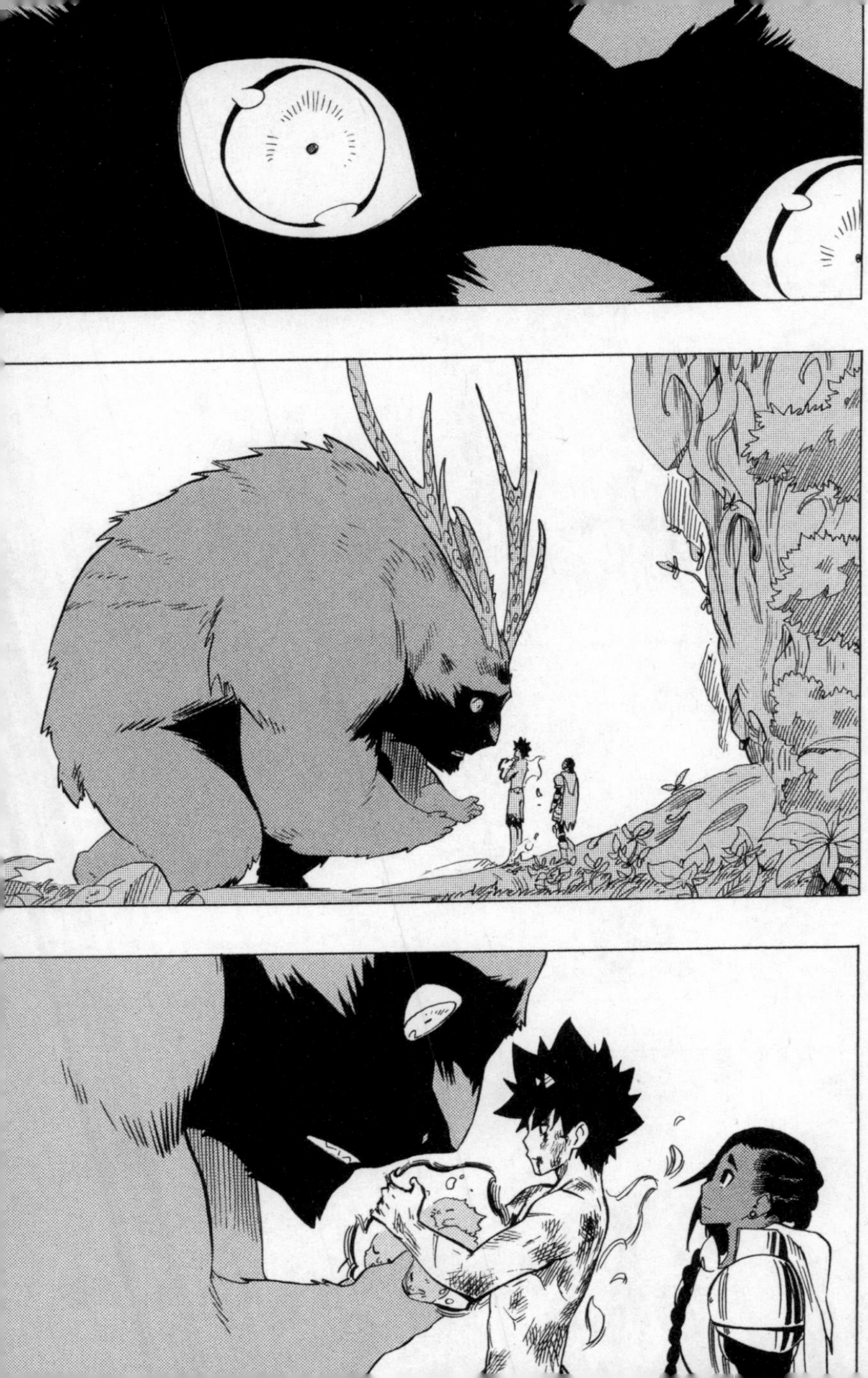

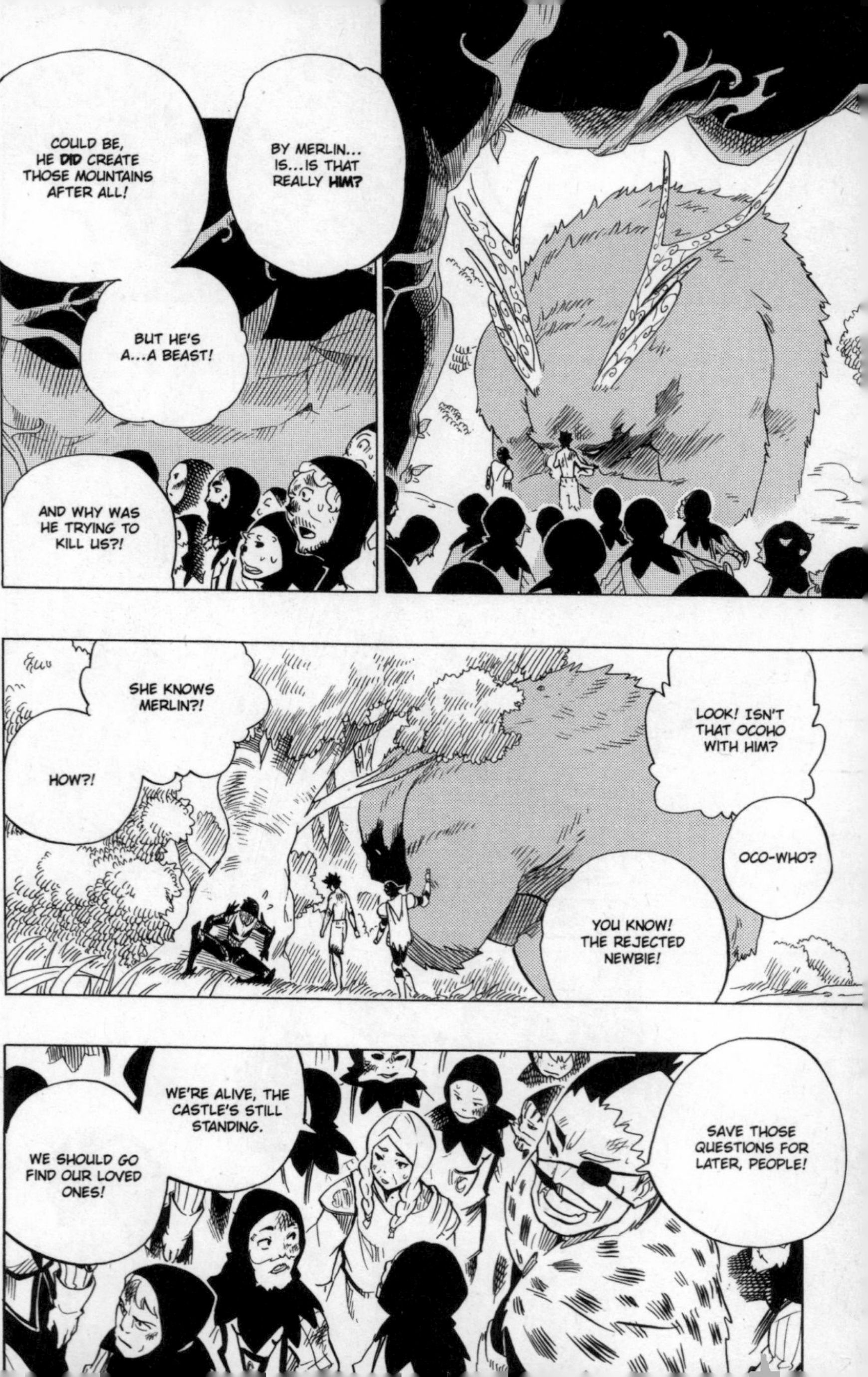
BY MERLIN... IS...IS THAT REALLY **HIM?**
COULD BE, HE **DID** CREATE THOSE MOUNTAINS AFTER ALL!
BUT HE'S A...A BEAST!
AND WHY WAS HE TRYING TO KILL US?!
LOOK! ISN'T THAT OCOHO WITH HIM?
OCO-WHO?
YOU KNOW! THE REJECTED NEWBIE!
SHE KNOWS MERLIN?!
HOW?!
SAVE THOSE QUESTIONS FOR LATER, PEOPLE!
WE'RE ALIVE, THE CASTLE'S STILL STANDING.
WE SHOULD GO FIND OUR LOVED ONES!

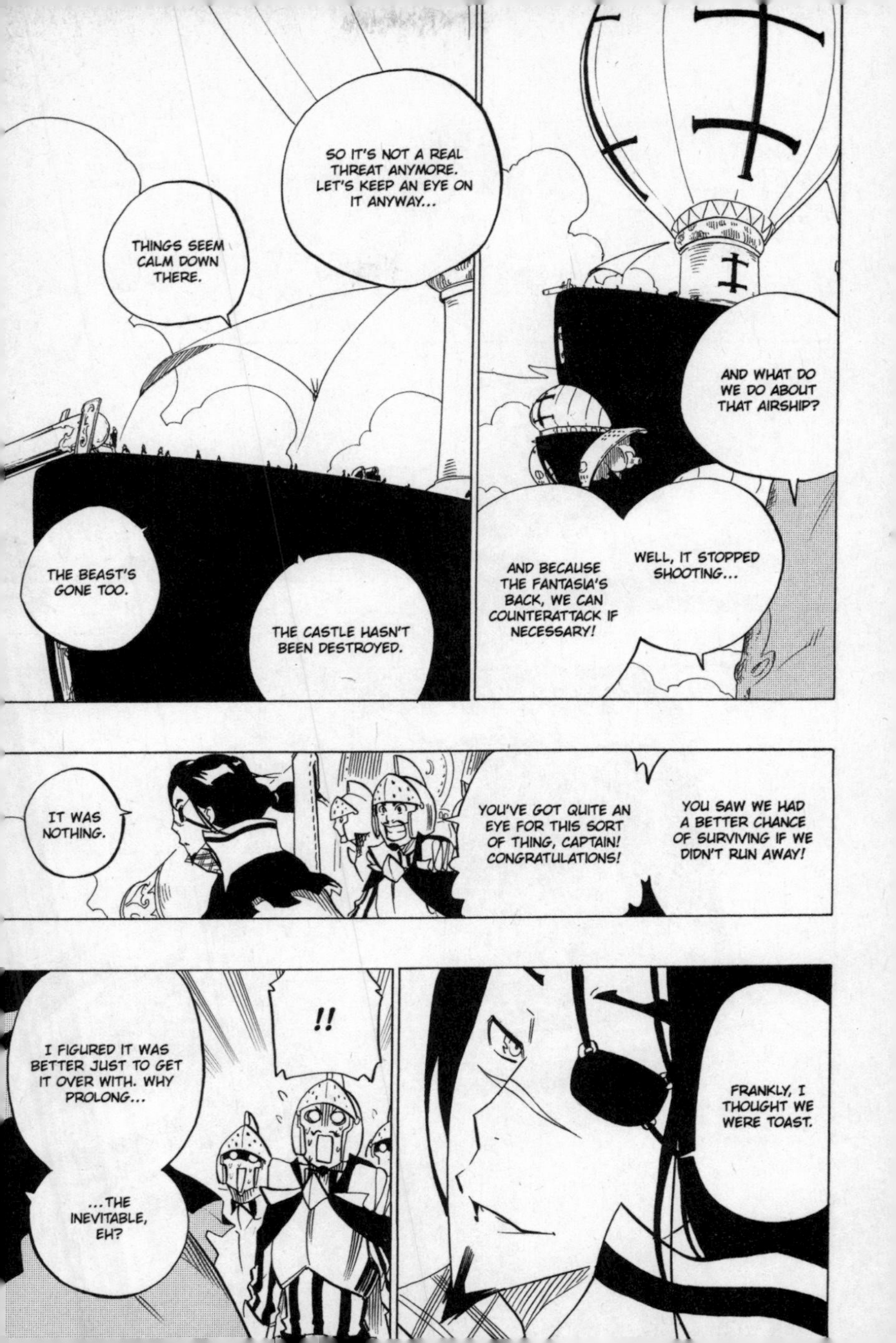

AND WHAT DO WE DO ABOUT THAT AIRSHIP?
WELL, IT STOPPED SHOOTING...
AND BECAUSE THE FANTASIA'S BACK, WE CAN COUNTERATTACK IF NECESSARY!
SO IT'S NOT A REAL THREAT ANYMORE. LET'S KEEP AN EYE ON IT ANYWAY...
THINGS SEEM CALM DOWN THERE.
THE CASTLE HASN'T BEEN DESTROYED.
THE BEAST'S GONE TOO.
YOU SAW WE HAD A BETTER CHANCE OF SURVIVING IF WE DIDN'T RUN AWAY!
YOU'VE GOT QUITE AN EYE FOR THIS SORT OF THING, CAPTAIN! CONGRATULATIONS!
IT WAS NOTHING.
FRANKLY, I THOUGHT WE WERE TOAST.
!!
I FIGURED IT WAS BETTER JUST TO GET IT OVER WITH. WHY PROLONG...
...THE INEVITABLE, EH?

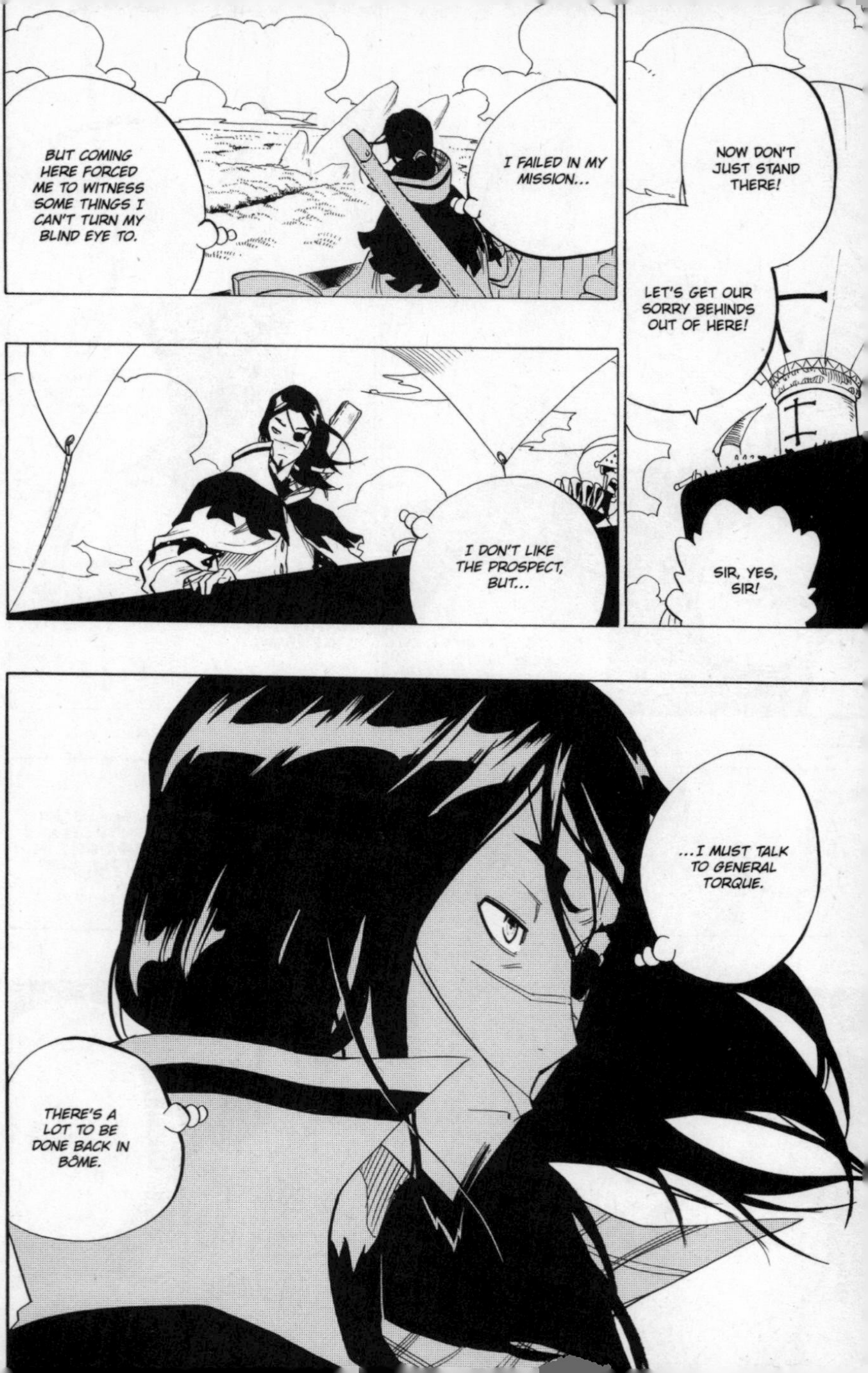
NOW DON'T JUST STAND THERE!
LET'S GET OUR SORRY BEHINDS OUT OF HERE!
SIR, YES, SIR!
I FAILED IN MY MISSION...
BUT COMING HERE FORCED ME TO WITNESS SOME THINGS I CAN'T TURN MY BLIND EYE TO.
I DON'T LIKE THE PROSPECT, BUT...
...I MUST TALK TO GENERAL TORQUE.
THERE'S A LOT TO BE DONE BACK IN BÔME.

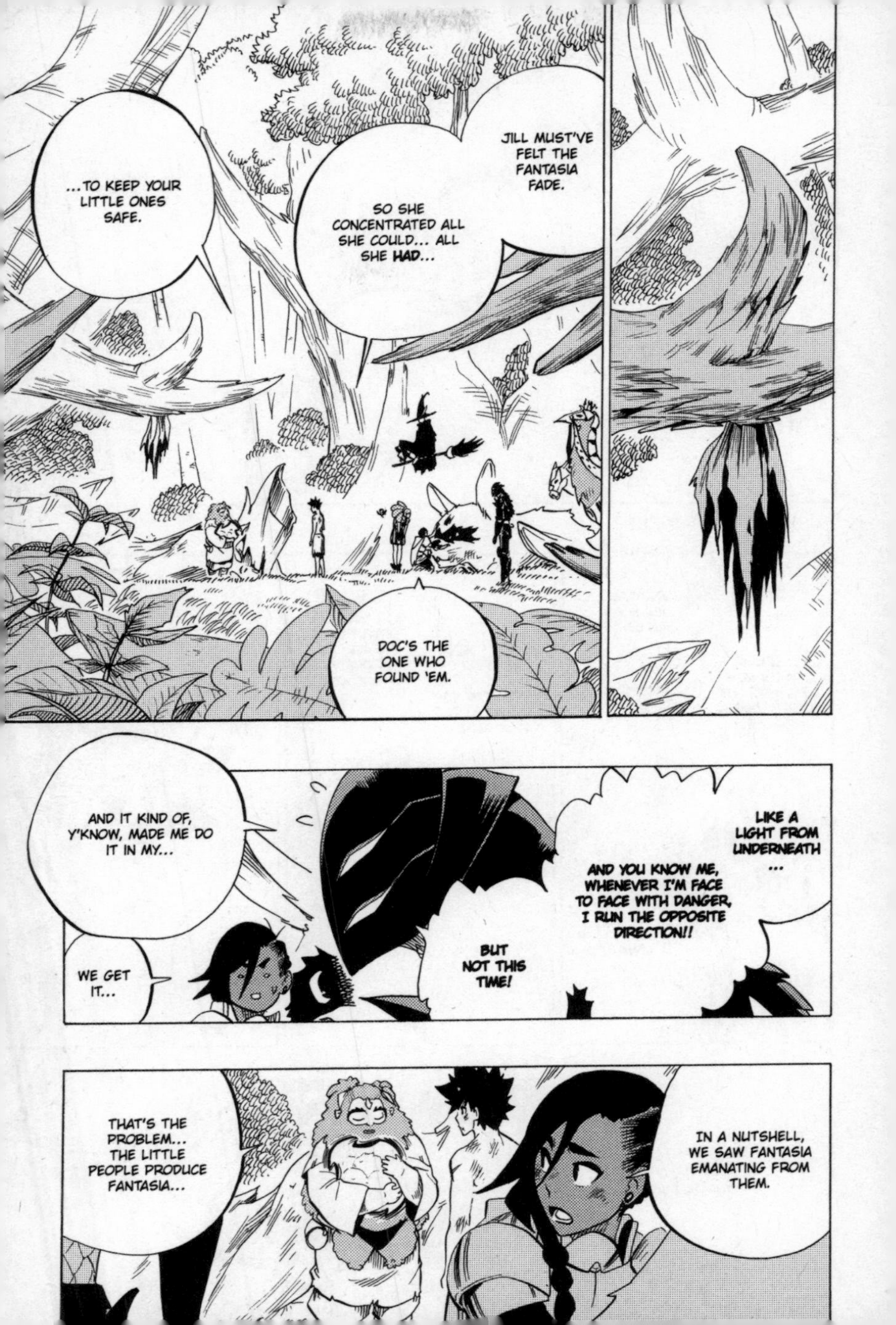
JILL MUST'VE FELT THE FANTASIA FADE.
SO SHE CONCENTRATED ALL SHE COULD... ALL SHE **HAD**...
...TO KEEP YOUR LITTLE ONES SAFE.
DOC'S THE ONE WHO FOUND 'EM.
LIKE A LIGHT FROM UNDERNEATH ...
AND YOU KNOW ME, WHENEVER I'M FACE TO FACE WITH DANGER, I RUN THE OPPOSITE DIRECTION!!
BUT NOT THIS TIME!
AND IT KIND OF, Y'KNOW, MADE ME DO IT IN MY...
WE GET IT...
IN A NUTSHELL, WE SAW FANTASIA EMANATING FROM THEM.
THAT'S THE PROBLEM... THE LITTLE PEOPLE PRODUCE FANTASIA...

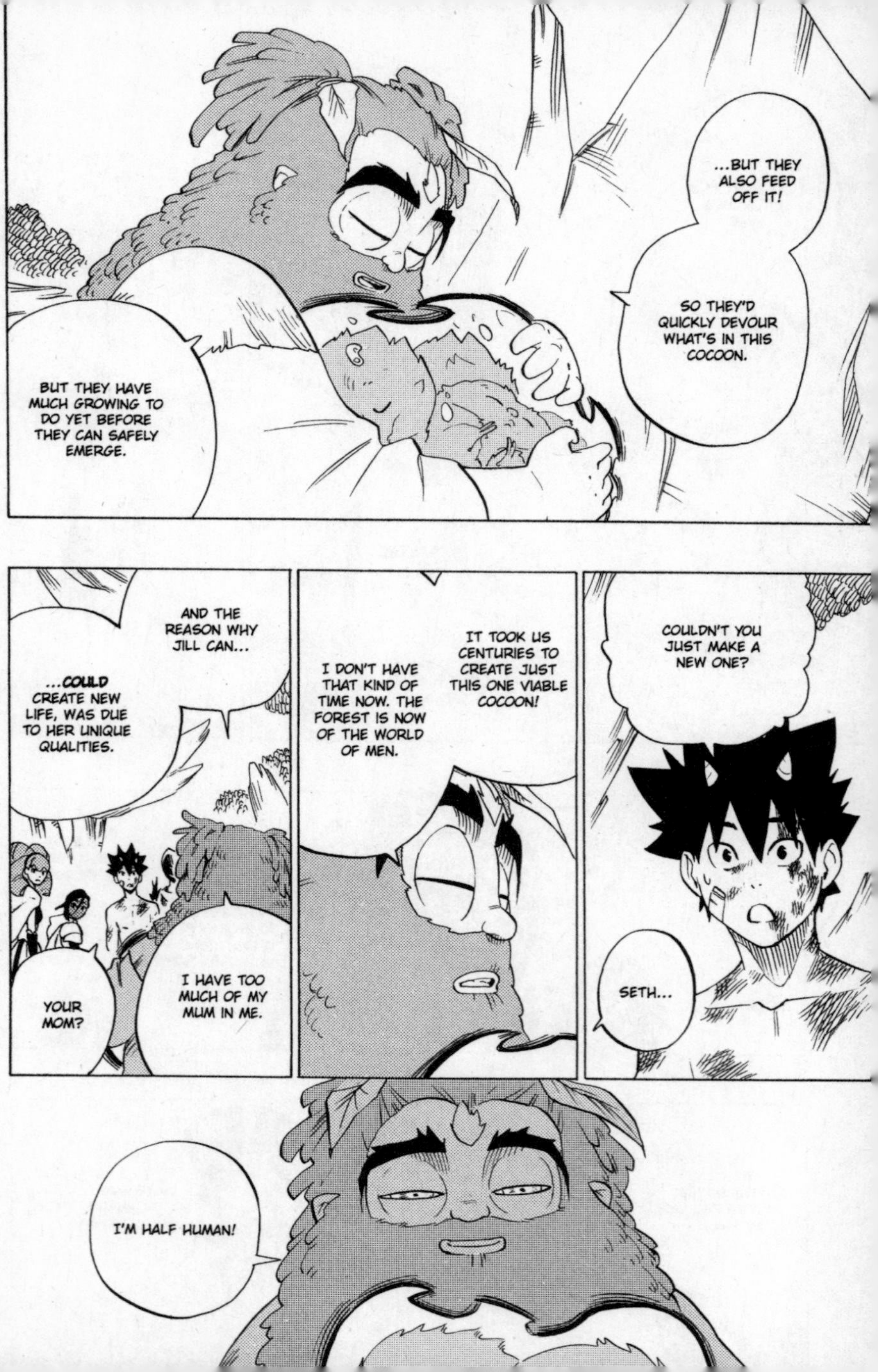
...BUT THEY ALSO FEED OFF IT!
SO THEY'D QUICKLY DEVOUR WHAT'S IN THIS COCOON.
BUT THEY HAVE MUCH GROWING TO DO YET BEFORE THEY CAN SAFELY EMERGE.
COULDN'T YOU JUST MAKE A NEW ONE?
SETH...
IT TOOK US CENTURIES TO CREATE JUST THIS ONE VIABLE COCOON!
I DON'T HAVE THAT KIND OF TIME NOW. THE FOREST IS NOW OF THE WORLD OF MEN.
AND THE REASON WHY JILL CAN...
...**COULD** CREATE NEW LIFE, WAS DUE TO HER UNIQUE QUALITIES.
I HAVE TOO MUCH OF MY MUM IN ME.
YOUR MOM?
I'M HALF HUMAN!

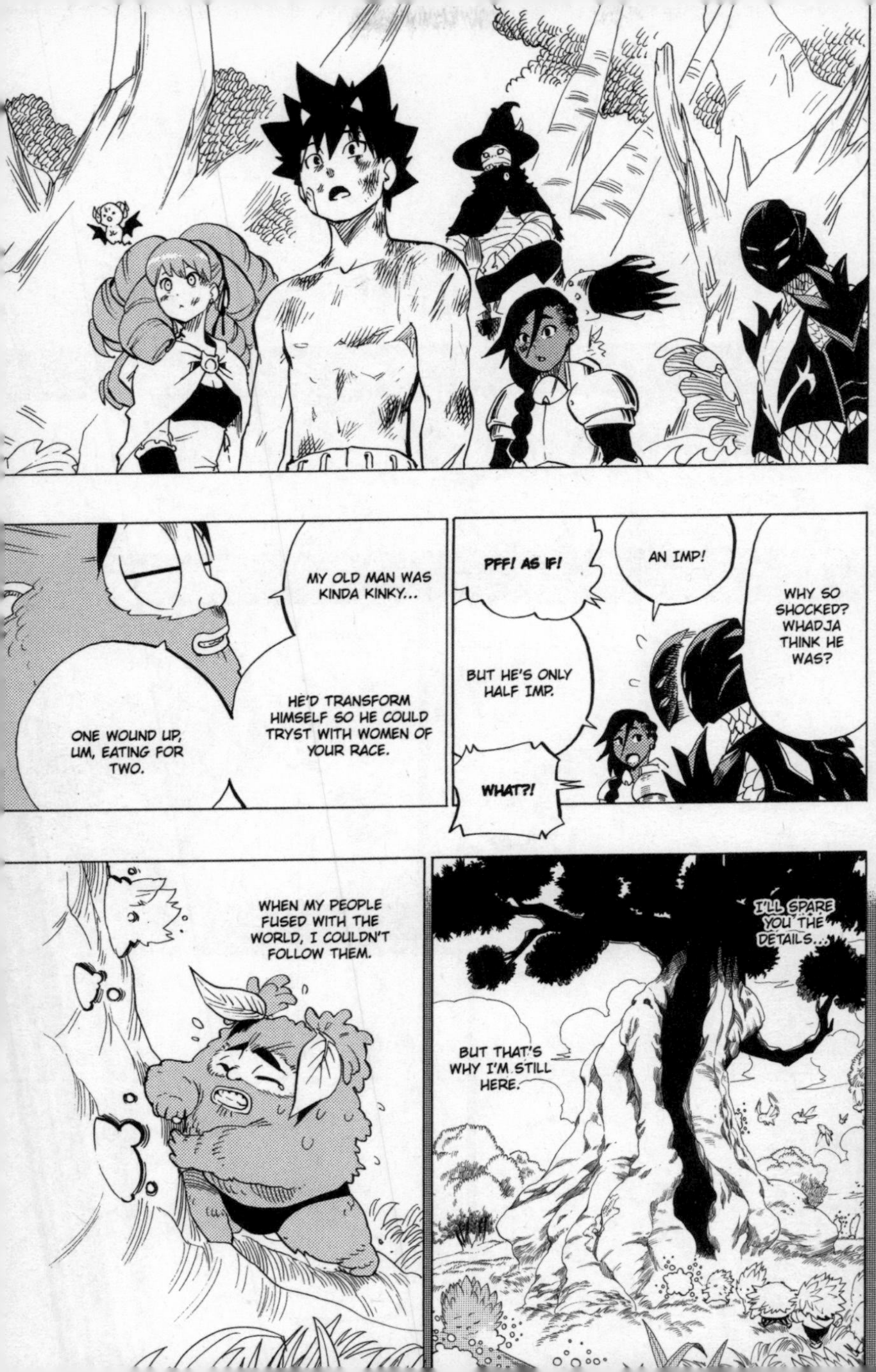
WHY SO SHOCKED? WHADJA THINK HE WAS?
AN IMP!
PFF! AS IF!
BUT HE'S ONLY HALF IMP.
WHAT?!
MY OLD MAN WAS KINDA KINKY...
HE'D TRANSFORM HIMSELF SO HE COULD TRYST WITH WOMEN OF YOUR RACE.
ONE WOUND UP, UM, EATING FOR TWO.
I'LL SPARE YOU THE DETAILS...
BUT THAT'S WHY I'M STILL HERE.
WHEN MY PEOPLE FUSED WITH THE WORLD, I COULDN'T FOLLOW THEM.

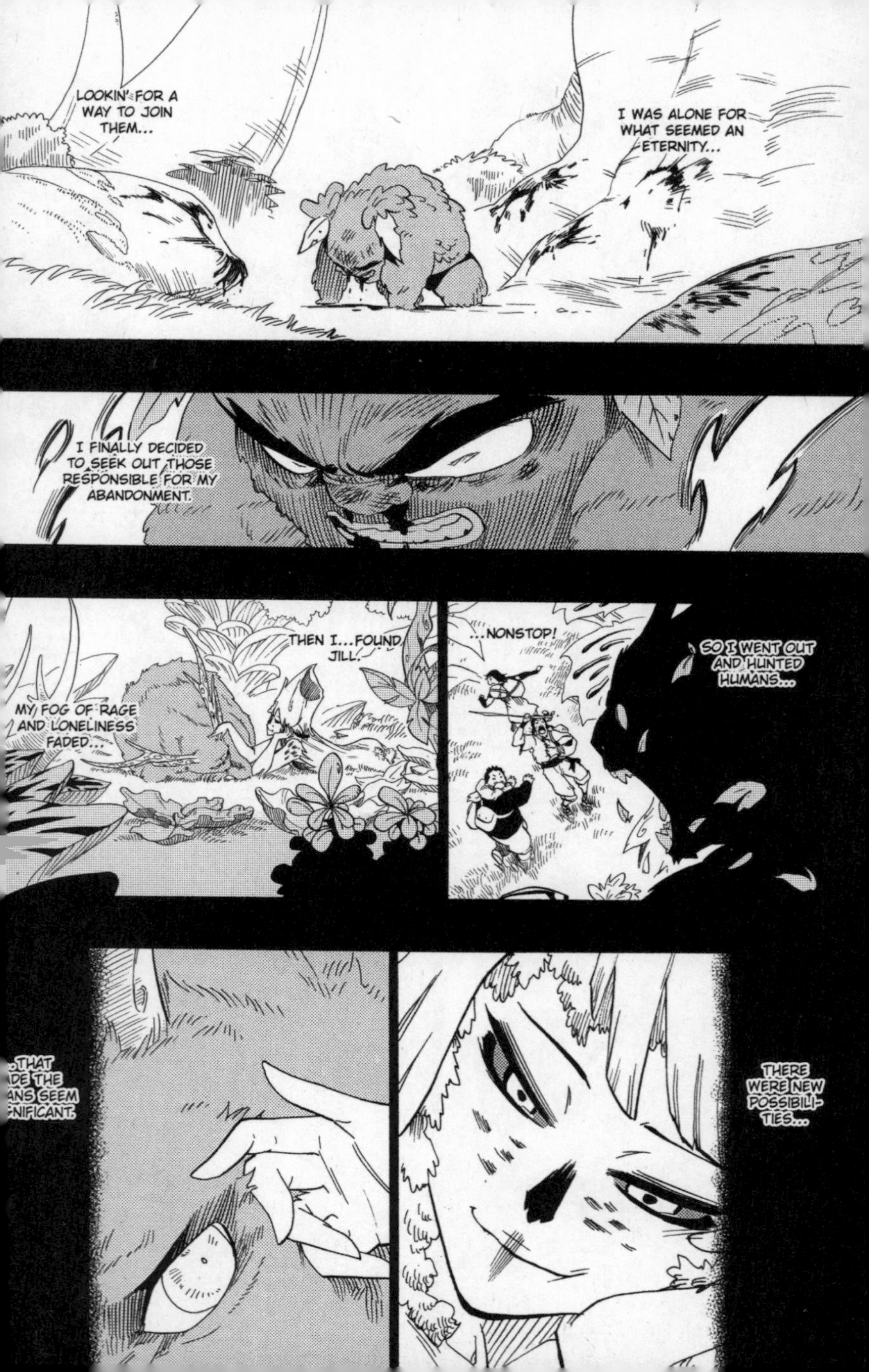
I WAS ALONE FOR WHAT SEEMED AN ETERNITY...
LOOKIN' FOR A WAY TO JOIN THEM...
I FINALLY DECIDED TO SEEK OUT THOSE RESPONSIBLE FOR MY ABANDONMENT.
SO I WENT OUT AND HUNTED HUMANS...
...NONSTOP!
THEN I...FOUND JILL.
MY FOG OF RAGE AND LONELINESS FADED...
THERE WERE NEW POSSIBILI-TIES...
THAT ADE THE ANS SEEM NIFICANT.

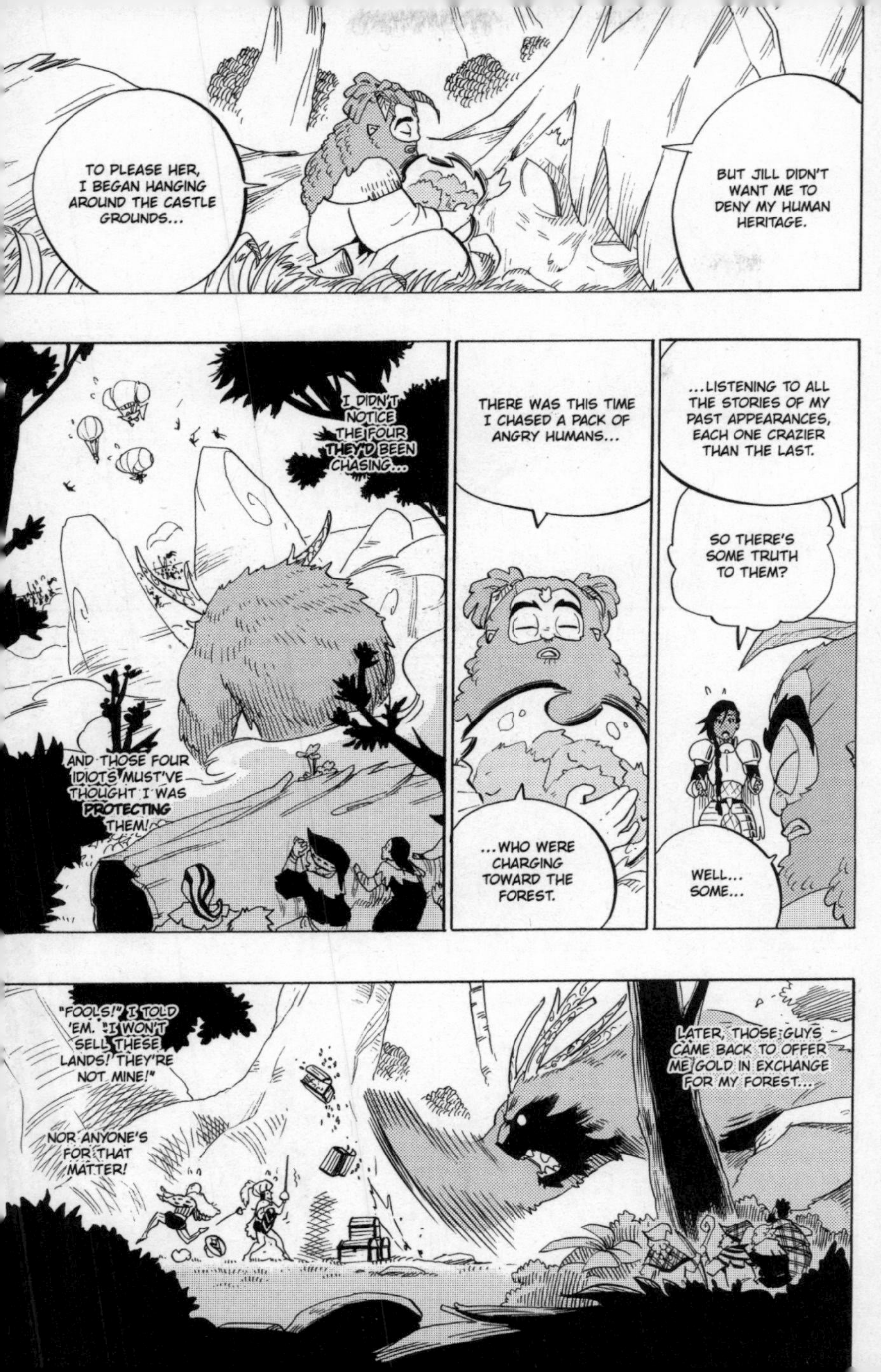
BUT JILL DIDN'T WANT ME TO DENY MY HUMAN HERITAGE.
TO PLEASE HER, I BEGAN HANGING AROUND THE CASTLE GROUNDS...
...LISTENING TO ALL THE STORIES OF MY PAST APPEARANCES, EACH ONE CRAZIER THAN THE LAST.
SO THERE'S SOME TRUTH TO THEM?
WELL... SOME...
THERE WAS THIS TIME I CHASED A PACK OF ANGRY HUMANS...
...WHO WERE CHARGING TOWARD THE FOREST.
I DIDN'T NOTICE THE FOUR THEY'D BEEN CHASING...
AND THOSE FOUR IDIOTS MUST'VE THOUGHT I WAS PROTECTING THEM!
LATER, THOSE GUYS CAME BACK TO OFFER ME GOLD IN EXCHANGE FOR MY FOREST...
"FOOLS!" I TOLD 'EM. "I WON'T SELL THESE LANDS! THEY'RE NOT MINE!"
NOR ANYONE'S FOR THAT MATTER!

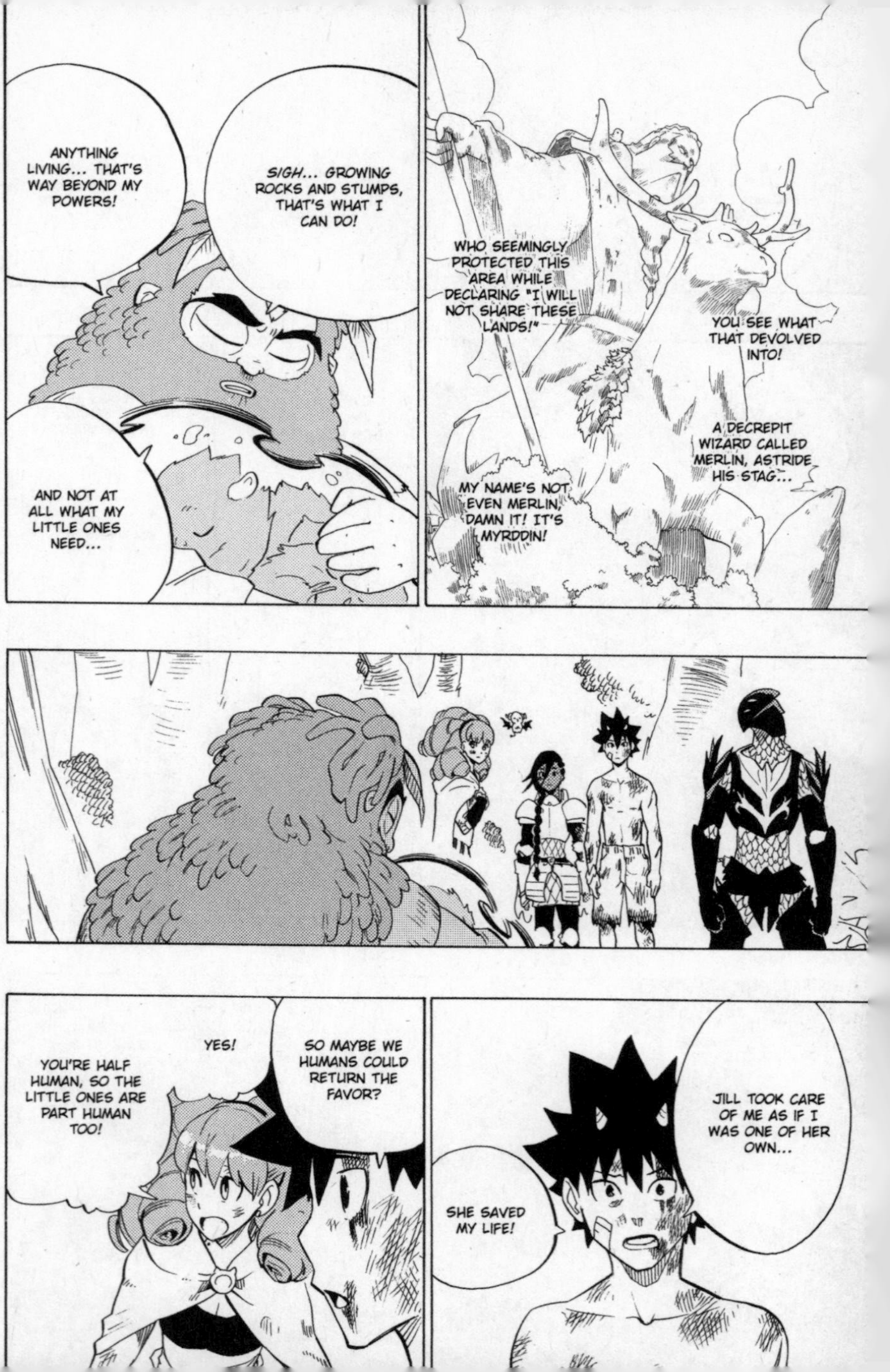
A DECREPIT WIZARD CALLED MERLIN, ASTRIDE HIS STAG...
WHO SEEMINGLY PROTECTED THIS AREA WHILE DECLARING "I WILL NOT SHARE THESE LANDS!"
YOU SEE WHAT THAT DEVOLVED INTO!
MY NAME'S NOT EVEN MERLIN, DAMN IT! IT'S MYRDDIN!
SIGH... GROWING ROCKS AND STUMPS, THAT'S WHAT I CAN DO!
ANYTHING LIVING... THAT'S WAY BEYOND MY POWERS!
AND NOT AT ALL WHAT MY LITTLE ONES NEED...
JILL TOOK CARE OF ME AS IF I WAS ONE OF HER OWN...
SHE SAVED MY LIFE!
SO MAYBE WE HUMANS COULD RETURN THE FAVOR?
YES!
YOU'RE HALF HUMAN, SO THE LITTLE ONES ARE PART HUMAN TOO!

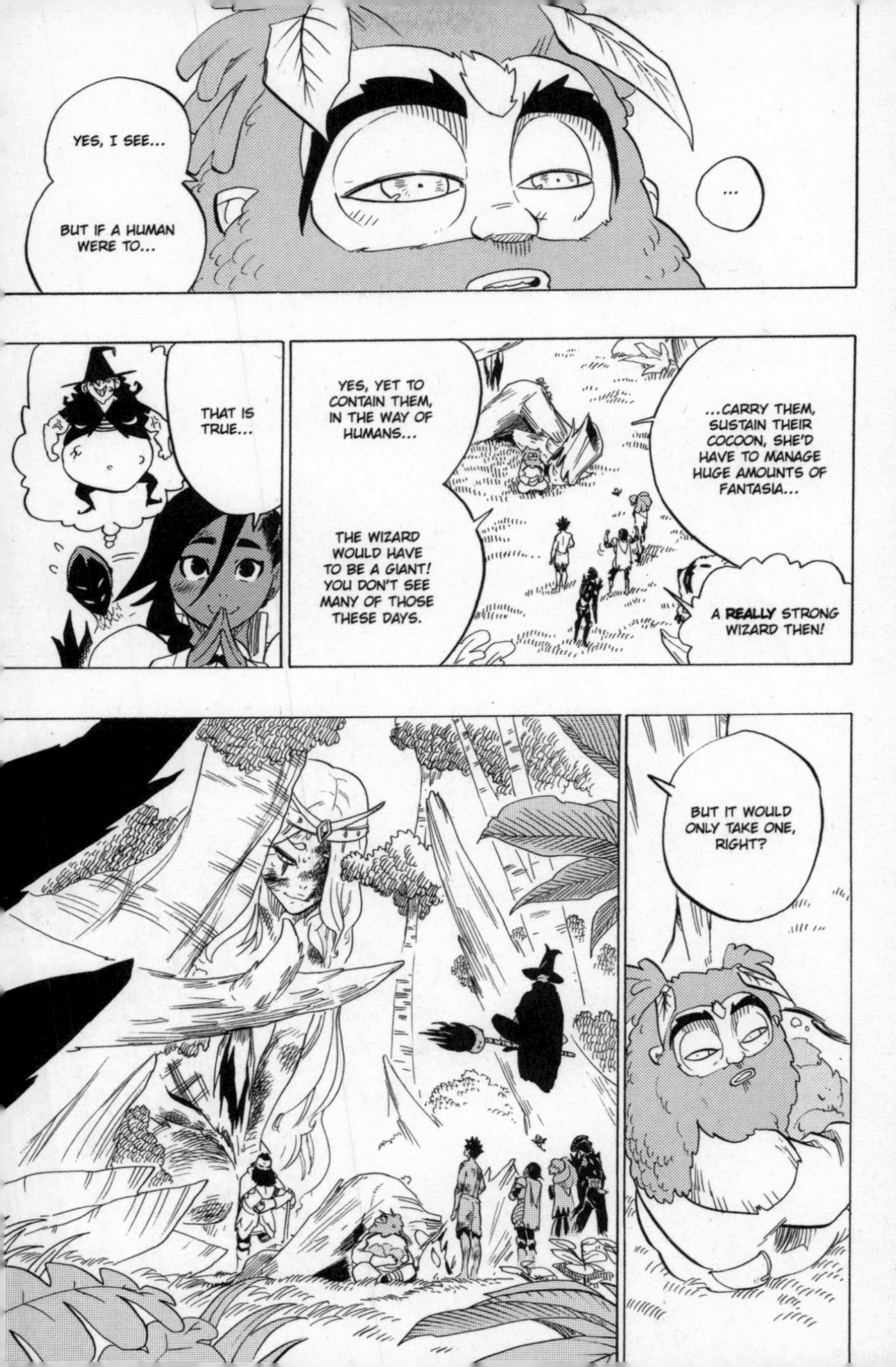
...
YES, I SEE...
BUT IF A HUMAN WERE TO...
...CARRY THEM, SUSTAIN THEIR COCOON, SHE'D HAVE TO MANAGE HUGE AMOUNTS OF FANTASIA...
A **REALLY** STRONG WIZARD THEN!
YES, YET TO CONTAIN THEM, IN THE WAY OF HUMANS...
THE WIZARD WOULD HAVE TO BE A GIANT! YOU DON'T SEE MANY OF THOSE THESE DAYS.
THAT IS TRUE...
BUT IT WOULD ONLY TAKE ONE, RIGHT?

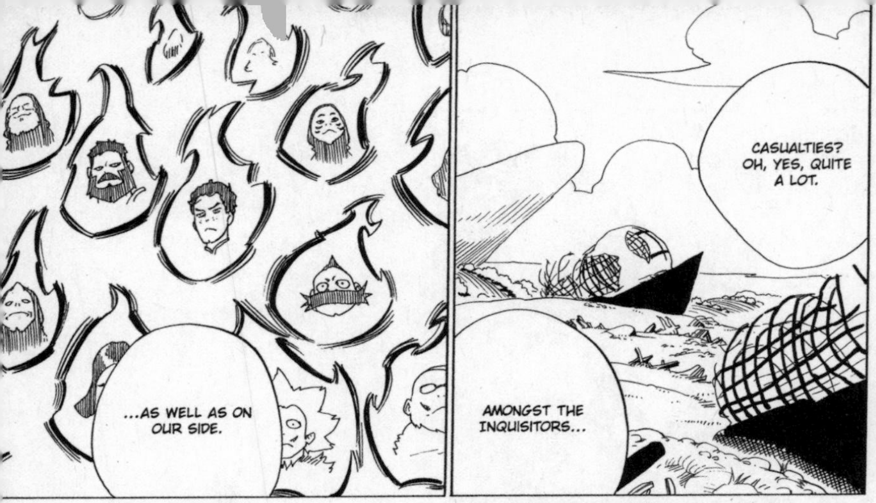
CASUALTIES? OH, YES, QUITE A LOT.
AMONGST THE INQUISITORS...
...AS WELL AS ON OUR SIDE.

Chapter 74

Take Off Your Masks

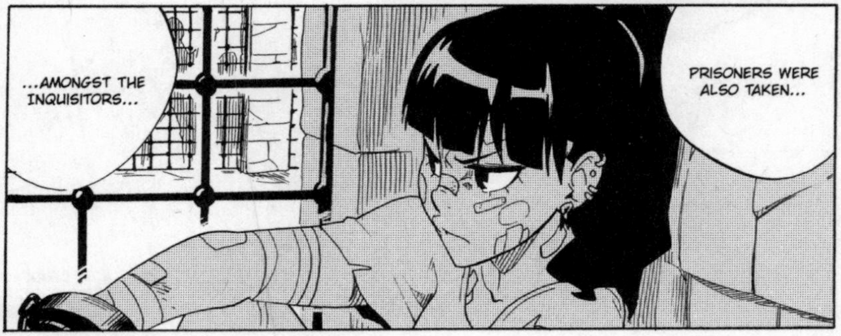
PRISONERS WERE ALSO TAKEN...
...AMONGST THE INQUISITORS...

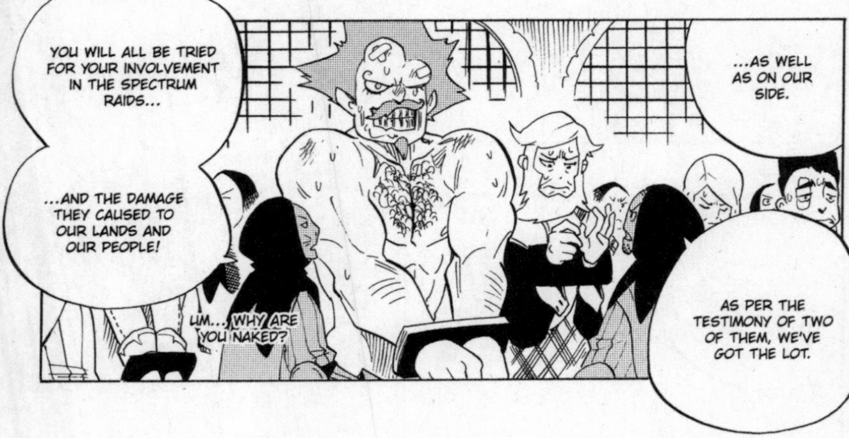
...AS WELL AS ON OUR SIDE.
AS PER THE TESTIMONY OF TWO OF THEM, WE'VE GOT THE LOT.
YOU WILL ALL BE TRIED FOR YOUR INVOLVEMENT IN THE SPECTRUM RAIDS...
...AND THE DAMAGE THEY CAUSED TO OUR LANDS AND OUR PEOPLE!
UM... WHY ARE YOU NAKED?

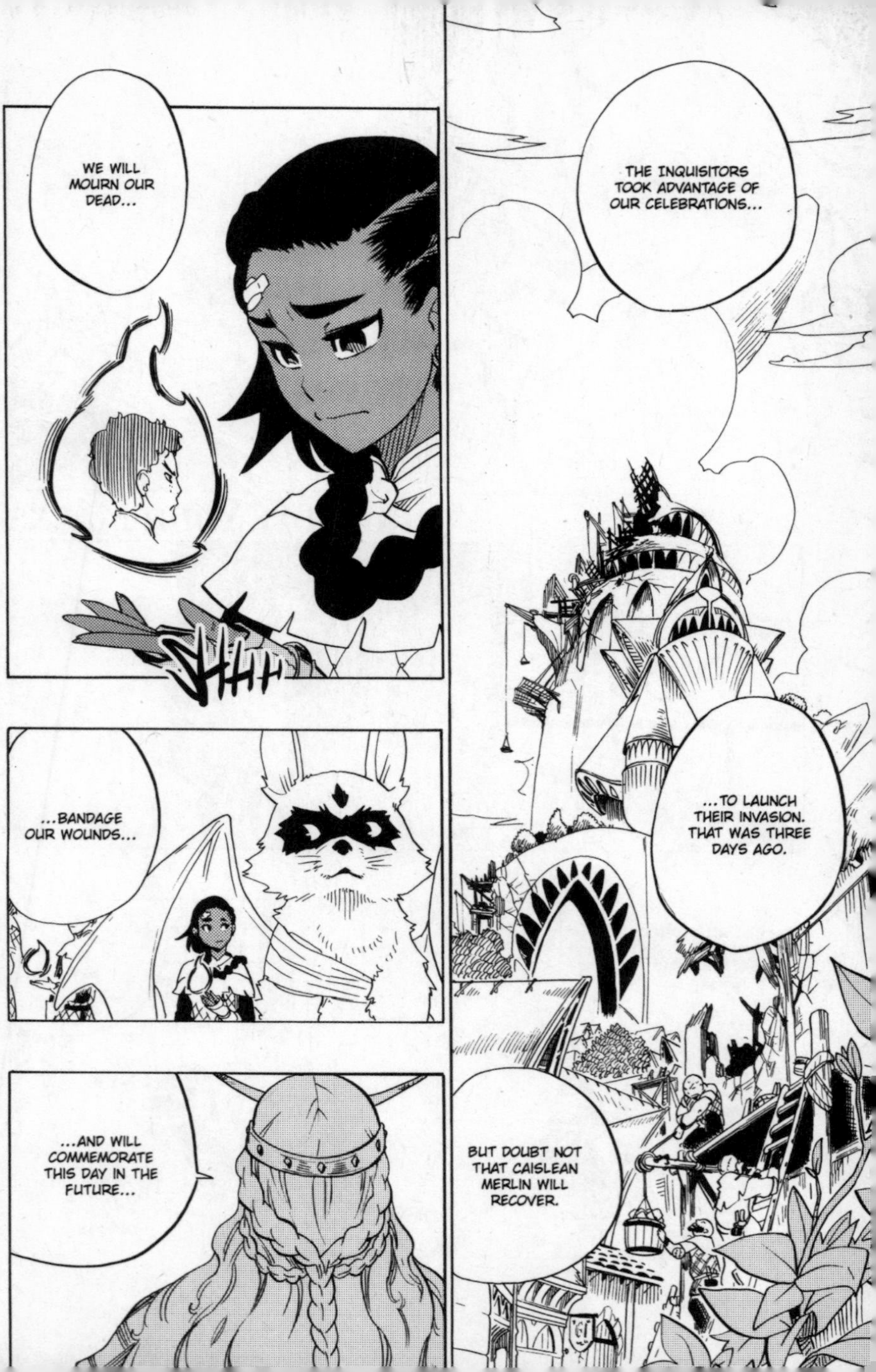
THE INQUISITORS TOOK ADVANTAGE OF OUR CELEBRATIONS...
...TO LAUNCH THEIR INVASION. THAT WAS THREE DAYS AGO.
BUT DOUBT NOT THAT CAISLEAN MERLIN WILL RECOVER.
WE WILL MOURN OUR DEAD...
...BANDAGE OUR WOUNDS...
...AND WILL COMMEMORATE THIS DAY IN THE FUTURE...

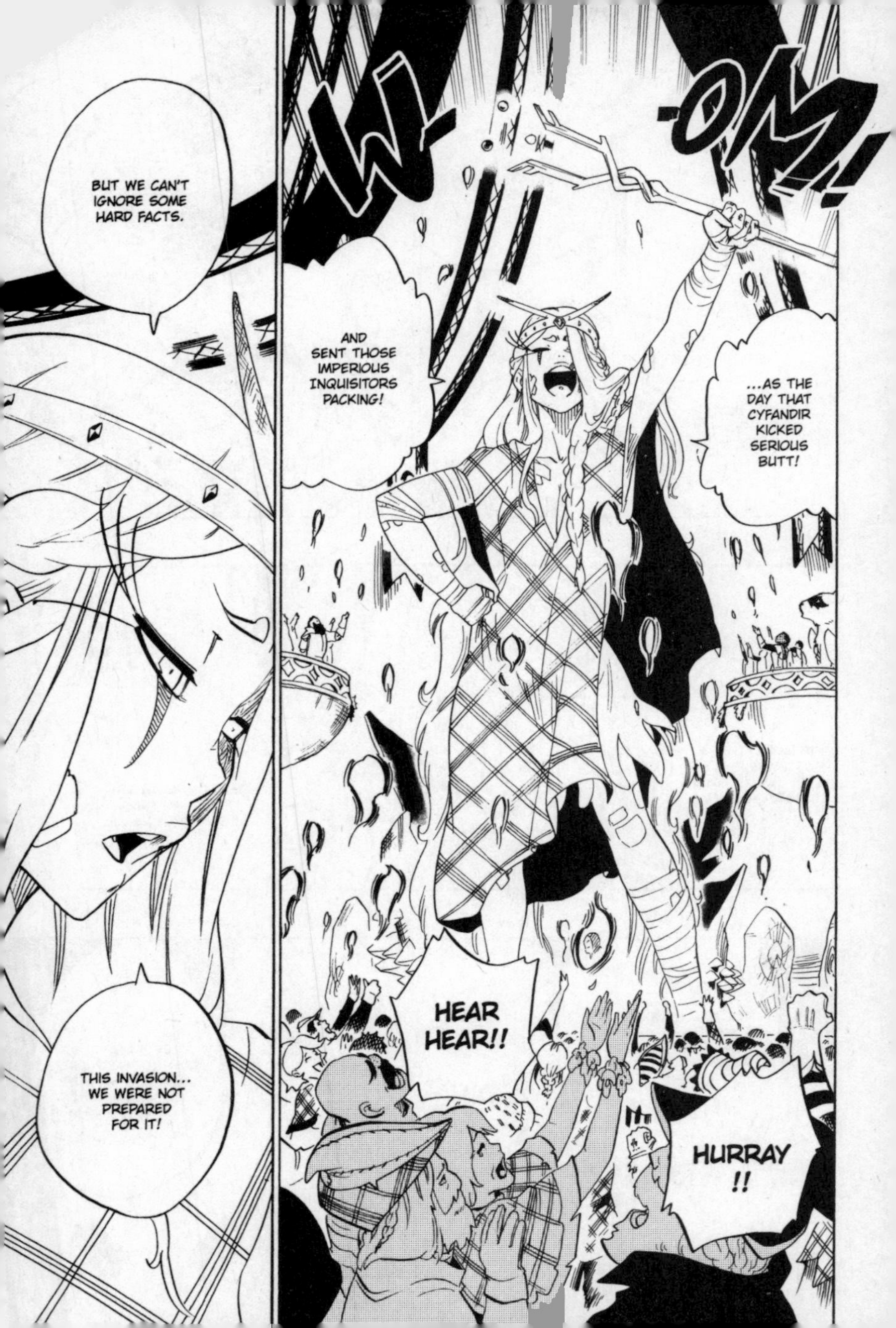
...AS THE DAY THAT CYFANDIR KICKED SERIOUS BUTT!
AND SENT THOSE IMPERIOUS INQUISITORS PACKING!
HURRAY!!
HEAR HEAR!!
BUT WE CAN'T IGNORE SOME HARD FACTS.
THIS INVASION... WE WERE NOT PREPARED FOR IT!

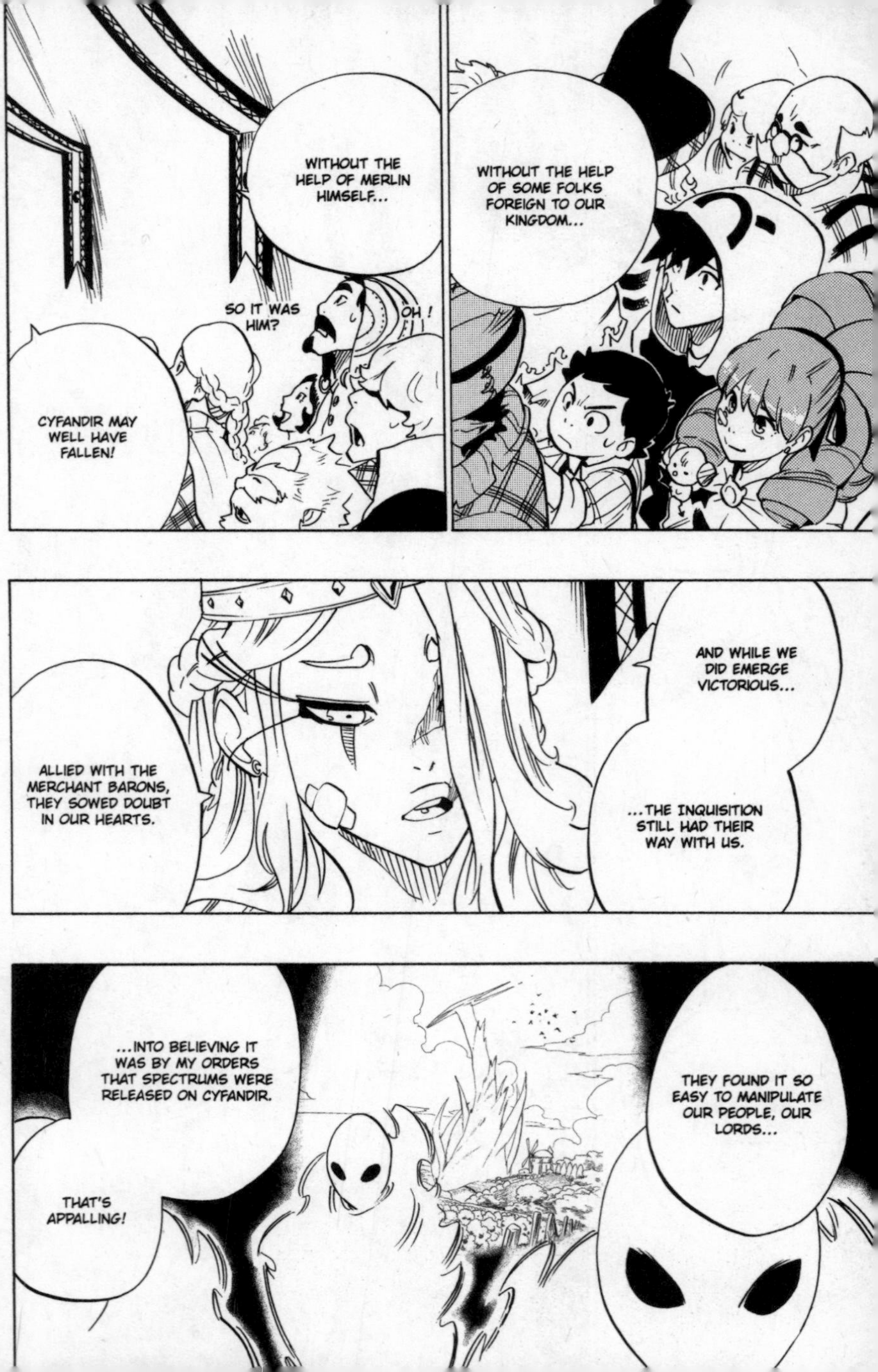
WITHOUT THE HELP OF SOME FOLKS FOREIGN TO OUR KINGDOM...
WITHOUT THE HELP OF MERLIN HIMSELF...
OH!
SO IT WAS HIM?
CYFANDIR MAY WELL HAVE FALLEN!
AND WHILE WE DID EMERGE VICTORIOUS...
...THE INQUISITION STILL HAD THEIR WAY WITH US.
ALLIED WITH THE MERCHANT BARONS, THEY SOWED DOUBT IN OUR HEARTS.
THEY FOUND IT SO EASY TO MANIPULATE OUR PEOPLE, OUR LORDS...
...INTO BELIEVING IT WAS BY MY ORDERS THAT SPECTRUMS WERE RELEASED ON CYFANDIR.
THAT'S APPALLING!

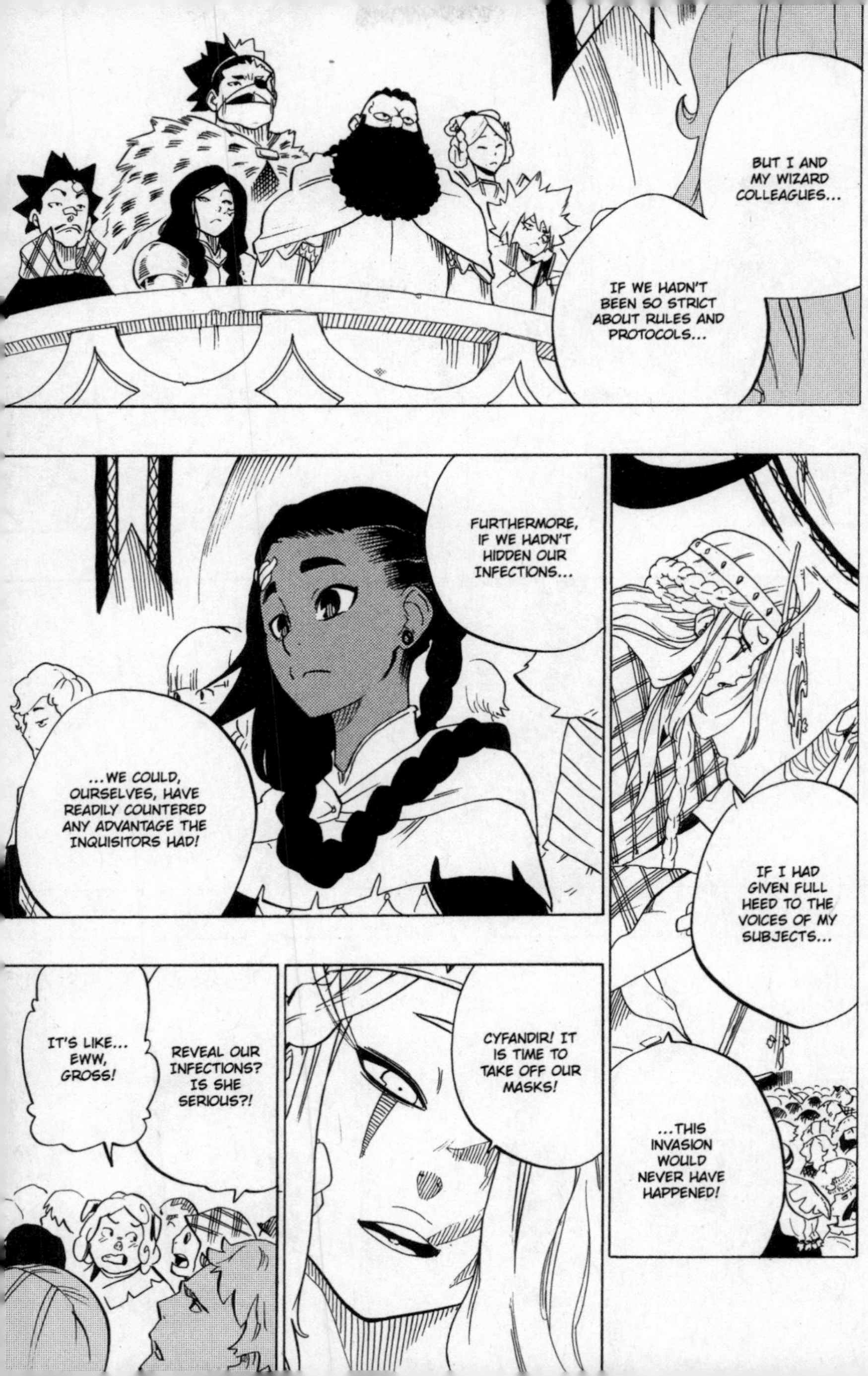
BUT I AND MY WIZARD COLLEAGUES...
IF WE HADN'T BEEN SO STRICT ABOUT RULES AND PROTOCOLS...
FURTHERMORE, IF WE HADN'T HIDDEN OUR INFECTIONS...
...WE COULD, OURSELVES, HAVE READILY COUNTERED ANY ADVANTAGE THE INQUISITORS HAD!
IF I HAD GIVEN FULL HEED TO THE VOICES OF MY SUBJECTS...
...THIS INVASION WOULD NEVER HAVE HAPPENED!
CYFANDIR! IT IS TIME TO TAKE OFF OUR MASKS!
REVEAL OUR INFECTIONS? IS SHE SERIOUS?!
IT'S LIKE... EWW, GROSS!

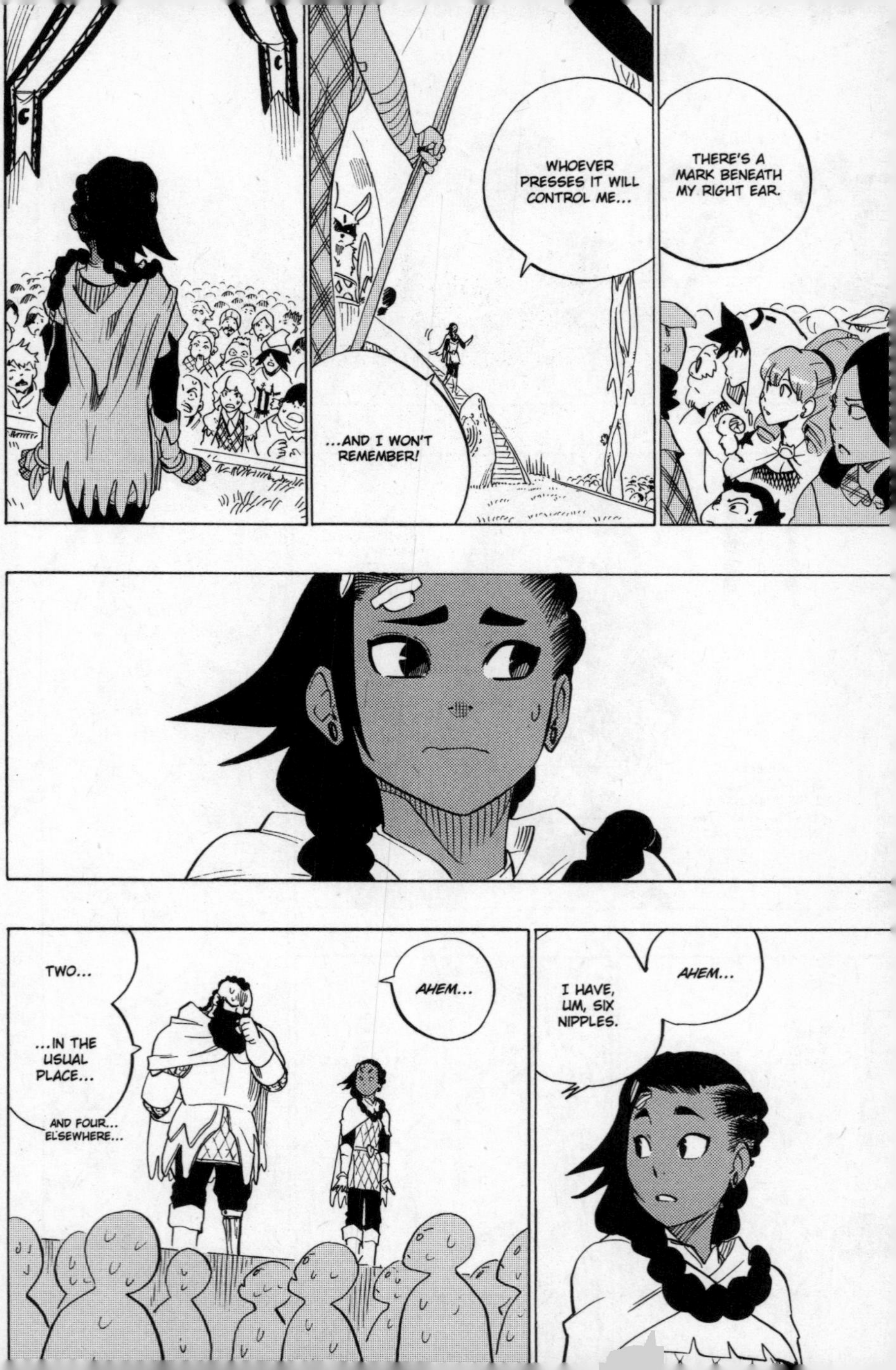
THERE'S A MARK BENEATH MY RIGHT EAR.
WHOEVER PRESSES IT WILL CONTROL ME...
...AND I WON'T REMEMBER!
AHEM...
I HAVE, UM, SIX NIPPLES.
AHEM...
TWO...
...IN THE USUAL PLACE...
AND FOUR... ELSEWHERE...

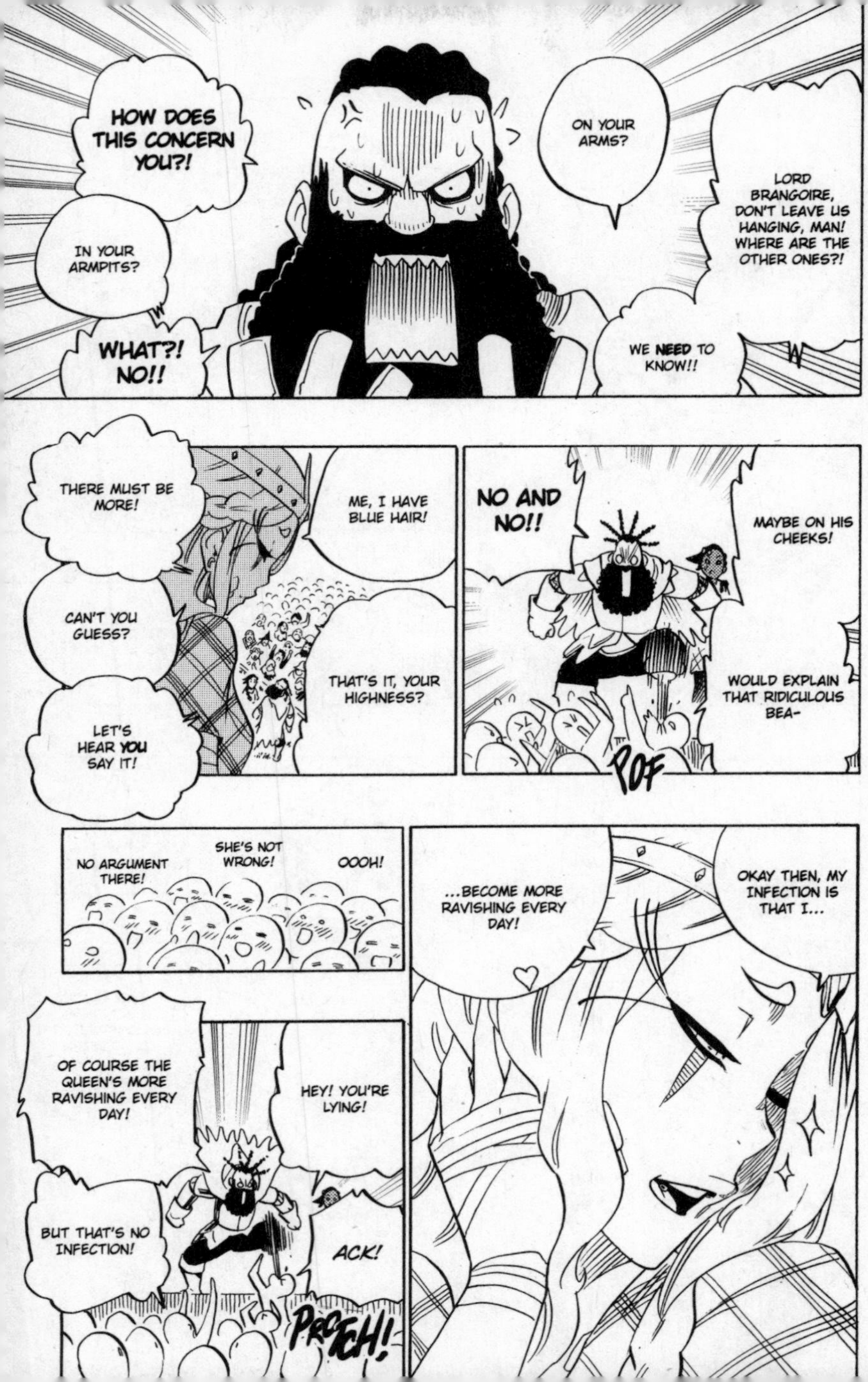
LORD BRANGOIRE, DON'T LEAVE US HANGING, MAN! WHERE ARE THE OTHER ONES?!
ON YOUR ARMS?
HOW DOES THIS CONCERN YOU?!
WE NEED TO KNOW!!
IN YOUR ARMPITS?
WHAT?! NO!!
MAYBE ON HIS CHEEKS!
NO AND NO!!
WOULD EXPLAIN THAT RIDICULOUS BEA-
POF
ME, I HAVE BLUE HAIR!
THERE MUST BE MORE!
CAN'T YOU GUESS?
THAT'S IT, YOUR HIGHNESS?
LET'S HEAR YOU SAY IT!
OKAY THEN, MY INFECTION IS THAT I...
...BECOME MORE RAVISHING EVERY DAY!
OOOH!
SHE'S NOT WRONG!
NO ARGUMENT THERE!
HEY! YOU'RE LYING!
OF COURSE THE QUEEN'S MORE RAVISHING EVERY DAY!
ACK!
BUT THAT'S NO INFECTION!

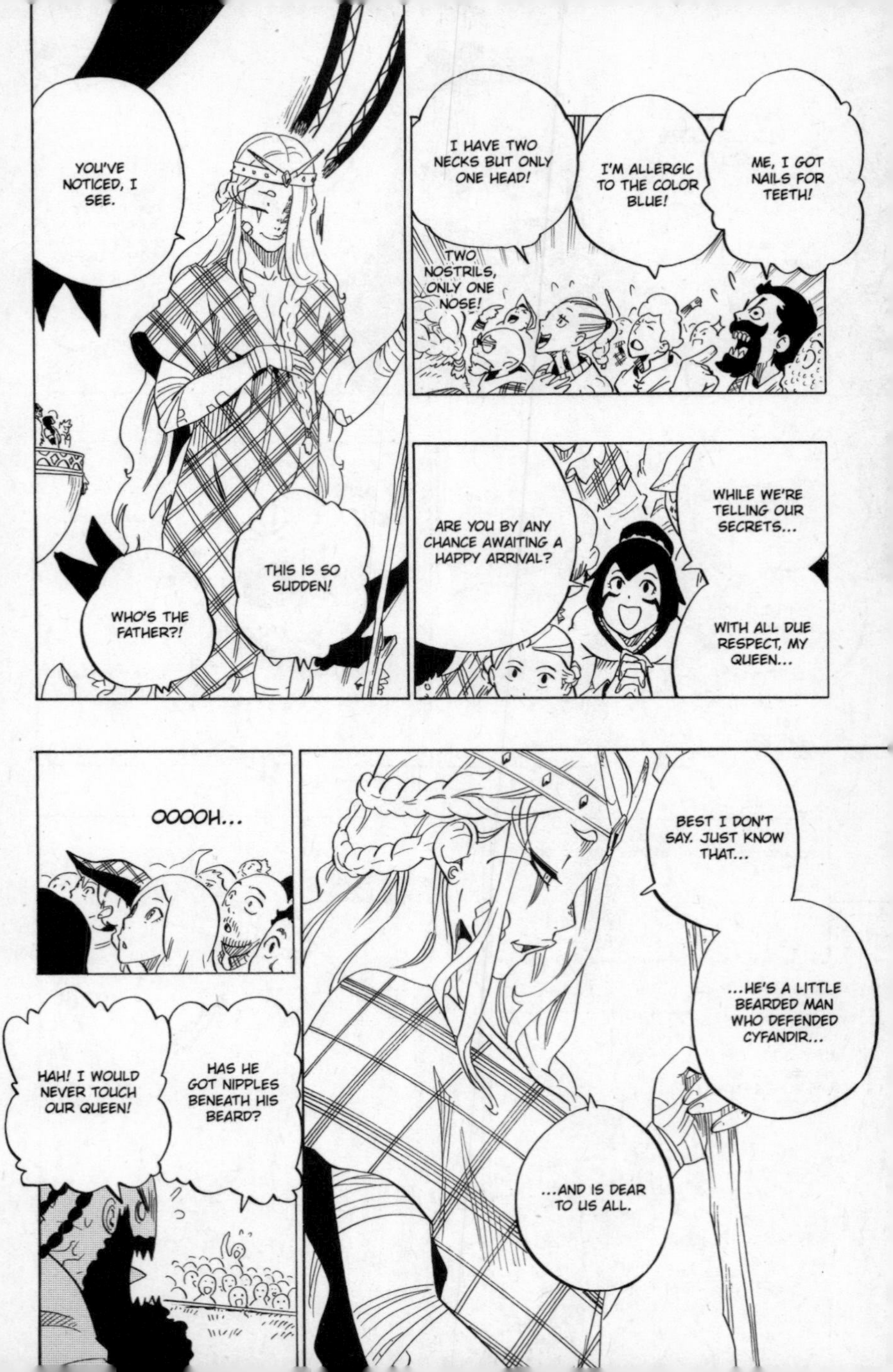

ME, I GOT NAILS FOR TEETH!
I'M ALLERGIC TO THE COLOR BLUE!
I HAVE TWO NECKS BUT ONLY ONE HEAD!
TWO NOSTRILS, ONLY ONE NOSE!
WHILE WE'RE TELLING OUR SECRETS...
WITH ALL DUE RESPECT, MY QUEEN...
ARE YOU BY ANY CHANCE AWAITING A HAPPY ARRIVAL?
YOU'VE NOTICED, I SEE.
THIS IS SO SUDDEN!
WHO'S THE FATHER?!
BEST I DON'T SAY. JUST KNOW THAT...
...HE'S A LITTLE BEARDED MAN WHO DEFENDED CYFANDIR...
...AND IS DEAR TO US ALL.
OOOOH...
HAS HE GOT NIPPLES BENEATH HIS BEARD?
HAH! I WOULD NEVER TOUCH OUR QUEEN!

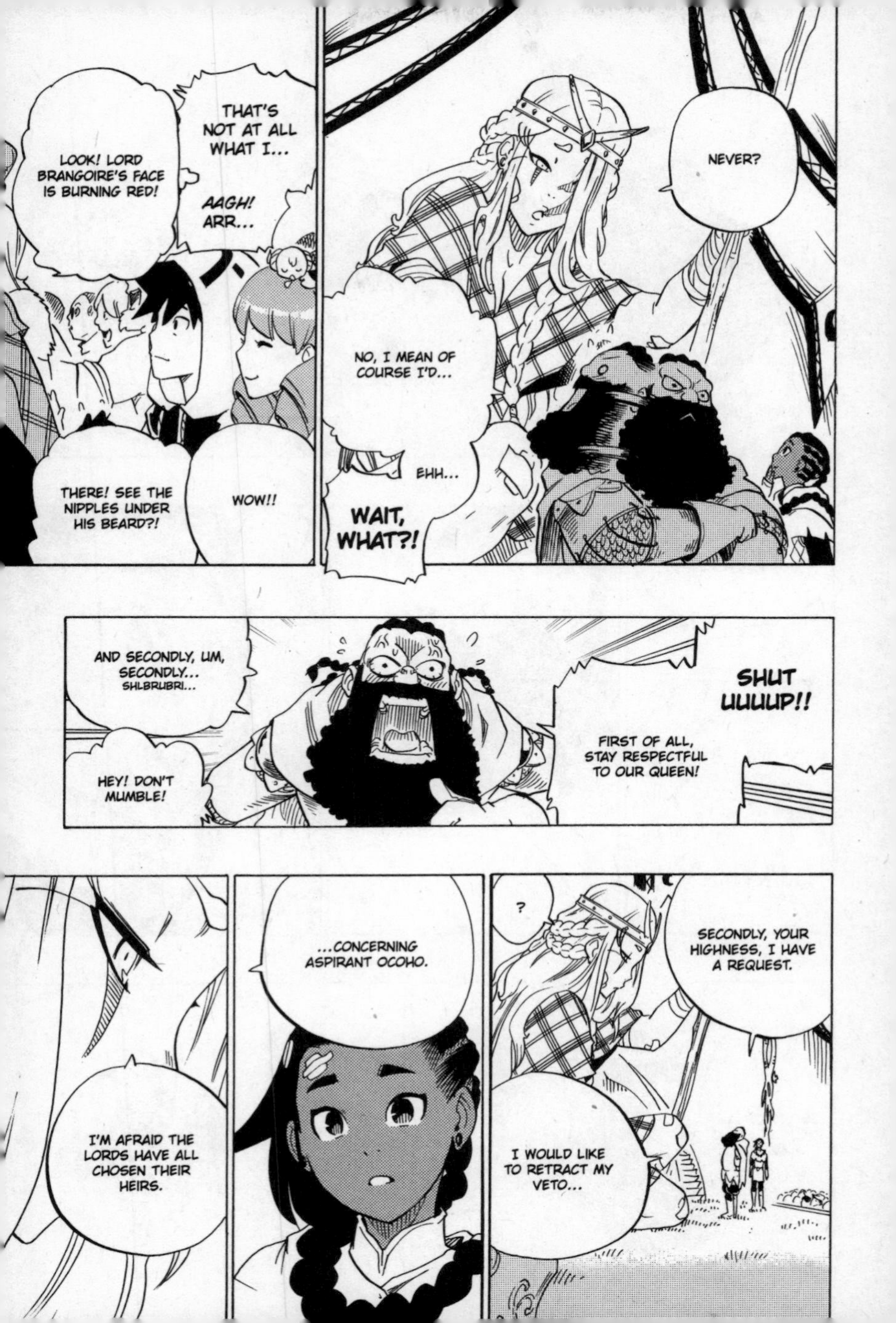
NEVER?
NO, I MEAN OF COURSE I'D...
EHH...
WAIT, WHAT?!
THAT'S NOT AT ALL WHAT I...
AAGH! ARR...
LOOK! LORD BRANGOIRE'S FACE IS BURNING RED!
WOW!!
THERE! SEE THE NIPPLES UNDER HIS BEARD?!
SHUT UUUUP!!
FIRST OF ALL, STAY RESPECTFUL TO OUR QUEEN!
AND SECONDLY, UM, SECONDLY... SHLBRUBRI...
HEY! DON'T MUMBLE!
?
SECONDLY, YOUR HIGHNESS, I HAVE A REQUEST.
I WOULD LIKE TO RETRACT MY VETO...
...CONCERNING ASPIRANT OCOHO.
I'M AFRAID THE LORDS HAVE ALL CHOSEN THEIR HEIRS.

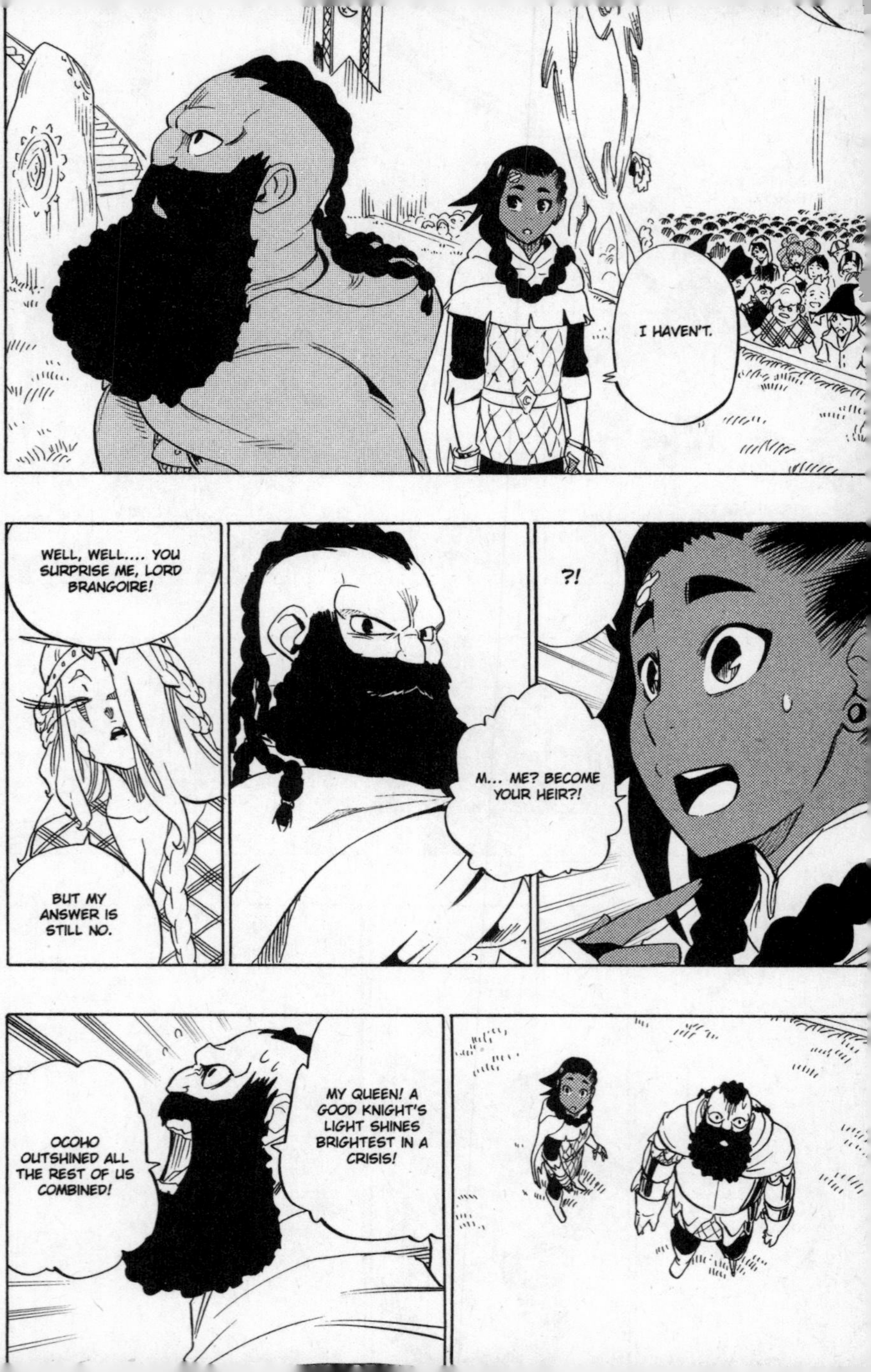
I HAVEN'T.
?!
M... ME? BECOME YOUR HEIR?!
WELL, WELL.... YOU SURPRISE ME, LORD BRANGOIRE!
BUT MY ANSWER IS STILL NO.
MY QUEEN! A GOOD KNIGHT'S LIGHT SHINES BRIGHTEST IN A CRISIS!
OCOHO OUTSHINED ALL THE REST OF US COMBINED!

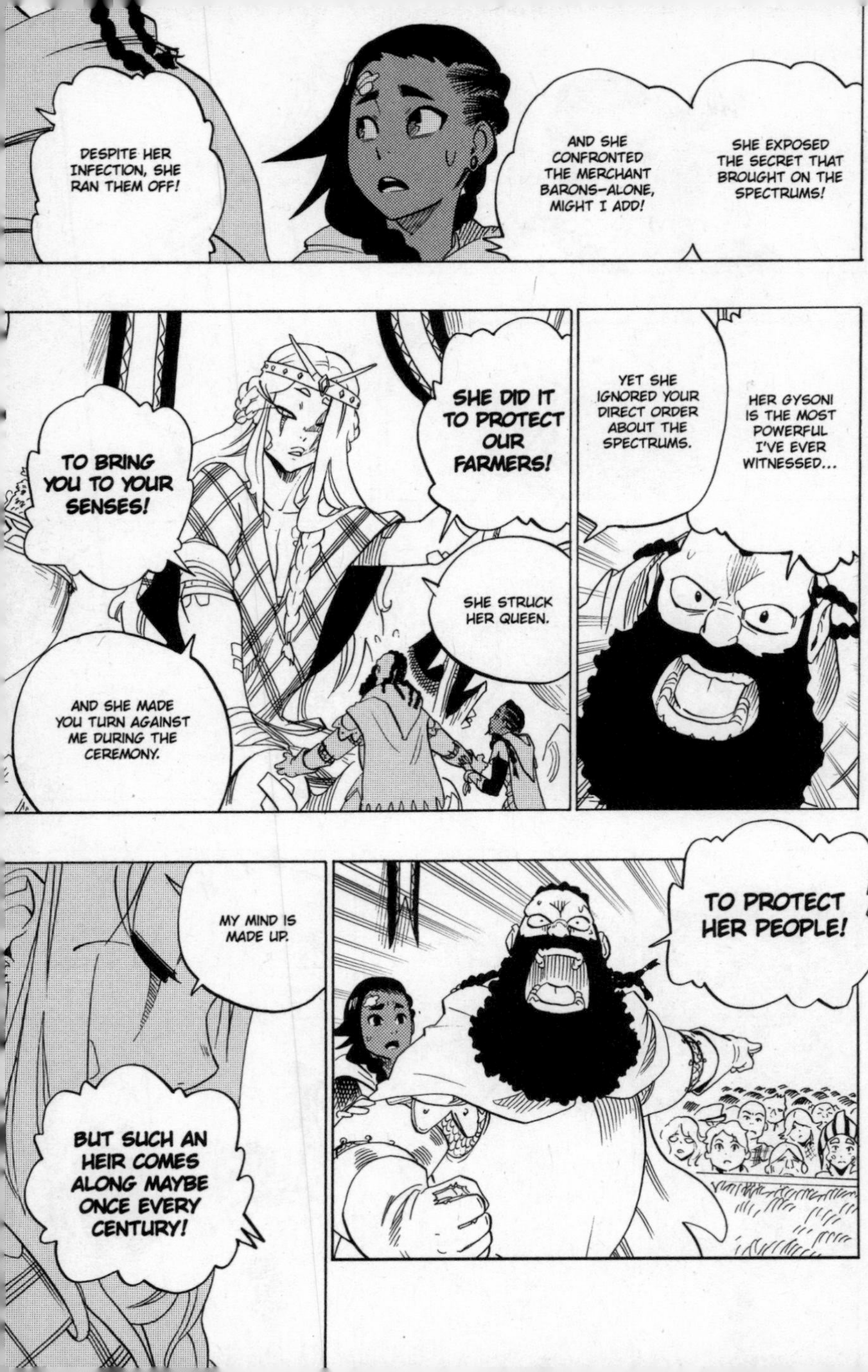
SHE EXPOSED THE SECRET THAT BROUGHT ON THE SPECTRUMS!
AND SHE CONFRONTED THE MERCHANT BARONS—ALONE, MIGHT I ADD!
DESPITE HER INFECTION, SHE RAN THEM OFF!
HER GYSONI IS THE MOST POWERFUL I'VE EVER WITNESSED...
YET SHE IGNORED YOUR DIRECT ORDER ABOUT THE SPECTRUMS.
SHE STRUCK HER QUEEN.
TO BRING YOU TO YOUR SENSES!
AND SHE MADE YOU TURN AGAINST ME DURING THE CEREMONY.
SHE DID IT TO PROTECT OUR FARMERS!
TO PROTECT HER PEOPLE!
MY MIND IS MADE UP.
BUT SUCH AN HEIR COMES ALONG MAYBE ONCE EVERY CENTURY!

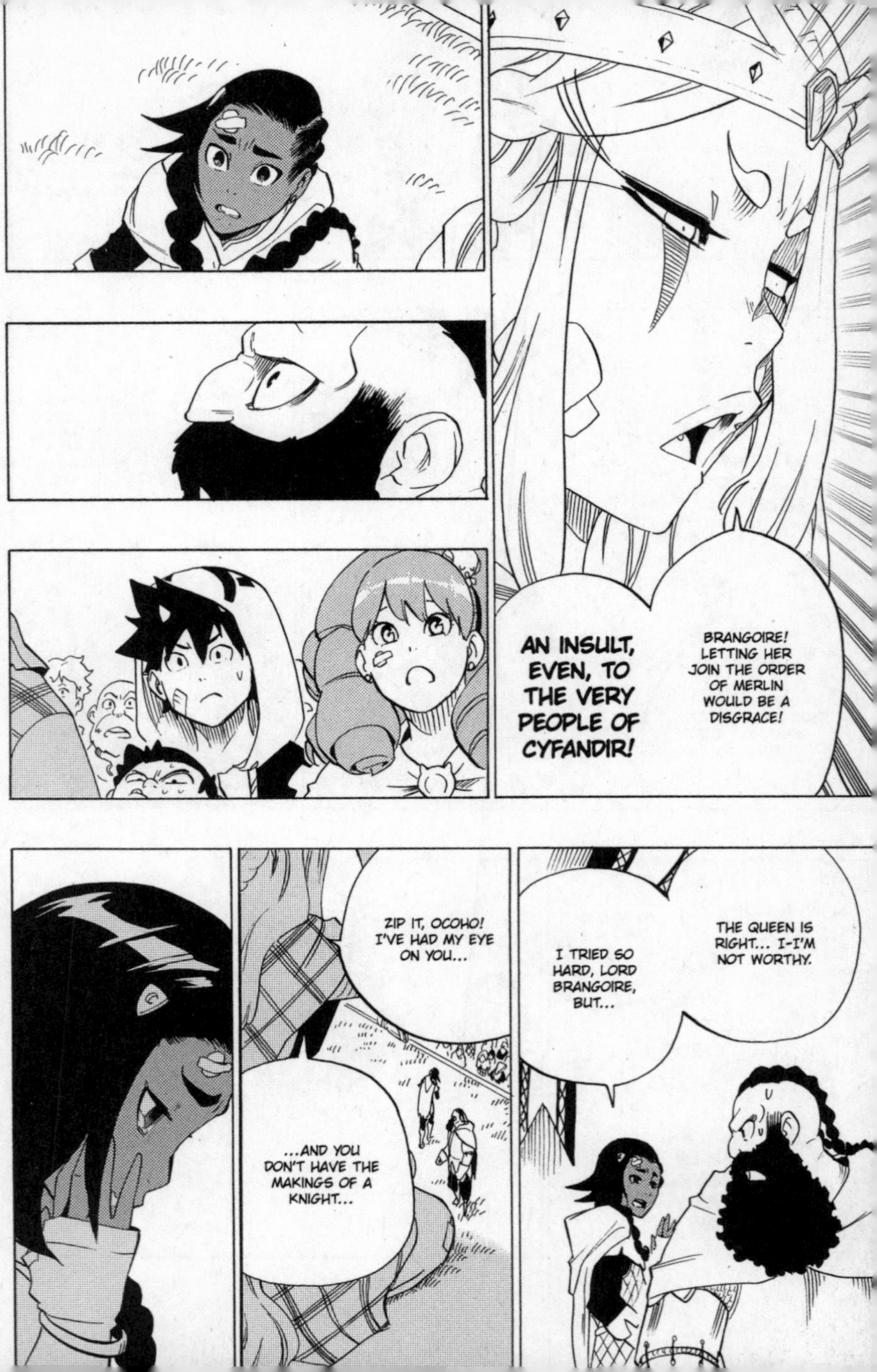
BRANGOIRE! LETTING HER JOIN THE ORDER OF MERLIN WOULD BE A DISGRACE!
AN INSULT, EVEN, TO THE VERY PEOPLE OF CYFANDIR!
THE QUEEN IS RIGHT... I-I'M NOT WORTHY.
I TRIED SO HARD, LORD BRANGOIRE, BUT...
ZIP IT, OCOHO! I'VE HAD MY EYE ON YOU...
...AND YOU DON'T HAVE THE MAKINGS OF A KNIGHT...

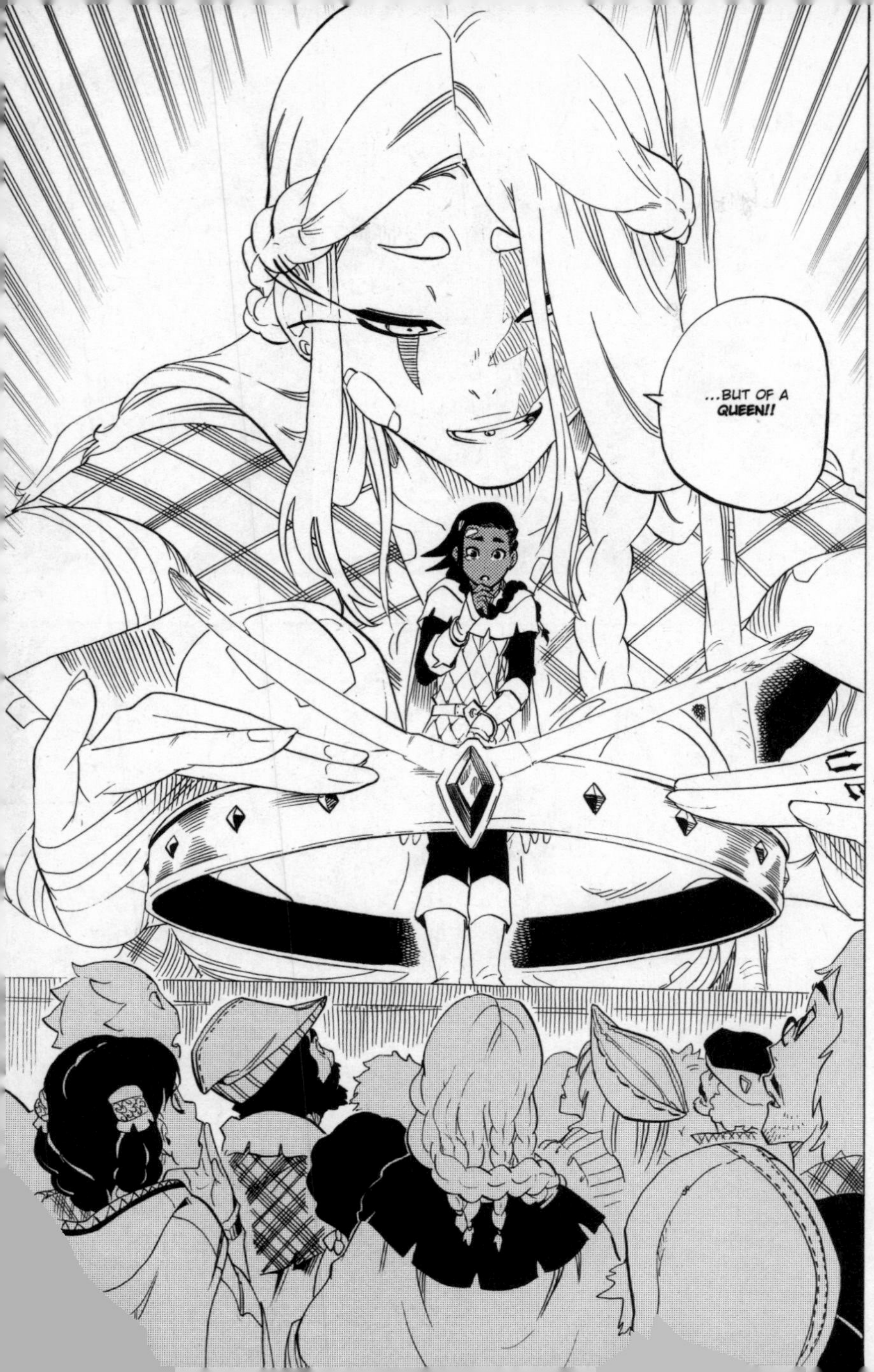
...BUT OF A QUEEN!!

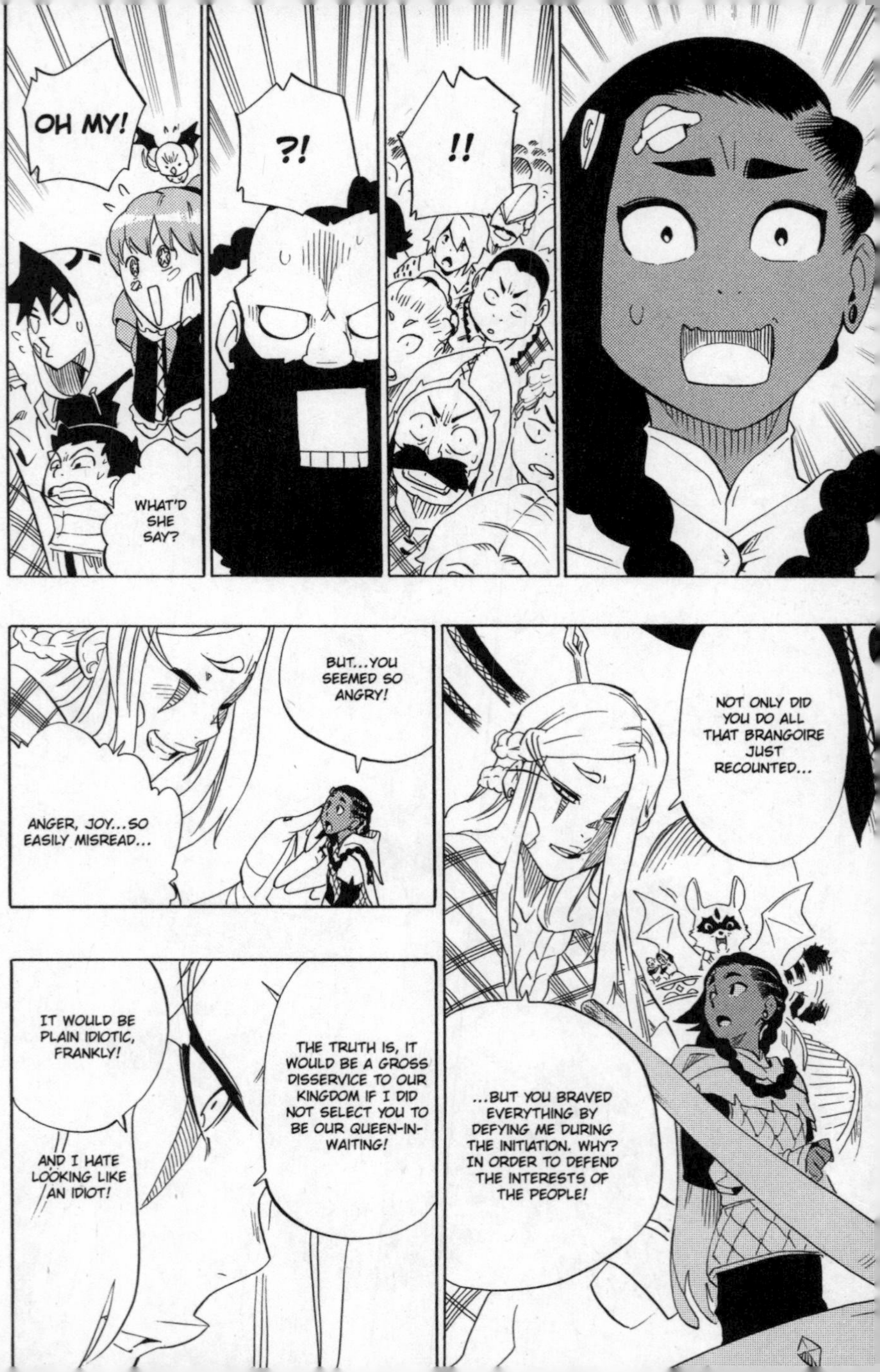
!!
?!
OH MY!
WHAT'D SHE SAY?
NOT ONLY DID YOU DO ALL THAT BRANGOIRE JUST RECOUNTED...
...BUT YOU BRAVED EVERYTHING BY DEFYING ME DURING THE INITIATION. WHY? IN ORDER TO DEFEND THE INTERESTS OF THE PEOPLE!
BUT...YOU SEEMED SO ANGRY!
ANGER, JOY...SO EASILY MISREAD...
THE TRUTH IS, IT WOULD BE A GROSS DISSERVICE TO OUR KINGDOM IF I DID NOT SELECT YOU TO BE OUR QUEEN-IN-WAITING!
IT WOULD BE PLAIN IDIOTIC, FRANKLY!
AND I HATE LOOKING LIKE AN IDIOT!

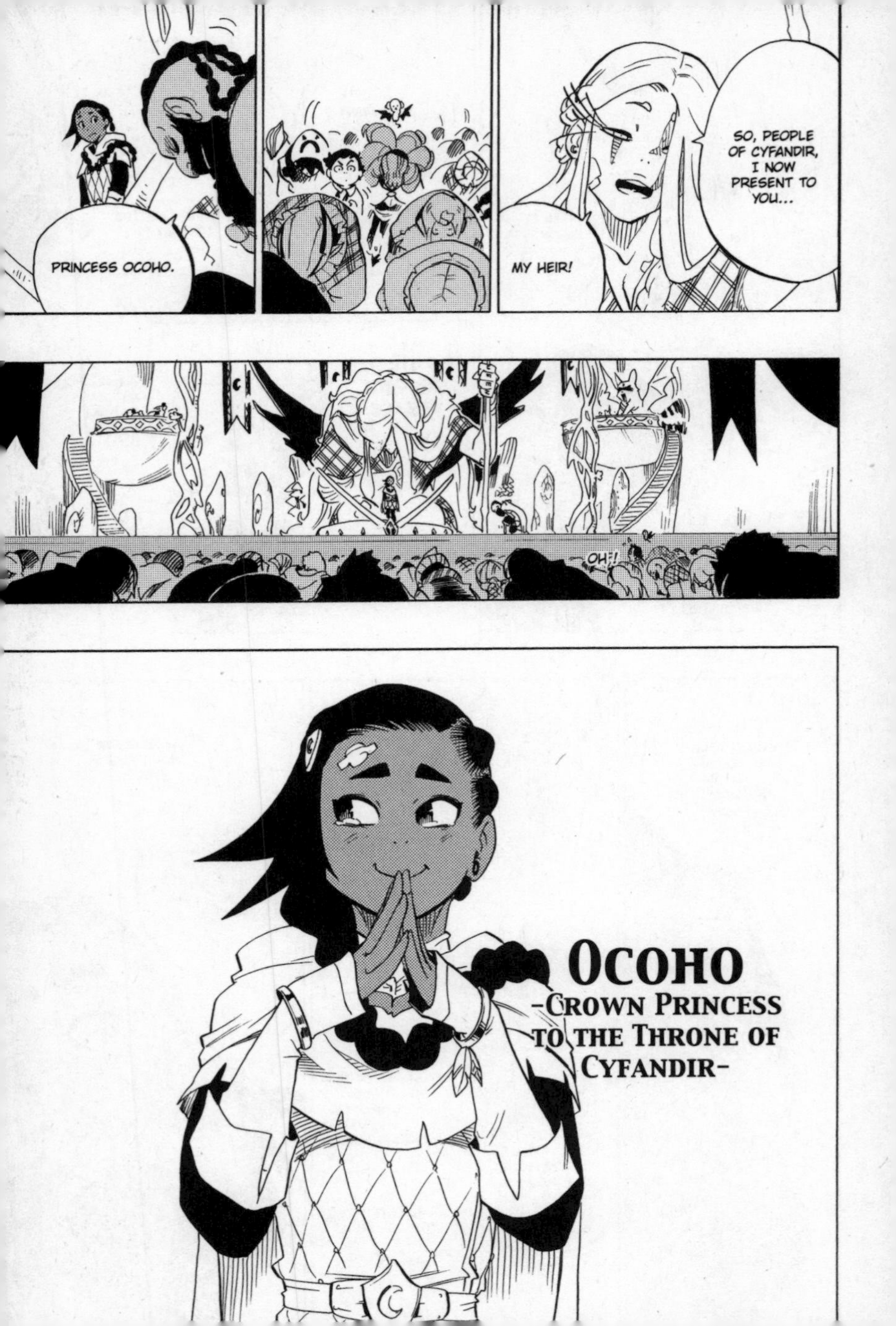
SO, PEOPLE OF CYFANDIR, I NOW PRESENT TO YOU...
MY HEIR!
PRINCESS OCOHO.
OH?!
OCOHO
-CROWN PRINCESS TO THE THRONE OF CYFANDIR-

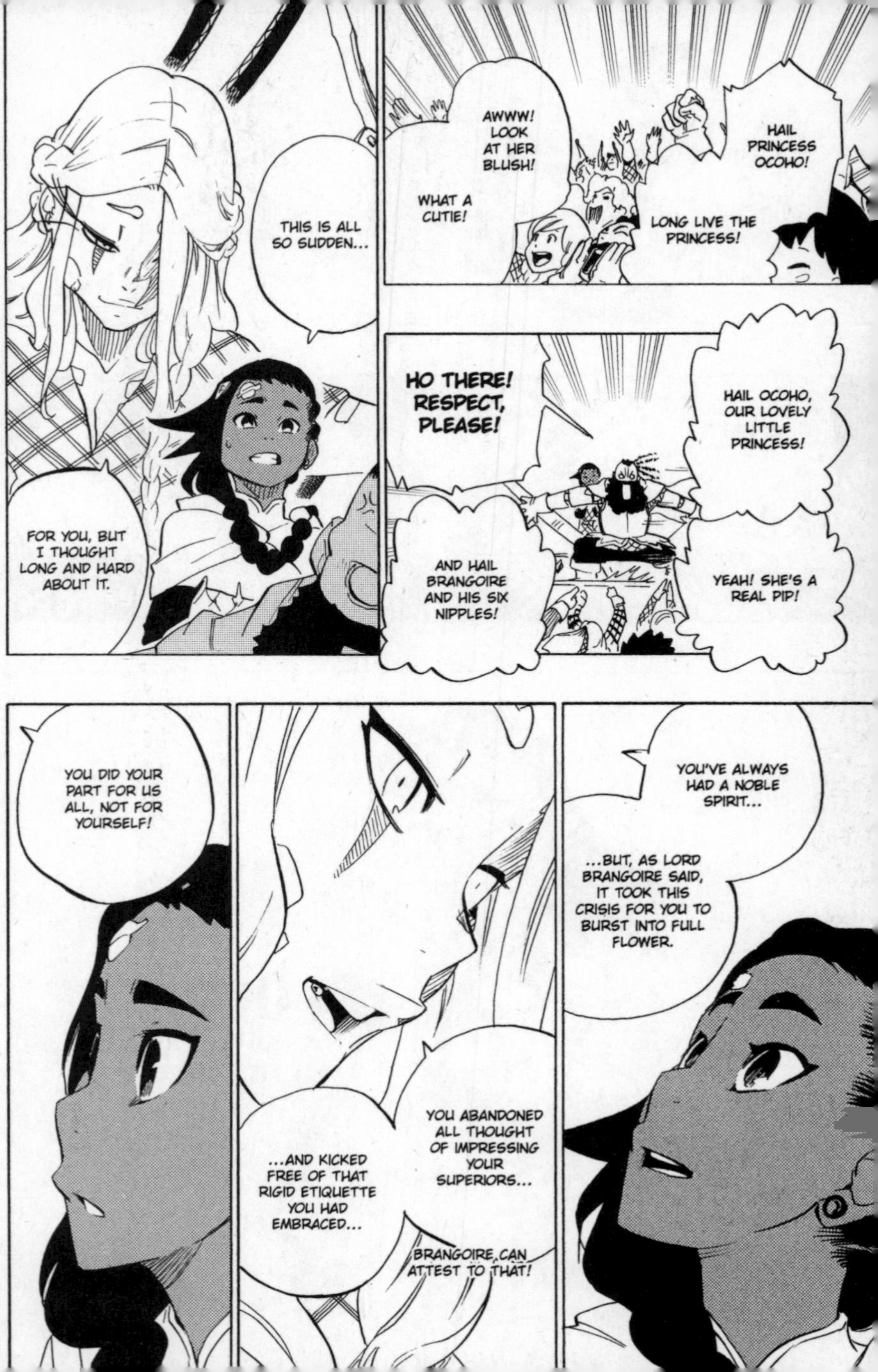
HAIL PRINCESS OCOHO!
AWWW! LOOK AT HER BLUSH!
LONG LIVE THE PRINCESS!
WHAT A CUTIE!
HAIL OCOHO, OUR LOVELY LITTLE PRINCESS!
HO THERE! RESPECT, PLEASE!
YEAH! SHE'S A REAL PIP!
AND HAIL BRANGOIRE AND HIS SIX NIPPLES!
THIS IS ALL SO SUDDEN...
FOR YOU, BUT I THOUGHT LONG AND HARD ABOUT IT.
YOU'VE ALWAYS HAD A NOBLE SPIRIT...
...BUT, AS LORD BRANGOIRE SAID, IT TOOK THIS CRISIS FOR YOU TO BURST INTO FULL FLOWER.
YOU ABANDONED ALL THOUGHT OF IMPRESSING YOUR SUPERIORS...
...AND KICKED FREE OF THAT RIGID ETIQUETTE YOU HAD EMBRACED...
BRANGOIRE CAN ATTEST TO THAT!
YOU DID YOUR PART FOR US ALL, NOT FOR YOURSELF!

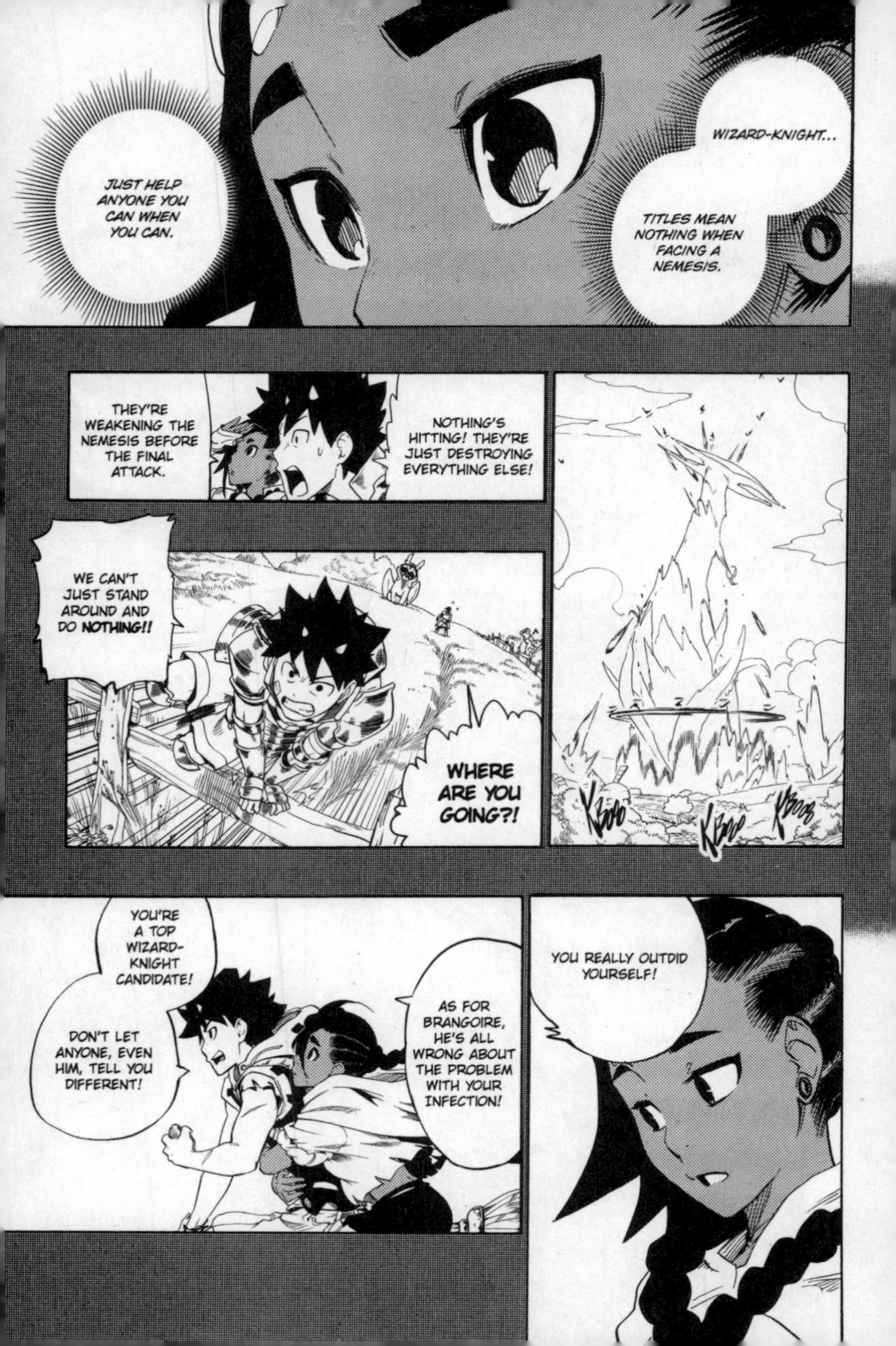
WIZARD-KNIGHT...
TITLES MEAN NOTHING WHEN FACING A NEMESIS.
JUST HELP ANYONE YOU CAN WHEN YOU CAN.
NOTHING'S HITTING! THEY'RE JUST DESTROYING EVERYTHING ELSE!
THEY'RE WEAKENING THE NEMESIS BEFORE THE FINAL ATTACK.
WHERE ARE YOU GOING?!
WE CAN'T JUST STAND AROUND AND DO **NOTHING!!**
YOU REALLY OUTDID YOURSELF!
AS FOR BRANGOIRE, HE'S ALL WRONG ABOUT THE PROBLEM WITH YOUR INFECTION!
YOU'RE A TOP WIZARD-KNIGHT CANDIDATE!
DON'T LET ANYONE, EVEN HIM, TELL YOU DIFFERENT!

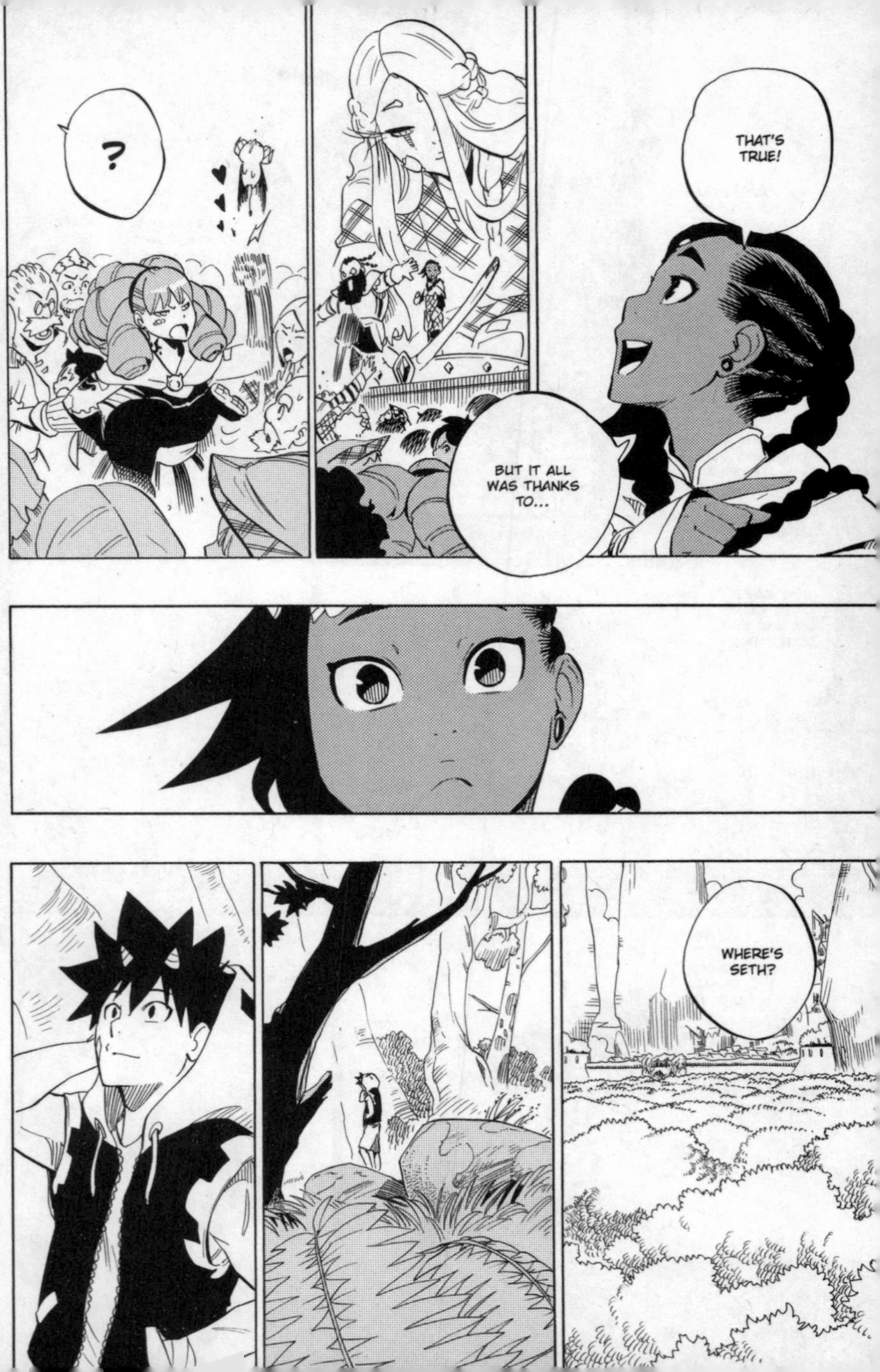
THAT'S TRUE!
BUT IT ALL WAS THANKS TO...
?
WHERE'S SETH?

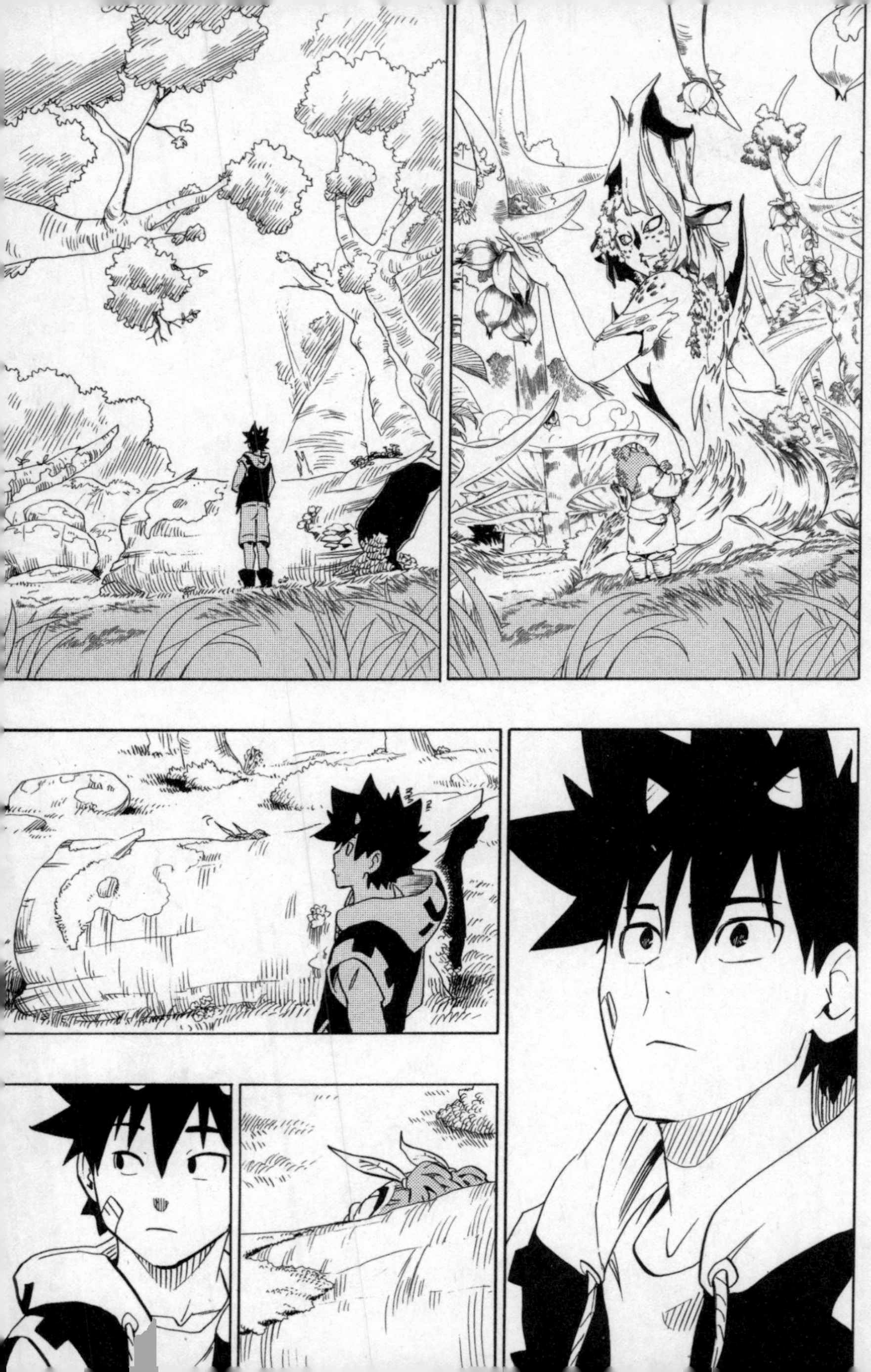

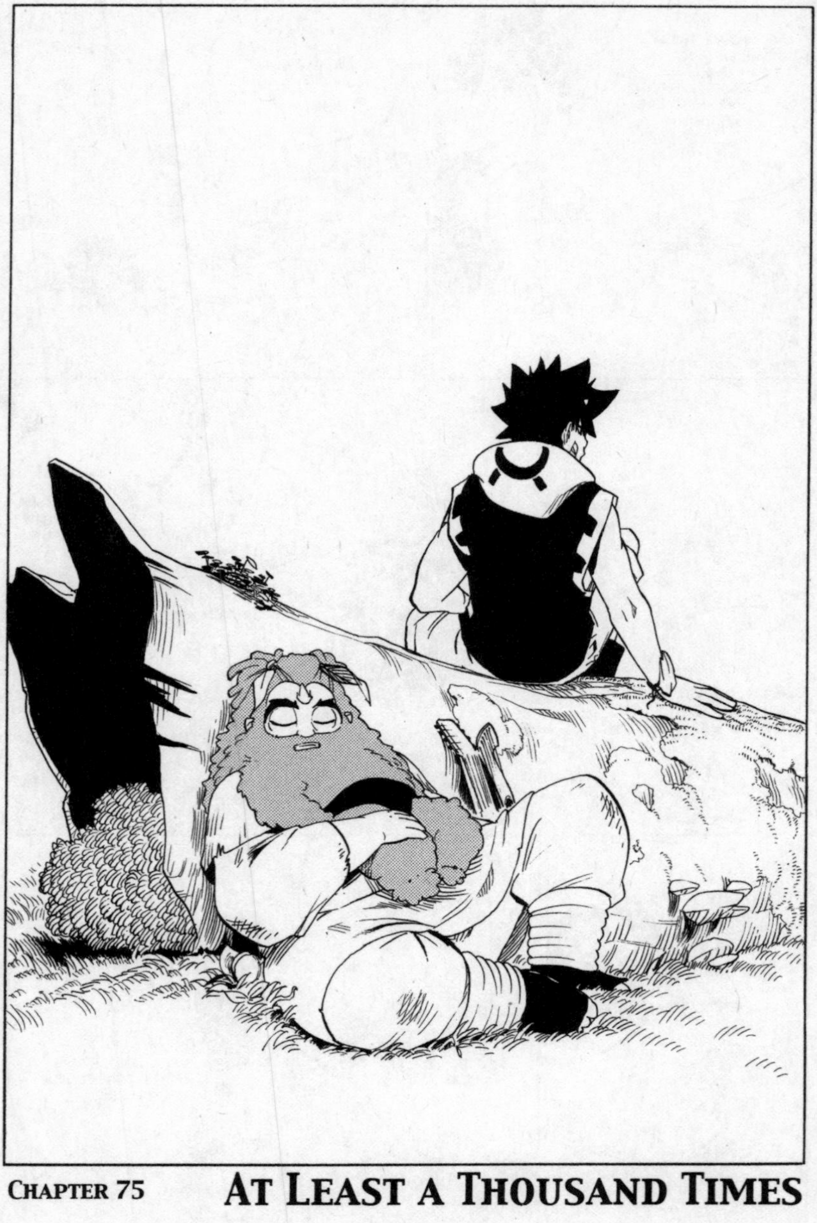

Chapter 75 At Least a Thousand Times

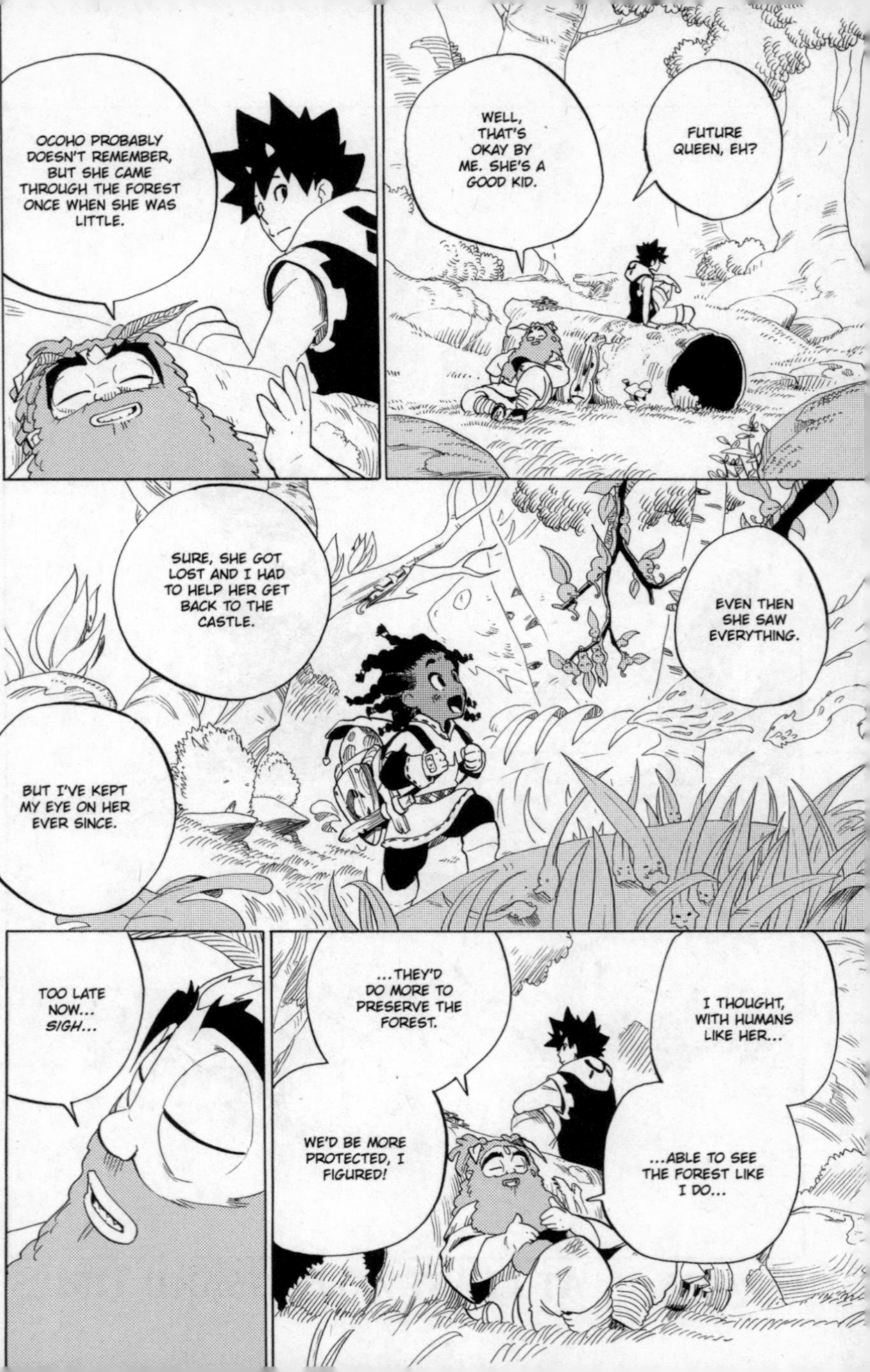
FUTURE QUEEN, EH?
WELL, THAT'S OKAY BY ME. SHE'S A GOOD KID.
OCOHO PROBABLY DOESN'T REMEMBER, BUT SHE CAME THROUGH THE FOREST ONCE WHEN SHE WAS LITTLE.
SURE, SHE GOT LOST AND I HAD TO HELP HER GET BACK TO THE CASTLE.
EVEN THEN SHE SAW EVERYTHING.
BUT I'VE KEPT MY EYE ON HER EVER SINCE.
I THOUGHT, WITH HUMANS LIKE HER...
...ABLE TO SEE THE FOREST LIKE I DO...
...THEY'D DO MORE TO PRESERVE THE FOREST.
WE'D BE MORE PROTECTED, I FIGURED!
TOO LATE NOW... *SIGH*...

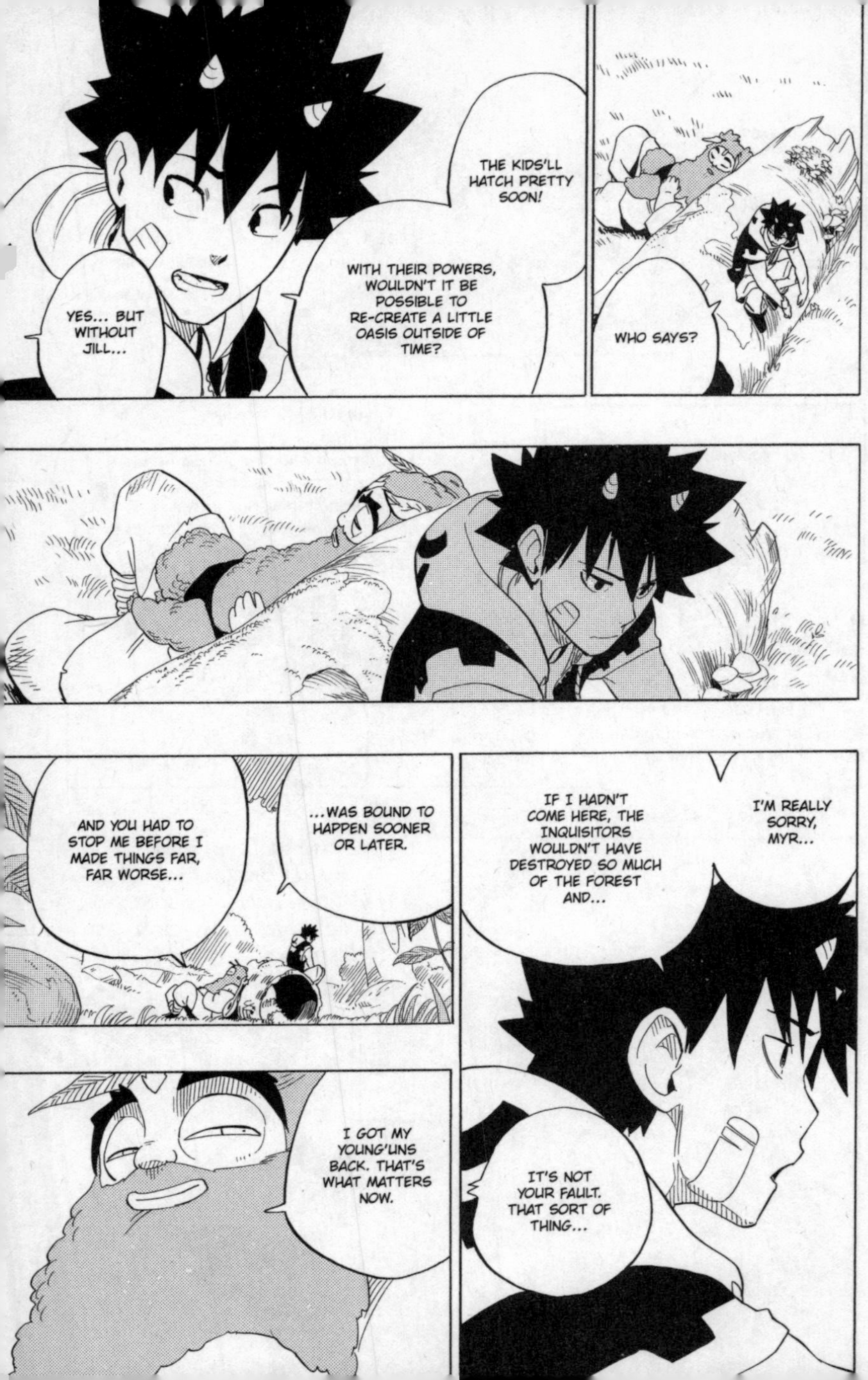
WHO SAYS?
THE KIDS'LL HATCH PRETTY SOON!
WITH THEIR POWERS, WOULDN'T IT BE POSSIBLE TO RE-CREATE A LITTLE OASIS OUTSIDE OF TIME?
YES... BUT WITHOUT JILL...
I'M REALLY SORRY, MYR...
IF I HADN'T COME HERE, THE INQUISITORS WOULDN'T HAVE DESTROYED SO MUCH OF THE FOREST AND...
IT'S NOT YOUR FAULT. THAT SORT OF THING...
...WAS BOUND TO HAPPEN SOONER OR LATER.
AND YOU HAD TO STOP ME BEFORE I MADE THINGS FAR, FAR WORSE...
I GOT MY YOUNG'UNS BACK. THAT'S WHAT MATTERS NOW.

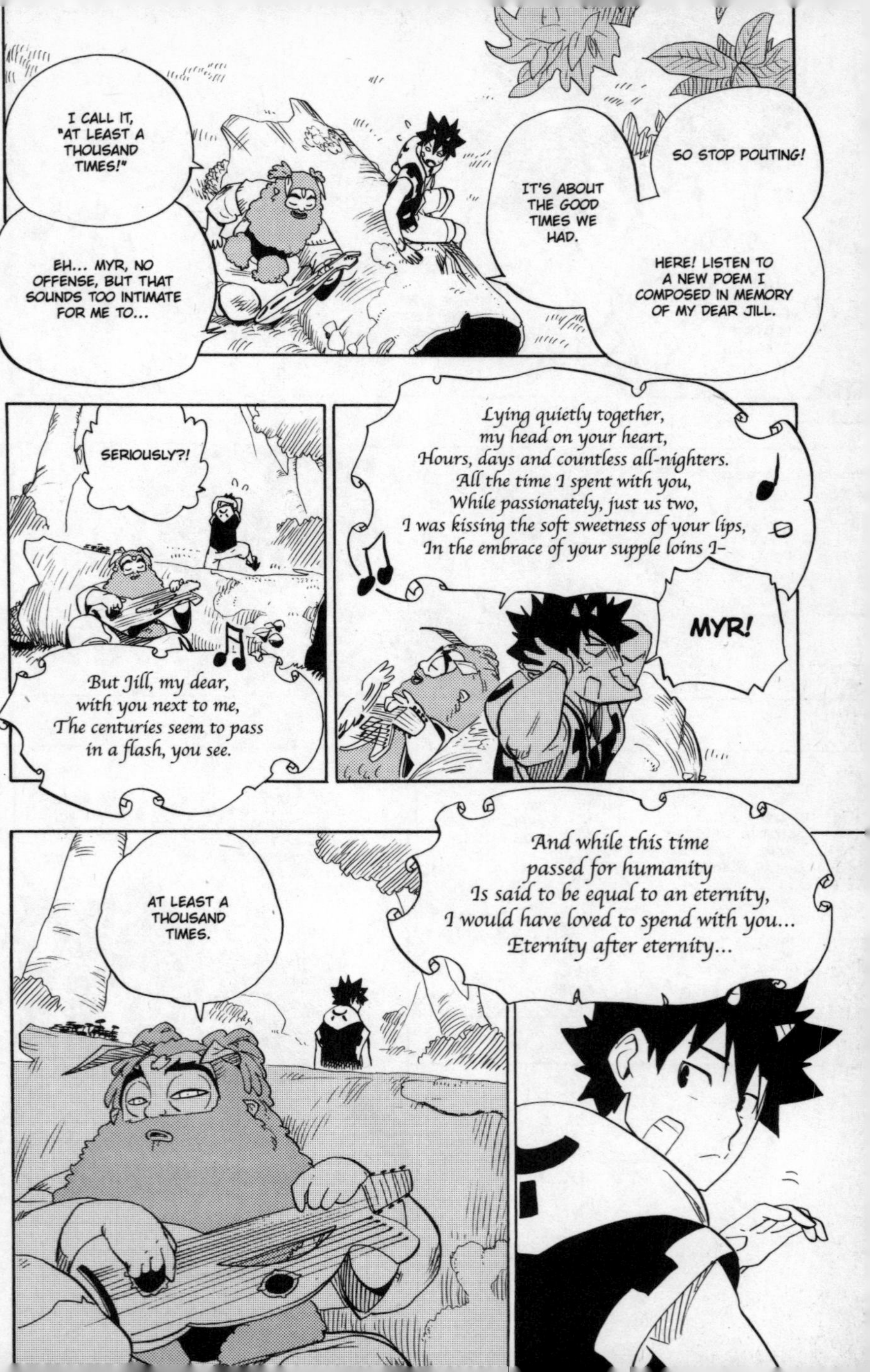
SO STOP POUTING!
HERE! LISTEN TO A NEW POEM I COMPOSED IN MEMORY OF MY DEAR JILL.
IT'S ABOUT THE GOOD TIMES WE HAD.
I CALL IT, "AT LEAST A THOUSAND TIMES!"
EH... MYR, NO OFFENSE, BUT THAT SOUNDS TOO INTIMATE FOR ME TO...
Lying quietly together, my head on your heart, Hours, days and countless all-nighters. All the time I spent with you, While passionately, just us two, I was kissing the soft sweetness of your lips, In the embrace of your supple loins I–
MYR!
SERIOUSLY?!
But Jill, my dear, with you next to me, The centuries seem to pass in a flash, you see.
And while this time passed for humanity Is said to be equal to an eternity, I would have loved to spend with you... Eternity after eternity...
AT LEAST A THOUSAND TIMES.

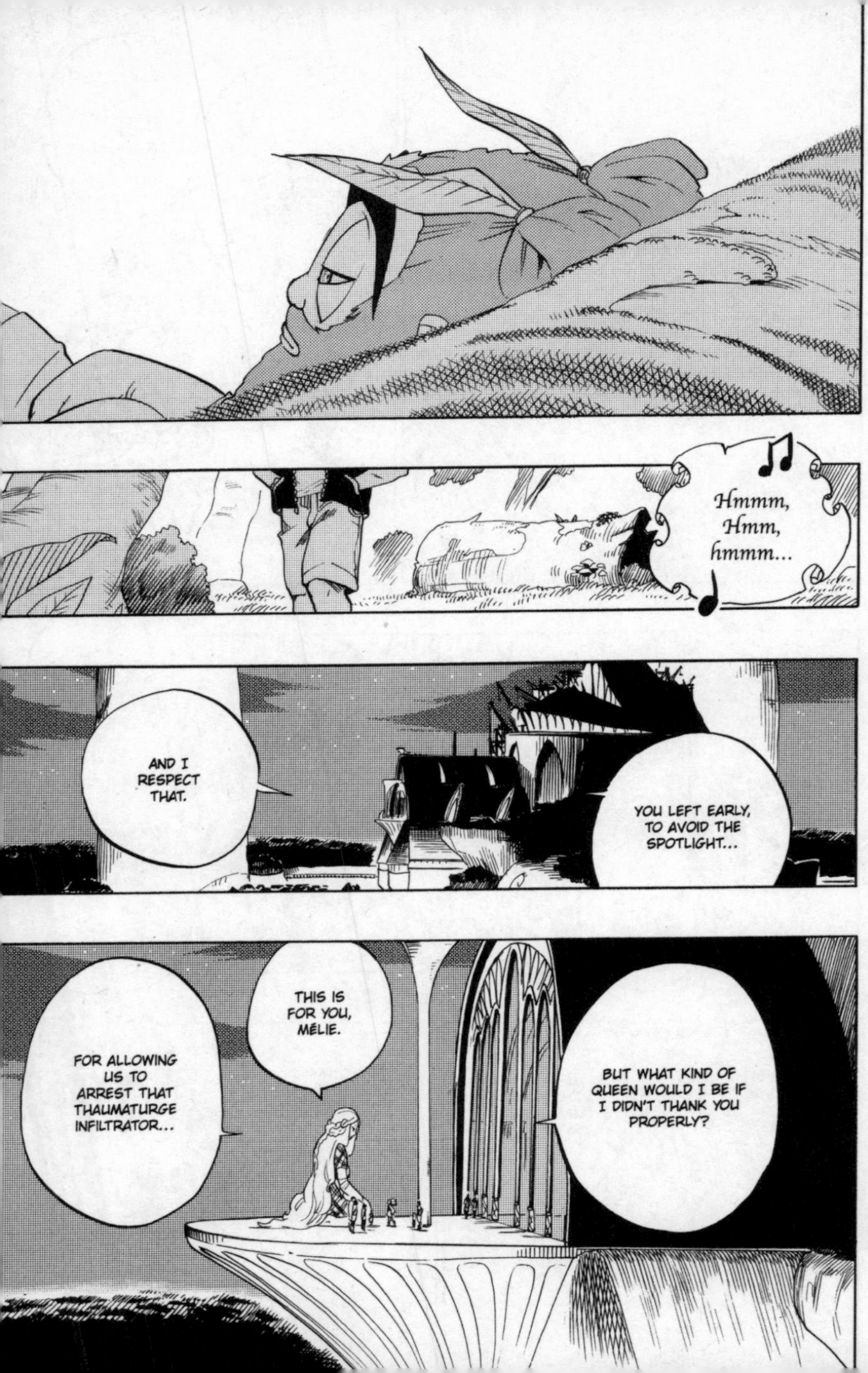
Hmmm, Hmm, hmmm...
YOU LEFT EARLY, TO AVOID THE SPOTLIGHT...
AND I RESPECT THAT.
BUT WHAT KIND OF QUEEN WOULD I BE IF I DIDN'T THANK YOU PROPERLY?
THIS IS FOR YOU, MÉLIE.
FOR ALLOWING US TO ARREST THAT THAUMATURGE INFILTRATOR...

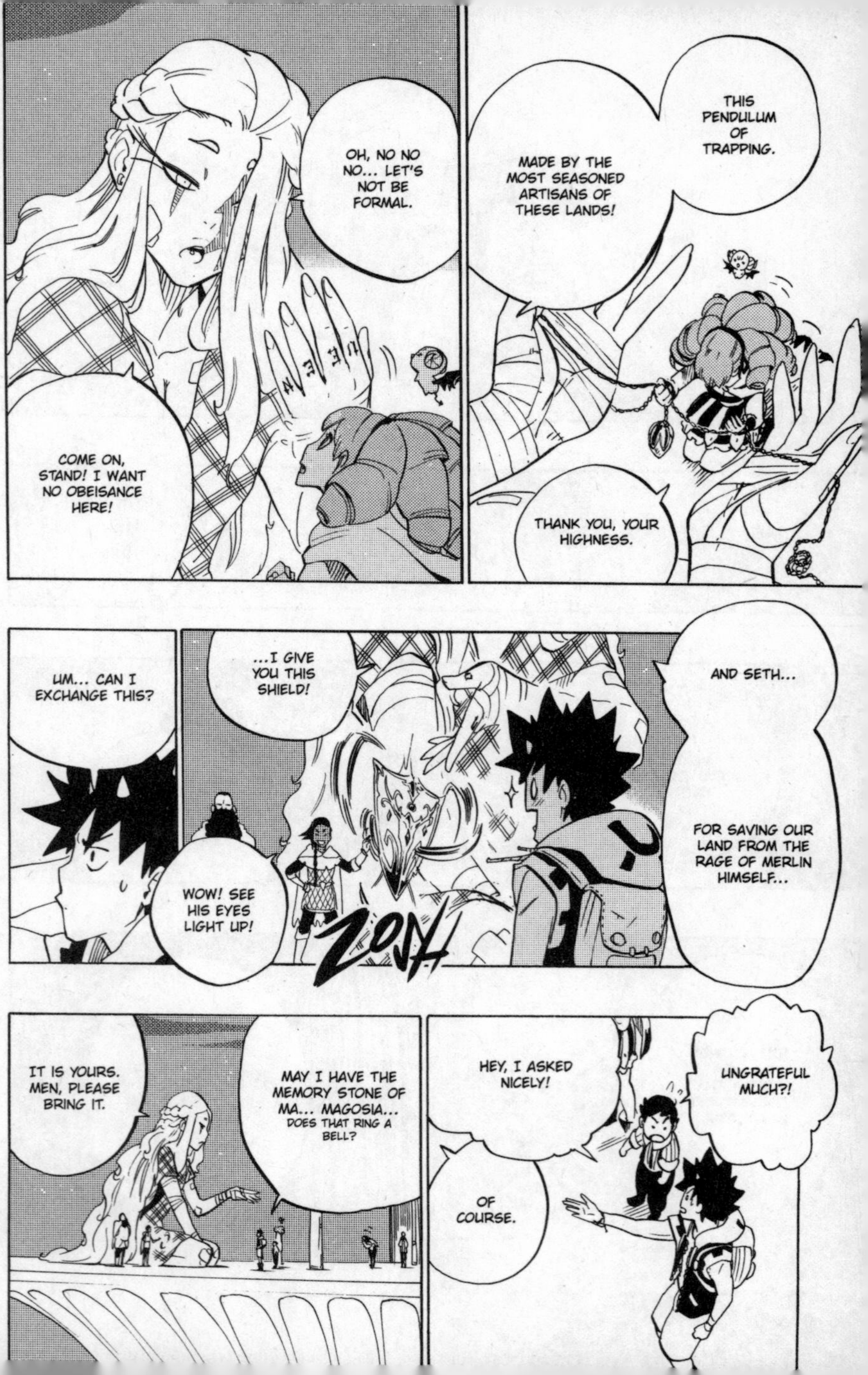
THIS PENDULUM OF TRAPPING.
MADE BY THE MOST SEASONED ARTISANS OF THESE LANDS!
THANK YOU, YOUR HIGHNESS.
OH, NO NO NO... LET'S NOT BE FORMAL.
COME ON, STAND! I WANT NO OBEISANCE HERE!
AND SETH...
FOR SAVING OUR LAND FROM THE RAGE OF MERLIN HIMSELF...
...I GIVE YOU THIS SHIELD!
ZOSH
WOW! SEE HIS EYES LIGHT UP!
UM... CAN I EXCHANGE THIS?
UNGRATEFUL MUCH?!
HEY, I ASKED NICELY!
OF COURSE.
MAY I HAVE THE MEMORY STONE OF MA... MAGOSIA... DOES THAT RING A BELL?
IT IS YOURS. MEN, PLEASE BRING IT.

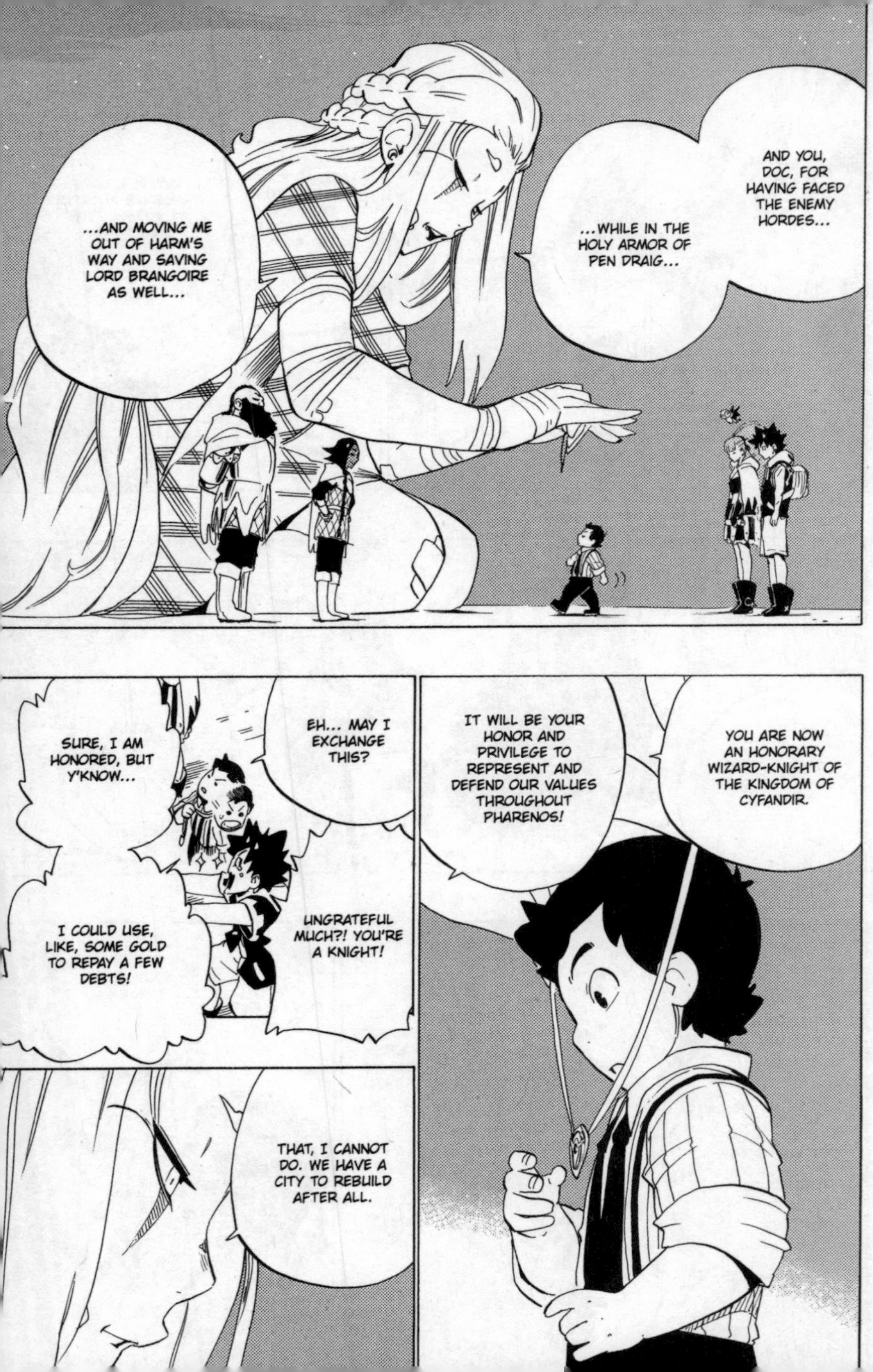
AND YOU, DOC, FOR HAVING FACED THE ENEMY HORDES...
...WHILE IN THE HOLY ARMOR OF PEN DRAIG...
...AND MOVING ME OUT OF HARM'S WAY AND SAVING LORD BRANGOIRE AS WELL...
YOU ARE NOW AN HONORARY WIZARD-KNIGHT OF THE KINGDOM OF CYFANDIR.
IT WILL BE YOUR HONOR AND PRIVILEGE TO REPRESENT AND DEFEND OUR VALUES THROUGHOUT PHARENOS!
EH... MAY I EXCHANGE THIS?
SURE, I AM HONORED, BUT Y'KNOW...
UNGRATEFUL MUCH?! YOU'RE A KNIGHT!
I COULD USE, LIKE, SOME GOLD TO REPAY A FEW DEBTS!
THAT, I CANNOT DO. WE HAVE A CITY TO REBUILD AFTER ALL.

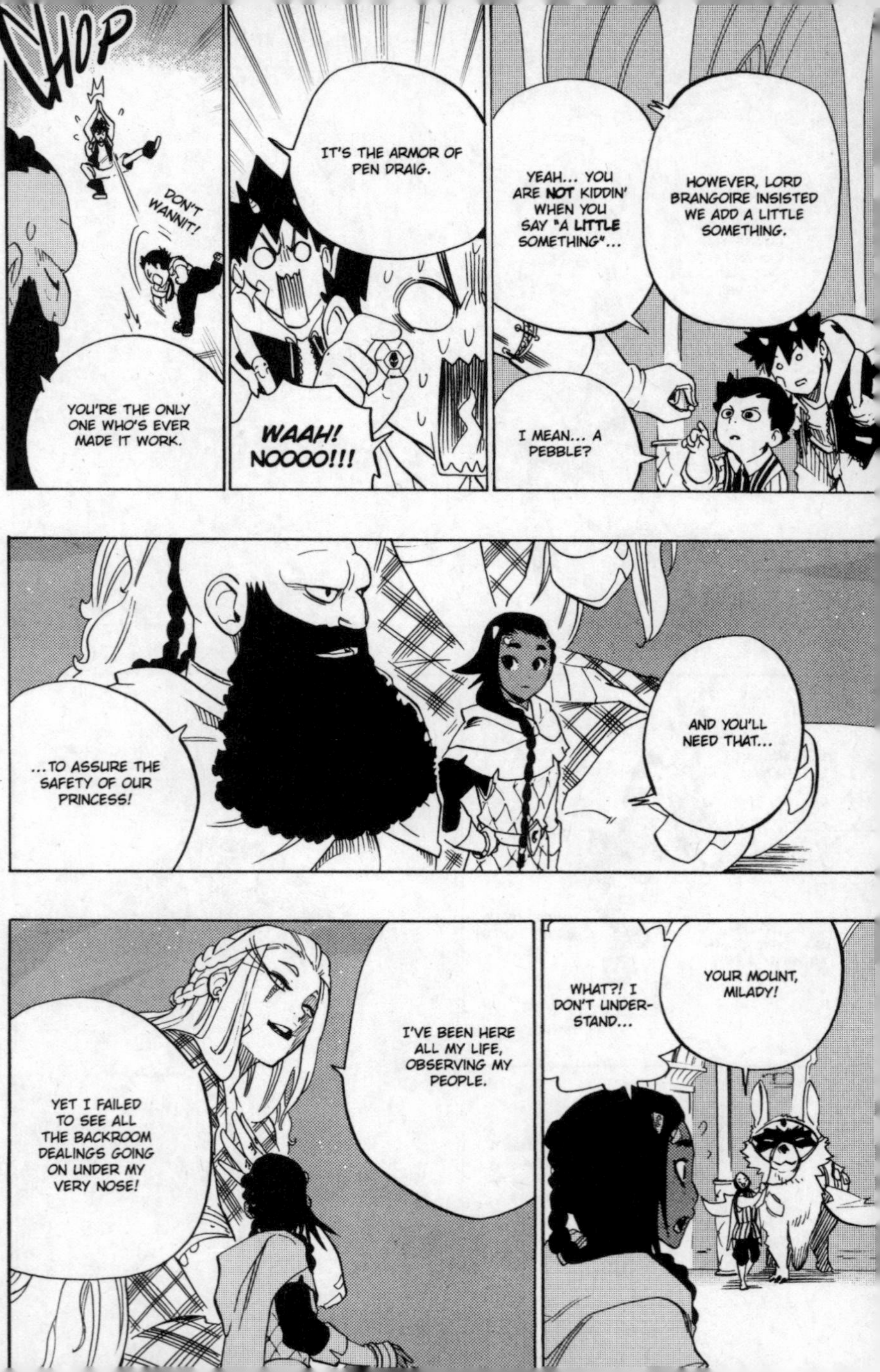
HOWEVER, LORD BRANGOIRE INSISTED WE ADD A LITTLE SOMETHING.
YEAH... YOU ARE NOT KIDDIN' WHEN YOU SAY "A LITTLE SOMETHING"...
I MEAN... A PEBBLE?
IT'S THE ARMOR OF PEN DRAIG.
WAAH! NOOOO!!!
CHOP
DON'T WANNIT!
YOU'RE THE ONLY ONE WHO'S EVER MADE IT WORK.
AND YOU'LL NEED THAT...
...TO ASSURE THE SAFETY OF OUR PRINCESS!
YOUR MOUNT, MILADY!
WHAT?! I DON'T UNDERSTAND...
I'VE BEEN HERE ALL MY LIFE, OBSERVING MY PEOPLE.
YET I FAILED TO SEE ALL THE BACKROOM DEALINGS GOING ON UNDER MY VERY NOSE!

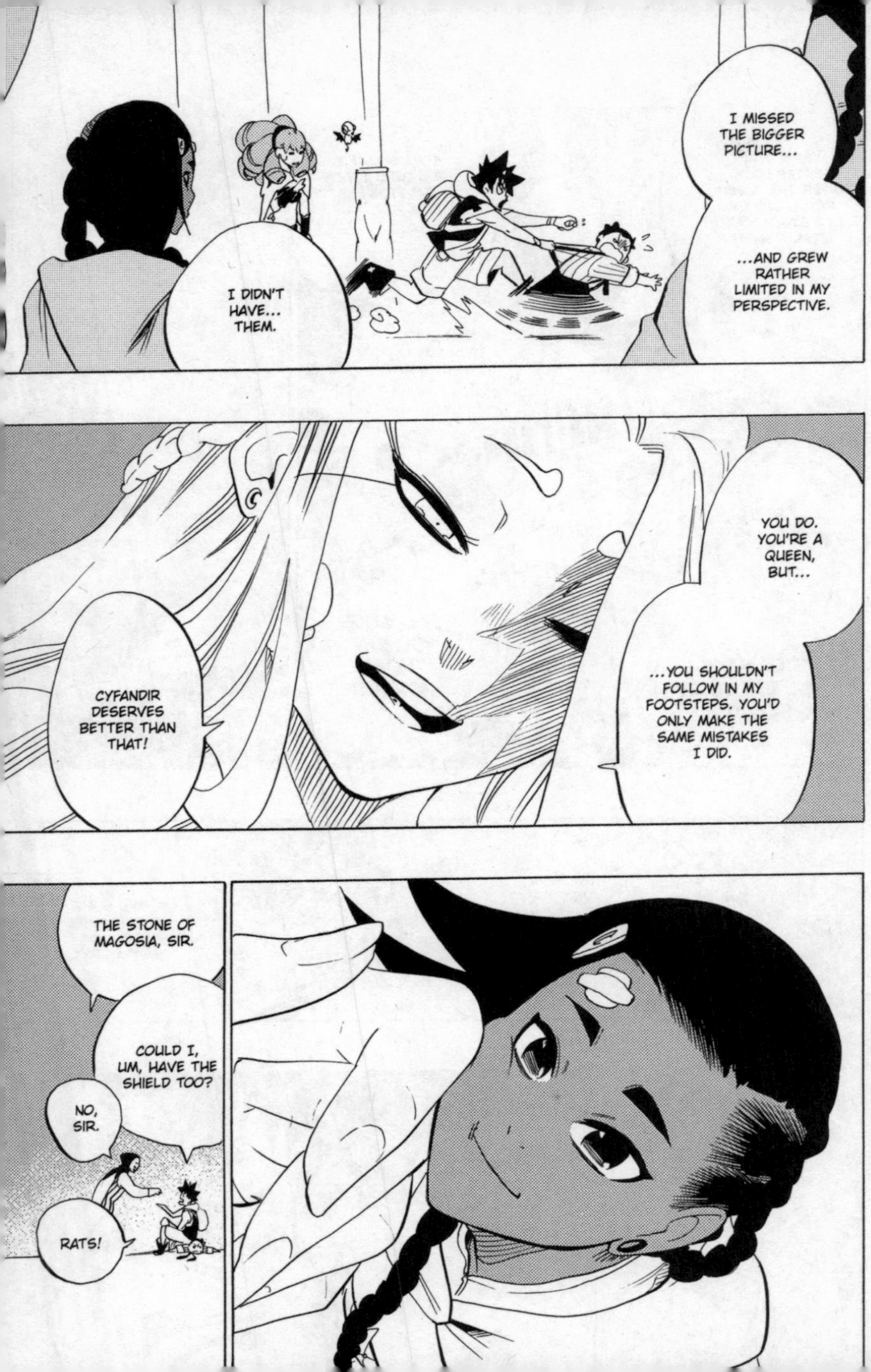
I MISSED THE BIGGER PICTURE...
...AND GREW RATHER LIMITED IN MY PERSPECTIVE.
I DIDN'T HAVE... THEM.
YOU DO. YOU'RE A QUEEN, BUT...
...YOU SHOULDN'T FOLLOW IN MY FOOTSTEPS. YOU'D ONLY MAKE THE SAME MISTAKES I DID.
CYFANDIR DESERVES BETTER THAN THAT!
THE STONE OF MAGOSIA, SIR.
COULD I, UM, HAVE THE SHIELD TOO?
NO, SIR.
RATS!

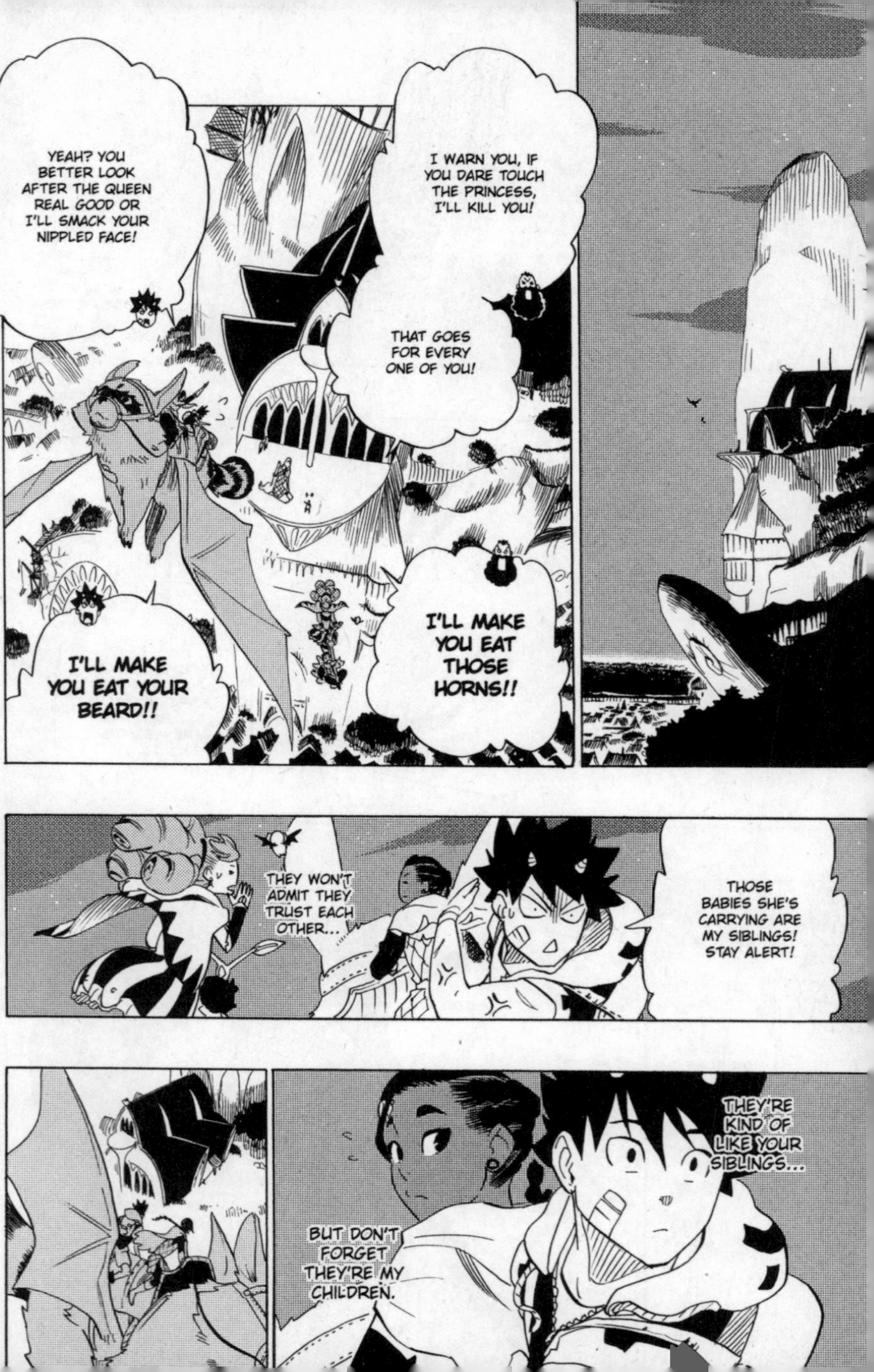
I WARN YOU, IF YOU DARE TOUCH THE PRINCESS, I'LL KILL YOU!
YEAH? YOU BETTER LOOK AFTER THE QUEEN REAL GOOD OR I'LL SMACK YOUR NIPPLED FACE!
THAT GOES FOR EVERY ONE OF YOU!
I'LL MAKE YOU EAT THOSE HORNS!!
I'LL MAKE YOU EAT YOUR BEARD!!
THOSE BABIES SHE'S CARRYING ARE MY SIBLINGS! STAY ALERT!
THEY WON'T ADMIT THEY TRUST EACH OTHER...
THEY'RE KIND OF LIKE YOUR SIBLINGS...
BUT DON'T FORGET THEY'RE MY CHILDREN.

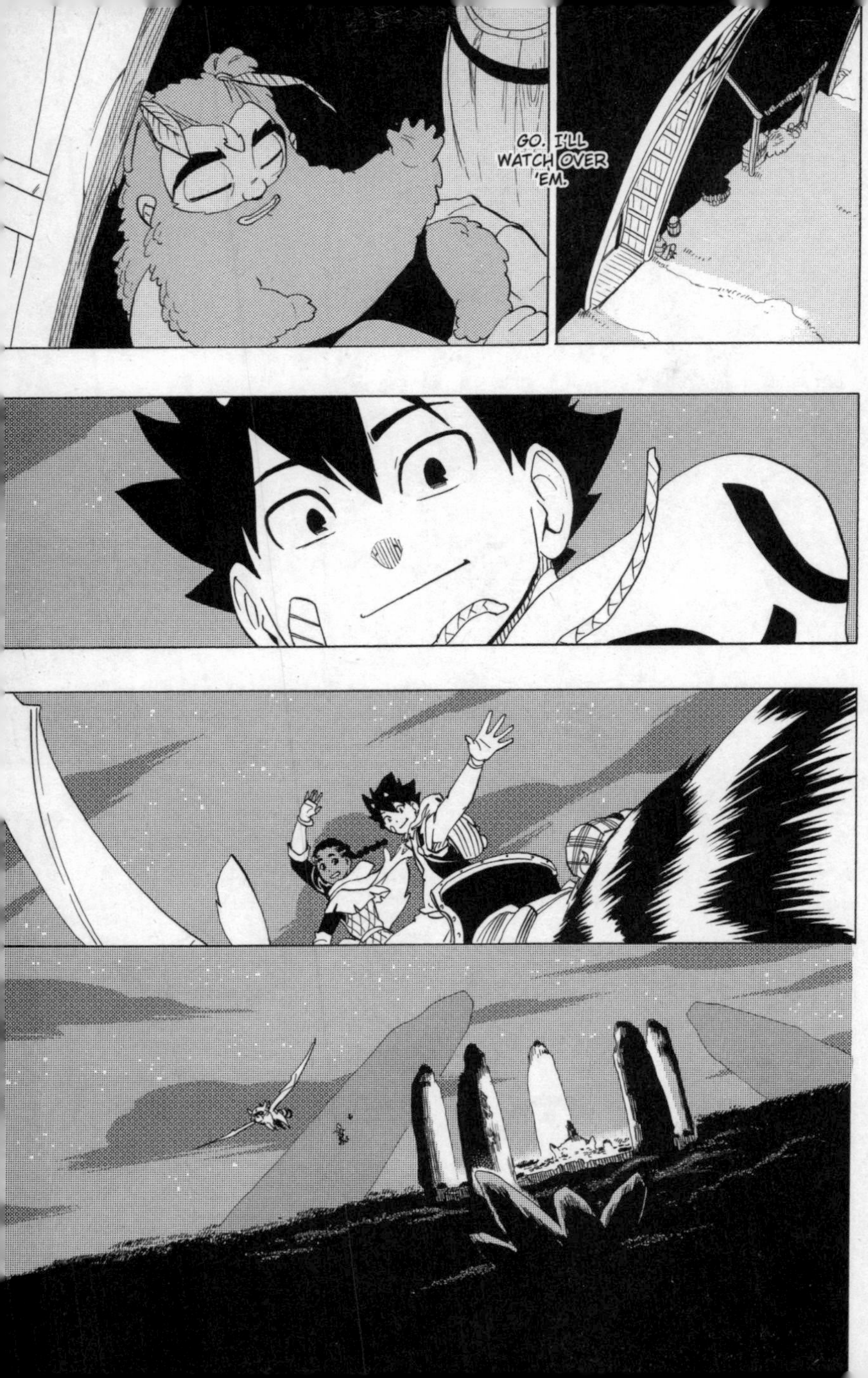
GO. I'LL WATCH OVER 'EM.

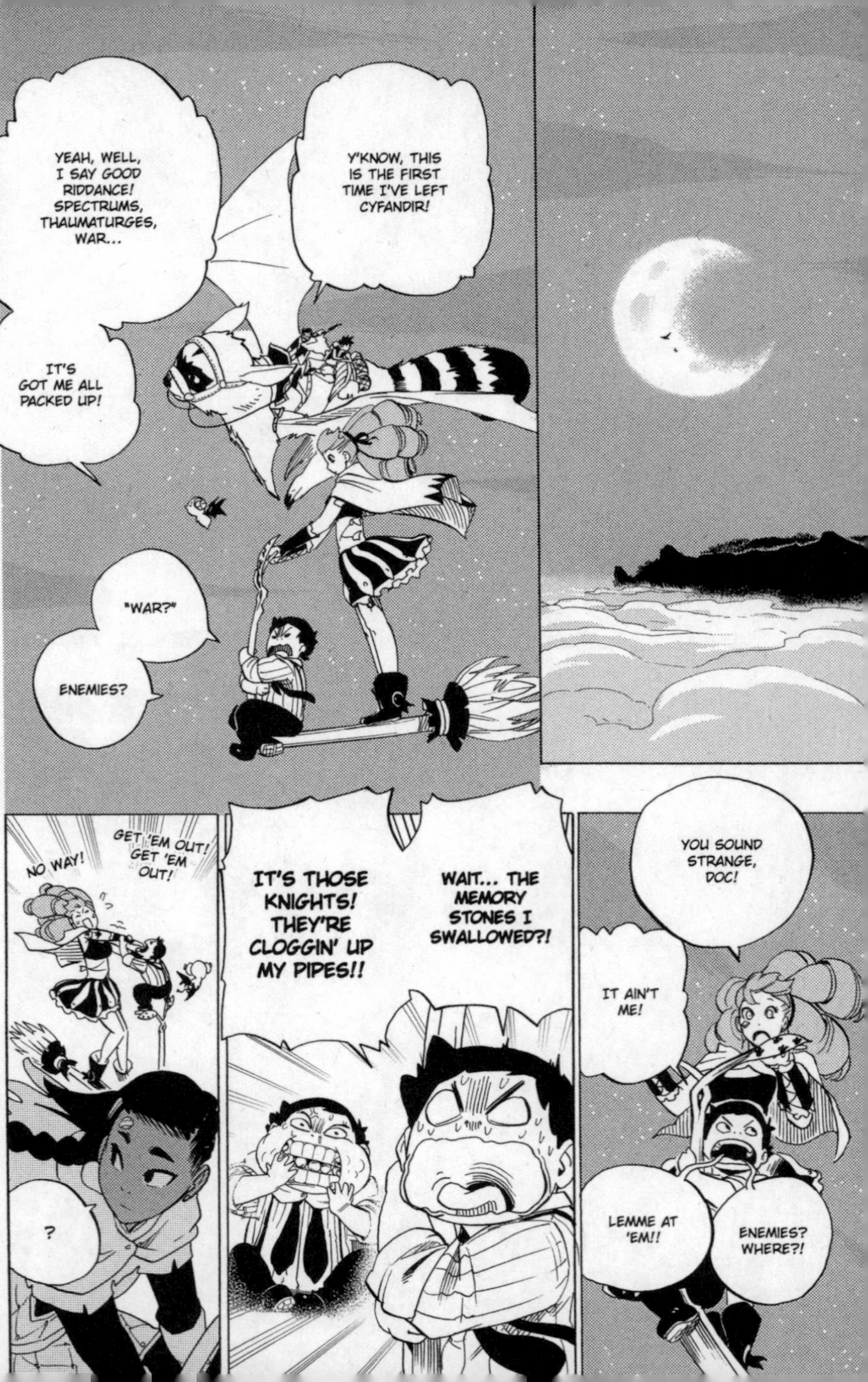
Y'KNOW, THIS IS THE FIRST TIME I'VE LEFT CYFANDIR!
YEAH, WELL, I SAY GOOD RIDDANCE! SPECTRUMS, THAUMATURGES, WAR...
IT'S GOT ME ALL PACKED UP!
"WAR?"
ENEMIES?
YOU SOUND STRANGE, DOC!
IT AIN'T ME!
ENEMIES? WHERE?!
LEMME AT 'EM!!
WAIT... THE MEMORY STONES I SWALLOWED?!
IT'S THOSE KNIGHTS! THEY'RE CLOGGIN' UP MY PIPES!!
GET 'EM OUT! GET 'EM OUT!
NO WAY!
?

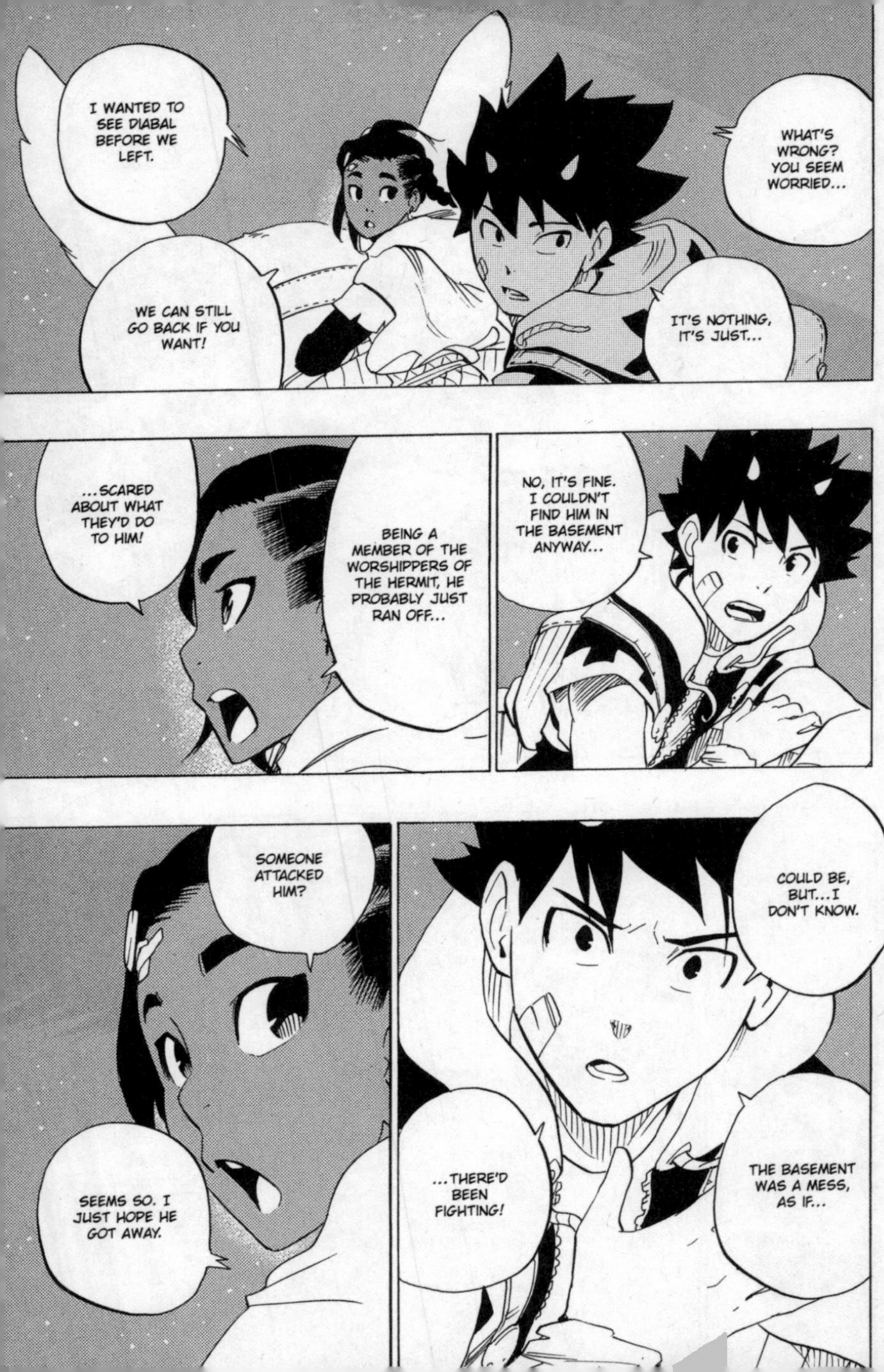

WHAT'S WRONG? YOU SEEM WORRIED...
IT'S NOTHING, IT'S JUST...
I WANTED TO SEE DIABAL BEFORE WE LEFT.
WE CAN STILL GO BACK IF YOU WANT!
NO, IT'S FINE. I COULDN'T FIND HIM IN THE BASEMENT ANYWAY...
BEING A MEMBER OF THE WORSHIPPERS OF THE HERMIT, HE PROBABLY JUST RAN OFF...
...SCARED ABOUT WHAT THEY'D DO TO HIM!
COULD BE, BUT...I DON'T KNOW.
THE BASEMENT WAS A MESS, AS IF...
...THERE'D BEEN FIGHTING!
SOMEONE ATTACKED HIM?
SEEMS SO. I JUST HOPE HE GOT AWAY.

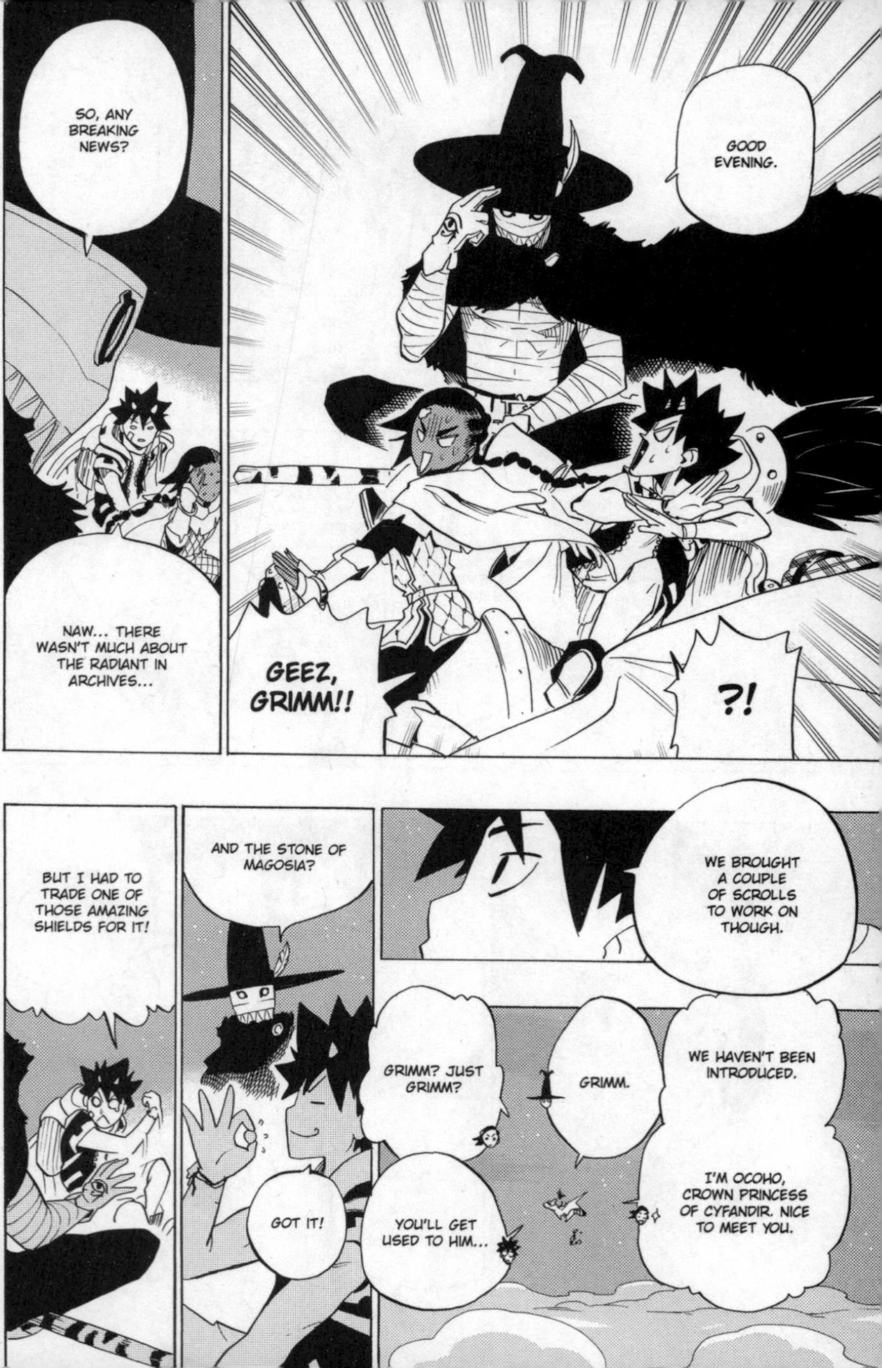
GOOD EVENING.
?!
GEEZ, GRIMM!!
SO, ANY BREAKING NEWS?
NAW... THERE WASN'T MUCH ABOUT THE RADIANT IN ARCHIVES...
WE BROUGHT A COUPLE OF SCROLLS TO WORK ON THOUGH.
WE HAVEN'T BEEN INTRODUCED.
I'M OCOHO, CROWN PRINCESS OF CYFANDIR. NICE TO MEET YOU.
GRIMM.
GRIMM? JUST GRIMM?
YOU'LL GET USED TO HIM...
GOT IT!
AND THE STONE OF MAGOSIA?
BUT I HAD TO TRADE ONE OF THOSE AMAZING SHIELDS FOR IT!

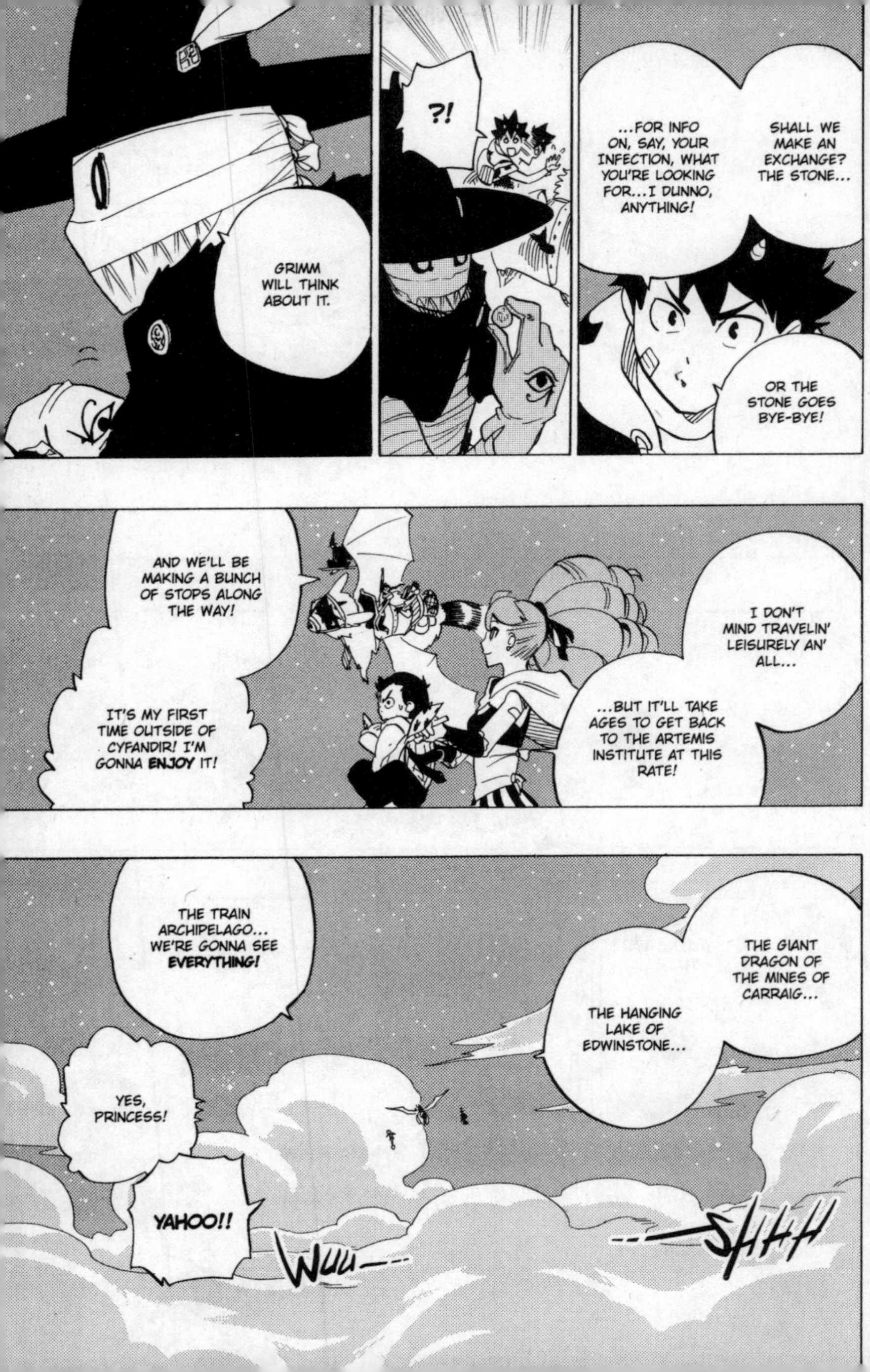
SHALL WE MAKE AN EXCHANGE? THE STONE...
...FOR INFO ON, SAY, YOUR INFECTION, WHAT YOU'RE LOOKING FOR...I DUNNO, ANYTHING!
OR THE STONE GOES BYE-BYE!
?!
GRIMM WILL THINK ABOUT IT.
I DON'T MIND TRAVELIN' LEISURELY AN' ALL...
...BUT IT'LL TAKE AGES TO GET BACK TO THE ARTEMIS INSTITUTE AT THIS RATE!
AND WE'LL BE MAKING A BUNCH OF STOPS ALONG THE WAY!
IT'S MY FIRST TIME OUTSIDE OF CYFANDIR! I'M GONNA **ENJOY** IT!
THE GIANT DRAGON OF THE MINES OF CARRAIG...
THE HANGING LAKE OF EDWINSTONE...
THE TRAIN ARCHIPELAGO... WE'RE GONNA SEE **EVERYTHING!**
YES, PRINCESS!
YAHOO!!
--SHHH
WUU---

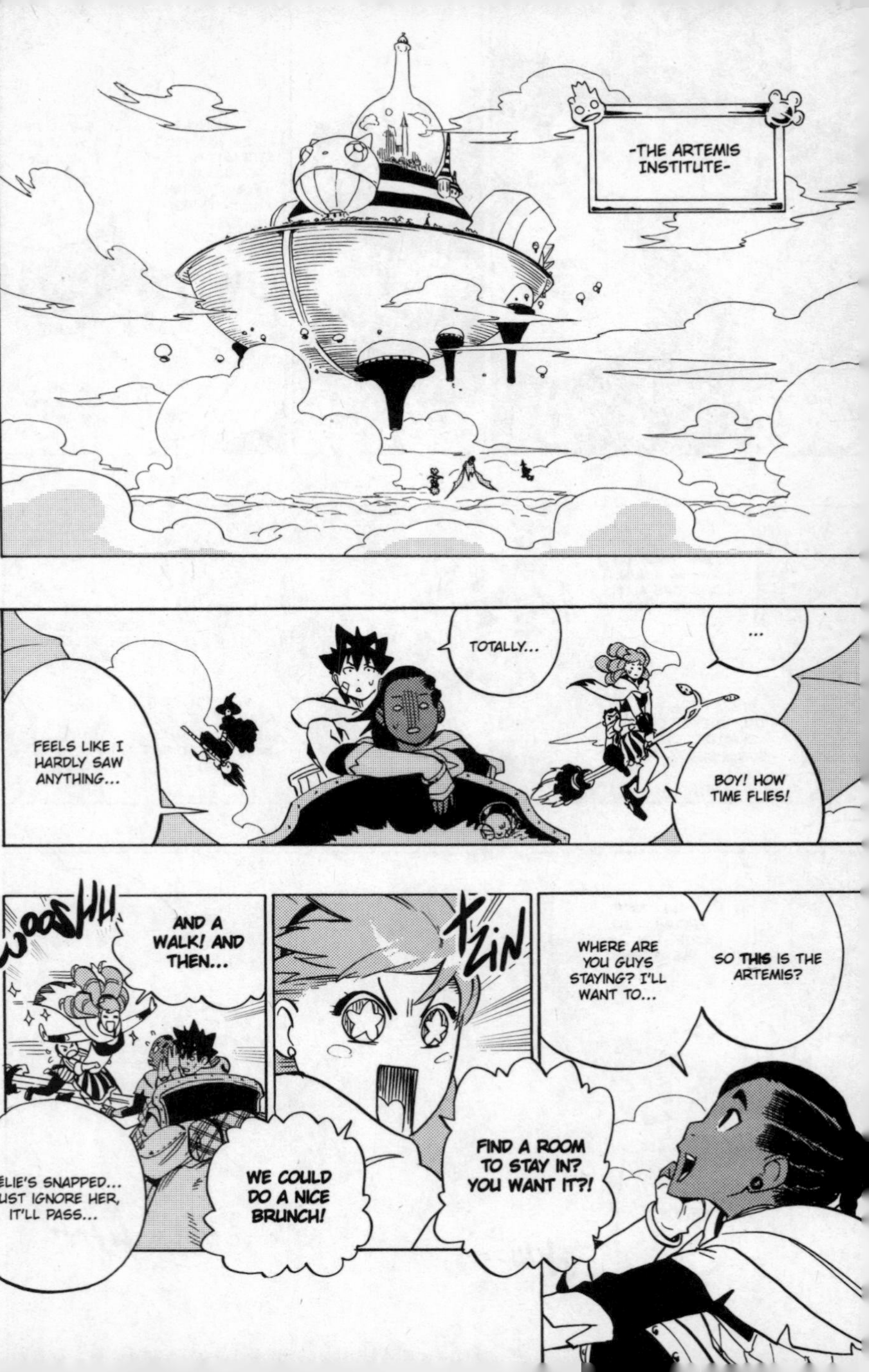
-THE ARTEMIS INSTITUTE-
...
BOY! HOW TIME FLIES!
TOTALLY...
FEELS LIKE I HARDLY SAW ANYTHING...
SO THIS IS THE ARTEMIS?
WHERE ARE YOU GUYS STAYING? I'LL WANT TO...
FIND A ROOM TO STAY IN? YOU WANT IT?!
TZIN
WE COULD DO A NICE BRUNCH!
WOOSHH
AND A WALK! AND THEN...
MÉLIE'S SNAPPED... JUST IGNORE HER, IT'LL PASS...

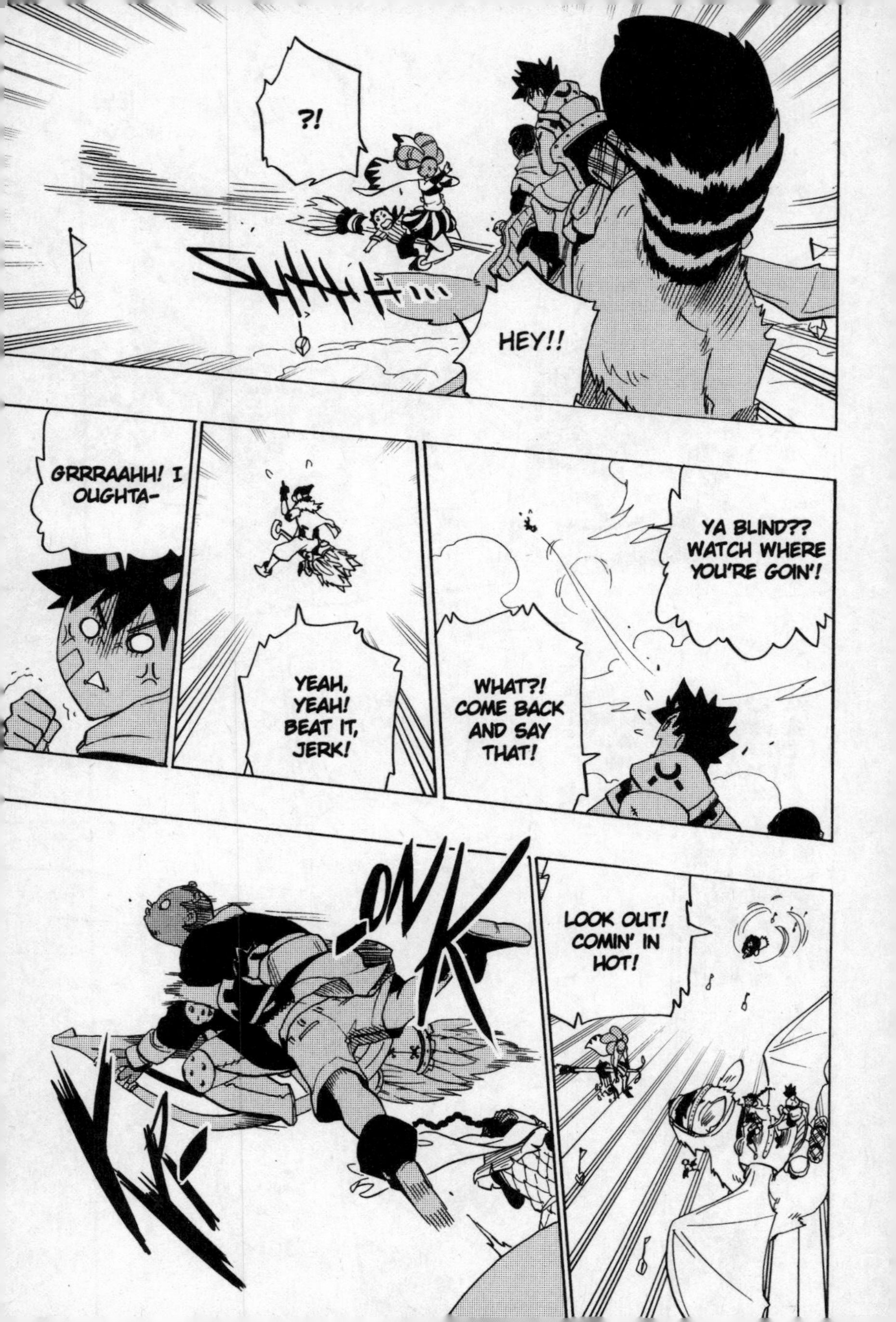
?!
HEY!!
YA BLIND?? WATCH WHERE YOU'RE GOIN'!
WHAT?! COME BACK AND SAY THAT!
YEAH, YEAH! BEAT IT, JERK!
GRRRAAHH! I OUGHTA-
LOOK OUT! COMIN' IN HOT!

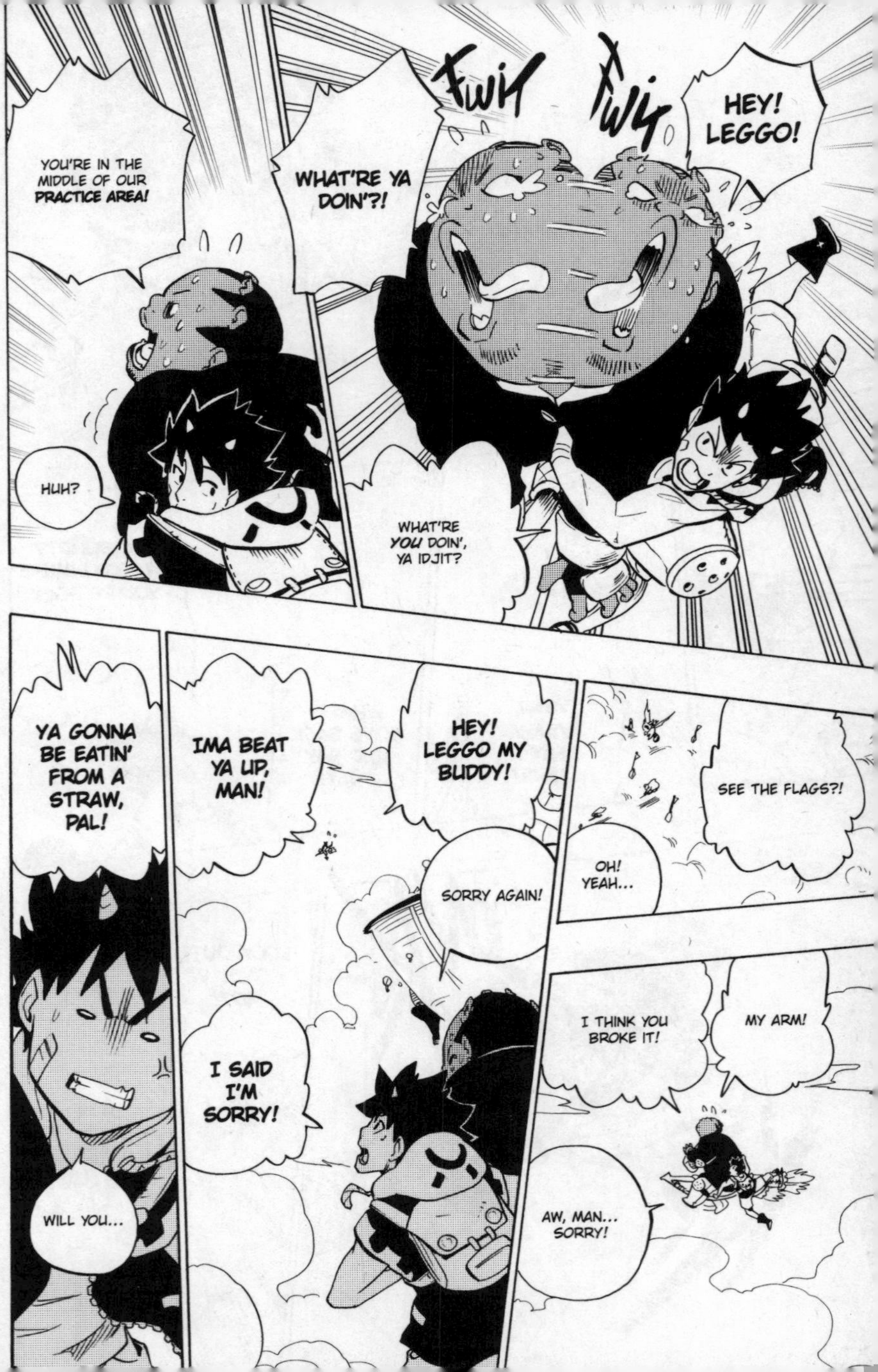
FWIP FWIP
HEY! LEGGO!
WHAT'RE YA DOIN'?!
WHAT'RE *YOU* DOIN', YA IDJIT?
YOU'RE IN THE MIDDLE OF OUR **PRACTICE AREA!**
HUH?
SEE THE FLAGS?!
OH! YEAH...
MY ARM!
I THINK YOU BROKE IT!
AW, MAN... SORRY!
HEY! LEGGO MY BUDDY!
IMA BEAT YA UP, MAN!
SORRY AGAIN!
I SAID I'M SORRY!
YA GONNA BE EATIN' FROM A STRAW, PAL!
WILL YOU...

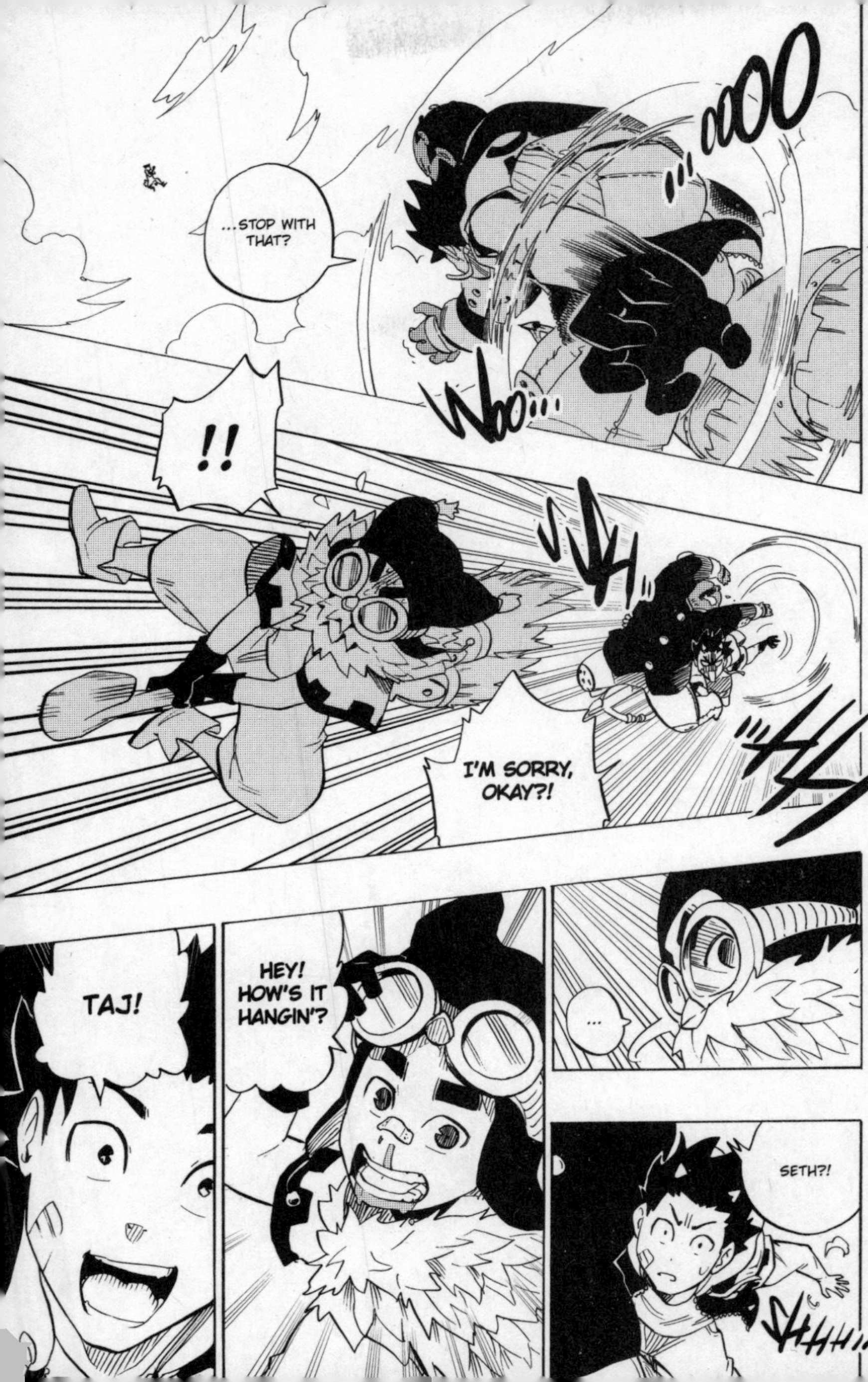
...STOP WITH THAT?
WOO...
!!
I'M SORRY, OKAY?!
...
SETH?!
HEY! HOW'S IT HANGIN'?
TAJ!

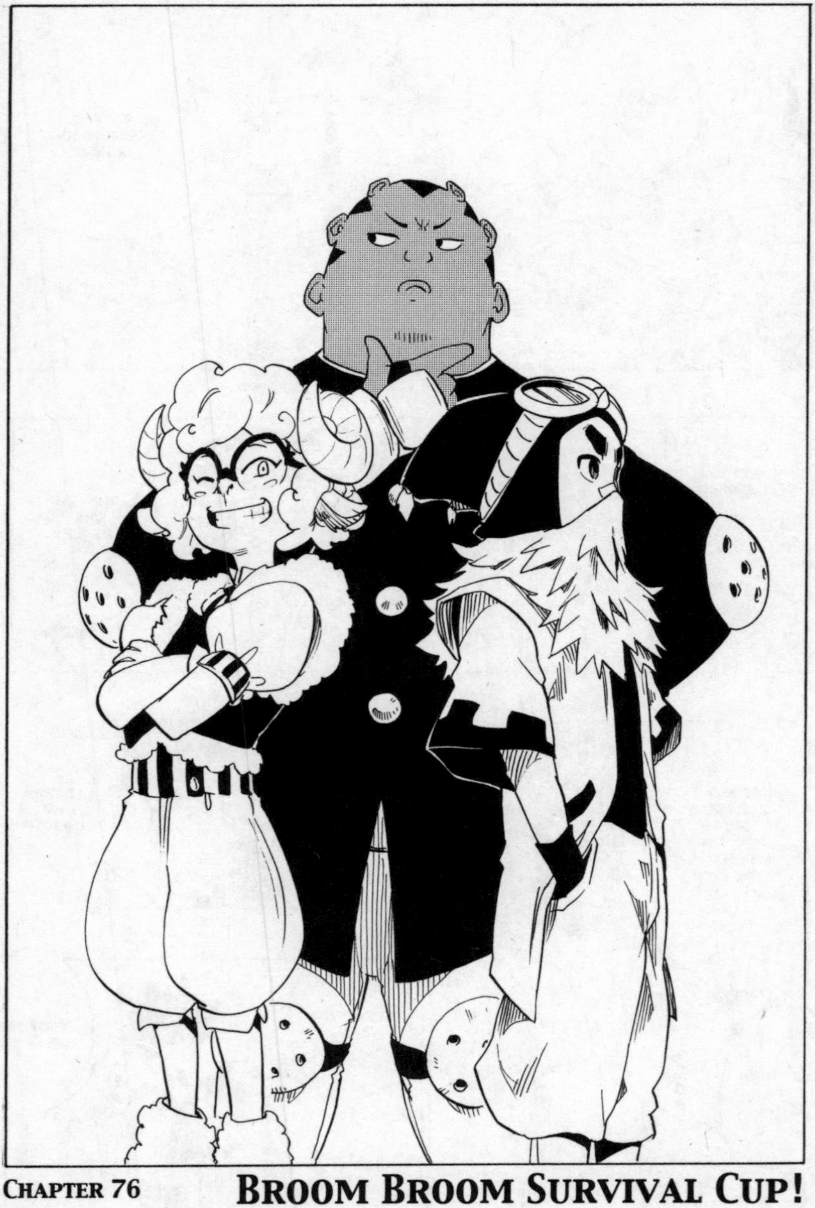

CHAPTER 76

BROOM BROOM SURVIVAL CUP!

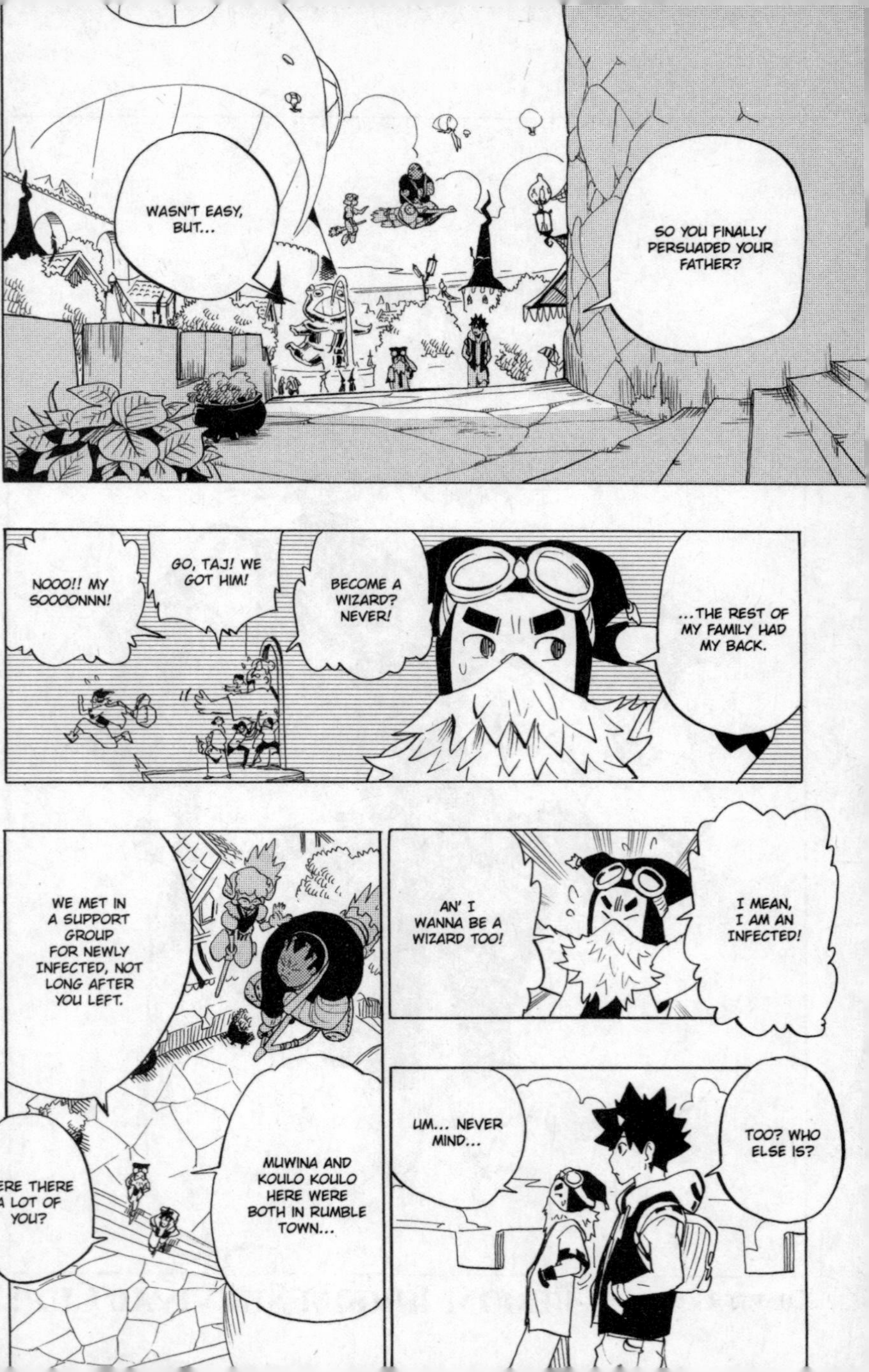
SO YOU FINALLY PERSUADED YOUR FATHER?
WASN'T EASY, BUT...
...THE REST OF MY FAMILY HAD MY BACK.
BECOME A WIZARD? NEVER!
GO, TAJ! WE GOT HIM!
NOOO!! MY SOOOONNN!
I MEAN, I AM AN INFECTED!
AN' I WANNA BE A WIZARD TOO!
TOO? WHO ELSE IS?
UM... NEVER MIND...
WE MET IN A SUPPORT GROUP FOR NEWLY INFECTED, NOT LONG AFTER YOU LEFT.
MUWINA AND KOULO KOULO HERE WERE BOTH IN RUMBLE TOWN...
WERE THERE A LOT OF YOU?

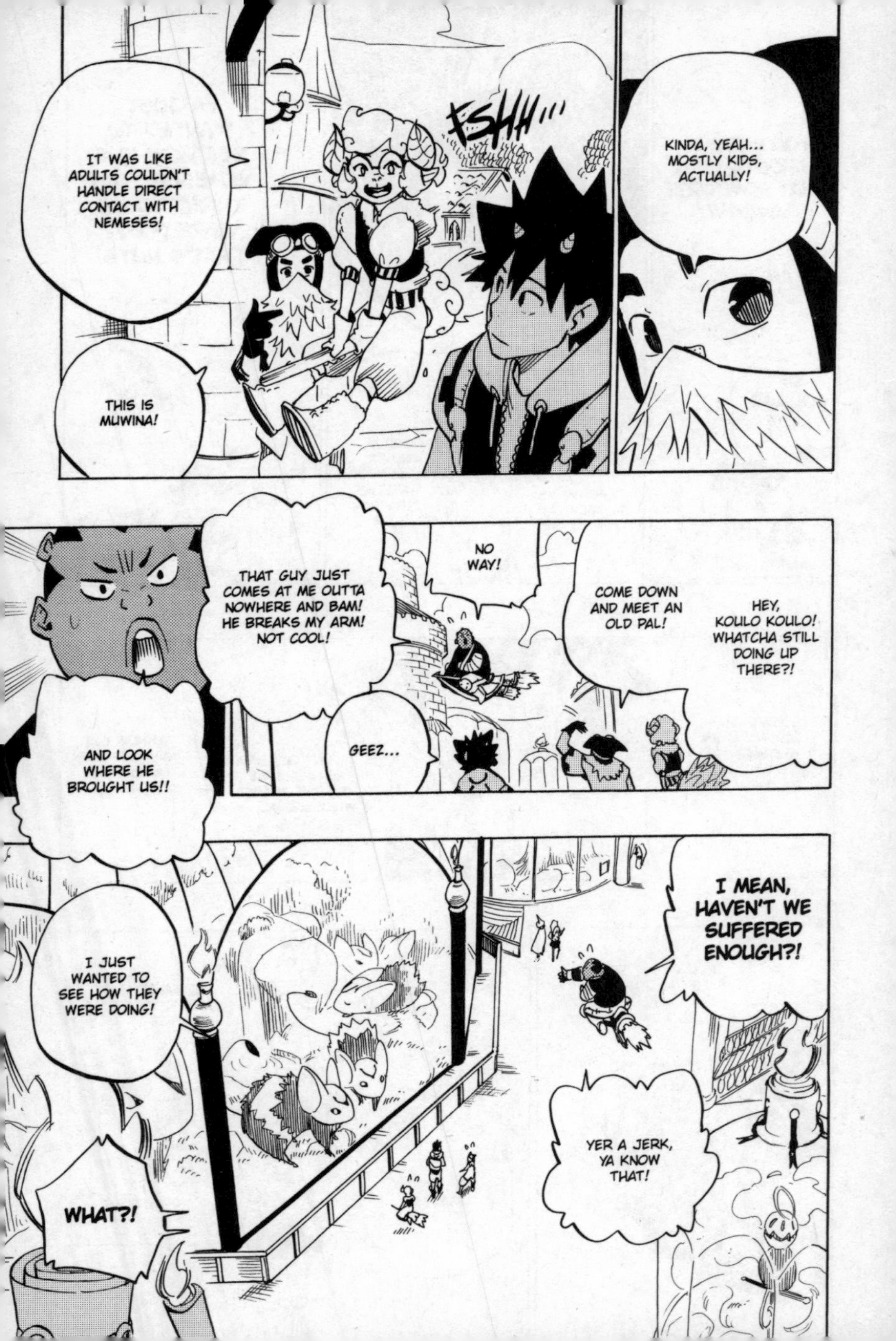
KINDA, YEAH... MOSTLY KIDS, ACTUALLY!
FSHH
IT WAS LIKE ADULTS COULDN'T HANDLE DIRECT CONTACT WITH NEMESES!
THIS IS MUWINA!
HEY, KOULO KOULO! WHATCHA STILL DOING UP THERE?!
COME DOWN AND MEET AN OLD PAL!
NO WAY!
THAT GUY JUST COMES AT ME OUTTA NOWHERE AND BAM! HE BREAKS MY ARM! NOT COOL!
GEEZ...
AND LOOK WHERE HE BROUGHT US!!
I MEAN, HAVEN'T WE SUFFERED ENOUGH?!
YER A JERK, YA KNOW THAT!
I JUST WANTED TO SEE HOW THEY WERE DOING!
WHAT?!

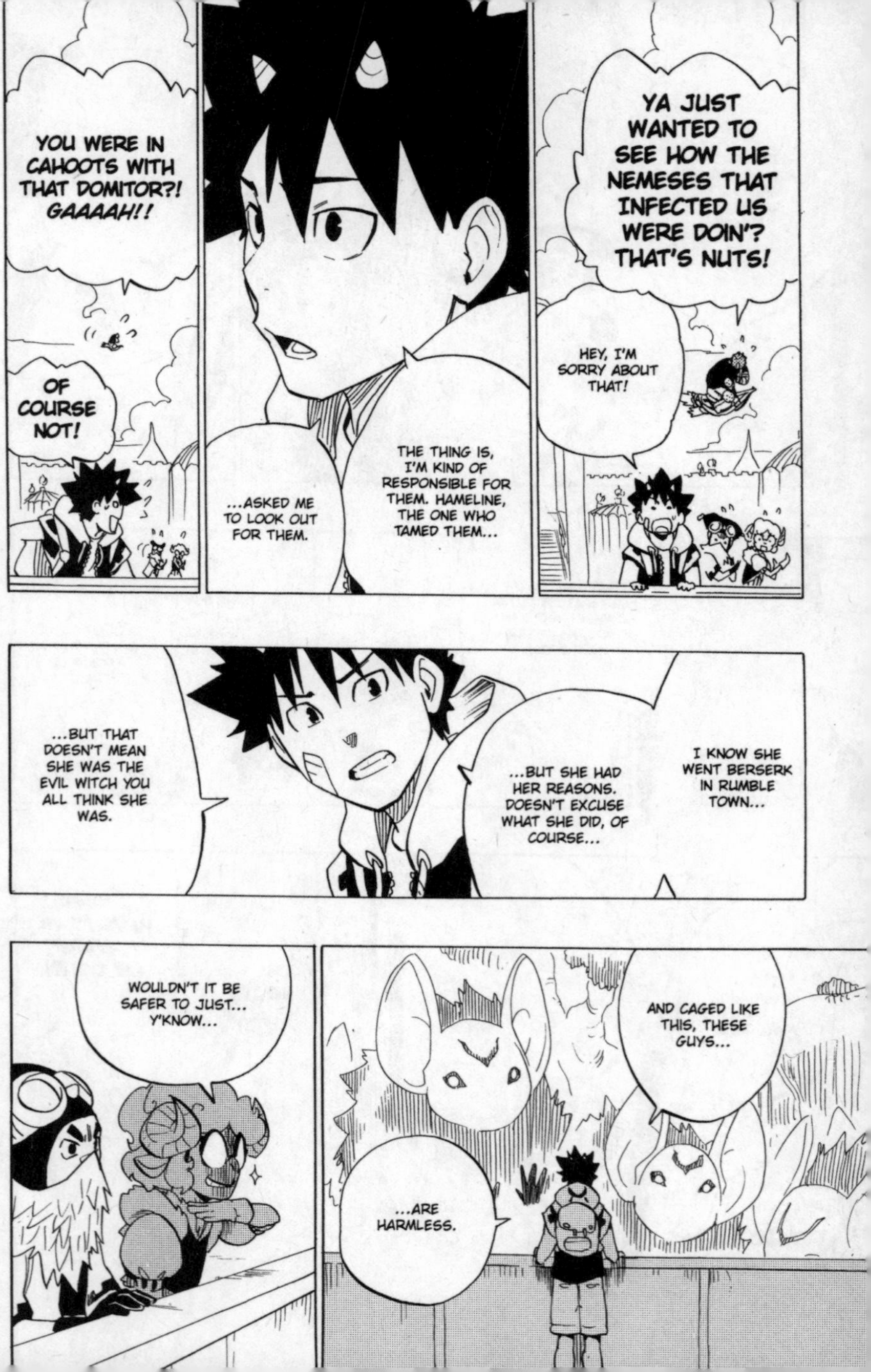
YA JUST WANTED TO SEE HOW THE NEMESES THAT INFECTED US WERE DOIN'? THAT'S NUTS!
HEY, I'M SORRY ABOUT THAT!
THE THING IS, I'M KIND OF RESPONSIBLE FOR THEM. HAMELINE, THE ONE WHO TAMED THEM...
...ASKED ME TO LOOK OUT FOR THEM.
YOU WERE IN CAHOOTS WITH THAT DOMITOR?! GAAAAH!!
OF COURSE NOT!
I KNOW SHE WENT BERSERK IN RUMBLE TOWN...
...BUT SHE HAD HER REASONS. DOESN'T EXCUSE WHAT SHE DID, OF COURSE...
...BUT THAT DOESN'T MEAN SHE WAS THE EVIL WITCH YOU ALL THINK SHE WAS.
AND CAGED LIKE THIS, THESE GUYS...
...ARE HARMLESS.
WOULDN'T IT BE SAFER TO JUST... Y'KNOW...

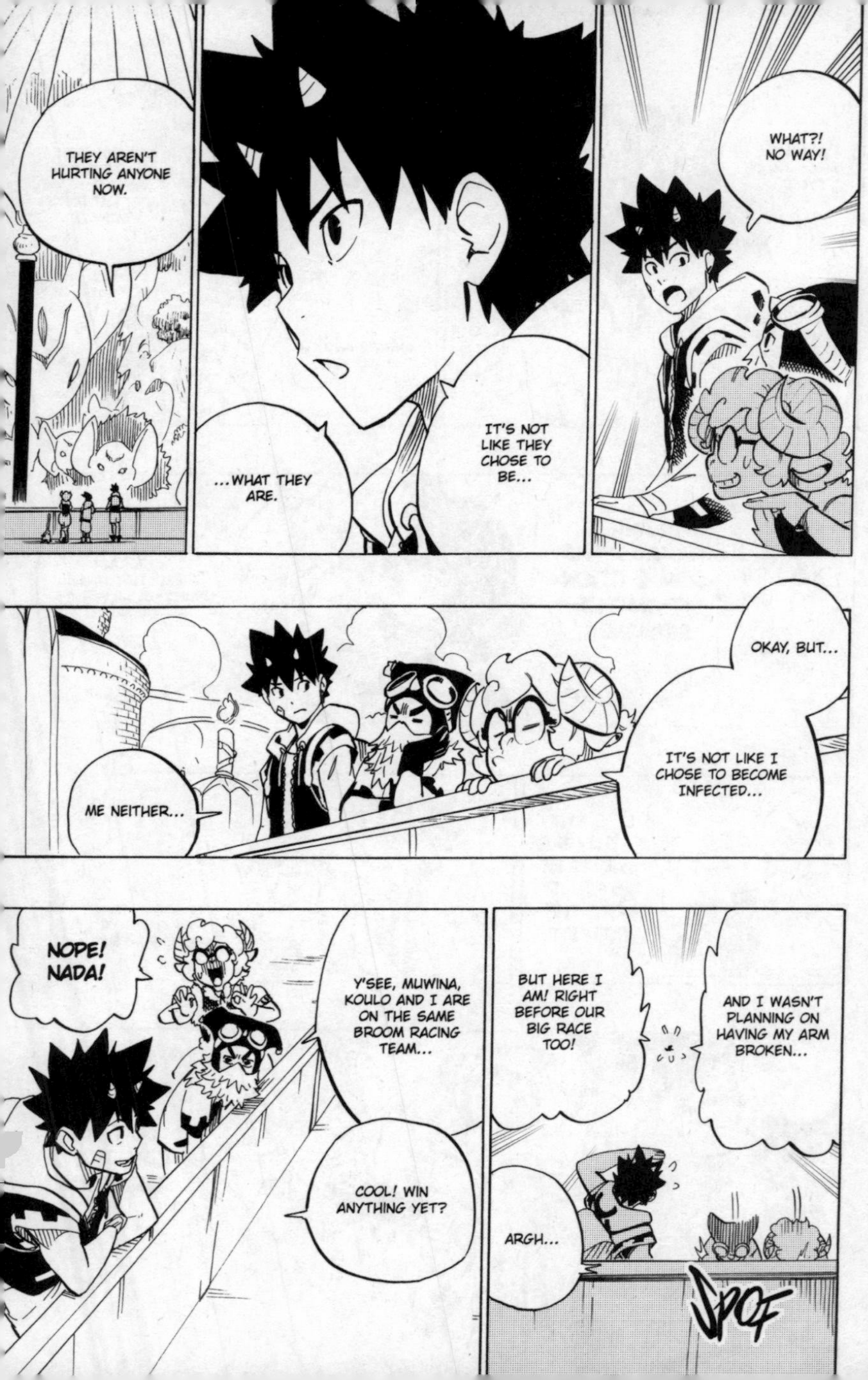
WHAT?! NO WAY!
IT'S NOT LIKE THEY CHOSE TO BE...
...WHAT THEY ARE.
THEY AREN'T HURTING ANYONE NOW.
OKAY, BUT...
IT'S NOT LIKE I CHOSE TO BECOME INFECTED...
ME NEITHER...
AND I WASN'T PLANNING ON HAVING MY ARM BROKEN...
BUT HERE I AM! RIGHT BEFORE OUR BIG RACE TOO!
ARGH...
SPOF
Y'SEE, MUWINA, KOULO AND I ARE ON THE SAME BROOM RACING TEAM...
COOL! WIN ANYTHING YET?
NOPE! NADA!

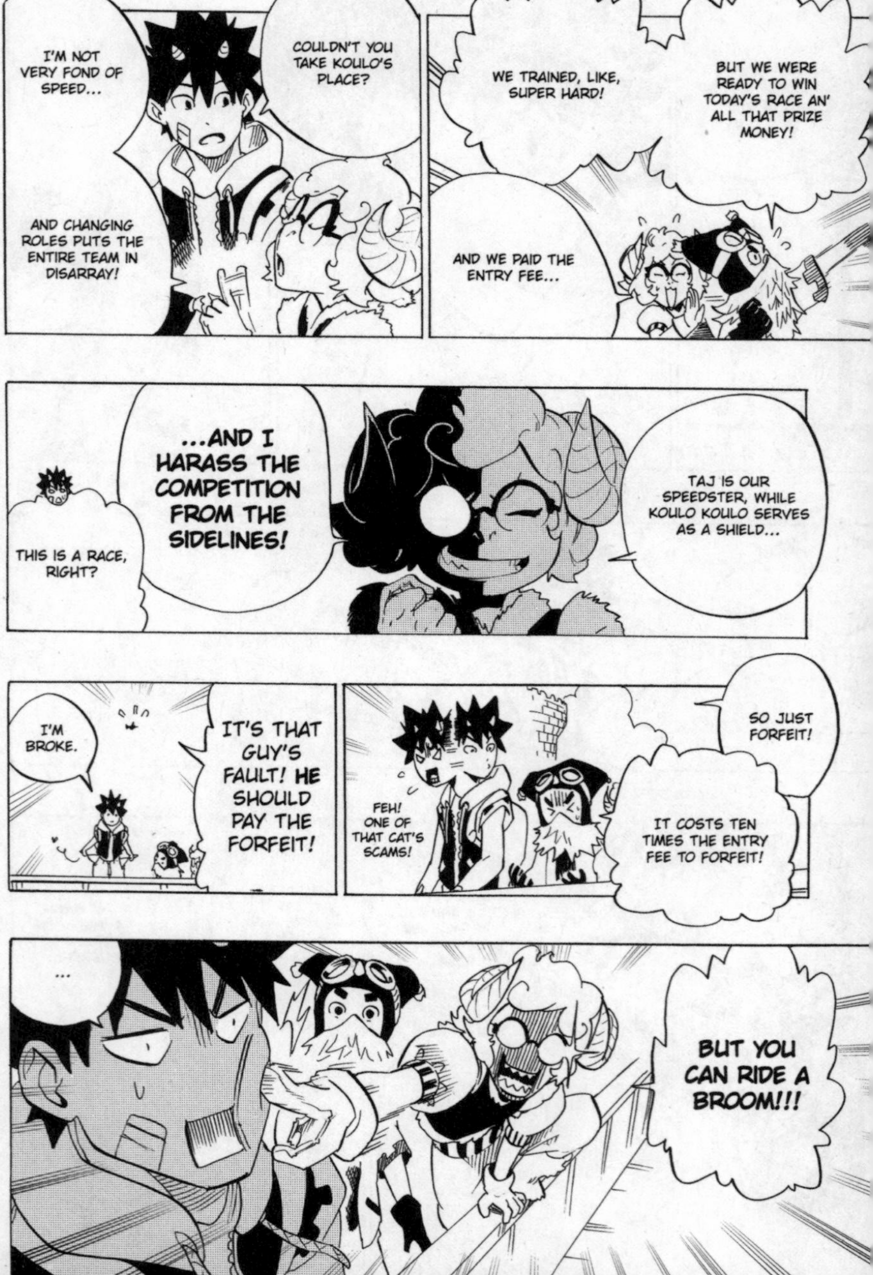
BUT WE WERE READY TO WIN TODAY'S RACE AN' ALL THAT PRIZE MONEY!
WE TRAINED, LIKE, SUPER HARD!
AND WE PAID THE ENTRY FEE...
COULDN'T YOU TAKE KOULO'S PLACE?
I'M NOT VERY FOND OF SPEED...
AND CHANGING ROLES PUTS THE ENTIRE TEAM IN DISARRAY!
TAJ IS OUR SPEEDSTER, WHILE KOULO KOULO SERVES AS A SHIELD...
...AND I HARASS THE COMPETITION FROM THE SIDELINES!
THIS IS A RACE, RIGHT?
SO JUST FORFEIT!
IT COSTS TEN TIMES THE ENTRY FEE TO FORFEIT!
FEH! ONE OF THAT CAT'S SCAMS!
IT'S THAT GUY'S FAULT! HE SHOULD PAY THE FORFEIT!
I'M BROKE.
BUT YOU CAN RIDE A BROOM!!!
...

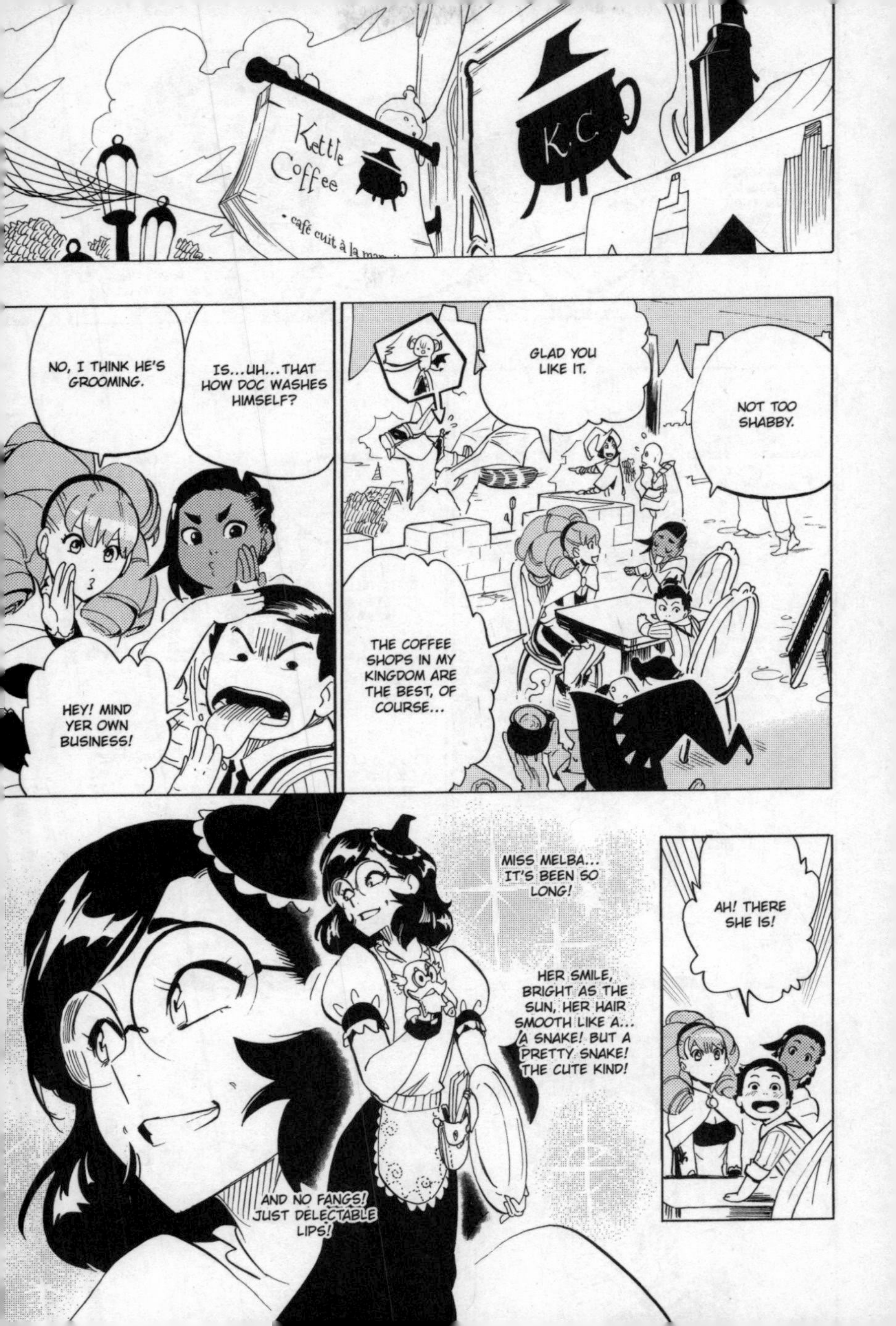
Kettle Coffee
K.C.
THE COFFEE SHOPS IN MY KINGDOM ARE THE BEST, OF COURSE...
NOT TOO SHABBY.
GLAD YOU LIKE IT.
IS...UH...THAT HOW DOC WASHES HIMSELF?
NO, I THINK HE'S GROOMING.
HEY! MIND YER OWN BUSINESS!
AH! THERE SHE IS!
MISS MELBA... IT'S BEEN SO LONG!
HER SMILE, BRIGHT AS THE SUN, HER HAIR SMOOTH LIKE A... A SNAKE! BUT A PRETTY SNAKE! THE CUTE KIND!
AND NO FANGS! JUST DELECTABLE LIPS!

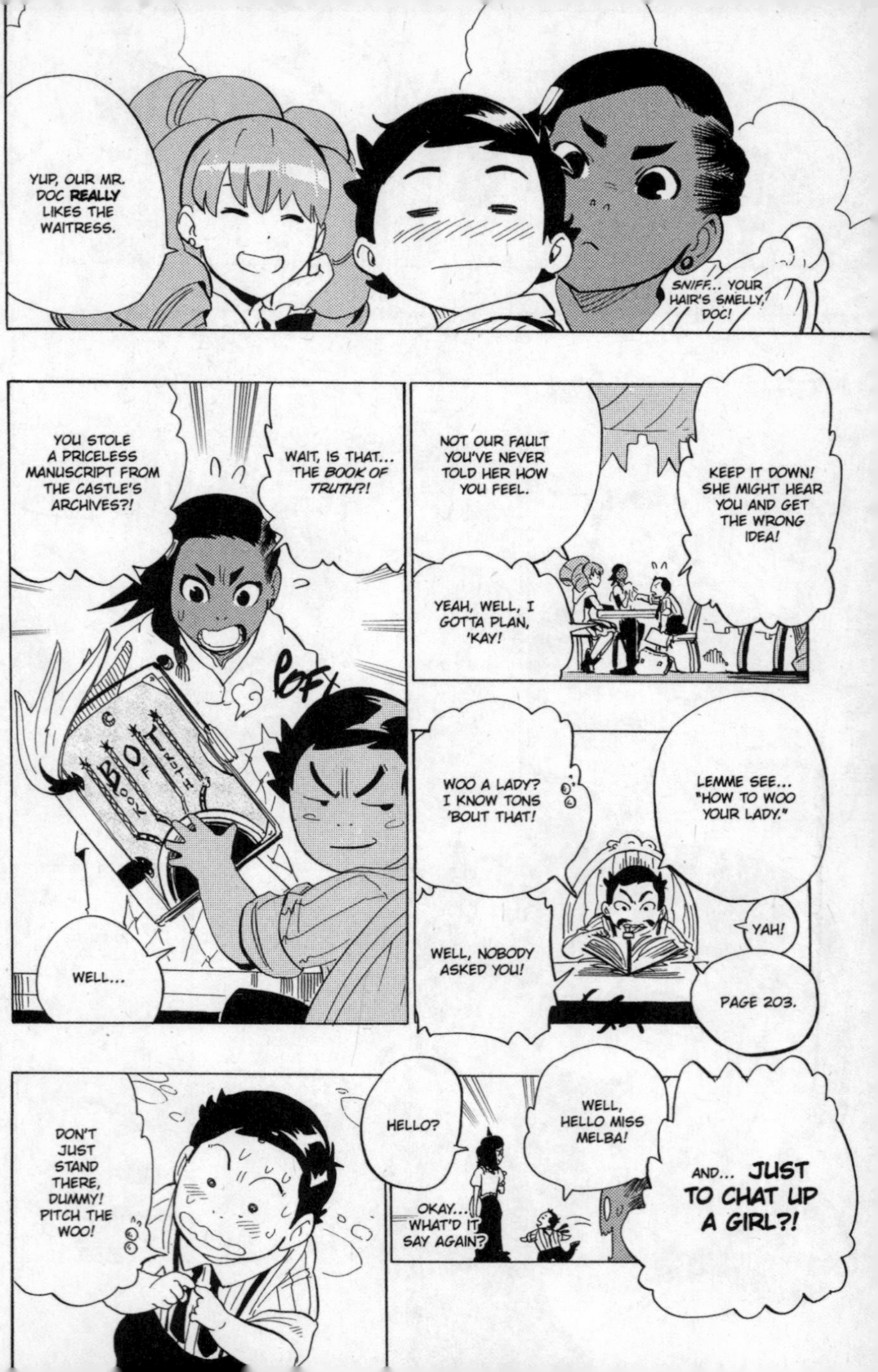
YUP, OUR MR. DOC **REALLY** LIKES THE WAITRESS.
SNIFF... YOUR HAIR'S SMELLY, DOC!
KEEP IT DOWN! SHE MIGHT HEAR YOU AND GET THE WRONG IDEA!
NOT OUR FAULT YOU'VE NEVER TOLD HER HOW YOU FEEL.
YEAH, WELL, I GOTTA PLAN, 'KAY!
LEMME SEE... "HOW TO WOO YOUR LADY."
WOO A LADY? I KNOW TONS 'BOUT THAT!
YAH!
WELL, NOBODY ASKED YOU!
PAGE 203.
WAIT, IS THAT... THE *BOOK OF TRUTH*?!
YOU STOLE A PRICELESS MANUSCRIPT FROM THE CASTLE'S ARCHIVES?!
WELL...
AND... **JUST TO CHAT UP A GIRL?!**
WELL, HELLO MISS MELBA!
HELLO?
OKAY... WHAT'D IT SAY AGAIN?
DON'T JUST STAND THERE, DUMMY! PITCH THE WOO!

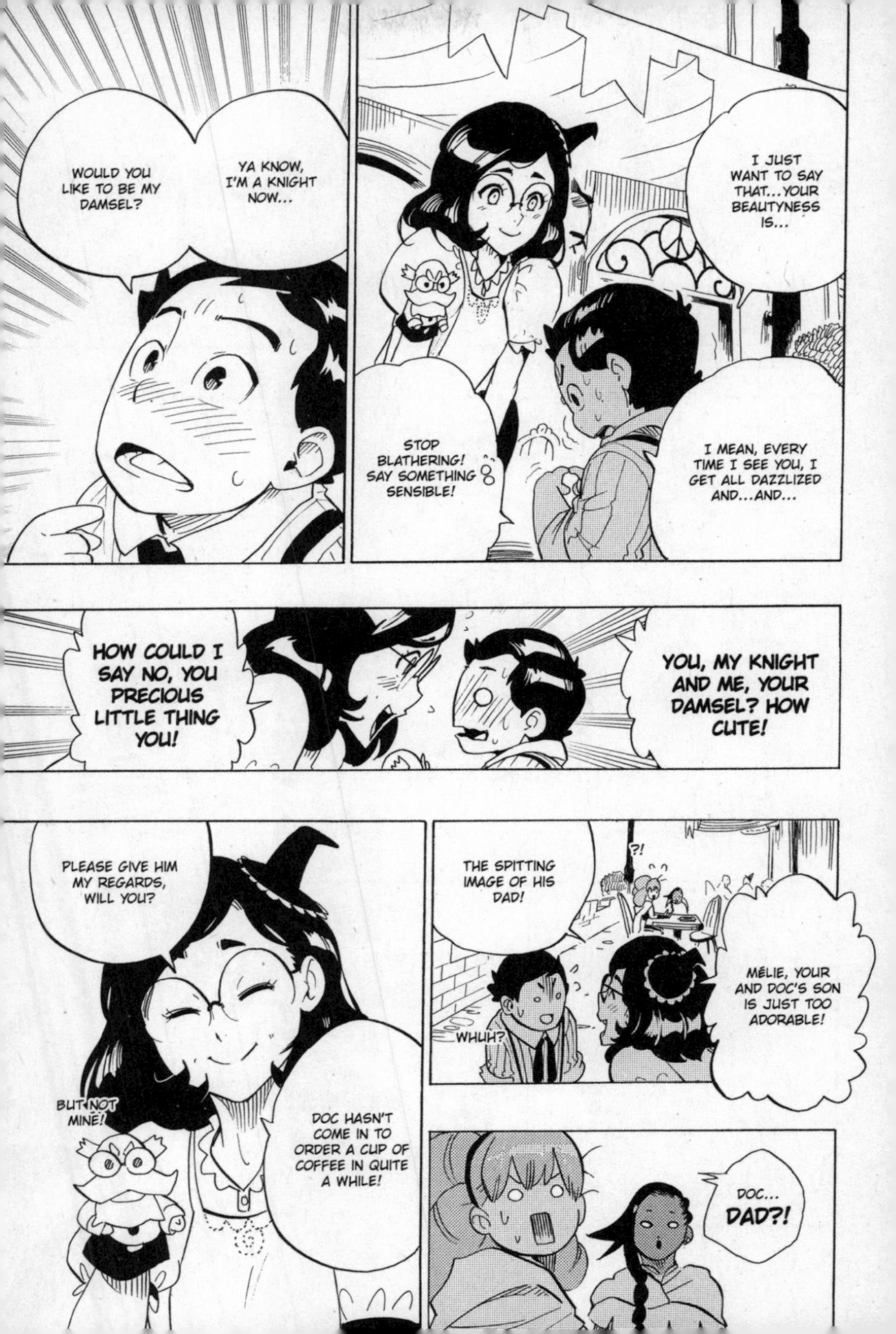
I JUST WANT TO SAY THAT...YOUR BEAUTYNESS IS...
I MEAN, EVERY TIME I SEE YOU, I GET ALL DAZZLIZED AND...AND...
STOP BLATHERING! SAY SOMETHING SENSIBLE!
YA KNOW, I'M A KNIGHT NOW...
WOULD YOU LIKE TO BE MY DAMSEL?
YOU, MY KNIGHT AND ME, YOUR DAMSEL? HOW CUTE!
HOW COULD I SAY NO, YOU PRECIOUS LITTLE THING YOU!
MÉLIE, YOUR AND DOC'S SON IS JUST TOO ADORABLE!
?!
THE SPITTING IMAGE OF HIS DAD!
WHUH?
DOC... DAD?!
PLEASE GIVE HIM MY REGARDS, WILL YOU?
DOC HASN'T COME IN TO ORDER A CUP OF COFFEE IN QUITE A WHILE!
BUT NOT MINE!

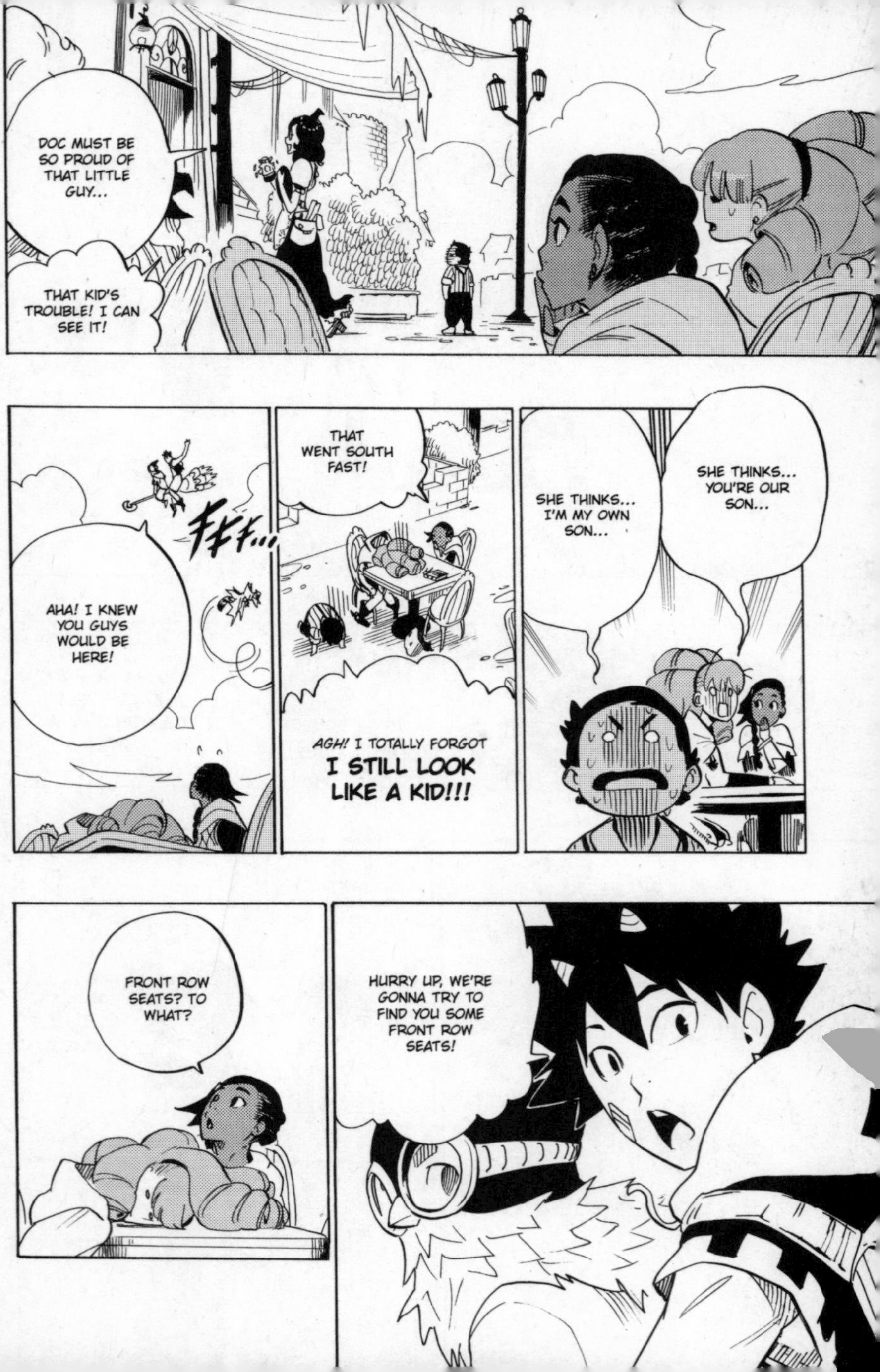
DOC MUST BE SO PROUD OF THAT LITTLE GUY...
THAT KID'S TROUBLE! I CAN SEE IT!
SHE THINKS... YOU'RE OUR SON...
SHE THINKS... I'M MY OWN SON...
THAT WENT SOUTH FAST!
AGH! I TOTALLY FORGOT I STILL LOOK LIKE A KID!!!
FFF...
AHA! I KNEW YOU GUYS WOULD BE HERE!
HURRY UP, WE'RE GONNA TRY TO FIND YOU SOME FRONT ROW SEATS!
FRONT ROW SEATS? TO WHAT?

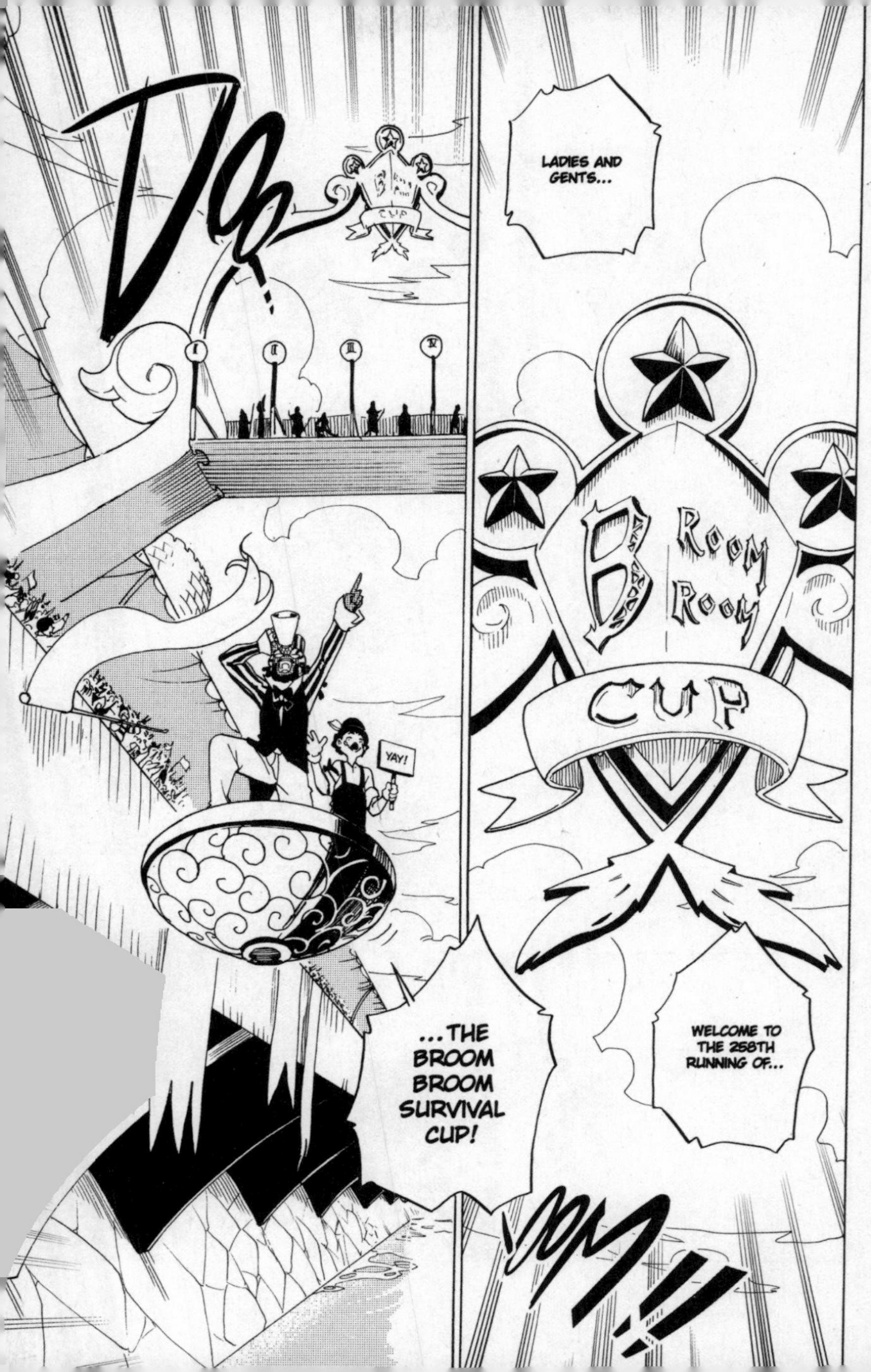
LADIES AND GENTS...
CUP
WELCOME TO THE 258TH RUNNING OF...
YAY!
...THE BROOM BROOM SURVIVAL CUP!

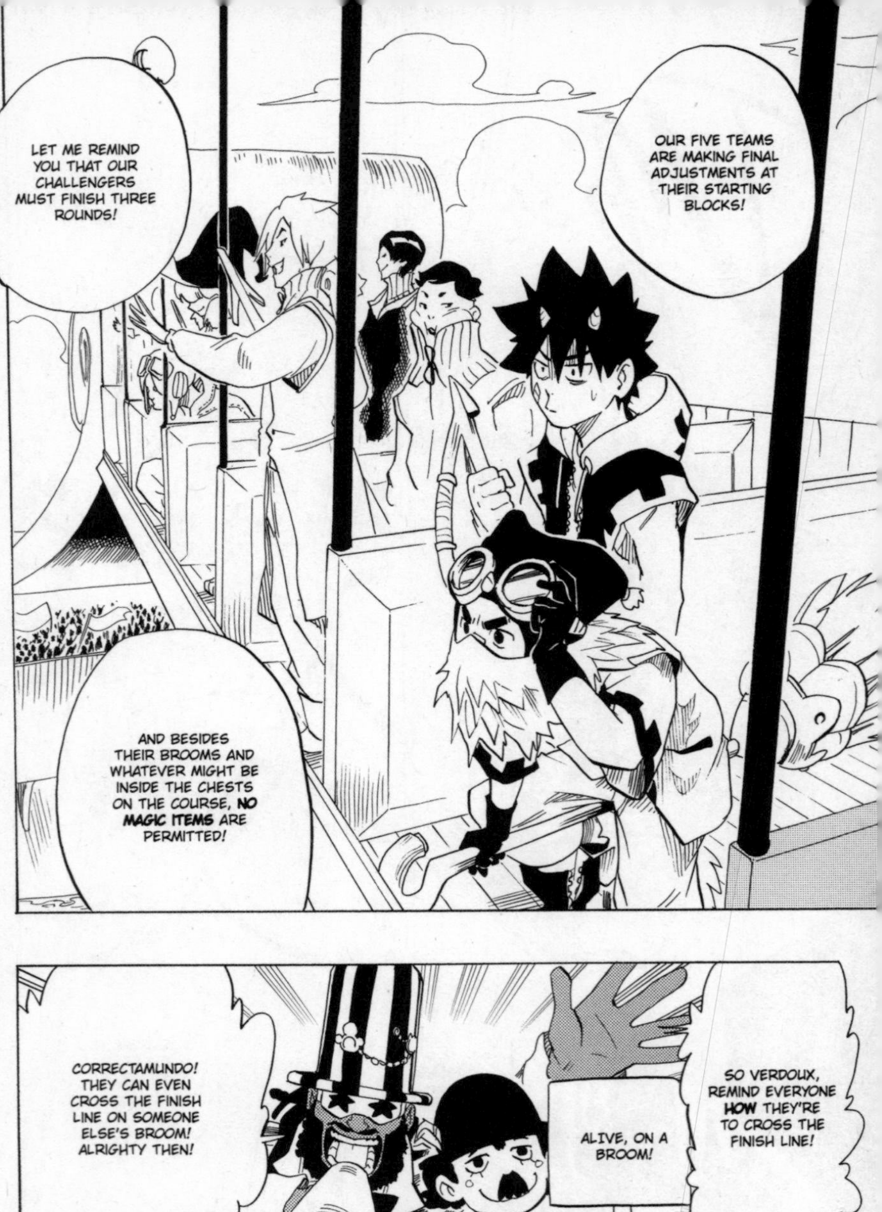
OUR FIVE TEAMS ARE MAKING FINAL ADJUSTMENTS AT THEIR STARTING BLOCKS!
LET ME REMIND YOU THAT OUR CHALLENGERS MUST FINISH THREE ROUNDS!
AND BESIDES THEIR BROOMS AND WHATEVER MIGHT BE INSIDE THE CHESTS ON THE COURSE, NO MAGIC ITEMS ARE PERMITTED!
SO VERDOUX, REMIND EVERYONE HOW THEY'RE TO CROSS THE FINISH LINE!
ALIVE, ON A BROOM!
CORRECTAMUNDO! THEY CAN EVEN CROSS THE FINISH LINE ON SOMEONE ELSE'S BROOM! ALRIGHTY THEN!

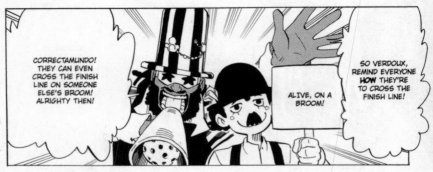

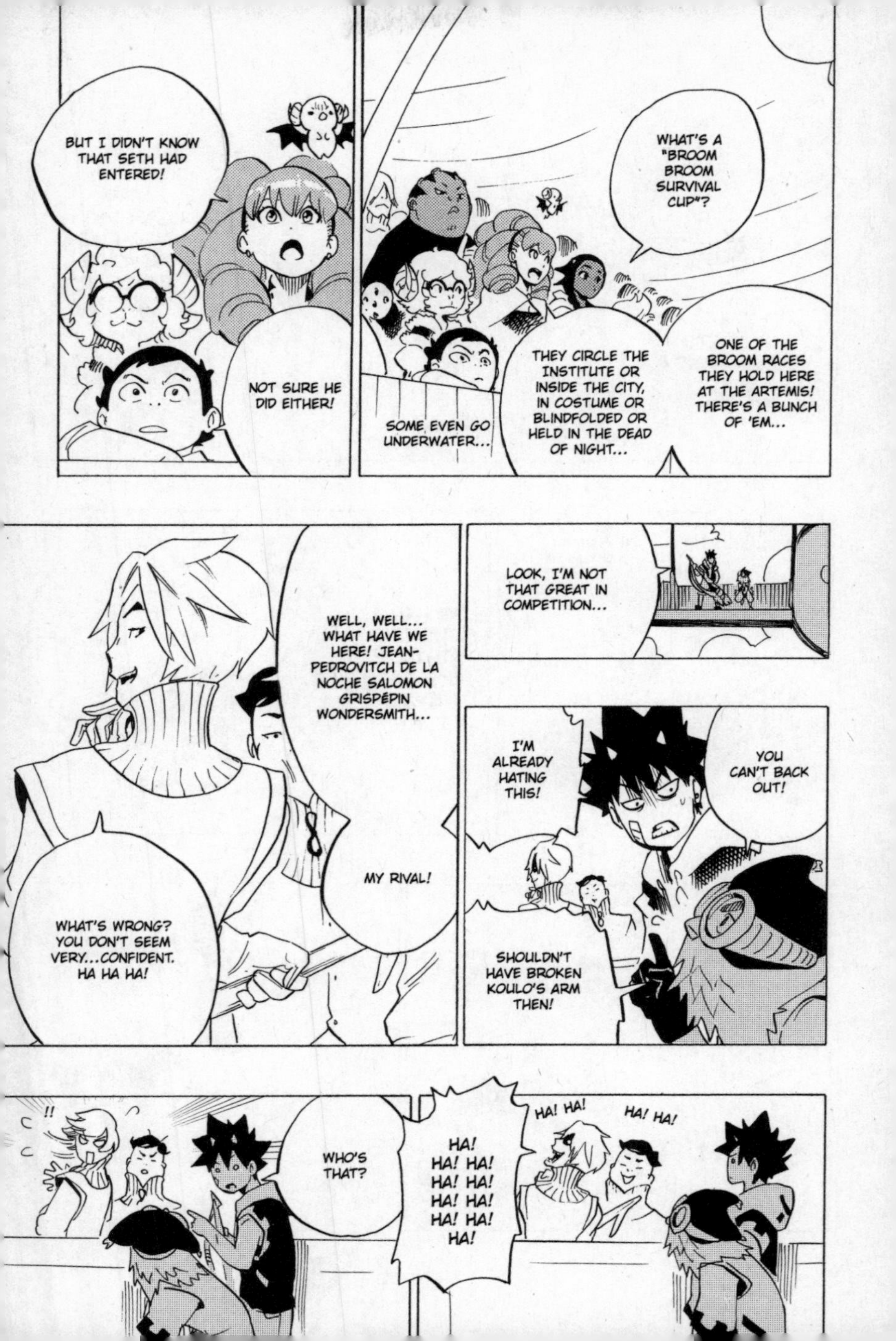
WHAT'S A "BROOM BROOM SURVIVAL CUP"?
ONE OF THE BROOM RACES THEY HOLD HERE AT THE ARTEMIS! THERE'S A BUNCH OF 'EM...
THEY CIRCLE THE INSTITUTE OR INSIDE THE CITY, IN COSTUME OR BLINDFOLDED OR HELD IN THE DEAD OF NIGHT...
SOME EVEN GO UNDERWATER...
BUT I DIDN'T KNOW THAT SETH HAD ENTERED!
NOT SURE HE DID EITHER!
LOOK, I'M NOT THAT GREAT IN COMPETITION...
YOU CAN'T BACK OUT!
I'M ALREADY HATING THIS!
SHOULDN'T HAVE BROKEN KOULO'S ARM THEN!
WELL, WELL... WHAT HAVE WE HERE! JEAN-PEDROVITCH DE LA NOCHE SALOMON GRISPÉPIN WONDERSMITH...
MY RIVAL!
WHAT'S WRONG? YOU DON'T SEEM VERY...CONFIDENT. HA HA HA!
HA! HA!
HA! HA!
HA! HA! HA! HA! HA! HA! HA! HA! HA! HA! HA!
WHO'S THAT?
!!

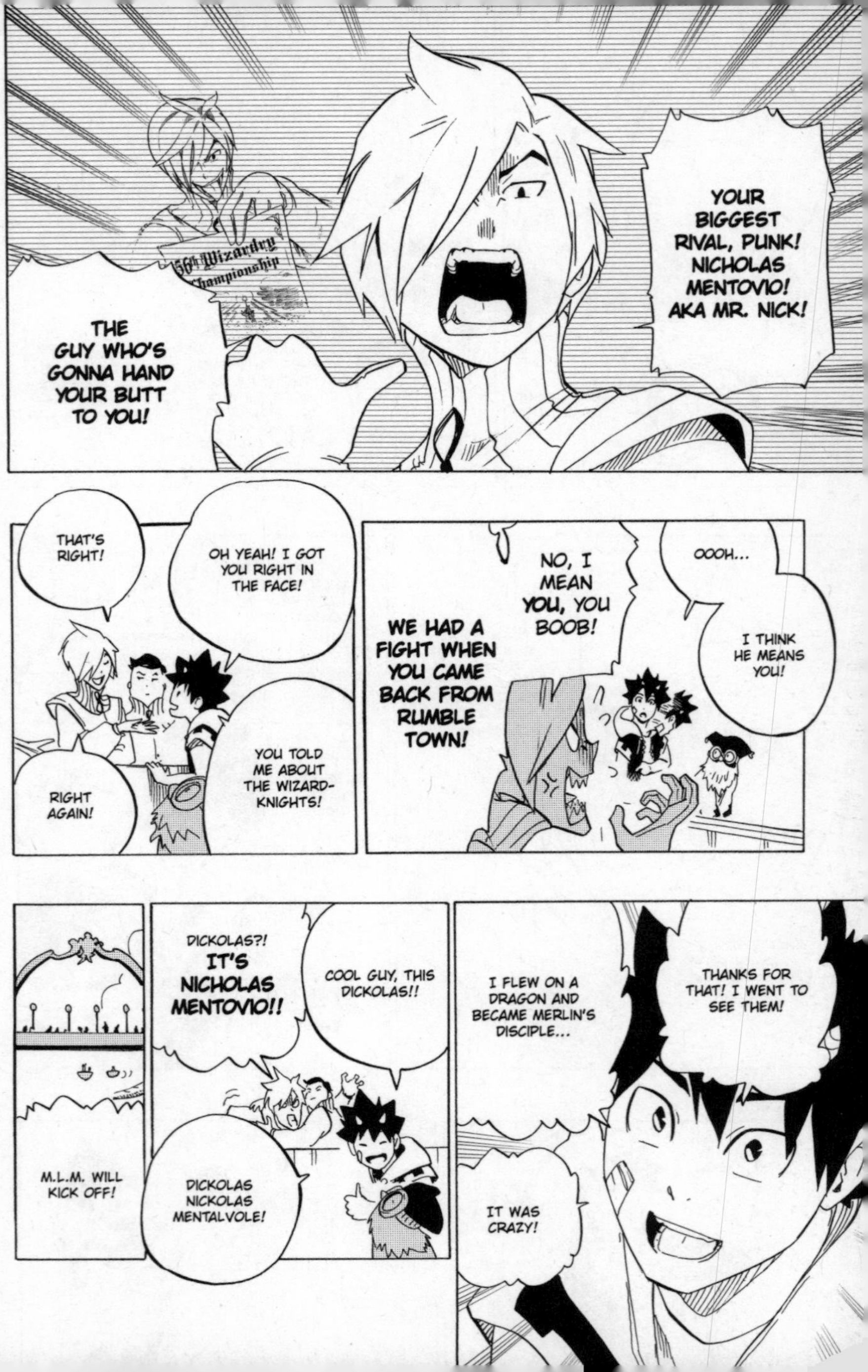
YOUR BIGGEST RIVAL, PUNK! NICHOLAS MENTOVIO! AKA MR. NICK!
56th Wizardry Championship
THE GUY WHO'S GONNA HAND YOUR BUTT TO YOU!
OOOH...
I THINK HE MEANS YOU!
NO, I MEAN YOU, YOU BOOB!
WE HAD A FIGHT WHEN YOU CAME BACK FROM RUMBLE TOWN!
OH YEAH! I GOT YOU RIGHT IN THE FACE!
THAT'S RIGHT!
YOU TOLD ME ABOUT THE WIZARD-KNIGHTS!
RIGHT AGAIN!
THANKS FOR THAT! I WENT TO SEE THEM!
I FLEW ON A DRAGON AND BECAME MERLIN'S DISCIPLE...
IT WAS CRAZY!
COOL GUY, THIS DICKOLAS!!
DICKOLAS?! IT'S NICHOLAS MENTOVIO!!
DICKOLAS NICKOLAS MENTALVOLE!
M.L.M. WILL KICK OFF!

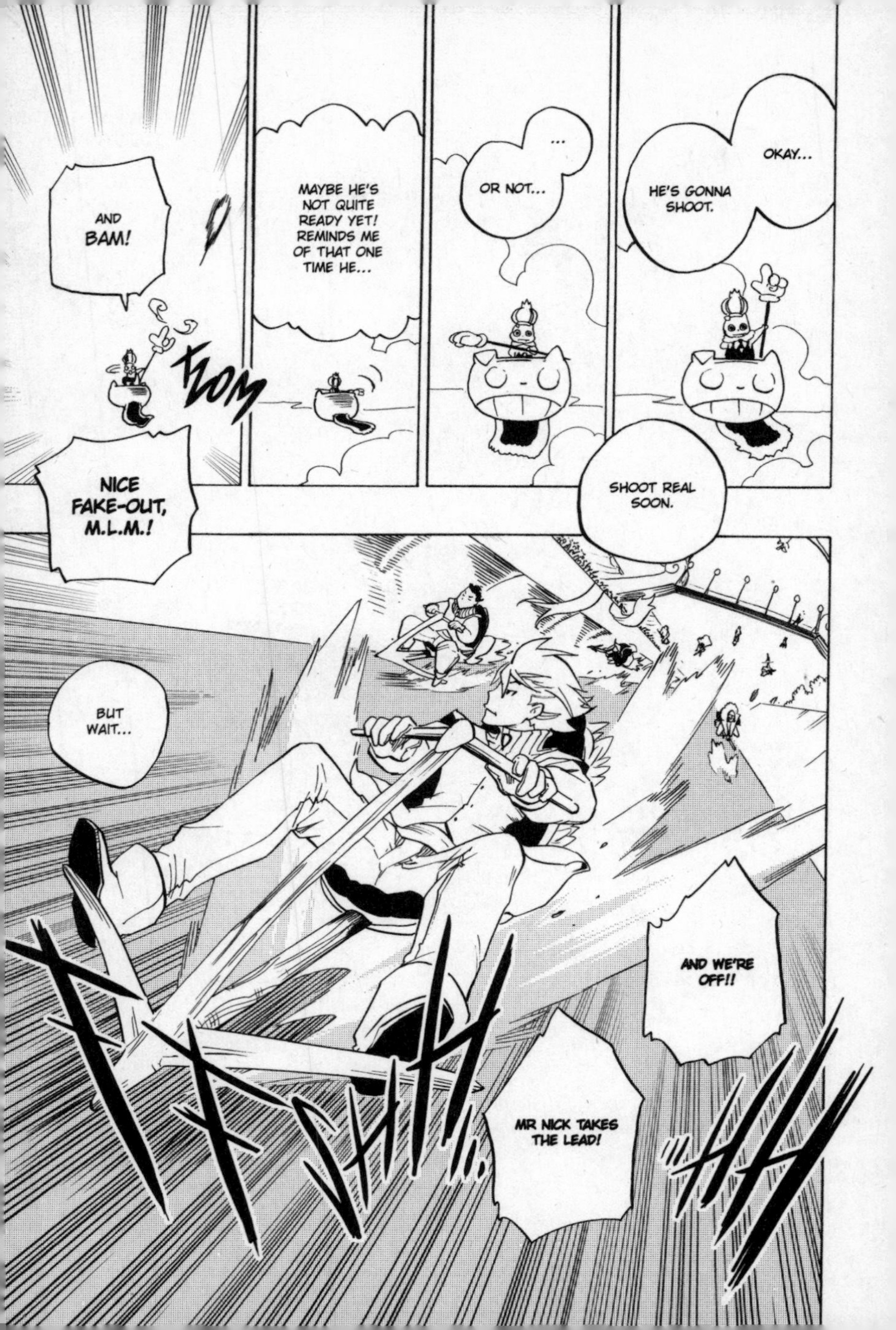
OKAY...
HE'S GONNA SHOOT.
SHOOT REAL SOON.
...
OR NOT...
MAYBE HE'S NOT QUITE READY YET! REMINDS ME OF THAT ONE TIME HE...
AND BAM!
FZOOM
NICE FAKE-OUT, M.L.M.!
AND WE'RE OFF!!
MR NICK TAKES THE LEAD!
BUT WAIT...

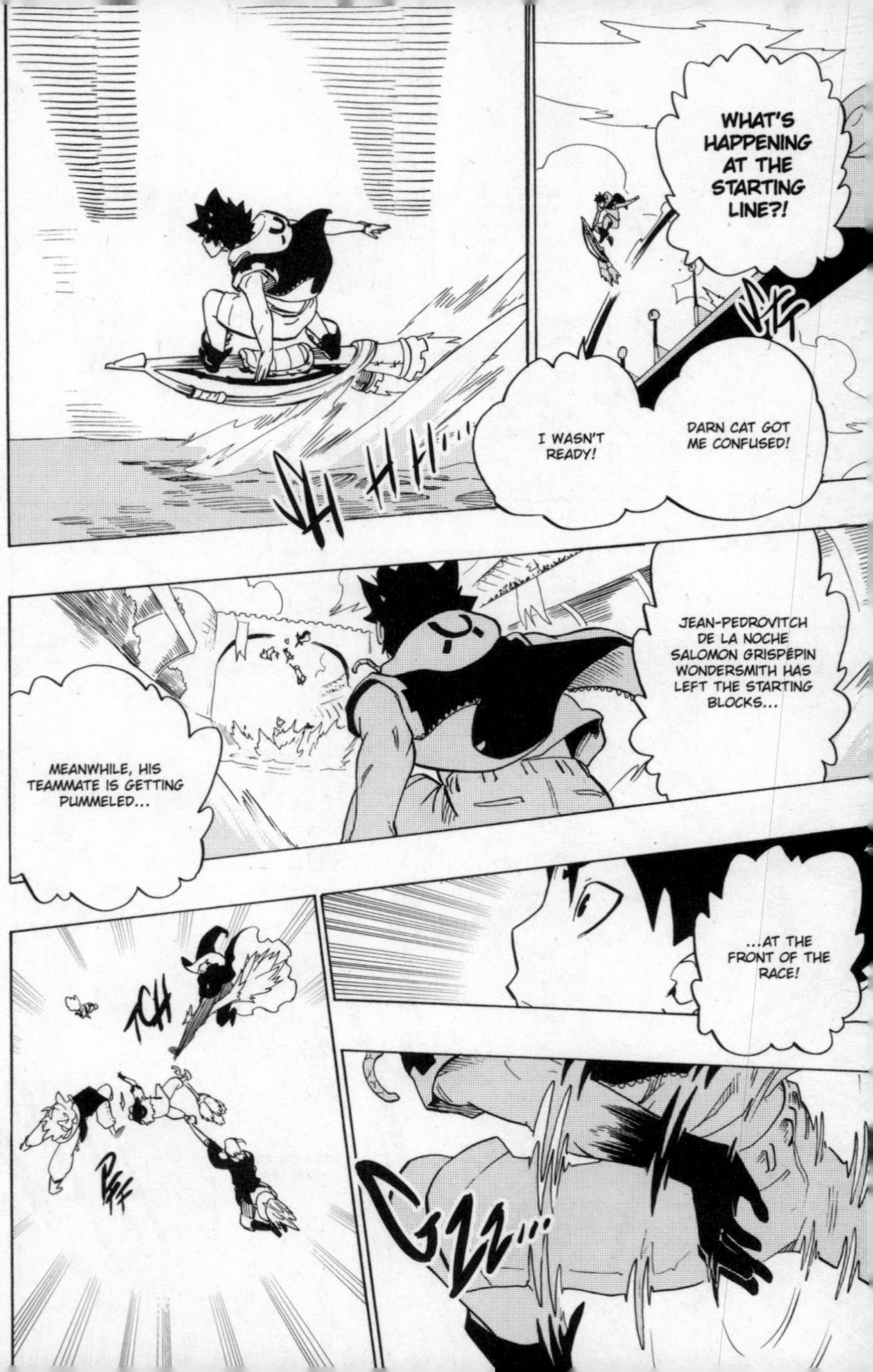
WHAT'S HAPPENING AT THE STARTING LINE?!
DARN CAT GOT ME CONFUSED!
I WASN'T READY!
JEAN-PEDROVITCH DE LA NOCHE SALOMON GRISPÉPIN WONDERSMITH HAS LEFT THE STARTING BLOCKS...
MEANWHILE, HIS TEAMMATE IS GETTING PUMMELED...
...AT THE FRONT OF THE RACE!
GZZ...
TCH

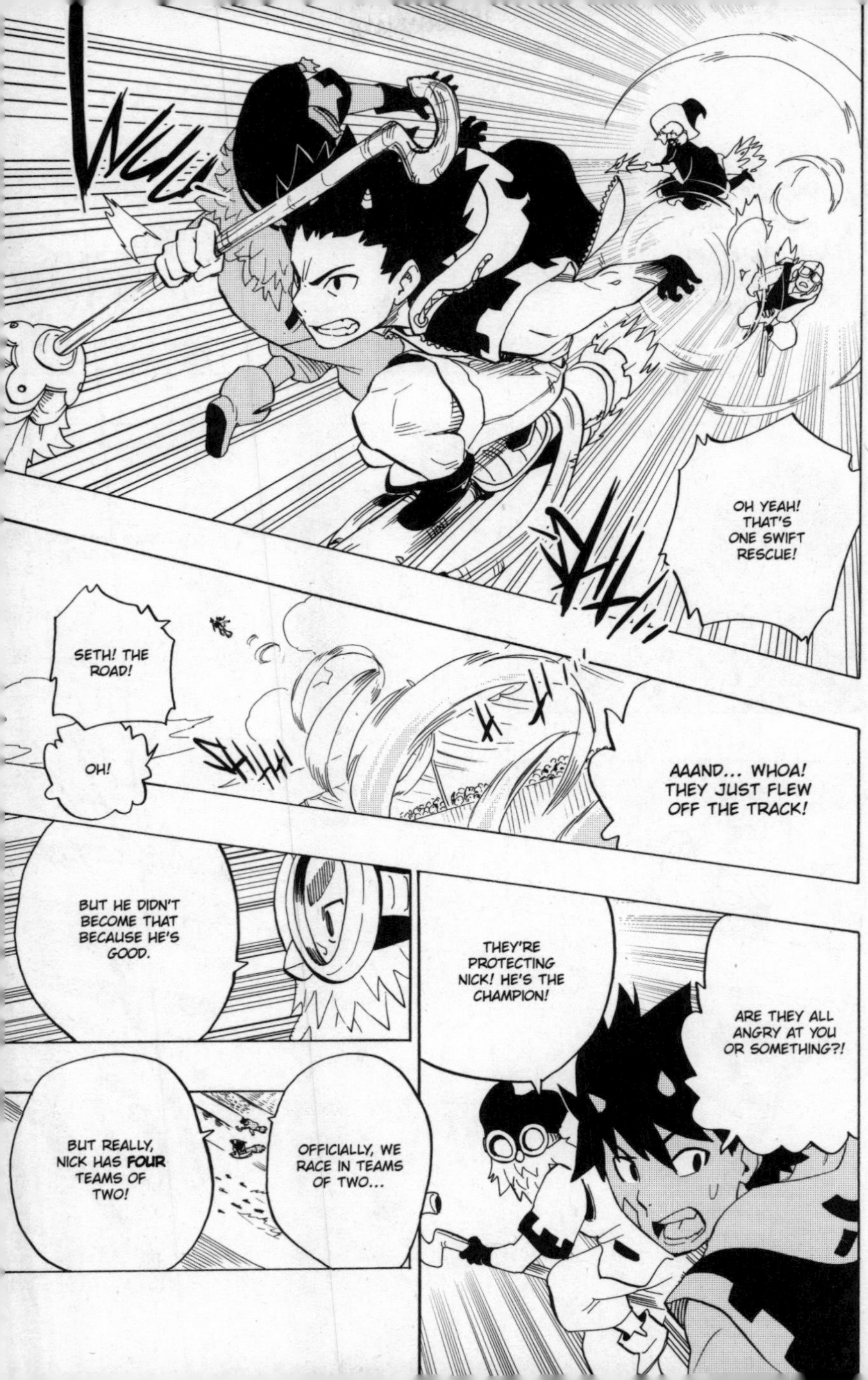
OH YEAH! THAT'S ONE SWIFT RESCUE!
AAAND... WHOA! THEY JUST FLEW OFF THE TRACK!
SETH! THE ROAD!
OH!
ARE THEY ALL ANGRY AT YOU OR SOMETHING?!
THEY'RE PROTECTING NICK! HE'S THE CHAMPION!
BUT HE DIDN'T BECOME THAT BECAUSE HE'S GOOD.
OFFICIALLY, WE RACE IN TEAMS OF TWO...
BUT REALLY, NICK HAS **FOUR** TEAMS OF TWO!

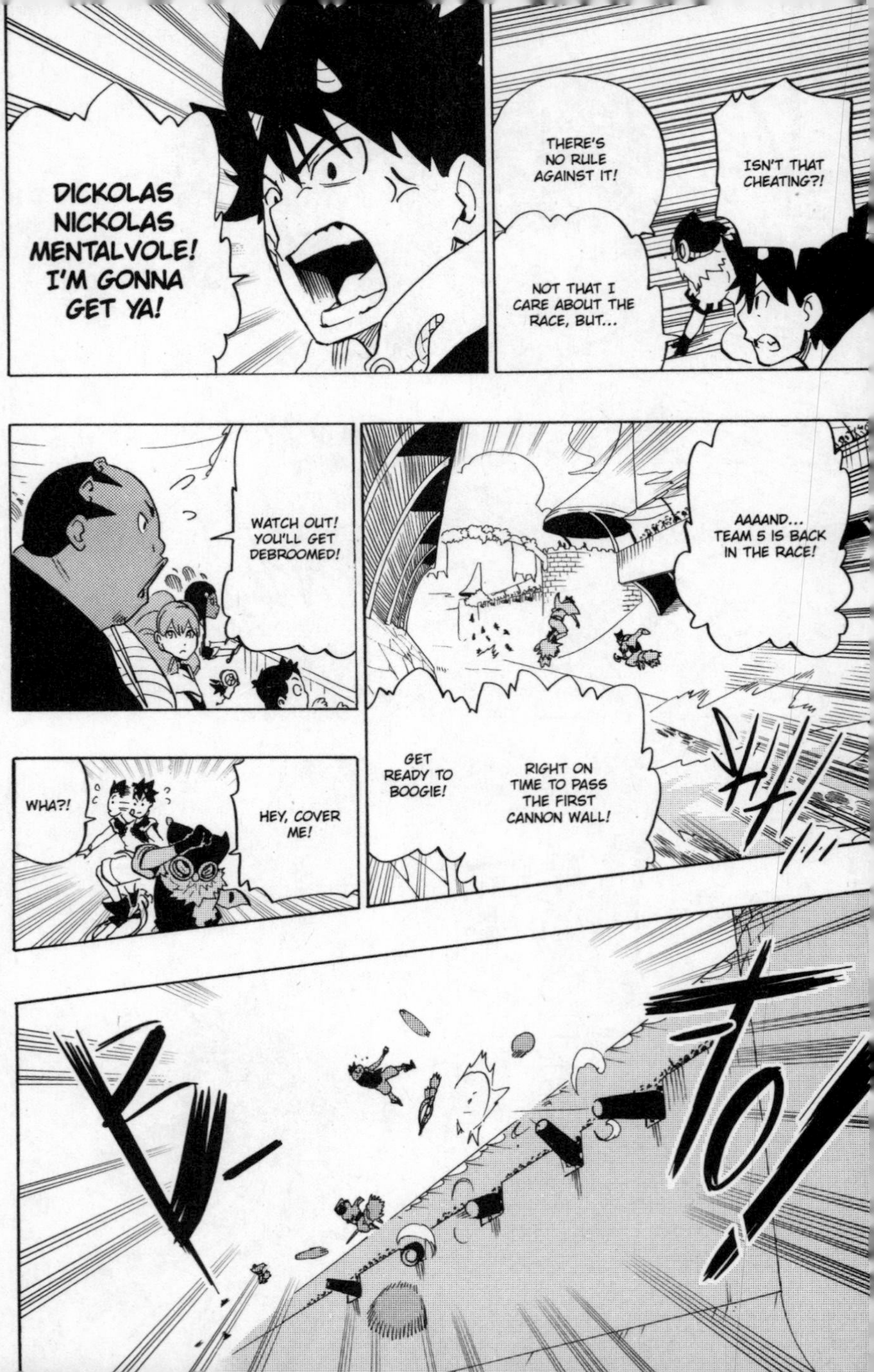
ISN'T THAT CHEATING?!
THERE'S NO RULE AGAINST IT!
NOT THAT I CARE ABOUT THE RACE, BUT...
DICKOLAS NICKOLAS MENTALVOLE! I'M GONNA GET YA!
AAAAND... TEAM 5 IS BACK IN THE RACE!
RIGHT ON TIME TO PASS THE FIRST CANNON WALL!
GET READY TO BOOGIE!
WATCH OUT! YOU'LL GET DEBROOMED!
HEY, COVER ME!
WHA?!

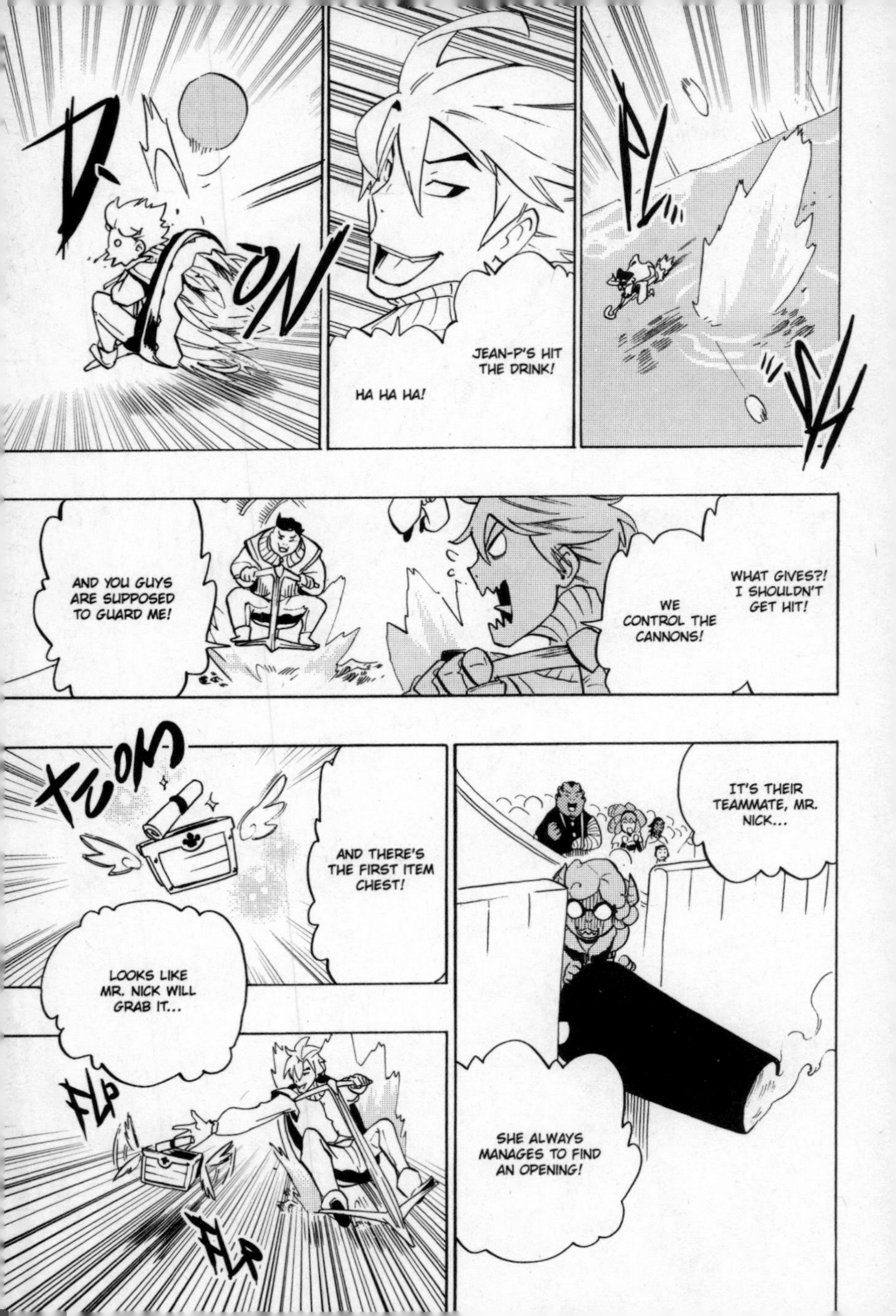
JEAN-P'S HIT THE DRINK!
HA HA HA!
WHAT GIVES?! I SHOULDN'T GET HIT!
WE CONTROL THE CANNONS!
AND YOU GUYS ARE SUPPOSED TO GUARD ME!
IT'S THEIR TEAMMATE, MR. NICK...
SHE ALWAYS MANAGES TO FIND AN OPENING!
AND THERE'S THE FIRST ITEM CHEST!
LOOKS LIKE MR. NICK WILL GRAB IT...

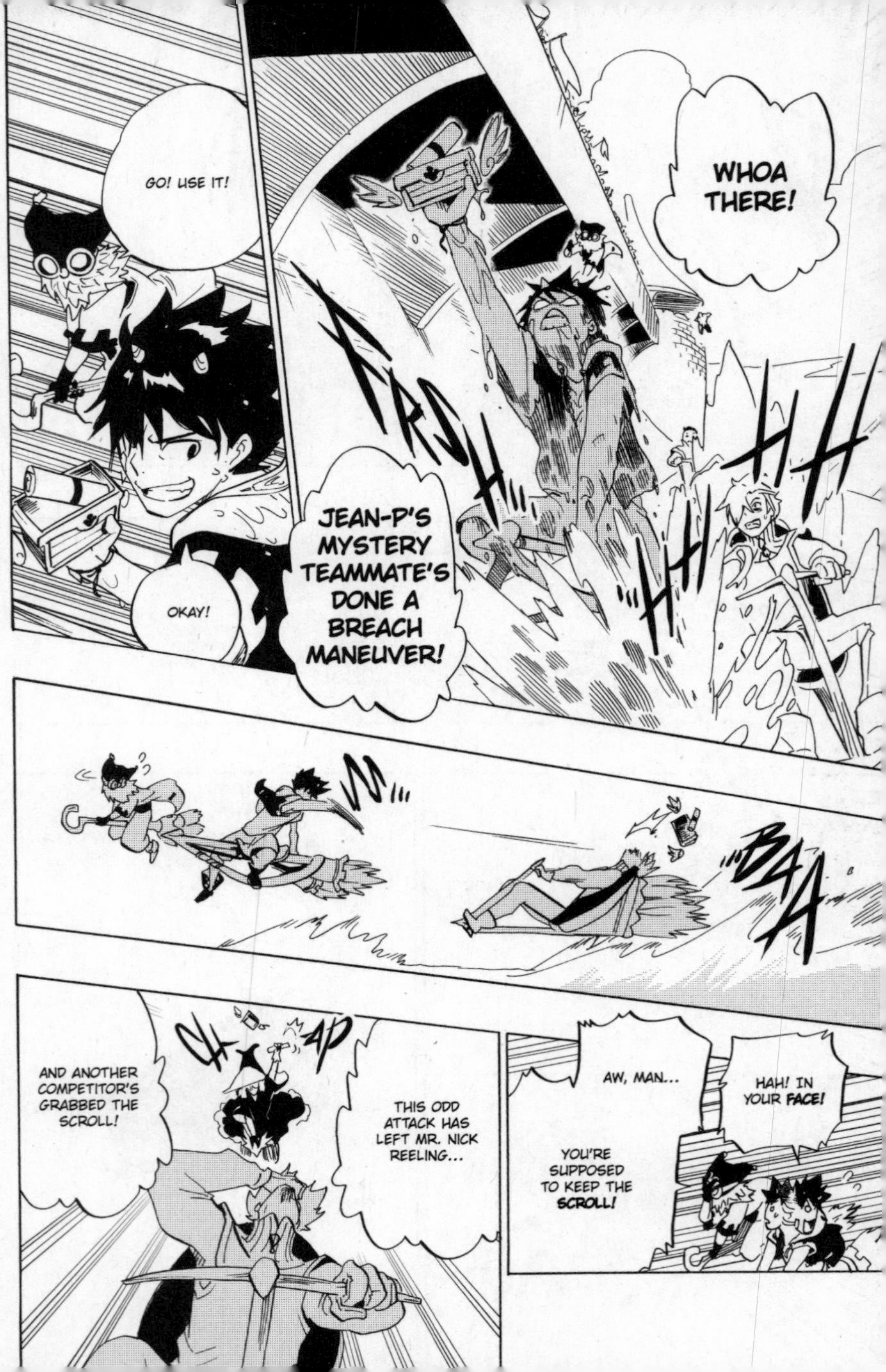
WHOA THERE!
FRSH
JEAN-P'S MYSTERY TEAMMATE'S DONE A BREACH MANEUVER!
GO! USE IT!
OKAY!
HAH! IN YOUR **FACE**!
AW, MAN...
YOU'RE SUPPOSED TO KEEP THE **SCROLL**!
THIS ODD ATTACK HAS LEFT MR. NICK REELING...
AND ANOTHER COMPETITOR'S GRABBED THE SCROLL!

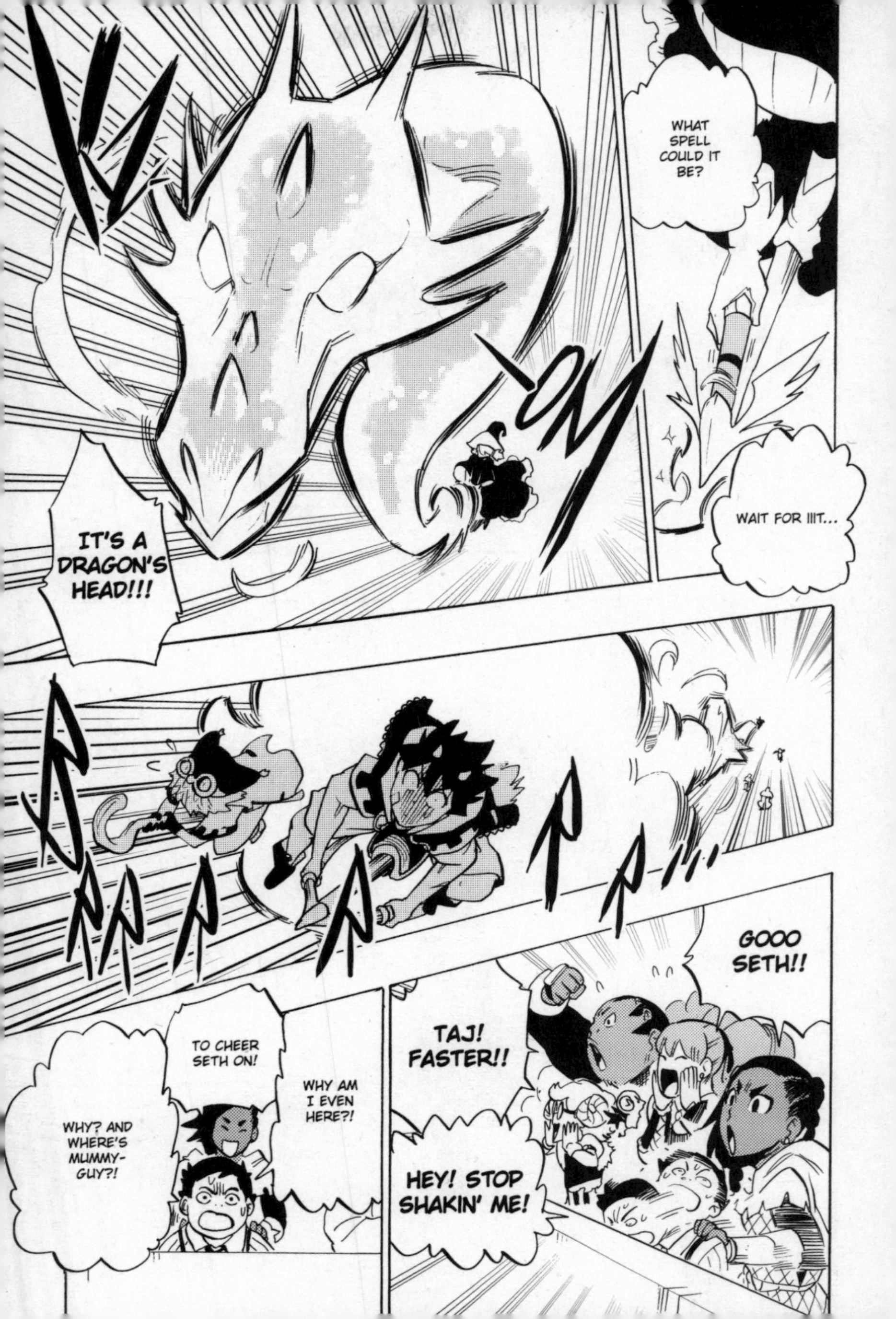
WHAT SPELL COULD IT BE?
WAIT FOR IIIT...
IT'S A DRAGON'S HEAD!!!
GOOO SETH!!
TAJ! FASTER!!
HEY! STOP SHAKIN' ME!
WHY AM I EVEN HERE?!
TO CHEER SETH ON!
WHY? AND WHERE'S MUMMY-GUY?!

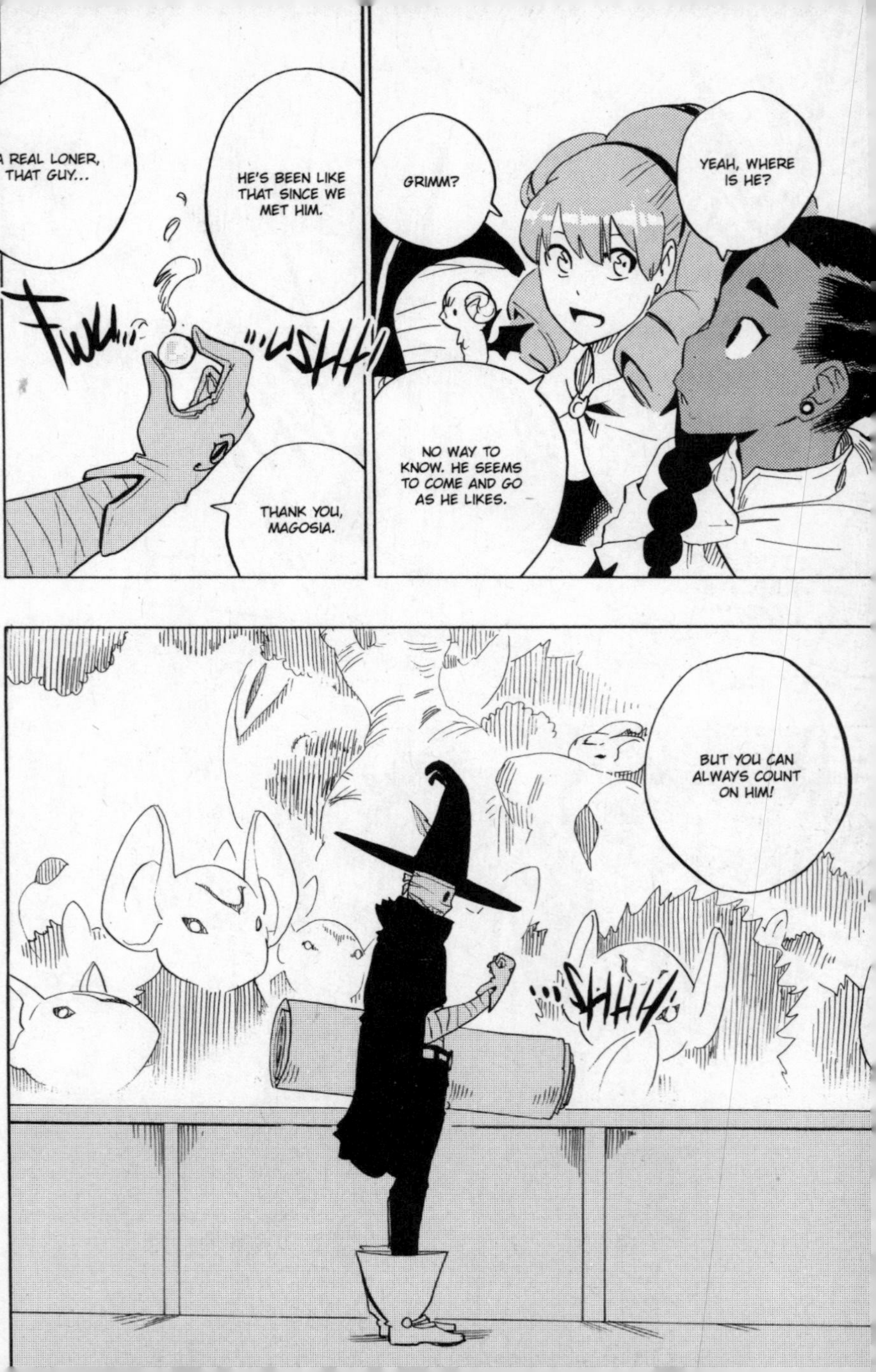
YEAH, WHERE IS HE?
GRIMM?
NO WAY TO KNOW. HE SEEMS TO COME AND GO AS HE LIKES.
HE'S BEEN LIKE THAT SINCE WE MET HIM.
A REAL LONER, THAT GUY...
FWU...USHH
THANK YOU, MAGOSIA.
BUT YOU CAN ALWAYS COUNT ON HIM!
SHHH

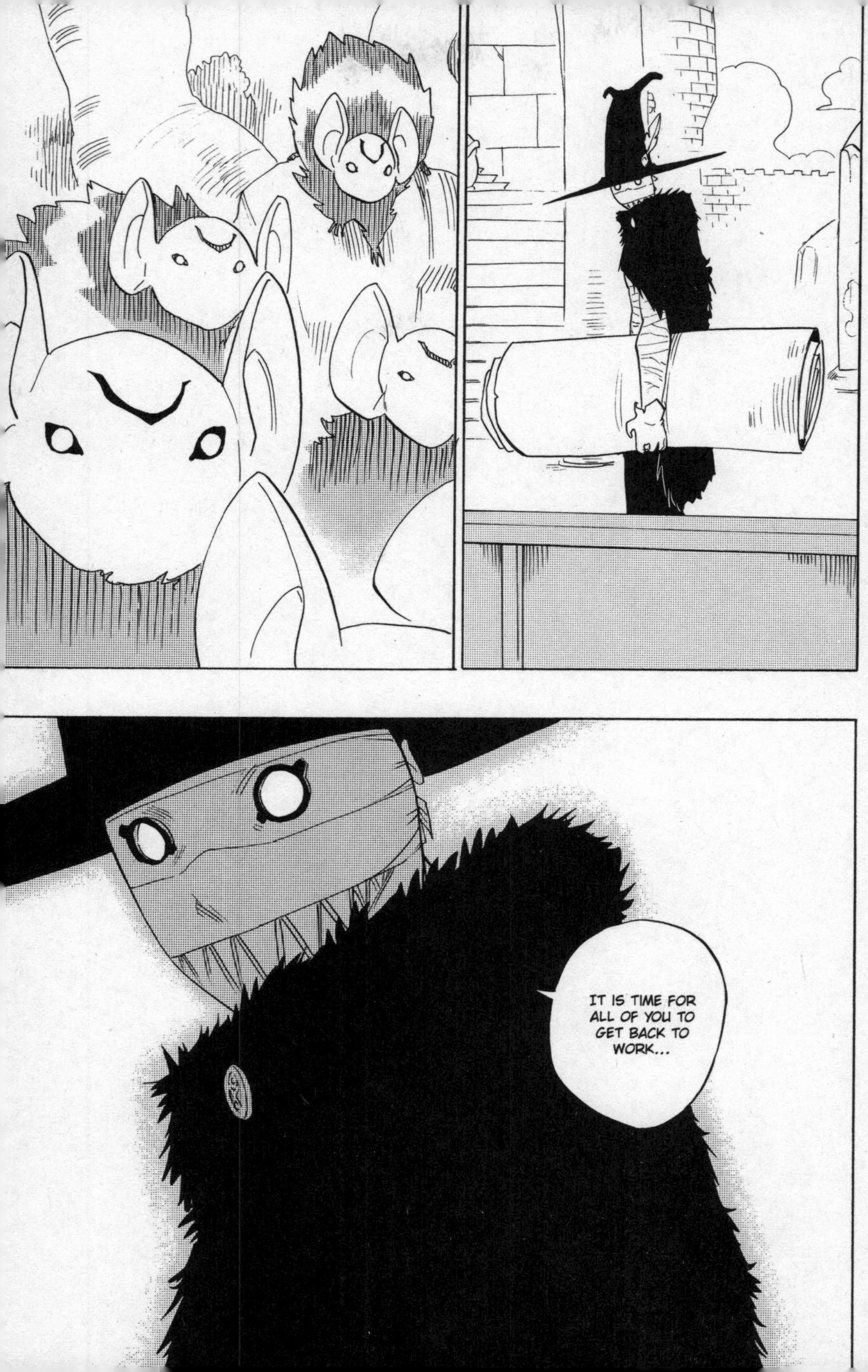
IT IS TIME FOR ALL OF YOU TO GET BACK TO WORK...

TO BE CONTINUED...

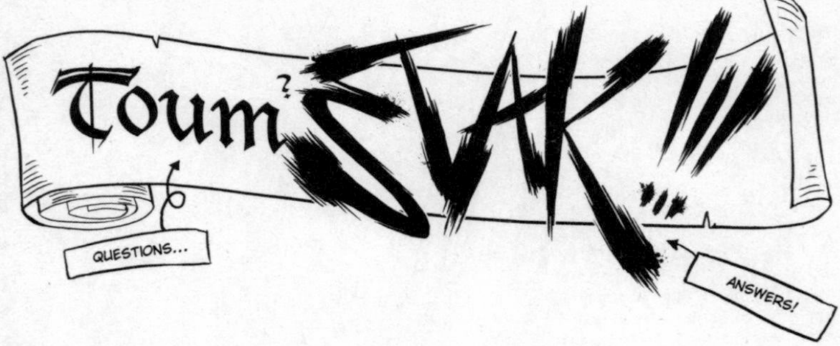
Toum
?
STAK!!
QUESTIONS...
ANSWERS!

A curious and admiring reader: Hi Tony, I had a little question about *Radiant* and more specifically about our little Inquisitor duo — Liselotte and Dragunov. Why does Liselotte keep calling Dragunov "Captain" and use such polite speech toward him even though he doesn't and they have the same rank? (Considering they're both Thaumaturge Captains) is it because she was his subordinate for a while in the past? Or was Von Teppes correct when he commented that his pretty eyes "distracted" her? Good luck on the next volumes :)

Tony Valente: It's more related to their personalities. Dragunov easily starts to act very colloquially, he doesn't care too much about hierarchy, but he also knows when he can and can't be nonchalant! With Torque, for example, there's no colloquial-ness whatsoever!!

Marvin O: Hello, I was digging through some videos on Youtube related to various topics for learning how to draw and becoming a mangaka, and that's when I came across one of your interviews. So I checked out your manga and I'm just so lucky to have found it now, because that meant I was able to go devour my way through the first eight volumes! Really great, loving the whole world you created! You really get attached to the characters.

Anyway, I know you always get the same type of questions because I read through all the "Toum Stak!!" sections, and yeah, after having read many tips on the internet and even books on learning how to draw, the only answer I see repeated over and over is to draw, just draw. Just about anything! And while it's not easy to find your own style, I lean more towards manga. So my question is: in that case, should I just draw manga over and over again in order to assimilate the style correctly?

I've been drawing since I was really young and I know how to copy stuff, but I can't draw anything original...

Tony Valente: So! First of all, you need to decide what style of manga you're interested in. Otherwise, it's like wanting to learn how to play music… But then the problem is still, what kind? If, for example, you like *shonen* manga, then which ones specifically? What kind of drawings do you like? What kind of scenes make you tick? And what about things outside of manga? Because one of the most important things is to figure out what you like and what works for you as a reader. Then you can start orienting your drawings and sceneries to what makes you as a reader excited. At that moment, as you progress, you'll more or less naturally start to get closer to something that is "your style," without copying from series A or B, but by responding to the audience that you yourself are!

I hope my answer wasn't too vague -_-

....

Oscar C.: Hello mister Valente!!!! First of all congratulations on your amazing work and congratulations on the anime adaptation!!! I had a few questions that have been bothering me, so here goes: will we see any new characters we don't know yet, who will join the team?

Tony Valente: Probably, yes!

- In volume 8 the Thaumaturge Ullmina says that general Torque is busy in Bôme dealing with the dangerous Domitor situation, so is it possible that Seth's next adventure will be going to Bôme and helping out the Domitors?

Probably, yes!

- And lastly, on the map of Pharenos in volume 5 we can see some dragons near Caislean Ceooch and the Islet of Borne. What do they represent?

Probably, yes! Oh, wait, you actually want a real answer this time... Eh... Let's just say that there are a lot of things that live in the Pharenos and I drew a couple of those things on the maps. Of course, whether those things are all real or just part of travelers' hallucinations, who knows...

....

Killian M.: Hello, good evening. While reading *Doc's Files [a bonus booklet with certain editions of volume 2, not yet available in English–ed.]*, I noticed a few things on the page about Hameline. It says her Infection is the zebra stripes all over her body, but that her pointy ears are just a feature of hers. So, that means she had the ears before her Infection. Is this just an aesthetic feature, or do her ears hide something about her more important like another race, or a mix between the Little People and the humans?

Tony Valente: Ah, yes, well, that is due to an oversight. Her Infection is a physical type and includes both her zebra stripes AND unusually shaped ears...

....

Steve V.: Hello, Tony. I just *devoured* the eight volumes of Radiant, congratulations on a job well done! I love a lot of the characters, the plot is the stuff of dreams, and the art is fabulous. So, now, we want an art book! When will you have time to make one?

Tony Valente: I'd love to make one, once there are enough illustrations to do that!!

- Also congratulations on the anime, looking forward to see what Seth looks like on TV. I was wondering, at what point are you involved in the creation of the episodes? Do you keep an eye on their work from afar, or are you more in a supervising role? How does that work?

I'm kind of like a consultant on that. They come to me for everything, from designs to the episode scripts. I okay them or give feedback, ask for some revisions... We talk about everything and try to get to the best compromises to fit the adaptation! So every week we have a Skype reunion with the series producer, and outside of those, there's also a lot of time spent on elements sent to me to be okayed. Actually, it's like I've got two jobs now! ^^

....

Clément F.: Hello hello, mister Valente! I have two questions: up until now, all the Nemeses we saw were in black and white. Is there any specific reason behind this, or is just a matter of preference? Personally, they kind of make me think of ying and yang...

Tony Valente: It's to create a visual identity that makes them easily recognizable within the manga pages, as they're normally black and white!

- Second question: Eh...eh...flshwhhublviou... AND DON'T MAKE ME REPEAT MYSELF!!!!

Yes, Milord!!!

....

Jade: Hi! I have a question I wanted to ask about the Nemeses. I noticed that Nemesis is the name of the Greek goddess of revenge and especially of "divine revenge." Since the Nemeses fall from the sky and destroy everything (like a divine punishment of sorts), I was wondering if there was a connection there or if it was just a coincidence??

Tony Valente: That was a deliberate choice, yes!

....

Vincent: Hello! I discovered *Radiant* not too long ago and I was really glad to have found it. It's like a cauldron with an intelligent mix of different ingredients in it that constitutes the best manga–*Dragon Ball, One Piece, Naruto* (and with *Naruto*, there must have been a lot of elements to sort through)... *Harry Potter!* First question: Is the title supposed to be pronounced "Ra-the-an", "Ra-the-ant", "Ray-dee-ant" (like in English) or is it "pudding"?

Tony Valente: What kind of question is that... It's pronounced "radish" (è_é)

- Second question: at the end of volume 5 you're talking about your experience in Japan when you went there for the Japanese release of volume 2. In it, your plane departs from North America. So I was wondering, you're French mangaka living in North America, meaning you've got a foot on three different continents?

That's right!

- And here's a question from Baron of Furgonde: Okay, so I don't understand. If he has a foot on three continents, one in Japan and the other in North America, that creates a bridge between his two legs. But I can't imagine what could be the third leg in the middle that goes all the way to France?

Baroness of Furgonde: Oh, I can imagine *very well!* And it sounds like a dream come true.

Baron of Furgonde: What's that, my dear?

XD

....

Randall M.: Hop, Tony Tony Chop... Sensei! First of all, thank you for coming up with this amazing work. I had a question that was bothering me ever since I noticed quite a strange phenomenon in a panel of volume 6, chapter 44, page 159. Is that a mushroom blowing bubbles in the water through his...butt?

Tony Valente: That's exactly it! But don't assume it's due to a lack of manners! He just heard about the existence of bubble baths that you can find in the more well-off establishments...so he just made do.

....

Dylan R. Hello mister Tony Valente. First things first, I have looooooooooved your manga since the first page of volume 1. I really love the world. I just saw the trailer for the anime adaptation of your manga and I'm already looking forward to watching episode 1. There's just one thing that bothers me: Seth's voice. But I'll get used to it. What did you think of the trailer? Do you think the anime will be able to recreate the manga's plot well?

Tony Valente: Firstly, thank you for reading *Radiant!* Regarding the trailer, you're not the only one who made the same remark about Seth's voice and, even if I myself do like it, I can understand where you're coming from. Every reader has his or her own idea when reading the manga and of course that means reality sometimes ends up different from that idea. The only thing I can say is to just be patient and first listen to the voices in the episodes to really understand how it is! As for the trailer, I think they absolutely *killed* it!! Obviously there's no way for me to not be biased about my own manga, so every time I open a volume I immediately fixate on what's wrong with it. But with the trailer, it was the first time I could be a viewer of the world that I built. It's definitely the kind of snippet that would have gotten me completely into the series. You can smell the adventure, the action is super good and the music completes it all! Anyway, I am very, very happy! (*u*)

....

Valentin: Hello, Tony. I've had this question I've been dying to ask you: how can a Merchant Baron also be an Inquisitor? I don't really get how that's possible.

Tony Valente: I assume you're talking about volume 4 when Santori is talking about the Merchant Baroness and Colonel Inquisitor Viviame of Hyres? Since Merchant Baron isn't like a rank or something like that, it's a title of nobility, there's nothing stopping a Baron from kickstarting a career as an Inquisitor while still maintaining his fortune!

....

Matthieu A.: So I bought volume 9 the day it came out to be able to read it as quickly as possible and there's really just one thing to say about it: it's still as amazing as ever! But I still have a few questions. How has Seth still not sprained his ankle wearing those boots of his??

Tony Valente: Thanks to his special training! The famous "Ultimate Death Training."

- The Armor of Pen Draig reminds me of the "Red Knight" skin in *Fortnite*. Is that a coincidence?

Huge coincidence! I don't play *Fortnite*. But I did get inspired by other video games. I don't play any FPS or other types of shooting games, but sometimes I look at the drawings and, for those that are futuristic in theme, you can often see these types of armors or exoskeletons that adjust to combat by boosting speed, jumps, etc. I wanted to do the same thing but with an ancient knight's armor!

- At one point there's a reference to a certain "Albur Fendragon." This is obviously a reference to King Arthur, so does this character have any relationship to Myr who, as we've learned, is actually Merlin?

That was just to find a name for a wizard who sounded like someone people would have heard of before!

....

Keryan B.: Hello mister Valente! As is the case for many others, I am a fan of your manga and the world you created. I wanted to know where the name Pharenos came from, if you completely came up with it yourself, or if you were inspired by elements in real life like you have for some of the Inquisitors?

Tony Valente: I did not invent the word Pharenos. It comes from a philosopher who used it to describe "the reality that we experience," meaning, not all of reality. For example, a blind person would experience our reality, but without the light; he's missing a big chunk of reality, so his Pharenos is different from that of someone who *can* see, even if those two perceptions of reality are both valid/correct. And those who can see, experience reality minus… Well, we don't know what we're missing! Ultrasounds, infra-sounds, ultraviolets etc… But there's definitely a lot more than just that. I thought that fit well with the world I was building where there's part of reality that people don't experience anymore: everything linked to the Fantasia, for example. It's part of their world, but most people can't perceive it. In conclusion: they miss out on part of the reality! Anyway, the term entails a lot of things that really interest me and I thought it was a pretty cool concept and the word looked nice too. Sooo… I took it! As for the name of the philosopher… Lost somewhere in the far ends of the Internet. Now, whenever I look up the word "Pharenos," the only hits I get are related to *Radiant*. Ah! That means that now I've gone and cut off part of our reality!! Sorry!

....

Yoh Ringo: Hey Tony sensei! First of all, congratulations on this great volume 10. It really shows your consistency as well on the art as the staging and the story that keeps on moving along well, just like the great mangaka we all know and love. (Yeah, I said volume 10, but with Caillte Forest and everything, you know!) I really have to admit there's a lot of humor in *Radiant* like in classic shônen series, but there's also this li'l French touch to your jokes and terms used by the characters (which is great btw!), so do the other foreign publishing companies ask you for your opinion at all? Do you somewhat manage the changes in the texts for the translated versions, or do you give them complete free rein?

Tony Valente: I am not at all involved in the translations, but I do know they try to make wordplays here and there where there are any, but making some adjustments as necessary.

- Next, I thought the fight between Seth v.s. Santori was really well done! How did you plan out the staging for this fight scene? Did you just go like "BAM! Seth does a big *Skulls Burst,* and then POW! Santori takes to the skies and unleashes his attack and SHTAK! dodged by Seth and… Whoa, I think I got kind of carried away ^^ Did you first imagine how it'd go inside your head or how did that all go?

I have to say that yes, when it comes to action scenes, it usually plays off inside my head before I write it down! And I try to also add some range, some volume, to the fights. See here, the background is kind of empty (just grass and nothing else around it), so we needed something to amp up the action. So I took advantage of Santori's Miracle and Seth who likes to jump all over the place to try and turn it into a scene with a lot of punch to it!

- Lastly, in volume 9, we finally discover that Myr was actually Merlin in what seems to be his actual form, only that we already knew about this in volume 6, pages 96-97, when he brings back Seth unconscious after his fight against Diabal. You sure you're not pulling an Oda on us here, Tony-sensei?

Ha ha! Well, I admit I like to have a little bit of foreshadowing here and there…and Oda is a master in the art of foreshadowing. But he's not the only one who does that! In the books that I read it's used very often, and one of the best in the biz is Robin Hobb. Sometimes certain actions will only make sense a few volumes later. Haah… Such mastery is just mesmerizing!!

Please send your questions to: radiant@ankama.com

So, we all know that plants consume carbon... But amongst certain varieties of trees, the older ones apparently send part of the carbon they absorb to the younger ones via a network of mushrooms that grow around their roots. And they seem to prefer sending their carbon to the younglings that grew from their own seeds! In other words, trees can recognize and feed their young! Think about it! Isn't that just crazy?! Trees that basically nurse their little sapling babies, I mean, come on! *_*

Anyway, this news made me fidget on my chair and that's partly how I came to imagine the whole story about the forest, Jill, Myr and their little ones...

With this volume, I declare the end to the Wizard Knight Arc! Not the entire series, of course! Just this arc!

—Tony Valente

Tony Valente began working as a comic artist with the series *The Four Princes of Ganahan*, written by Raphael Drommelschlager. He then launched a new three-volume project, *Hana Attori*, after which he produced *S.P.E.E.D. Angels*, a series written by Didier Tarquin and colored by Pop.

In preparation for *Radiant*, he relocated to Canada. Through confronting caribou and grizzlies, he gained the wherewithal to train in obscure manga techniques. Since then, his eating habits have changed, his lifestyle became completely different and even his singing voice has changed a bit!

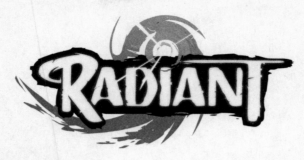

RADIANT VOL. 10
VIZ MEDIA Manga Edition

STORY AND ART BY **TONY VALENTE**
ASSISTANT ARTIST **TPIU**

Translation/**(´・∀・｀)ｻｧ?**
Touch-Up Art & Lettering/**Erika Terriquez**
Design/**Julian [JR] Robinson**
Editor/**Gary Leach**

Published by arrangement with MEDIATOON LICENSING/Ankama.
RADIANT T10

Printed in the U.S.A.

Published by VIZ Media, LLC
P.O. Box 77010
San Francisco, CA 94107

10 9 8 7 6 5 4 3 2 1
First printing, March 2020

VIZ MEDIA
viz.com

PARENTAL ADVISORY
RADIANT is rated T for Teen and is recommended for ages 13 and up. This volume contains fantasy violence.

RATED T TEEN ratings.viz.com

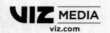

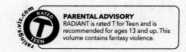

DEMON SLAYER

KIMETSU NO YAIBA

Story and Art by

KOYOHARU GOTOUGE

In Taisho-era Japan, kindhearted Tanjiro Kamado makes a living selling charcoal. But his peaceful life is shattered when a demon slaughters his entire family. His little sister Nezuko is the only survivor, but she has been transformed into a demon herself! Tanjiro sets out on a dangerous journey to find a way to return his sister to normal and destroy the demon who ruined his life.

Black ✤ Clover

STORY & ART BY YŪKI TABATA

Asta is a young boy who dreams of becoming the greatest mage in the kingdom. Only one problem—he can't use any magic! Luckily for Asta, he receives the incredibly rare five-leaf clover grimoire that gives him the power of anti-magic. Can someone who can't use magic really become the Wizard King? One thing's for sure—Asta will never give up!

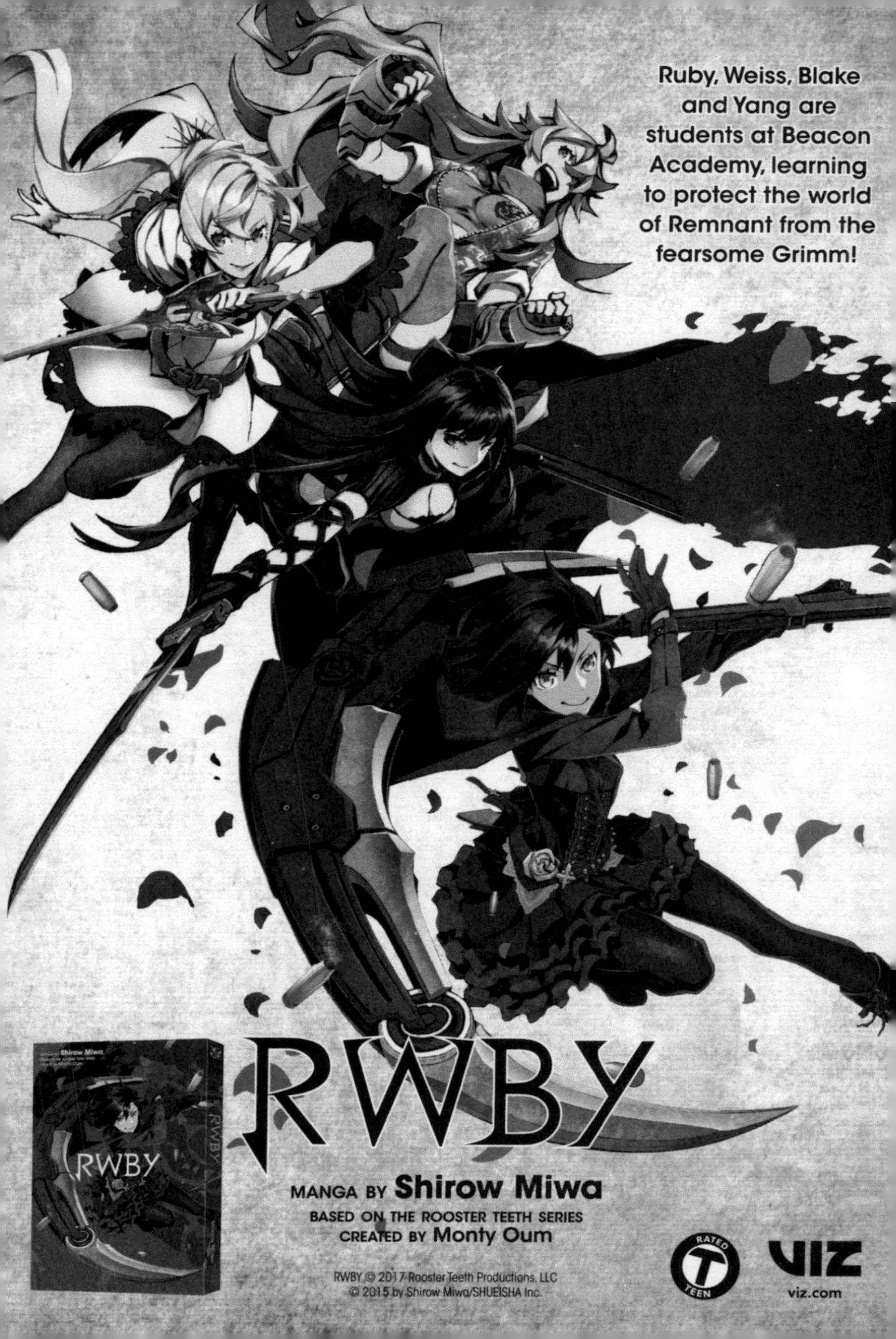
Ruby, Weiss, Blake and Yang are students at Beacon Academy, learning to protect the world of Remnant from the fearsome Grimm!
RWBY
MANGA BY Shirow Miwa
BASED ON THE ROOSTER TEETH SERIES
CREATED BY Monty Oum
RWBY © 2017 Rooster Teeth Productions, LLC
© 2015 by Shirow Miwa/SHUEISHA Inc.
RATED T TEEN
VIZ
viz.com

MY HERO ACADEMIA
SMASH!!

Story and Art by Hirofumi Neda
Original Concept by Kohei Horikoshi

HILARIOUS HIJINKS
featuring the characters
and story lines of
MY HERO ACADEMIA!

The superpowered society of *My Hero Academia* takes a
hilarious turn in this reimagining of the best-selling series! Join
Midoriya, All Might and all the aspiring heroes of U.A. High, plus
memorable villains, in an irreverent take on the main events
of the series, complete with funny gags, ridiculous jokes and

NARUTO

the Seventh Hokage
and the Scarlet Spring

STORY AND ART BY
MASASHI KISHIMOTO

In the years since the great ninja war, peace has bloomed in the ninja world, and a new generation has begun to take root. Naruto's work as an adult seems to be pretty mundane, but his son, Boruto, is constantly demanding attention. Luckily for Naruto, he can make clones of himself to babysit his son. But Sasuke's daughter, Sarada, could be the target of a mysterious figure who has connections to the Uchiha clan!

www.viz.com

A Dragon Ball fan's greatest dream is getting to live in the Dragon Ball universe and fight alongside Goku and his friends! But one particular fan is in for a rude awakening when he suddenly dies and gets reincarnated as everyone's favorite punching bag, Yamcha!

Based on Dragon Ball by Akira Toriyama, Art by dragongarow LEE

ASTRA
LOST IN SPACE

CAN EIGHT TEENAGERS FIND THEIR WAY HOME FROM 5,000 LIGHT-YEARS AWAY?

It's the year 2063, and interstellar space travel has become the norm. Eight students from Caird High School and one child set out on a routine planet camp excursion. While there, the students are mysteriously transported 5,000 light-years away to the middle of nowhere! Will they ever make it back home?!

YOU'RE READING THE WRONG WAY

RADIANT reads from right to left, starting in the upper-right corner, meaning that action, sound effects, and word-balloon order are completely reversed from English order.

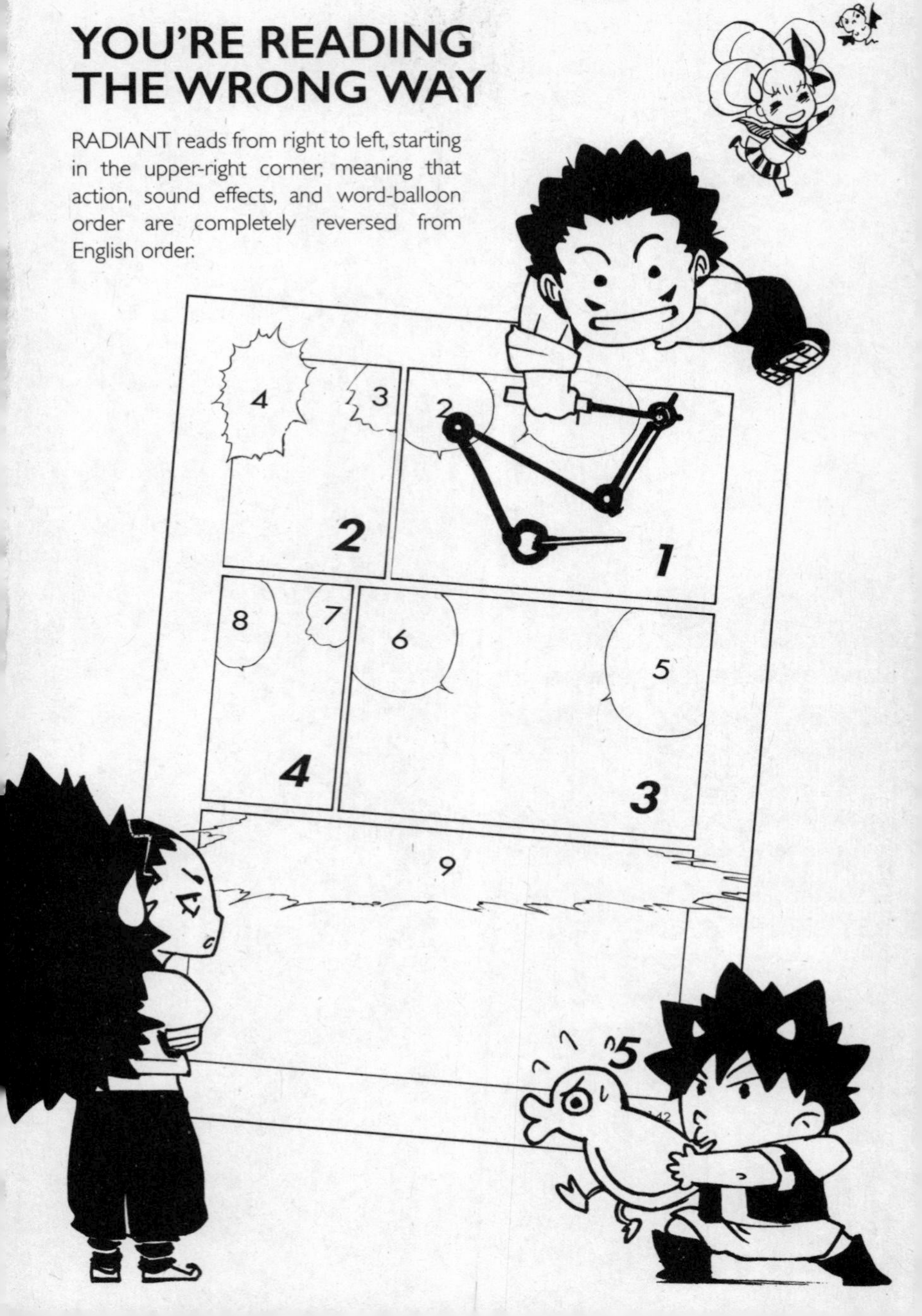

1
2
3
4
2
1
2
3
4
5
6
7
8
9
5